The Sounds of Capitalism

The Sounds of
CAPITALISM

Advertising, Music, and the
Conquest of Culture

TIMOTHY D. TAYLOR

University of Chicago Press
Chicago and London

The University of Chicago Press, Chicago 60637
The University of Chicago Press, Ltd., London
© 2012 by The University of Chicago
All rights reserved. Published 2012.
Paperback edition 2014
Printed and bound by CPI Group (UK) Ltd, Croydon, CR0 4YY

23 22 21 20 19 18 17 16 15 14   2 3 4 5 6

ISBN-13: 978-0-226-79115-9 (cloth)
ISBN-13: 978-0-226-15162-5 (paper)
ISBN-13: 978-0-226-79114-2 (e-book)
10.7208/chicago/9780226791142.001.0001

Portions of chapters 1 and 2 first appeared in an earlier form as "Music and Advertising in Early Radio," *echo* 5 (Spring 2003), http://www.echo.ucla.edu/volume5-issue2/taylor/index.html. A portion of chapter 3 appeared in an earlier form as "The Rise of the Jingle," *Advertising and Society Review* 3 (2010), http://muse.jhu.edu/journals/advertising_and_society_review/v011/11.2.taylor.html. One portion of chapter 9 appeared as "The Changing Shape of the Culture Industry; or, How Did Electronica Music Get into Television Commercials?" *Television and New Media* 8 (August 2007): 235–58; another portion of chapter 9 appeared as "Advertising and the Conquest of Culture," *Social Semiotics* 4 (December 2009): 405–25.

Library of Congress Cataloging-in-Publication Data

Taylor, Timothy Dean, author.
    The sounds of capitalism : advertising, music, and the conquest of culture / Timothy D. Taylor.
        p.   cm.
    Includes bibliographical references and index.
    ISBN-13: 978-0-226-79115-9 (cloth : alk. paper)
    ISBN-10: 0-226-79115-7 (cloth : alk. paper)   1. Music in advertising—United States.
2. Advertising—United States—History—20th century.   3. Mass media and music—United States.   I. Title.
    ML3790.T395 2012
    306.4'8420973—dc23
                                                                                    2011041483
⊗ This paper meets the requirements of ANSI/NISO Z39.48-1992 (Permanence of Paper).

For Sherry

Art imitates life and commercials imitate art.

—Composer/lyricist Peppy Castro, 1988

CONTENTS

ILLUSTRATIONS

Figures

Tables

EXAMPLES

All audio and video examples referenced in the text can be found at *The Sounds of Capitalism* website, www.soundsofcapitalism.com.

1.1. *Eveready Hour* with Martha Copeland, broadcast excerpt, 1928

1.2. *Clicquot Club Eskimos*: "Clicquot Club Foxtrot," 1926

1.3. *Roxy and His Gang*, 17 September 1928

2.1. *The Fleischmann's Yeast Hour*, opening excerpt, 19 December 1935

3.1 Billy Murray, "In My Merry Oldsmobile," 1907

3.2. Billy Murray, "Under the Anheuser Bush," 1904

3.3. The Happiness Boys, "How Do You Do?," 1925

3.4. The Interwoven Pair, late 1920s

3.5. Singin' Sam, the Barbasol Man, "Barbasol, Barbasol," ca. 1943

3.6. *The Jell-O Program*, theme song, 1930s

3.7. "Tastyeast Is Tempting," early 1930s

3.8. "Hurrah for the Wonder Bakers!"

3.9. "The Cantor Cantata"

3.10. *The Life and Love of Dr. Susan*, opening, 1939

3.11. *The Life and Love of Dr. Susan*, closing, 1939

3.12. The Wheaties Quartet, "Have You Tried Wheaties?," 1926

ACKNOWLEDGMENTS

Since this book has been over a decade in the making, there are many people to thank.

First appreciations must go to the various good people at archives around the country for their help and expertise. I began this project while at the National Humanities Center, which offers easy access to the John W. Hartman Center for Sales, Advertising, and Marketing History at Duke University. I would like to thank all the good people at the NHC, and, at the Hartman Center, Jacqueline Reid and Ellen Gartrell. I would also like to thank Suzanne Adamko and Mike Henry at the Library of American Broadcasting, University of Maryland; Richard L. Pifer at the NBC archive at the Wisconsin Historical Society, Madison; David Haberstich, Kay Peterson, and Wendy Shay at the National Museum of American History, Washington, DC; Jeanette M. Berard and Klaudia Englund at the Thousand Oaks Library in Thousand Oaks, California, repository of the Rudy Vallée Collection; Michael Oppenheim, Collections Reference Services Librarian, Rosenfeld Management Library, University of California, Los Angeles; and Gerald Fabris of the Thomas Edison National Historical Park. If I have forgotten anyone, I apologize. Librarians and archivists rule.

Deepest thanks also go to friends across the country who housed me on my trips to archives: Louise Meintjes in Durham, North Carolina, and Ron Radano and Colleen Dunlavy in Madison, Wisconsin.

Joyce Kurpiers was of great assistance more than once when I needed additional materials from the Hartman Center at Duke University. And she kindly provided me with her excellent dissertation on advertising music, which has been very helpful in writing this book.

Many students helped over the years as research assistants and music digitizers, and I would like to name them here: Rachel Adelstein, Hyun Kyong Chang, Kate Grossman, Elizabeth Keenan, Toby King, Julianne Lindberg, Maria Sonevytsky, Wyatt Stone, and Melanie Work. Liz Macy and Chloe Coventry also deserve recognition for their expert skills in transcribing the interviews.

The audio examples for which original recordings do not exist ("Hurrah for the Wonder Bakers!" and "The Cantor Cantata") were recorded by Hyun Kyong Chang, piano, and Jeremy Mikush, tenor. The recording was engineered by Jan Stevens in his studio and coproduced by Jan and me. Thanks are due to all for bringing these old tunes back to life after many decades.

I am also indebted to Nancy Tomes, whose advice and encouragement helped a great deal when the research for this project was in its early stages at the National Humanities Center in 2000.

I am grateful for various audiences in different venues who allowed me to try out some of these chapters as presentations. I am also indebted to graduate students at Columbia University and the University of California, Los Angeles, who took courses on the subjects represented in this book.

I am especially grateful to all those in the commercial music industry who gave me their time and shared their experiences, and I would like to name them all here: Brian Albano, Bill Backer, Georg Bissen, Andy Bloch, Anne Bryant, Marit Burch, Dan Burt, Suzanne Ciani, Randy Crenshaw, Ron Dante, Nick DiMinno, Fritz Doddy, Bernie Drayton, Roy Eaton, Herman Edel, Scott Elias, Janie Fricke, Victoria Gross, Susan Hamilton, David Horowitz, Jessica Josell, Steve Karmen, Chuck Kinsinger, Andrew Knox, Bernie Krause, Mitch Leigh, Joey Levine, Barry Manilow, Tom McFaul, Spencer Michlin, Shahin Motia, Hunter Murtaugh, Linda November, Loren Parkins, Anne Phillips, Ben Porter, Josh Rabinowitz, Sid Ramin, Artie Schroeck, Howard Schwartz, David Shapiro, Ron Smith, Marissa Steingold, Anthony Vanger, and Chris Washburne. Interviews with research subjects were approved for this study by the Office for the Protection of Research Subjects at the University of California, Los Angeles, as study number G08-06-065-02.

This research was supported by grants from the National Humanities Center and the American Council of Learned Societies in 2000, the Charles A. Ryskamp Fellowship for 2004–6 from the American Council of Learned Societies, and the Academic Senate at UCLA.

Special thanks need to go to those few people who read the entire manuscript: Linda Scott, who was gracious, supportive, and extremely helpful; one anonymous reviewer for the University of Chicago Press, and the other, the unanonymous Charles McGovern, whose ideas and recommendations were most useful. Douglas Mitchell, editor extraordinaire, was a pleasure to work with, as were Tim McGovern and Renaldo Migaldi at the University of Chicago Press. Thanks also go to copy editor Susan J. Cohan.

Last and most of all, I thank Sherry B. Ortner for her many insights throughout this project, but especially for her unflagging devotion, support, advice, and dedication for, now, many years.

The consumption engineer is the big job of the immediate future. He will outrank the sales manager and give orders to the
production manager. It is not his job to sell what the factory
makes, but to teach the factory to make what the consumer
will buy.
—Legendary adman Earnest Elmo Calkins, 1930

The magic of consumption offers an opportunity for utilizing
our increased productive ability in the positive form of a better standing of living.
—Arno H. Johnson, J. Walter Thompson Company, 1955

Capitalism, Consumption, Commerce, and Music

Music has power. Musicians know it, listeners know it. And
so do advertisers.

This book tells the story of how the advertising industry
through most of the twentieth century and into the twenty-
first has employed music to sell goods, slowly imprinting
into our collective DNA the sounds of songs that sell. The
story is one of increasingly close relationships between
the advertising industry and the other cultural industries;
the increase in efficiency and specificity in marketing to
particular segments of the population; the decrease—to
negligibility—of the difference between "advertising music" and "music"; the almost unrestricted growth of the advertising industry; the almost unrelenting rise in consumption as a practice of everyday life; and the myriad clever

and complex ways that products have been insinuated into people's consciousness through lyrics and music.

In the cultural studies literature, much has been made of the resistant and even liberatory aspects of popular culture. If one examines particular cases, it is indeed possible to locate instances of people's resistance to what has been foisted upon them by the cultural industries. But if one examines the long haul of the production of the cultural industries, as this book does, it becomes clear that, while there may be cases here and there—even many instances—of resistance to and liberation through popular culture, it is nonetheless unarguable that the cultural industries have triumphed, and are continuing to triumph, over the nearly century-long history covered in this book. When this book begins, in the 1920s, the United States was primarily an industrial and agricultural economy. Today, it is a consumer economy. When this book begins, Americans fashioned selves by drawing on Victorian conceptions of character. Today, we fashion selves mainly through the products we purchase.

The question, of course, is, how did we get here from there? While I have long resisted what one might call music exceptionalism—the idea that music occupies a more important place in our culture than other forms of expression or cultural production—in this book, I argue that the various uses of music in advertising chronicled in what follows have played not just an important role, but a singular one, in shaping consumption patterns in the United States. More than that: music in advertising has helped make us into the consumers we are, for music's relationship to the body and its ability to address listeners emotionally have made it a powerful tool for advertisers at least since the rise of broadcasting in the 1920s.

This book begins in that tumultuous decade, examining the uses of music in advertising from the beginning of broadcasting to the present. Its main purpose is to narrate this almost entirely unknown history, but it will also examine the changing nature of various forms of American capitalism and the role that consumption has played, and continues to play, in American culture. It is now commonplace to hear contemporary American culture described as a consumer society, but only in the last couple of decades has consumption become an object of study, in part because of the long-standing focus on production. Scholars in the last couple of decades have sought to balance the productivist perspectives of Marxian and other studies, and there have been several histories of consumption in the United States that will inform what follows, such as those by Lizabeth Cohen, Gary Cross, and Charles F. McGovern.[1]

I also hope to situate this book in historical studies of the music industry as an industry, particularly since, as I will show, the advertising and music industries are increasingly intertwined today. Histories of the music industry in the United States, by Karl Hagstrom Miller and David Suisman, provide an important complement to the history of the advertising industry to follow.[2]

This book also takes its place beside the small number of those to address the American advertising industry historically, books by David Ewen, Jackson Lears, and Roland Marchand, even though these and virtually all of the scholarly literature on advertising focus on print advertisements, not ads with sound and moving images.[3] Advertisers' and advertising agencies' arguments over what kind of music to air are revealing, divulging a good deal about who they think their audience is, instructing us about how they think of themselves, as well as giving us a way to understand the workings of American capitalism over nearly a century.

In some ways, this book tells a simple story. A new music, or technology, or demographic, or medium, can result in effective advertising, advertising that those in advertising agencies can use as an example of the importance of their work. But once audiences become inured to these new modes of enticement, their effectiveness wanes. Until another one comes along.

Capitalism and the Production of Consumption

As useful as the writings on consumption are, capitalism is not always a salient part of their stories, which tend to be more concerned with analyzing consumption as a social practice that plays various important roles: in conceptions of citizenship, identity formation, the sign-values of commodities, and more. I, however, am interested in capitalism, and the role consumption plays in supporting it, driving it, and how individual subjects have slowly, over the course of the twentieth century, become increasingly, and primarily, defined as consumers. Examining how commercials were fashioned not only to sell goods and services but also to inculcate listeners and viewers into their roles as consumers forms an important part of this book. That is, I am mainly concerned with the production of consumption, rather than consumption as social practice, about which much has been written. And I am less interested in "reading" these commercials as entities in and of themselves (for which there is also an extensive literature, though mainly focusing on print).[4] I am, rather, concerned with commercials as expressions of an ideology designed to sell not only a particular commodity but consumption itself.

Several classic theorists have placed consumption at the center of their understanding of the workings of capitalism as a response to the productivist orientation of Karl Marx and much post-Marxian thought. Probably the most central of these is Werner Sombart, whose *Luxury and Capitalism,* first published in 1913, posited that the consumption practices in French courtly life led to increased consumption more generally in the early modern period.[5] Following Sombart and others such as Arjun Appadurai, I seek to emphasize the role that consumption played, and continues to play, in both promoting and perpetuating American capitalism since the end of the nineteenth century in the United States.[6] In this context, it is clear that the shift of the manufacture of goods for production—tools, railroads, and more—gave way to the increased production of consumer goods, which were sold through new venues such as department stores and lengthy catalogs such as those published by Sears, Roebuck and Montgomery Ward.[7] With the rise of the advertising industry in the late nineteenth century, advertising more than anything else began to propel consumption practices. Today it's clear, of course, that consumption plays a powerful role in driving capitalism; one hears routinely from news sources that the American economy is supported by consumer spending; and there are, of course, George W. Bush's and Rudolph Giuliani's exhortations to Americans after the September 11, 2001, attacks that their most important duty was not to sacrifice but to spend.

This book follows three waves of increased consumption and the increased inculcation of consumption in American life beginning, in the 1920s, with radio, a powerful new advertising medium; followed by television in the 1950s; and, finally, the explicit sacralization of consumption by Ronald Reagan in the 1980s, a wave that was later buttressed by the rise of the Internet and in particular the World Wide Web in the 1990s.[8]

My approach to studying American consumer capitalism in the last ninety years or so is by now a familiar one among interpretive social scientists, employing a combination of Marxian criticism of capitalism as a system that is usually implicit, combined with a Weberian attention to concrete historical processes. That is, Marx, for all his insistence on the materialist conception of history, was rather long on materialism and rather short on history. Max Weber provides this, at least with respect to one of the origins of capitalism, and provides as well a model of how one can persuasively theorize out of a detailed history, in this case, the history of music as a particularly compelling affective form that, when used in advertising, has played a potent role in making goods and consumption part of our habitus.

In this, I suppose, this book is not that different from the voluminous and influential writings of Theodor Adorno on the subject of music in capitalist cultures, though, indeed, there has been little writing on music and capitalism since Adorno that has been as sophisticated.[9] (There haven't been many sustained treatments of music and capitalism at all, with a few exceptions, such as Jacques Attali's *Noise: The Political Economy of Music*).[10] Yet, though I may agree with him occasionally, Adorno's work is replete with problems. It is short on empirical data, whether historical or ethnographic, the author preferring simply to "read" history and culture out of musical (or other) "texts." Sometimes this works spectacularly and convincingly; other times, less so. And Adorno was unreflexive about his own positionality, or, as Pierre Bourdieu would have it, he failed to objectify objectivity.[11] His privileged position as a middle-class academic permitted him to write about the degradations of "mass culture," as if everyone had previously listened to music attentively and in a kind of philosophically receptive mode in which he himself seemed to relate to western European classical music. Most seriously, the relative lack of empirical data led him to generalizations and conclusions that aren't always sustainable. Capitalism isn't as monolithic as it comes across in many of his writings, people aren't always duped by the cultural industries, music isn't always a commodity, and, if it is, isn't always a commodity in the same way. If we have learned one important thing from the Marxian study of culture after Adorno—from Raymond Williams—it is that the world is always in flux, that processes, even the most draconian effects of American capitalism, cannot be captured with snapshots of particular cultural moments, or examinations of a single work or two.[12]

Thus, detailed empirical data over the long term are required if we are truly going to attempt to understand how capitalism and cultural production work. This book offers such a study, covering nearly a century of advertising and music practices, showing how capitalism adapted to and created new modalities of consumption, and the role that music played in them. If, in the end, the book seems to arrive at a set of conclusions that might be recognized as Adornian, it is a result of long study of a very long historical moment, not a nostalgia for a past that never actually existed—except, perhaps, for a tiny social elite—or an almost pathological disdain for popular culture and its consumers.

The Chapters

The Sounds of Capitalism gathers together, for the first time, the myriad practices of advertising and music production and places them in a historical narrative (though admittedly multipronged) from the beginning of broadcasting in the 1920s to the present. This massive body of music has been remarkably neglected by scholars; there is almost no humanistic or social science writing on this subject apart from a handful of items, none of which are historical.[13]

In the early days of radio advertising, the subject of chapter 1, advertisers normally sponsored entire programs, a practice that made the choice of music crucial for attracting the audience the advertiser desired, and thus the history of the early period of broadcasting reveals the advertising industry desperate to discover what Americans wanted to hear, while at the same time offering them what advertisers thought was best suited to sell goods. Leery of direct selling in the home, the industry first settled on a "goodwill" strategy, trying to provide music that listeners would like, which, it was hoped, would generate goodwill for the advertiser's product. In some cases, advertising agencies chose a genre or style that allowed them to attempt to impart a "personality" to a brand through music; for example, snappy, effervescent banjo music was thought to be the best way to sell Clicquot Club Ginger Ale in the 1920s. Advertising music was entirely functional in this era, designed to animate products and little else.

Chapter 2 explores the many paths pursued by advertisers and advertising agencies as they attempted to ascertain who was listening to their programs, and what kind of musical programs listeners preferred. Accustomed to print, advertising agencies were not prepared to broadcast their programs into a void. They thus encouraged listeners to write in for free photographs of the stars, postcards, and other items. In the early days of radio advertising, listener letters were scrutinized for quality of paper, penmanship, and style. Polling listener preferences also appeared in the 1920s, growing increasingly sophisticated.

The onset of the Depression meant that the goodwill model was exchanged for hard-sell tactics in an attempt to influence consumers directly, a move that is perhaps best registered by the late 1930s with the rise of the "singing commercial" or jingle, the happy, memorable tune with lyrics singing the praises of the product that dominated advertising music into the 1980s (chapter 3).

Since some successful jingles were recorded as songs in their own right, escaping the narrowly commercial world in which they originated, music produced for purely commercial purposes began to have an impact on the broader world of popular culture as popular music stars recorded song versions of jingles, such as the famous "Chiquita Banana" song from 1944. Chapter 5 continues the examination of the jingle, particularly how its sound came to be standardized in the postwar era in a sound that was derived from mainstream popular musics of the 1950s and 1960s and featured a chorus that became known as the Madison Avenue Choir. This chapter also chronicles the fall of the jingle as it became increasingly seen as uncool and unhip in the 1980s and after.

Chapter 4 interrupts the history of the jingle to examine the rise of television in the 1950s and the tensions that emerged between the hard-sell tactics of the Depression and the newer, and subtler, modes of selling that were often described as "psychological," reflecting the penchant for Freudianism in the postwar era. Approaches to selling began to emphasize emotional appeals over rational ones, and some musicians were at the vanguard of this movement, articulating a discourse about affect, and a practice of evoking it, in advertising music. By the late 1970s, employing music to attempt to manipulate consumers' emotions in complex ways was commonplace, having become the norm in the realm of all commercial music to the extent that extremely subtle gradations of mood are common in discussions of commercial music today.

The boundary between advertising music and other music continued to blur so that by the early 1970s advertising songs were becoming popular hits in their own right with increasing frequency, as in the 1971 Coca-Cola song "I'd Like to Teach the World to Sing"; advertisers began to pull away from the jingle in favor of the original song that could become a hit. The real difference from the past, a difference that continues to inform the industry's practices to this day, was to seek assiduously the youth market by employing popular music in commercials as part of what Thomas Frank has called the "conquest of cool," a strategy of co-opting the cool and the hip in popular culture for use in advertising and marketing in order to appeal to youth.[14] As a result, commercial music became even less segregated from other musics, increasingly infiltrating the listening lives of Americans, whether or not audibly marked as "advertising music." The effects of baby boom youth were so powerful that a new form of capitalism has emerged that has been profoundly shaped by the counterculture's critique of earlier forms of capitalism (chapter 6).

Chapter 7 examines the rise of market segmentation and the use of music to target specific groups of consumers, while at the same time, the advent of Music Television (MTV) in the early 1980s made the usage of music even more common, garnering for some musicians millions of dollars in fees as some advertisers continued to attempt to reach as broad a group as possible. This occurred in an era that witnessed a new wave of consumption, driven in part by Ronald Reagan's and others' promotion of consumption as a public good. A raft of mergers and consolidations in the advertising industry meant that there was ever greater attention to the bottom line and efficiency, which made advertising work for musicians less rewarding than it had been in the past.

In the mid-1980s, baby boomers' ascension to positions of power in the advertising and marketing industry meant that, instead of following popular music trends, advertising agency executives began to attempt to be trend-setters themselves by using existing popular music in commercials instead of commissioning jingles, and by seeking unknown music to feature in commercials in order to position advertising as the new arbiter of the hip and cool (chapter 8). The "conquest of cool," I argue, has become the conquest of culture itself. This conquest was aided in this period by MTV and new digital technologies, marking one of the most decisive changes in advertising music for decades, all signaling the beginning of the end of a clear boundary between "advertising music" and "popular music." Because of the dominance of these technologies, today's commercial musicians move fluidly between playing in bands; producing recordings; and making music for film, television, or advertising, taking their musical tastes and styles with them wherever they go. Sounds developed for advertising have found their way into mainstream popular musics, and vice versa, in what has become a constant interchange.

Thus, while advertising music for decades simply echoed contemporary popular music styles (and frequently lagging behind), by the 1950s, advertising music had begun to become closely intertwined with the production of popular music generally. The rise of the baby boomers and postboomers to power in the advertising industry and the increased flexibility of workers in the realm of commercial music has meant that there is no popular music that is not, to varying degrees, advertising music, whether or not listeners hear it as such. The long-standing distinction between art and commerce much debated by advertising industry workers and those who study them has become moot: the sounds of capitalism are everywhere.

The concluding theoretical chapter discusses the social group responsible for promulgating the ideology of the hip and the cool, what Bourdieu has called the new petite bourgeoisie, and the new form of capitalism they are involved in promoting and perpetuating, a new capitalism that is more culturalized than earlier ones, drawing on the skills of people in this group to continue to promote consumption. A salient feature of this new capitalism in the field of cultural production of this new petite bourgeoisie is the main trope in the advertising industry—"creativity," which operates as a kind of Weberian calling in today's capitalism.

Finally, a note on sources. The empirical basis of this book is archival research, reading of the voluminous trade press, and interviews with workers in the advertising industry, past and present. Doubtless there are some historians who will quibble with my use of some or all of the above, for theirs is the task of separating truth from fabrication. But the goal I have set for myself in this book is only partially that of telling the "true" story of music used in advertising; I am just as interested in uncovering the ideologies, the discourses, that circulated in particular periods in American history when the music in question was produced. To that end, what people say in print or to me is all fair game: they are articulating the ideologies of their field of cultural production in their time, and these should be of no less interest to us than empirical history. I am thus making what is probably a commonplace distinction between historical approaches and ethnographic ones, and hope my attempts to combine them will be clear in what follows.

Last, I should note that, while this book covers a large amount of history, it is mainly focused on national advertising campaigns, which are well represented in the major archives, the trade press, and the national press. Local and regional campaigns are largely absent due to the impracticality of scouring small archives across the country, though a few scholars, particularly in the South, have offered some of this work.[15]

But that, I hope, does not diminish the book's contribution. It is the first history of its kind, a history of music that many—even most—Americans know, but know nothing about.

The Radio is a one-sided institution; you can listen, but you
cannot answer back. In that lies its enormous usefulness to
the capitalist system. The householder sits at home and takes
what is handed to him, like an infant being fed through a tube.
It is a basis upon which to build the greatest slave empire in
history.

—Upton Sinclair, Oil!, 1926

1

Music and Advertising in Early Radio

This chapter begins with the early history of radio broadcasting and examines how this new communications technology became conceptualized and employed as an advertising medium. It charts the slow rise of radio advertising
through the later processes of informing reluctant advertisers and advertising agencies of the usefulness of radio, the
translation of print advertising techniques to sound, and
the debates over which music to use in broadcast advertising.[1] It also examines two early programs, the *Clicquot Club
Eskimos* and *Aunt Jemima*.

Before proceeding, it must be understood that the rise
of radio, and advertising, can be grasped only in a larger
framework of changing patterns of American consumption
beginning in the final decades of the nineteenth century. A
complex series of factors marked this change, beginning, of

course, with the rise of industrial production. Mass production necessitated an increase in wages so that workers could also participate in the economy as consumers. Coupled with this development, the growing banalization of work with the implementation of Taylorist and Fordist models of management and production also meant that the consumption of goods and services came to occupy a larger role in American life. Old American ideals of thrift and self-sacrifice ceased to serve an economy that increasingly demanded spending as American workers were transformed into consumers.[2] To quote one observer from 1935: "As modern industry is geared to mass production, time out for mass consumption becomes as much a necessity as time in for production."[3]

The growth of consumption in this period was aided by changes in American spending habits: the practice of credit rose, and the use of the installment plan accelerated greatly.[4] Settings of consumption increased the allure of purchased goods, as new department stores became increasingly like churches, temples of consumption.[5] Goods were designed to be more attractive to consumers.[6] And movies helped promote the idea of lavish lifestyles.[7]

Herbert Hoover, according to William Leach, used his presidency to legitimate the "bureaucratic language of consumption" with terms such as *mass leisure, mass consumption,* and *mass services,* terms that entered everyday usage and shaped Americans' thinking about consumption. Hoover's conception of government was that it should not only protect its citizens but help them realize their needs and desires as well.[8] In a 1925 speech before the Associated Advertising Clubs of the world, he articulated his conception of "desire," praising advertisers for their role in raising the standard of living:

The older economists taught the essential influences of "wish," "want" and "desire" as motive forces in economic progress. You have taken over the job of creating desire. . . . In economics the torments of desire in turn create demand, and from demand we create production, and thence around the cycle we land with increased standards of living.[9]

Edward A. Filene, of department store fame, said in the 1920s that in a new era of mass production and consumption, businessmen "must produce customers as well as saleable goods."[10] This, he believed, would free modern people from everyday drudgeries and allow them to appreciate the higher things in life. Filene began his 1932 book *Successful Living in This Machine Age* with this definition:

Mass Production is not simply large-scale production. It is large-scale production based upon a clear understanding that increased production demands increased buying, and that the greatest total profits can be obtained only if the masses can and do enjoy a higher and ever higher standard of living.

This will result in the raising of wages, shortening of work time, and lowering of prices, so that class thinking will be erased.

But it is not standardizing human life. It is liberating the masses, rather, from the struggle for mere existence and enabling them, for the first time in human history, to give their attention to more distinctly human problems.[11]

And the masses were not to feel anonymous. As a 1930 editorial in *Collier's* said:

The old kings and aristocrats have departed. In the new order the masses are master. Not a few, but millions and hundreds of millions of people must be persuaded. In peace and in war, for all kinds of purposes, advertising carries the message to this new King—the people.

Advertising is the king's messenger in this day of economic democracy. All unknowing a new force has been let loose in the world. Those who understand it will have one of the keys to the future.[12]

As Hoover's speech makes clear, advertisers were well aware of their mission, which they conceived not simply as selling goods but as promoting consumption more generally, even equating their mission with that of civilization.[13] The influential advertising industry trade magazine *Printers' Ink* said in 1923 that advertising was a means of efficiently creating consumers and homogeneously "controlling the consumption of a product through advertising."[14] An entry in *The Encyclopedia of the Social Sciences* in 1922 said, "What is most needed for American consumption is training in art and taste in a generous consumption of goods, if such there can be. Advertising is the greatest force at work against the traditional economy of an age-long poverty as well as that of our own pioneer period; it is almost the only force at work against Puritanism in consumption."[15] In 1929, an article in the trade magazine *Advertising and Selling* about the future of advertising held, "Having learned the value of advertising as a commercial expression . . . the world will next turn to advertising to make itself articulate in a broad social way. By 1950 men will have learned to express their ideas, their motives, their experiences, their hopes and ambitions as human beings, and their desires and aspirations as groups, by means of printed or painted advertising, or of messages projected through the air."[16] Advertising, to put it bluntly, was viewed by its practitioners and proponents as a powerful force of modernization, designed to obliterate the "customs of ages; [to] . . . break down the barriers of individual habits of limited thinking," according to a 1922 observer. Advertising viewed itself as "at once the destroyer and creator in the process of the ever-evolving new. Its constructive effort [was] . . . to superimpose new conceptions of individual attainment and community desire."[17]

In an era of increasing rural-to-urban migration, much of what was sold in the early twentieth century were goods that played to people's fears of standing out in the crowd, with body odor or other attributes that were thought to indicate poor hygiene. Consumers weren't simply being told to buy—they were being indoctrinated by fear into thinking that unless they purchased certain products, they might offend others. This, of course, was an old strategy; Lynn Dumenil writes that advertising campaigns devoted to personal hygiene items were second only to those for food in the 1920s.[18] This claim is borne out by publications of the period.[19]

Selling Goods, Selling Radio

Thus, through medicine-show-style scare tactics and other strategies, the shift toward a consumer culture was well under way in this era. A question for broadcasters and potential advertisers, however, concerned how the new medium of radio was to be paid for; early funding mechanisms for radio were unclear at the beginning. And the earliest radio broadcasts were a haphazard affair: radio stations would put on the air whatever was convenient, available, and free, and this was usually music, for it was easier and often cheaper to employ an existing ensemble to perform than to hire writers and actors for dramatic works. And most musicians weren't paid until about 1925 since there was no revenue before broadcast advertising.[20] One early musician recalled what it was like: no pay, but "people did it for kicks—or for laughs or for—just for the sheer novelty and fun of it"; this musician played the piano and chatted, a practice called "songs and patter" at that time. But then, the [radio station] management realized or perhaps planned ahead of time that they had a commodity here that they could sell to advertisers—and they garnered a contract with the manufacturer of a very fine coffee—called Martinson's Coffee—it was a class kind of coffee—it was a little more expensive than the average—and I found myself on the air—at a—I won't say a very healthy fee—but enough to make it interesting—I believe it was once or twice a week—for Martinson's Coffee—doing what I had been doing gratis.[21]

It wasn't long, however, before big money started to turn to radio and advertising, selling radio to the American public in order to give advertisers a new way to sell goods.[22]

Selling Radio to Advertisers

At first, radio programs were designed to sell radios (about which, more later), but purveyors of hardware soon learned that the best way to sell radios was to sell programs. There was an expectation, as one writer said in 1923, that "when a radio manufacturer sells a receiving instrument he is more or less morally obligated to supply the purchaser with entertainment. . . . Our manufacturers have learned that they must sell programs instead of instruments."[23]

And Merlin H. Aylesworth, the first president of the National Broadcasting Company, the first network (or "chain" as they were known then), wrote in 1929 that NBC was incorporated for the "purpose of promoting the presentation of good radio programs" in order to entice people to purchase radio equipment. NBC was owned by the Radio Corporation of America, General Electric, and Westinghouse, each of which owned, respectively, 50 percent, 30 percent, and 20 percent of NBC, and all of which manufactured radio parts. Aylesworth observed:

A radio receiving-set is of no value intrinsically, as it stands in your house with the switch turned off. Its only value is created by what comes out of it. Our business, therefore, is to do everything possible to give the public high-class broadcasting so that it will purchase equipment, either from the manufacturers who own our Company or from their competitors.[24]

Yet convincing advertisers, and advertising agencies, that radio was a worthwhile medium for broadcasting required a good deal of effort by broadcasters.

Significant amounts of money were spent on the promotion of radio, some-times resulting in rather overblown claims; a document produced by NBC in 1929 stated boldly, "Because Broadcast Advertising appeals to the prospective purchaser through the medium of his ear instead of his eye, it acts on him in a subconscious manner, supplementing all other advertising to him," employ-ing language from psychology that increasingly found its way into advertis-ing discourse following World War I.[25] People's emotions were preyed upon, whether fear or something more pleasant. "Soup can produce emotion," said Edith Lewis of J. Walter Thompson in 1923; "you can write as emotionally about ham as about Christianity."[26]

The National Broadcasting Company and its younger, upstart rival, the Columbia Broadcasting System, produced countless lavish brochures on products, as well as on programs, stars, and their overall stable of entertain-ers in order to hype themselves to potential advertisers (I will examine some of these below).[27] NBC would also send materials that touted previous suc-cesses, including sample scripts, recommendations for music, and more. And the networks would offer free items to listeners who wrote in. Erik Barnouw writes that in the June 1932 issue of *Chain Store Management* magazine, the Kellogg Company told its dealers how merchandising through *Singing Lady* program, a children's show, was working:

> Just think of this: 14,000 people a day, from every state in the Union, are send-ing tops of Kellogg packages to the Singing Lady for her song book. Nearly 100,000 tops a week come into Battle Creek. And many hundreds of thousands of children, fascinated by her songs and stories and helped by her counsel on food, are eating more Kellogg cereals today than ever before. This entire program is pointed to *increase consumption*—by suggesting Kellogg cereals, not only for breakfast but for lunch, after school and the evening meal. It's another evidence of the Kellogg policy to build business—and it's building.[28]

Selling Radio to Advertising Agencies

NBC and, later, the Columbia Broadcasting System also attempted to sell ra-dio to advertising agencies using some of the same strategies just discussed. Typical of early solicitation letters sent to advertising agencies was this one from an NBC representative (no signature was on the carbon) to a representa-tive at the Philip Kobbé Company Inc. in New York City dated 17 February

1925, which included a list of rates and the results of a survey that revealed that radios were in relatively affluent homes—"They can afford luxuries"—and a list of advertisers, followed by this pitch:

> These representative advertisers have found Radio Broadcasting to be an ef-
> fective means of gaining the friendship of the buying public, and a powerful
> medium for indelibly impressing the name of their product on its memory.
> Doesn't it follow quite naturally that when the radio audience is entertained
> by the "Eveready Entertainers"—"The Astor Coffee Orchestra"—"The Happi-
> ness Candy Boys"—"The A & P Gypsies" each group composed of professional
> talent of the highest caliber, the result is bound to be a pleasant remembrance
> of the names "Eveready," "Astor Coffee," etc. One proof of this is the thou-
> sands of letters of commendation and appreciation addressed to the "Eveready
> Entertainers"—"The Astor Coffee Orchestra" or "The Happiness Candy Boys"
> in the files of their respective clients.[29]

Once advertising agencies began to be convinced of the usefulness of radio in advertising—a process that did not happen all at once, some agencies
being slower to get on the bandwagon than others—broadcasters and advertising agency radio department staff members devoted much of their to time
informing their clients and potential clients about what radio, and advertising
on the radio, was all about. Essentially, they had to promote radio to their colleagues who had learned advertising as a print business, and who saw themselves as rather highbrow. This was especially true at the J. Walter Thompson
Company, the biggest advertising agency in America at the time; Stanley Re-
sor, who with others had purchased the company from Thompson in 1916,
was the first head of a major advertising firm who had a college degree, and
his was from Yale.

The Thompson Company staff meeting minutes in the late 1920s reveal
a good deal of proselytizing on behalf of radio by members of the agency's
newly formed radio department. The first head of this department, William H. Ensign, defended radio to his bosses and colleagues in the meeting of
11 July 1928 by saying, "As far as J. Walter Thompson is concerned, the latest
developments are along lines of loss of ground rather than making progress as
far as billing is concerned," because two of their clients had decided to cancel
most of their radio programs. Ensign nonetheless defended the new medium:
the problem was not radio but the clients' cold feet, and once new sales data

were in, the clients could be urged to resume broadcasting. Ensign went on to mention broadcasting plans for other clients, and then produced his main evidence in favor of radio, that "15 national advertisers and 6 semi-national or local have entered the ranks of broadcast advertisers" in the previous six months, and he included a list of Thompson competitors that had started radio departments.[30]

Attempts to convince colleagues continued in other company venues. J. Walter Thompson's *News Letter* from 15 September 1928 displayed on its first page an article by one of the company's first radio program producers, Gerard Chatfield, who was a classically trained musician formerly employed by NBC. Chatfield began his article, "Advertising Agency Should Recognize and Use Radio," by writing, "Radio broadcasting has become a major medium in record-breaking time. It should be considered as such and not as a freakish mystery, a plaything or an experiment. It is simply another means of gaining entrance into approximately 10,000,000 of the most prosperous homes in the United States."[31]

In the staff meeting of 3 April 1929, Henry P. Joslyn (who had succeeded Ensign the previous month) provided several examples of how music had been used on the air to sell products. His first, and best, example concerned the *Lucky Strike Hour*, described as a "straight jazz program of dance music, interspersed with the reading [by the announcer] of anti-fat testimonials taken from the printed advertising." No famous jazz orchestra was hired; "no name, such as Paul Whiteman [a famous bandleader], was used to make this campaign stand out." George Washington Hill, the imperious president of Lucky Strikes' manufacturer, the American Tobacco Company, wrote to the president of NBC to say that sales rose more than 47 percent, an impressive figure since the American Tobacco Company had suspended most of its other advertising during a two-month trial period of advertising on the radio.[32]

Joslyn also listed some "local" examples—that is, the so-called spot advertisements that aired only on one station that had a link, or what was called a tie-in, to a local dealer.[33] Tie-ins were usually simply a plain poster or print ad, but often more. A brochure about Ipana Toothpaste produced by NBC in 1928 included photos of the tie-ins that Ipana provided to customers who wrote in: a "Magic Radio Time Table" pad so that listeners could write down their favorite programs; a bridge scorecard; a photo of the Ipana Troubadours, the program's resident musicians; a card with a paean to the smile. All of these items had the Ipana name prominently displayed. Then there was the tie-in

Figure 1.1 Ipana Troubadours, 1920s. (Author's collection.)

material made available to dealers: posters, brochures, a "radio applause card" that listeners could take to send in comments on the program, and more.[34] The troubadours also played for Ipana salesmen at conventions. All this was devised for a program that not only carried the brand name, but with musicians whose costumes bore the colors of Ipana, colors mentioned in the radio announcements, "pioneering the technique of package identification over the air," as the vice president of Bristol-Myers, Ipana's manufacturer, put it.[35]

One popular and influential program, *The Eveready Hour* (early radios were battery-powered), even issued playing cards with figures from the program on them in addition to the more normal postcard. The first major radio variety program (beginning in December 1924), *The Eveready Hour* featured some of the leading Broadway and other musicians of the day and was the first program that paid its talent to appear (example 1.1).[36]

Fan clubs would also form around favorite singers. Some were organized by listeners themselves; others were stimulated by advertisers. Douglas Duff Connah writes of a case of Kate Smith singing for La Palina cigars, which resulted in organic fan clubs that "led the sponsor to encourage formation of other groups. Elaborate Kate Smith–La Palina Club charters were printed, signed by Kate and presented to each new group, which was given an official number, and the chartering of each new club was announced over the air by the star."[37]

By the mid-1930s, consumers could be positively bombarded by advertisers in a highly organized campaign, as the accompanying figure from an NBC promotional brochure shows (fig. 1.2).[38] In this illustration, the sponsored radio program is represented as the primary advertising force, surrounded by an array of various modes of print advertising and tie-ins. NBC was obviously emphasizing the idea of the centrality of radio broadcasting, and also providing a useful diagram for how the ideology of consumption was entering the home, and American culture more generally, via every conceivable avenue.

Early Strategies

At the beginning of radio, there were countless debates about how it would be funded. It was a convoluted and arduous journey to advertising as the solution, yet it quickly became so dominant that networks in this period did little more than provide studio space and lease airtime.[39] Many programs were produced by advertising agencies in this period; those programs that were produced by

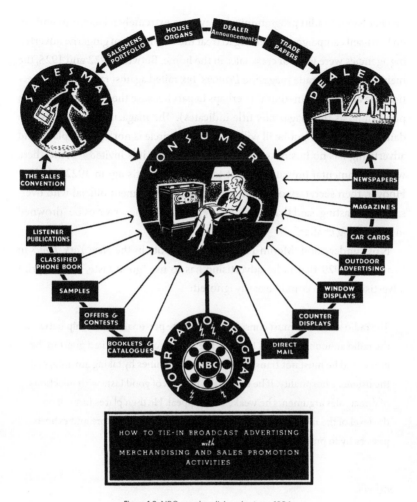

Figure 1.2 NBC merchandising chart, ca. 1936.

the networks were called "sustaining programs" (usually high-prestige shows such as the *NBC Music Appreciation Hour*, with conductor Walter Damrosch). Because of this production arrangement, in the early days of radio it is virtually impossible to separate broadcasting from advertising. So, at least in the 1920s and into the early 1930s, a history of music and broadcast advertising is less about advertisements than about programs themselves, into which mentions of brand names and sales pitches could be built.

Even though advertisers triumphed in their desire to provide the funding mechanism for radio programming, they were extremely reluctant to embark on hard-sell campaigns, preferring to treat the new medium gingerly; advertising agencies were wary of crass sales in the home. Between 1922 and 1925, the main advertising trade magazine *Printers' Ink* railed against radio as an "objectionable advertising medium" (perhaps in part because the editors focused on publishing, as the magazine's title indicates). The magazine emphasized the dangers of creating public ill will: "The family circle is not a public place, and advertising has no business intruding there unless it is invited." [40] And there was governmental pressure against too much advertising: in 1922, Herbert Hoover, then secretary of commerce and the government official who oversaw broadcasting, said that it was unacceptable that the airwaves be "drowned in advertising chatter."[41]

NBC understood. Merlin H. Aylesworth wrote in the *New York Times* in September 1929 that radio advertising has to use "good taste," unlike print advertising, which could be easily ignored:

> The radio advertiser must consider the intimate personal relationship between the radio announcer and his hearers. The announcer is an invited guest in the home, and he must not transgress the social amenities by taking advantage of the listener's hospitality. If he breaks the bounds of good taste with injections of direct sales arguments he weakens his appeal. He then places himself on the level of the merchant who stands in the doorway of his store and exhorts passers-by to purchase his goods.[42]

Goodwill

Thus, the first model of broadcast advertising that evolved emphasized goodwill: sponsored programs were developed to generate goodwill in the audience, whose members, it was hoped, would purchase the products advertised out of gratitude to the sponsor for providing the program. The idea of goodwill became the dominant advertising and broadcasting strategy at the beginning of radio.

Radio programs, in order to generate goodwill, had to provide something that people couldn't hear any other way. According to Orrin E. Dunlap, "Mechanical [i.e., recorded] music on the radio does not generally create goodwill, because it can be heard at home without the use of a radio set."[43] Another early radio writer acknowledged the goodwill strategy, and observed:

If, then, you can draw on a large body of material which is fairly certain to have general appeal and not to hurt anyone's feelings, you are doing the wise thing from the commercial standpoint. Such a body of material exists. It is based on the primal occupations of ordinary human beings. A girl with a charming voice singing "Thank God for a Garden" will offend no one but a few atheists. . . . The "Four Indian Love Lyrics," the Barcarolle from the "Tales of Hoffman" [by Jacques Offenbach], "O, Promise Me," and a few thousand other things are in the same category.

And, of course, modern music had to be avoided: "Why should they [broadcasters] monkey with dangerous artistic creations which, while they are new, are likely to arouse passions and interfere, perhaps, with the sale of goods?" wrote one commentator in 1928.[44]

Earning goodwill was not viewed as being particularly difficult. Hard-sell pitches were kept to a minimum, and entertainment, mostly music, was chosen to appeal to a broad audience. In 1929, Orrin E. Dunlap described a program sponsored by the Dixie Cup Company that began broadcasting in 1928:

The Dixie Circus goes on the air with Uncle Bob Sherwood, "the last of P. T. Barnum's clowns" taking two little friends, Dorothy and Dick, to the big tent. The overture is "Dixie." The circus atmosphere is supplied by the roars and grunts of the animals, the circus band, and last but not least the calliope. Uncle Bob tells interesting facts about the circus and the animals as the trio stops at the various cages. The incentive for the program is to create goodwill for Dixie sanitary cups.

Dorothy and Dick spy the circus lemonade! They ask Uncle Bob if they can have a drink. He agrees that lemonade is part of the circus, "but you youngsters don't have to drink out of half-washed glasses as we used to do. You can have yours in fresh, individual Dixies." This has been classed by some critics as too much advertising. But, nevertheless, the calliope makes a big hit. A dozen listeners in a Massachusetts town signed one letter pleading for at least ten minutes of the calliope instead of a few short blasts at the conclusion of the program.[45]

This passage reveals a number of the broadcast advertising strategies of the era. The *Dixie Circus* program included the name of the company in the program's title to inform listeners who was paying for their entertainment. And it used the tried-and-true fear of germs, of contaminated "half-washed glasses," to induce the listening public to purchase its cups.

The idea of goodwill seems to have been fairly successful at first. Not only did sales of sponsors' products frequently rise, but audience members wrote letters to sponsors to express their appreciation, some of which were published in the trade press. "It may interest you to know," wrote a listener from Philadelphia to the Whittall Rug Company, sponsor of the Whittall Anglo-Persians (an orchestra conducted by Louis Katzman that played standards and an occasional "oriental" work), "as a result of the Whittall Anglo-Persian concerts, which are enjoyable to no ordinary extent, we have just purchased three large and two small Anglo-Persian rugs. Otherwise and as heretofore, we would have 'shopped around.'"[46]

George C. Biggar, production manager at WLS Chicago, which had begun broadcasting the *Jamesway Barn Warming* in 1930, wrote that Jamesway Barn Equipment was hoping for the kind of reaction that it ultimately received when an Indiana representative of the company visited a farmer. "'I'm the Jamesway man,' he said, introducing himself. 'Say, I'm sure glad to meet you,' replied the farmer, 'I know you because I hear you on WLS every Tuesday night.' Needless to say, this farmer felt that he was meeting an old friend, and sales resistance had been cut to a minimum."[47] And one commentator in 1930 recounted the story of a farmer who drove twenty-five miles to the branch office of a utility company to express his appreciation for its radio band, saying, "I have come to the conclusion that any company that has sufficient enterprise to furnish radio audiences with such concerts free of charge is a good company in which to invest my money and I have come here to buy some of your stock."[48]

Occasionally, radio stations would hold a contest in an attempt to generate goodwill. In the early 1930s, WOAI, in San Antonio, Texas, regularly broadcast a "Mexican orchestra," including the occasional vocalist, sponsored by Gebhardt Chili Powder Company. The company and its advertising agency wanted a broader audience and thought the program should be changed to feature "snappy American music with a little Mexican atmosphere." But, unable to decide, it elected to air the original program juxtaposed with a new one to see what the audience preferred. The company offered a free can of its deviled sandwich spread and new recipe book as a goodwill offering to those who wrote in with their preference. The Mexican program won.[49]

The advertising that did find its way into programs in this era was referred to as "indirect advertising," which would incorporate a message or two in the program, often including the product name in the program title, as we have seen. Sometimes the sponsor's name would appear in the name of the band or orchestra as well, occasionally even insinuating the product name into the names of individual performers. *The Palmolive Hour*, which aired from 1927 to 1931, for example, featured singers "Olive Palmer" (whose real name was Virginia Rea) and "Paul Oliver" (Frank Munn). "The naming of the musical unit in such a way that the company's name can be included with each entertainment announcement is psychologically sound," wrote P. H. Pumphrey, manager of the radio department of the advertising agency Fuller, Smith & Ross Inc. "When the listener hears that 'The Lucky Strike Dance Orchestra now plays Baby's Birthday Party,' or that 'Ernö Rapee and his General Electric Orchestra will bring us the finale from Beethoven's Fifth Symphony,' the commercial name registers, but except to the most captious, does not appear as an intrusion."[50]

The Depression, and advertisers' desire to improve flagging sales, meant the eventual demise of the goodwill strategy. By late in 1932, *Fortune* magazine wrote, "The advertiser has become tired of thinking about goodwill or publicity and insists upon thinking about sales."[51] And the *Wall Street Journal* offered a parody of the goodwill strategy in 1938 that captures the lengths to which some advertisers went:

Friends of the radio audience: The Aunt Sally Superior Horseradish Company, sponsoring this program for your enjoyment, does not believe that radio listeners want their concerts interrupted by long advertising announcement[s]. Therefore the makers of Aunt Sally Superior Horseradish will not delay this program more than a few moments. They appreciate the fact that you are more interested in the next number than in the excellent qualities of Aunt Sally Superior Horseradish. And since the beginning of its weekly broadcasts the Aunt Sally Superior Horseradish Company has felt that in giving you an hour of music it is accomplishing more than by taking your time telling you about Aunt Sally Superior Horseradish. If you will listen closely you will find that the Aunt Sally Superior Horseradish Company uses only seven words in its radio advertising announcement. And those words are "Aunt Sally Superior Horseradish Really Is Superior." The next selection by the Aunt Sally Superior Horseradish Company will be a selection of Victor Herbert favorites, played for you by the Aunt Sally Superior Horseradish Orchestra.[52]

Which Music?

Advertisers learned early on that musical programs were popular with audiences, so much so that sponsored musical programs quickly became common on the airwaves by the late 1920s; the catchphrase among advertisers was that music was radio's "safety first."[53] NBC executive Frank A. Arnold wrote in 1931, "In the early days of national broadcasting the thing which probably saved the day was the discovery that 'the great common denominator of broadcasting' was music," because the great variety of regions, languages, classes, and so forth made it difficult to devise a program with mass appeal.[54] For Arnold, it was music that had created the national audience for radio; regardless of language or country of origin, "every one in his group knew and appreciated the language of music."[55] P. H. Pumphrey concurred in the same year, writing, "With rare exceptions, the largest and the surest audiences are built by musical programs."[56]

Deciding what music should be featured on a sponsored program was normally the subject of a great deal of debate between the sponsor and its advertising agency, for there were competing ideas about which music was most appropriate: sponsors wanted music that they felt best projected the image they wanted for their product and addressed the market as they saw it; advertising agencies frequently had differing thoughts about this; and then there was the thorny question of audiences and their musical preferences, which arose slightly later.

The records of the J. Walter Thompson Company suggest that the production of broadcast musical programs was well under way before higher executives began to wonder about it. When they did finally begin to take it more seriously, the first issue they wanted addressed with respect to the use of music in advertising was the question concerning classical music or jazz. This matter was confronted by J. Walter Thompson executives in their staff meeting on 3 April 1929, at which point their broadcasting department had been active for over a year. So, according to Henry P. Joslyn, head of the radio department at the time, "The question as it came to me was the question of jazz and classical music as media for radio advertising." Joslyn patiently explained to the gathered executives, still thinking in terms of print, that that was the wrong question; clients like different musics, as do audiences.[57] The subtext, though, concerned the "quality" of programming. Classical music, even in its lighter forms, was seen as more highbrow than jazz, and thus a more suitable music for advertising, at least in the ears of the J. Walter Thompson executives. But as one contemporary guidebook to radio advertising put it, advertising agencies needed to chart a path between "popularity" and "distinctiveness" (i.e., between music considered to be highbrow and lowbrow, two buzzwords in this period).[58] Agencies and/or clients wanted to put "good" programming on the air—which for them usually meant classical music—but the listening public might want something else.

And the listening public might actually listen to music differently—inattentively—further influencing the choice of music. A 1930 article by Jarvis Wren, radio advertising specialist at Kenyon and Eckhardt in New York City, argued that many musical programs tended not to grab the undivided attention of the listener, at least if they featured unobjectionable music. In such cases, the sales message might be lost. This was a particular problem when the music was of a "dreamy type," such as Hawaiian guitars. Wren thought, however, that musical programs could attract a large audience.

For Wren, musical programs were the most effective when the product was already well known, or when the sales message was simple and straightforward, or when the program was going to be supplemented by a good deal of print advertising. In other cases, such as launching a new product, he believed the dramatic program to be superior.[59] His ideas appeared in a more formulaic way in a 1931 publication, which said that questions of which music was the most appropriate went beyond the image desired for a particular product, the sponsor's preferences, or even the preferred audience, revealing a prejudice against the audiences for popular musics. From the more highbrow perspective of advertising agencies and their clients, popular music audiences were thought to possess short attention spans, necessitating reinforcement of the radio program by print advertising, and were thought to be unable to digest longer sales campaigns. Classical music audiences were assumed to be more intelligent, and broadcasting classical music could still generate goodwill in this select audience, grateful for classical music in an environment increasingly cluttered by various kinds of popular music.[60]

Undoubtedly, one of the considerations about what kind of music to broadcast was cost. An article from the late 1930s broke down the cost for various ensembles, indicating that a symphony orchestra of forty people cost $425, while a dance orchestra with twelve people cost $96 or $135, depending on the amount of rehearsal time. At the low end, a "harmony duo" and

"male or female trio" cost \$35; a male or female soloist cost anywhere from
\$15 to \$200.[61]

Classical or Jazz?

The early debates about which music was most suitable usually coalesced
around the question of whether to broadcast classical music or jazz. Advertising agencies tended to prefer classical music because of the prestige and legitimacy it conferred on their young and somewhat disreputable profession, an
attitude aided by a potent public discourse about the power of radio to uplift
the tastes of the nation.[62] Sponsors, however, tended to advocate music that
would enhance their product's image, or sell the product, and that was usually
music more popular than classical music. And sometimes meddlesome sponsors sought to choose music themselves.[63]

The debate about classical music versus jazz has been discussed by two
major radio historians, Susan J. Douglas and Michele Hilmes, who take these
terms largely at face value.[64] Both authors assume that *jazz* and *classical* mean
much the same now as they did then. In fact, however, the terms as used in
broadcasting were not very far apart in this period.[65] *Jazz* referred not to a
music with a high improvisational content performed mainly by African
Americans but, rather, highly arranged quasi-classical dance tunes performed
by white musicians, many with classical musical training and backgrounds.
Paul Whiteman is the best example of a "jazz" musician in this discourse, and
indeed was the most prestigious and influential figure in this music in this
era. *Classical* in the late 1920s and 1930s in broadcasters' discourse referred
not to "classics" but mainly to light works, light classics, and a few warhorses.
Frank A. Arnold provided a script for the *General Electric Hour* that aired on
WEAF in New York City on 8 November 1930 (an hour-long program that
featured speeches by Floyd Gibbons, "famous journalist and adventurer," and
music, mainly on the lighter side, performed by the General Electric Orchestra, conducted by Walter Damrosch). The selections on that particular program included "Suite from 'Henry VIII'" by Saint-Saens [*sic*]; "Second and
Fourth Movements from 'Symphony in G'" by Haydn; "Whispering of the
Flowers" by von Bloom; and "Overture to 'Rienzi'" by Wagner. There were
many such lists that contained a similar smattering of warhorses (usually excerpted, as in the Haydn symphony above) and many light works.

When more demanding music did appear on the air, especially when conducted by its composer, advertisers frequently objected. Alfred P. Sloan Jr., president and chairman of General Motors, which sponsored the *General Motors Symphony Concerts* in the mid-1930s, complained to NBC president Aylesworth in a letter from 2 January 1935:

> I understand that some Conductor—whoever he may be, is inconsequential—was permitted to perpetrate, on the radio audience, a composition of his own, which is a very sore point with me. I have given instructions, time and time again, that this should not be done....
>
> I am informed further, that the concert was far from tuneful—another point which I have urged....
>
> Now please understand, Mr Aylesworth, that I do not believe in jazz. Nobody hates it more than I do, but I do contend that there is plenty of music available, if one will adjust their thinking to its importance, that has some melody in it, and at the same time is not of the jazz order....
>
> I am going to have the programs reasonably tuneful, at the same time not of the jazz order, and I am going to prevent Conductors from perpetrating their own compositions on an unsuspecting public, at the expense of General Motors stockholders, or else there is not going to be any program at all.[66]

Aylesworth and General Motors' advertising agency agreed. Sloan replied, "I have tried to convey the idea, be it right or wrong, that the fundamental thing I am contending for is music with a reasonable amount of harmony. The reason I want a ban placed on conductors playing their own compositions, is because, while they may be very high in technique, they are very low in melody and appeal to the masses."[67]

Debates over the most appropriate music for broadcasting resulted in endless solicitations of fan mail, mailing of questionnaires, and other means of acquiring data about listener tastes. In 1927, a nationwide poll of listeners resulted in a list of favorite compositions. Some are well known—Beethoven's Fifth Symphony, Schubert's Eighth Symphony, and Wagner's Overture to *Tannhäuser* heading the list—but over half were light classics, such as Rudolph Friml's *The Firefly*, Victor Herbert's "Dagger Dance" from *Natoma*, and Edwin Poldini's "Poupée Valsante."[68] A different survey from 1927 revealed:

> Fully 70 per cent of the letters written to WEAF by admiring listeners in 1922 were in response to dance or jazz programs, 25 percent to classical programs,

and 5 per cent to so-called educational features. A year later, jazz dropped to about 35 per cent of the response, classical music rose to 35 per cent, and educational talks . . . increased to 35 percent. These figures were brought forward as evidence that the radio audience had improved greatly in its tastes.[69]

The author accounted for the popularity of jazz by noting that many stations solicited requests, and that the "poor musical quality of reception then attainable simply exaggerated the more raucous element of jazz music."[70] Nationally, however, by the late 1920s, jazz or dance music was the most popular music on the air, though classical music never disappeared.[71]

Building a Program

Let me now turn to the question of devising a program, and the question of translating print advertising practices to sound. Because advertisers and ad agencies were accustomed to thinking in terms of print, radio did not immediately present itself as a medium for advertising; radio in its infancy was not viewed as a primary medium for advertising but rather one that supplemented print advertising. Few advertising executives in this era could conceive of selling a product solely through sound.

Early discussions of sound were thus frequently analogized to print, as NBC president Aylesworth wrote in a 9 April 1932 article in *Adcrafter*: "Sometimes, the use of a popular star to attract an audience is compared with the use of a headline in very bold type, while the use of a large orchestra with a conductor of the highest caliber may be said to resemble the commissioning of a famous artist to paint special pictures for four-or-five color magazine advertisements," but he cautioned also that radio is its own medium and such analogies cannot be pushed too far.[72] And in one of the earliest books on radio advertising, published in 1929, *New York Times* radio writer Orrin E. Dunlap delineated how radio music functions compared to print advertising:

> The headline of a printed advertisement is extremely important. It catches the eye. The headline of an ethereal [i.e., broadcast] advertisement must attract the ear. It is usually done by the opening announcement or in some case an orchestra plays an introductory musical selection before a word is spoken. It is often easier to lure the ear with a snappy musical selection than with words.[73]

Dunlap seemed even more convinced about the function of music in radio advertising as he continued, for by the next page he opined confidently, "Music is more captivating than words on the radio."[74] He offered several examples, including the *Maxwell House Concert* program, which took as its theme song the "Old Colonel March," and wrote, "The old southern colonel referred to is no other than the gentleman often pictured in the magazine advertisements, on billboards . . . holding up the empty cup as he remarks, 'Good to the last drop.'"[75] In this way, advertisers could remind listeners of their sponsored programs and reinforce the sales work done by their programs.

Once advertisers were more accustomed to dealing with sound, the issue was addressed more frequently in the trade press; a 1941 article tackled the question in some depth. The author described a musical program called *Blue Velvet*, which offered "music for music's sake." But conductor Mark Warnow's newer program, *The Lucky Strike Hit Parade*, was "music for advertising's sake." The author wondered if all musical programs were the same, whether or not they were sponsored by an advertiser. According to Warnow, there was a difference: "When I and my orchestra accept a commercial program," he said, "we become part of an advertisement and it is our job to function as part of a radio advertisement just as the artwork, the layout and the typography of a printed advertisement would."[76]

Lucky Strike's program was built around the ten most popular tunes of the week. One way that Warnow viewed the program as an advertisement was to present the songs in arrangements that were as close to the popular versions as possible. (An arrangement is a different orchestration or instrumentation of the known version; the practice of arranging exploded in the radio era as a way of making a hit tune last longer.) "That is making your music good advertising," he said. "It would be just as silly to experiment with these numbers as it would to experiment, say, with the [famous Lucky Strike] slogan, 'It's toasted.'" The music was also to be played simply and clearly so that songs would be easily recognized by the audience. And the public's taste was carefully monitored. "A certain kind of tempo or rhythm may grow into popular favor. Therefore, if Mr. [George Washington] Hill [president of the American Tobacco Company, maker of Lucky Strike cigarettes] suggests that a rhythmic number should have more 'shake,' while he may not be using a musical term, he is using a term based on an observation that I can translate into music."[77] In this way, musical programs were slowly conceptualized and shaped to convey advertising messages that might appeal to listeners.

The Audience

In the late 1920s, market research was rudimentary, often mainly anecdotal, so that concocting programs was essentially little more than a hit-or-miss proposition. In the case of a cigar campaign described in a trade press article in 1929, advertising man Sherman G. Landers of the Aitken-Kynett Company of Philadelphia described his audience as men over thirty, but that was all.[78] Landers also proffered what was at the time something of a marketing insight: "We . . . set out to design a program that would attract the type of man who had already become a cigar smoker or the married man with a family looking for relaxation in the form of entertainment."[79] (This was actually a strategy ahead of its time, for most broadcasters knew so little of their audience that they tended to design programs around the product, not its market.) Given this crude grasp of the market, Landers and his company decided to stay away from the "craze" for dance orchestras, which they thought would have attracted too young an audience for their product. Instead, their "final decision was to recreate the black face days of yore in an old-fashioned minstrel show" as the *Dutch Masters Minstrels* program.

The normal ideal was a program that could appeal to large and diverse audiences while offending the fewest people. As NBC put it, "Tell it to the masses, and the classes will understand."[80] There was a consensus in general that the broadest possible audience had to be reached; as a writer for the *Saturday Evening Post* put it in 1924:

> The radio audience includes everybody. Therefore it wants about everything
> transmissible through the air. The ideal program is one made up to appeal
> to every taste every day, pleasing everybody at some point, not somebody at
> every point.[81]

Reaching everybody meant providing something for everybody.

The Clicquot Club Eskimos

Thus, the early approach was generally not to decide on a desired audience but, rather, to devise a program with general appeal. Advertisers were more concerned about the best way to represent the product, believing that their job was to find a way to select or fabricate a musical sound or program that would somehow resonate with—or create—perceptions of the product itself. Frank A. Arnold wrote in 1931, "A sparkling water, or a ginger ale, or a summer drink, chooses for its copy program, a type of music suggestive of and thoroughly in keeping with the product itself."[82]

Arnold was probably thinking of the music for the *Clicquot Club Eskimos* program, a show sponsored by a ginger ale company whose product was sold by the Clicquot Club Eskimos, a band led by virtuoso banjo player Harry Reser.[83] This program aired from 1923 to 1926, originating in New York City on WEAF, NBC's flagship station. Orrin E. Dunlap wrote in 1929, "The Eskimos play 'sparkling' music because their ginger ale sparkles. They open their program with the Clicquot March and the bark of the Eskimo dogs [example 1.2]. They hope that when listeners see the bottle with the Eskimo on the label they will recognize it as the same Clicquot that made the loudspeakers sparkle with pleasant banjo tunes."[84] No recordings of this program exist from this era, but there is at least one script, so below is what was probably a typical opening of their program, which captures something of the flavor of the show.[85]

> Announcer: Look out for the falling snow, for it's all mixed up with a lot of
> ginger, sparkle, and pep, barking dogs and jingling bells and there we have a
> crew of smiling Eskimos, none other than the Clicquot Club Eskimos trip-
> ping along to the tune of their own march—"Clicquot."
> Orchestra: (Plays "Clicquot"; the trademark overture.)
> Announcer (Continuing):
> After the long breath-taking trip down from the North Pole, the Eskimos
> stop in front of a filling station for a little liquid refreshment—and what else
> would it be, but Clicquot Club Ginger Ale—the ginger ale that's aged six
> months. Klee-ko is spelled C-L-I-C-Q-U-O-T. You'll know it by the Eskimo
> on the bottle. (Slight pause.) Up in Eskimo-land where the cold wind has a
> whistle all its own and a banjo is an instrument of music, the Eskimos spell
> melody with a capital "M," and tell us that "It Goes Like This."
> Orchestra: (Plays "It Goes Like This.")[86]

Note how the product advertisement is woven into the continuity (the connecting prose) of the program in this era of "indirect advertising."

The *Clicquot Club Eskimos* program was so successful that NBC produced

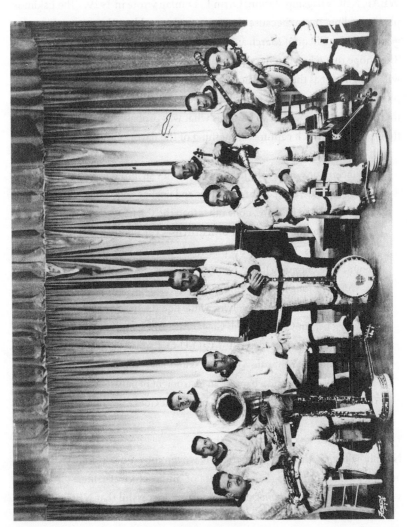

Figure 1.3 The Clicquot Club Eskimos, 1920s. Harry Reser, center. (Author's collection.)

Figure 1.4 Harry Reser: "Clicquot Fox Trot March," cover, 1926.

a lavish brochure in 1929 that touted the program to potential advertisers. Calling the Eskimos "among the most unique salesmen in the history of commerce," the brochure set out to sketch the program's attributes, including the theme song.[87] The sheet music, published in 1926, featured Reser and the other members of the group (mostly banjo players) and the Clicquot mascot, a cherubic "Eskimo" holding a bottle of ginger ale much too big for him.[88] The music was given away to fans writing in to the program; NBC claimed in 1929 that fifty thousand requests had been made.[89]

NBC said that the Clicquot Club program was probably the first to use a "trademark overture," a piece of music that "is probably as well-known in introducing the Clicquot Club Company's program as 'Over There' is in announcing a war picture." Continuing, employing language from print advertising:

> The value of this from an advertising standpoint can hardly be overestimated. Millions of people from coast to coast are put into a receptive frame of mind to hear the Clicquot Club Eskimos' program by the familiar jingle of sleigh-bells, the rhythmic crack of the whip and the bark of the huskies as they bring the Eskimos on to the radio stage for their weekly program. This musical preface and epilogue are "headline" and "signature" to the Clicquot Club Company's air advertisement.[90]

The literalness driving such a conception of music is interesting here; even though, as various advertising scholars have noted, tactics derived from psychological warfare employed in World War I found their way into advertising practices in the 1920s and after, the music used in the beginning of radio was not usually selected primarily for its affective qualities but, rather, its ability to reinforce imagery and text, to animate the product. Early radio advertising with music is a kind of throwback to earlier advertising practices of selling the product based on its qualities, which are reinforced by sound, especially music, instead of attempting to use psychology to incite consumers to purchase.

Aunt Jemima

The *Aunt Jemima* program, also produced by the J. Walter Thompson Company, speaks to the question of attempting to match a product to music. J. Walter Thompson's Gerard Chatfield wrote in the company's *News Letter* in 1928 that some products simply suggest a kind of program, saying, "Aunt Jemima"—of pancake mix fame—"should croon folk songs of the South," for example.[91] And the program shows how radio producers in advertising agencies were piggybacking radio onto earlier forms of entertainment that were known to be popular, namely, minstrelsy, as in the *Dutch Masters Minstrels* program. J. Walter Thompson's executives thought a minstrel program was perfectly natural for selling pancake mix. This supposed naturalness, however, still had to be framed and introduced to everyone associated with the product.

Perceptions of the quality (or lack thereof) of sponsored programs occupied many of the J. Walter Thompson staff meeting minutes. Henry P. Joslyn described one of Thompson's own ads, for Aunt Jemima's Pancake Flour, in the meeting on 3 April 1929, an ad that

> advertised by a troop [sic] of darkies who sing and play for the white folks
> at Col. Higbee's plantation. They are real Negroes, headed by J. Rosamond
> Johnson and Taylor Gordon who have toured Europe and America as concert
> singers. They are famous under their own names but go on the air as Uncle Ned
> and Little Bill. Aunt Jemima herself is one of the characters in the troop [sic]
> and a small orchestra, quartette and chorus is built around them. The dialogue
> brings the name "Aunt Jemima" to the listening ear between each number. The
> "act" is one of the best on the air today. Occasional jazz is used. Spirituals and
> old-time favorites are more frequent.[92]

Unmentioned by Joslyn, the title character was played by the Italian American vaudevillian Tess Gardella.

As one might guess from the foregoing, the scripts for these early shows were written entirely in dialect. Musical selections were sometimes named, sometimes not. Occasionally, the script directions would simply say "Quartette—Lively Spiritual" or "Lively instrumental," and refer to Aunt Jemima and her friends as either "docile" or "lively."

J. Walter Thompson Company staff nonetheless found the program effective. The company News Letter from 15 December 1928 includes a report from the company's Chicago office that described the program, concluding:

> The Aunt Jemima selling talk was worked in very unobtrusively and naturally.
> The whole entertainment hung together beautifully and did not drag for a
> single moment. It was apparent to every one present that the whole thing was a
> very distinctive piece of work and far above the average of radio programs.[93]

Aunt Jemima sales figures climbed steadily after the introduction of the radio program. In a staff meeting on 16 April 1930, John Reber, by summer of 1929 the head of the radio department, presented his colleagues with the following figures: sales for 1928 were up 14 percent over the previous year; 1929, up 30 percent; 1930, up 35 percent in January.[94]

Personality

Advertising with sound was used in one strikingly novel way beyond simply animating a product: sound could be used to make a program's stars, and even products, come to life by bestowing on them "personality."[95] Historian Warren I. Susman has written influentially of the twentieth-century move away from the nineteenth-century emphasis on "character" to "personality," of self-sacrifice giving way to self-realization, locating evidence for this change in the advice manuals published between 1900 and 1920. The key quotation that Susman finds in almost all these manuals is "'Personality is the quality of being Somebody.'"[96]

The impetus for developing one's personality came, Susman says, from the problem of living in a crowd, a mass culture, in which distinguishing oneself from others became a prime concern.[97] This new culture of mass consumption, mass production, mass media, and mass society began to emphasize not just personality but the fascinating, stunning, attractive, magnetic, glowing, masterful, creative, dominant, or forceful. Cultivating one's personality was a way to stand out from the crowd, which could be accomplished by the consumption of self-help books, elocution lessons, charm courses, and beauty aids—all designed to help consumers construct personalities, fashion selves. The personality manuals examined by Susman stressed that one's personality is something to be performed; "every American was to become a performing self." F. Scott Fitzgerald described personality in the *Great Gatsby* as "an endless series of successful gestures."[98]

Conceptions of personality were also shaped by the mass media. David Suisman writes that cultivating personality of recording stars such as Enrico Caruso early in the twentieth century was important in marketing the phonograph.[99] Warren Susman does not examine radio, but his analysis of the role of film is striking. Until about 1910, he writes, the studios concealed the identities of film actors. But in that year, the movie star was born, necessitating the use of the press agent and the skills of the advertising agency; the movie star was increasingly marketed as a personality. And, in this nascent consumer culture, movie stars came to represent leisured lives fulfilled by commodities.[100]

Figure 1.5 Samuel L. "Roxy" Rothafel. (Courtesy of Ross Melnick.)

Radio advertisers clearly meant to capitalize on this new emphasis on personality, and, indeed, they helped drive it. Their discourses, and those of their performers, are replete with references to the importance of personality. In 1924, one commentator wrote, "There is such a thing as 'screen personality' the motion picture directors tell us. Already broadcasting directors are convinced that there is also a 'voice personality.'"[101] Also in 1924, Samuel L. Rothafel, one of the first radio superstars, known affectionately to early radio listeners as "Roxy," host of a popular music program (example 1.3), said:

I am convinced that the radio performer's personality is more important than his voice, his subject or the occasion. Any of these may be poor or inopportune and still a speaker will succeed. But if his personality is flat, his purpose vague, he certainly will not command respect on the radio circuit.[102]

Again and again, the concept of personality emerges in early discussions of radio performance strategies. Singer Olive Palmer (Virginia Rea) wrote in an article for *Etude* magazine in 1931:

> I am frequently asked whether it is possible to project personality through the voice alone. I suppose it depends on the individual. I do know that the test of a radio singer is whether he can convey to others through the voice what he feels. A tear, for instance, must carry over to the unseen listener, or else the song is ineffective. A smile, a bit of whimsy, of rollicking good humor, longing, tenderness, a caress—all these and many more must register on the listener through the ear solely.[103]

Advertising men recognized the importance of personality as well. Roy Durstine, one of the first advertising agency men to enter radio broadcasting, wrote in 1928 that radio advertising "can create a personality so that millions will feel that they know him intimately."[104] Another influential adman of the era, William Benton, chairman of the board of Benton and Bowles, described in some detail how "personality" was "added" to a program. He explained the success of an "inexpensive little program" in 1935 featuring crooner Lanny Ross by saying that his company "built an atmosphere around him." Ross's program, *The Log Cabin Inn* (sponsored by Log Cabin syrup) was popular, according to Benton, because the audience liked Ross, followed his exploits, and rooted for him:

> This whole factor of personalization, of sympathetic settings and background, of illusion—is, in our judgement, the most fascinating and important in any study of the future of radio: How to get more of it, how better to personalize the stars, how to put them in situations where the public is with them and wants them to succeed and your product along with them.[105]

More generally, William H. Ensign of J. Walter Thompson said in 1928, "National Advertisers find that radio . . . carries their names or the names of their products into millions of homes in a way which is not only conducive to good will building—but which stamps those names with a personality that makes them mean more than just something to be bought," as though consumers were not merely purchasing a product but personality itself.[106]

Such was the importance of the concept of personality that NBC used a standard form for auditioning new readers and musicians, and one of the criteria to be addressed by the auditioner was personality (along with "Quality," "Musicianship," and others).[107]

Advertising agencies extended the concept of personality to goods themselves in fairly short order. The advertising literature of the day was filled with discussions of how to give a product personality. As early as 1929, an NBC promotional book on broadcast advertising said that advertisers and their agencies realized that they could devise programs to stimulate the listener's imagination, "so that he cloaks an inanimate product in living personality."[108]

Inevitably, music frequently played a role in developing a product's personality, and discussions of musical programs by broadcasters trumpeted this. NBC concluded in its brochure on the *Clicquot Club Eskimos* program, "Even a ginger ale may be personalized and dramatized."[109] The brochure discussed the selection of music, which was designed to emphasize the "ginger, pep, sparkle, and snap" of the product: "Manifestly, peppy musical numbers of lively tempo were in order. The banjo, an instrument of brightness and animation, was deemed most suitable in typifying the snap of Clicquot Club personality."[110]

A different brochure produced by NBC about the Ipana Troubadours program claimed that the broadcast advertising of the toothpaste "has given *personality* to a Tooth Paste."[111] Not coincidentally, both of these were popular programs with well-known musicians. This interest in imparting personality to a product persisted until well into the television era, though it was slowly supplanted by the use of music to add mood (see chapter 4).[112]

Advertisers and their agencies imbued programs such as these with the ideologies of modern consumer culture. Radio programs educated listeners about their roles as consumers in an era widely viewed as a kind of technological modernity, encouraging people to fashion selves not through their experience in their communities, in churches, in schools, in unions, but through mass-marketed goods made real and vivid—and desirable—on the radio.

The greatest advertising medium in the world is radio.
—Rudy Vallée, 1930

Media is a question of how many seats and how many arses.
—Phil Richardson, head of the first corporate
media department in the United States
(Procter and Gamble), 1930s

The Classes and the Masses in the 1920s and 1930s

"Tell it to the masses and the classes will understand," wrote the National Broadcasting Company of its program *The Clicquot Club Eskimos* in 1929.[1] This chapter addresses the question of the audience: how it was investigated and studied by the networks and advertising agencies, and how it was eventually commodified. The writings on the subject of the audience in this period are influential though few in number. They are also mainly theoretical, or concentrate on the rise of audience studies around major figures such as sociologist Paul Lazarsfeld.[2] It is important, however, to examine the problem historically: How were audience preferences obtained? What were the processes that resulted in the construction of the audience? The central tension for broadcasters and advertisers in this era was to cast a broad net. But at the same time, identifying audiences to

target was important, as broadcasters wanted to be able to attract the wealthi-
est consumers to market expensive goods to, as well as a large middle group
of listeners.

Constructing the Mass Audience

Radio played a powerful role in the rise of mass culture in the United States,
although Americans had a concept of the "mass" before. Indeed, this was one
of the central tensions of late nineteenth- to early twentieth-century thought,
as has been studied by T. J. Jackson Lears and others. Lears argues that ur-
ban-industrial transformation in the nineteenth century gave rise to changes
in Americans' everyday lives; urban life as anonymous individuals instead of
known neighbors in villages and the countryside, as well as modern conve-
niences that removed people from the daily experience of the outdoors resulted in much hand-wringing about a perceived loss of individuality. Lears
quotes a magazine writer from 1909: "We *are* a mass. As a whole, we have lost
the capacity for separate selfhood."[3]

The advent of radio did not create a sense of mass; it only emphasized a
tendency already under way. Yet, at the same time, radio imparted a feeling
of togetherness, since everyone knew that listeners were hearing the same
programs at the same time. Millions of people could read popular books and
magazines, or see a movie, or listen to a phonograph record, though one commentator observed in 1923 that there is "a lack of immediate contact with the
audience" when playing phonograph records.[4] With radio, however, those
millions were listening *simultaneously*, but not as a group. As one early observer wrote the same year:

> How easy it is to close the eyes and imagine the other listeners in little back
> rooms, in kitchens, dining-rooms, sitting-rooms, attics; in garages, offices,
> cabins, engine-rooms, bungalows, cottages, mansions, hotels, apartments; one
> here, two there, a little company around a table away off yonder, each and all
> sitting and hearing with the same comfort just where they happen to be.[5]

This writer continues to imagine the far-flung audience, united in time and in
their rapture at hearing organ music emanating from their radios.

Roy Durstine, one of the founders of BDO (Barton, Durstine and Osborn)
in 1919, which founded the first radio department in 1925, wrote in 1928,

Radio comes right into the middle of the family circle. It speaks and plays and sings for millions, but those millions are divided into countless audiences of one or two or perhaps three or four. At most a small group of friends is gathered together.

This is no mass psychology.[6]

By early 1929, according to Charles Henry Stamps (on whom I am relying heavily for this history of audiences), the radio audience was becoming seen as something more complicated than an undifferentiated mass or as a collection of individuals. Merlin H. Aylesworth, the first president of NBC, wrote in June 1929 that to understand radio advertising, one must remember that radio

cannot be an appeal to crowd psychology. We hear so much about the radio audience of many millions that we are inclined to visualize it as a vast throng sitting together, listening to what comes over the air. Of course it's nothing of the kind. It is almost invariably made up of family groups of not more than four or five people who select the evening's entertainment with increasing care and discrimination.[7]

Radio was thus an unprecedented technology, making people feel alone and together, simultaneously.

Who Is Listening?

But sentiments such as the above were mainly based on conjecture, for, unlike print advertising, whose sales could be measured in magazines and newspapers sold, broadcasters and advertisers had little idea who was listening, or how they were listening. A 1923 article in *Radio Broadcast* said, "It would be illuminating to have on record not the number of the *possible* radio audience, but the *actual* number of the audience listening, on a particular evening, to any particular programme."[8] From the beginning of radio, broadcasters, advertisers, and advertising agencies were desperate to discover everything they could about their audiences; people attempted to extrapolate from figures of radios sold, numbers of fan letters received, and so on.

In the absence of hard data about audiences, the most common assumption was that if one person liked it, everybody could like it. But who was this everybody? Most influential was the notion that the "average mental age" of an American was somewhere between the ages of twelve and fourteen. This information was derived from a pool of one hundred thousand American soldiers who were tested for their IQ in World War I and found to have an average mental age of thirteen, a figure that was taken as gospel by people in broadcasting and advertising for much of the period before World War II and which played a powerful role in the rise of discourses about the "mass" nature of broadcasting for several decades.[9] An exasperated editorial in *Fortune* in 1942 said, "For nearly a generation, the people of this country have been suffering patiently from a curious mental illness, a peculiar delusion about themselves. That disease is the wide acceptance of a fallacious axiom: that they have an average mental age of a thirteen-year-old child."[10]

Before the establishment of a system to rate listenership in 1929, advertisers and sponsors gauged the success of programs by the quality and volume of listener response. They often offered samples in order to gather information about listeners who mailed in their responses; and they sponsored contests whose main purpose was to solicit listener feedback.[11] One contest, sponsored by Gilmore Oil Company Ltd., manufacturer of Blu-Green Gas, solicited verses to its program's theme song, entitled, unimaginatively, "Blu-Green Gas." In 1931, the vice president of Gilmore's advertising agency wrote an article for the trade press, reporting, "To date more than 25,000 verses have been received, which we believe justifies our calling the Blu-Green Gas Song the longest song in the world."[12]

Another tactic was to hint that a program was about to be canceled in order to generate fan mail, which seems to have worked; I have seen a number of sets of fan mail in various archives complaining about the announced cancellation of a program. A variant on this strategy was mentioned in a 1931 letter in the NBC archives, which says, "Sometimes, we will take a program off the air in order to find if public opinion expresses itself in the form of a protest."[13]

But the main measure of a program's success in the early days was to read listener mail, however it was solicited. Roy Durstine wrote of fan mail in 1930,

> It is a part of the agency's work in connection with radio to keep a record of this fan mail. This record is not merely a count of replies analyzed by localities. It is a careful study of the type of stationery, the sex and apparent age of the writer, a rough classification of good, fair, and poor responses, and a thoughtful reading of the letters for suggestions in building future programs.[14]

Mail was read not just for content but, as it were, ethnographically: Frederick Lumley wrote of CBS studying letters and searching for clues to social group by examining the type of paper, grammar, spelling, punctuation, and sentence structure.[15]

Early radio listeners seem to have been avid letter writers. A letter from E. P. H. James, sales promotion manager at NBC, to Harcourt Parrish of Ivy Lee and Associates, a public relations firm in New York City, in July of 1931 said that in 1930, NBC received 2,180,000 letters from the public with comments on programs, some with criticisms. "These criticisms are carefully read and every attempt made to offer programs which will please as many members of the general listening public as possible," he observed, and went on to note that there are a variety of tastes. Tastes changed quickly, which means that NBC had to offer a variety of programs and "watch the reception of each type of program very closely."[16] Parrish had evidently asked about inducements in order to solicit mail response, and James responded with a tally of what 143 NBC advertisers had done, as of 1 May 1931. The majority (34 percent) made no offer; 19 percent offered a booklet, 14 percent a sample, 9 percent recipes, 6 percent novelties, 4 percent miscellaneous, 4 percent dealer's name, 3 percent photographs, 3 percent club membership, 2 percent songs, 1 percent program suggestions, and 1 percent comic newspaper.[17]

In January 1930, the J. Walter Thompson Company began airing the *Davey Tree Hour*, a weekly program featuring light classics and sentimental songs, including a lecture on trees by Martin L. Davey, the son of the company's founder. Davey published an article in 1932 on the success of his program, saying that he believed the public's appetite for jazz to be satiated, and that "a very small percent of the people really understand and appreciate classical music of the more difficult sort."[18] Because of this low number, Davey believed that familiar melodies would offer the most appeal though variety was also necessary. To that end, "We made sure that every other piece was fast and every other piece was slow. We made an effort to have a variety of songs of racial origin, including English, Scotch, Irish, Welsh, German, Italian, etc."[19]

This program generated a good deal of mail that pleased John Reber, head of the J. Walter Thompson Company Radio Department, and his colleagues. Reber said at the staff meeting of 14 January 1930 that the company received about six hundred unsolicited letters in praise of the program. "Never before . . . have we had letters of such a high quality; they were even considerably higher quality than those received as a result of one classical music program that we had. The stationery, the English and the evidences of culture on the part of the writers were decidedly higher than the average."[20] Davey himself wrote that the letters the company received regarding its program were almost never rude, and that "a majority of them come from people of education and culture." Yet, he noted, "We have received a very large number of letters written on cheap paper and in poor English."[21] Davey nonetheless maintained that these writers were intelligent people.[22]

Despite the broad audience that Davey sought with his program, however, he still felt that the program appealed to a higher class of people (than, perhaps, jazz programs, though he didn't say this). Davey, echoing the worries of advertisers and agencies in this period, also admonished the reader that since radio programs come into people's homes, broadcasters had an obligation "to respect the feelings and taste of the better class of citizens."[23]

Attention to fan mail dropped with the rise of more sophisticated means of measuring audiences through polling; there may also have been suspicions about fan mail. Merrill Denison wrote in 1934, in an assertion that I have not encountered anywhere else, "Fan mail was highly regarded until the discovery was made that supplying it had become a racket,—that any interested person could buy letters to New York at so much a ton."[24] Accurate or not, by the mid- to late 1930s, fan mail was less important as a way of measuring audience reactions. "To-day," wrote one commentator in 1937, "executives read only exceptional letters, depending upon audience-mail tabulators to record, file and analyze letters and their contents. Favorable and unfavorable reactions are recorded on punched file-cards, enabling one to see statistically what the fans are saying. Machines, each with a daily capacity of 5,000 cards, compile the records."[25]

Polling

Countless polls and surveys were conducted in order to construct a profile of the average audience member and what he or she wanted. Advertisers and sponsors also used polls about listener preferences to conceive programs.[26] Depending on how the poll was worded and the kinds of musical categories employed, the poll results usually favored dance music, though classical music fared better in some polls.

Taking polls and encouraging listener responses was the first step away from simple assertions of advertisers' and sponsors' musical tastes in programming

Table 2.1 The "ideal program," 1923

Classical and operatic music	2.6 hours	30%
Jazz	2.5 hours	29%
Market reports and weather	0.8 hours	9%
Speeches and lectures	1.7 hours	20%
News and sports	1.2 hours	12%
[Total]	8.8 hours	100%

Source: "Radio Audience Decides Programs," *Wireless Age*, August 1923, 29.

and reliance on fan mail. In a broadcasting environment in which advertising paid for programming, obtaining accurate information on listeners' preferences was crucial, and polling and audience surveys quickly became prevalent, and increasingly scientistic.[27] These polls and listener surveys helped advertisers and advertising agencies tailor programs to fit the target audience, based on the kind of music used.

The earliest polls were mainly designed to assess audience desires about broadcasting generally, as in this 1923 poll about the ideal program, with the following responses tabulated in table 2.1. Note how classical music and jazz are the only two music categories, as this is the generic fault line of the debate over what kind of music should be aired, a debate that lasted for much of the 1920s.

Later polls addressed more specific listener preferences, especially about music. The categories are revealing of the tastes of the time, with categories such as "old-time songs," "Hawaiian music," "mixed quartettes," "saxophone," "pipe organ," "religious music," "Mexican music," and others.[28]

What was reported as the first survey of the radio audience was conducted in 1928 by Daniel Starch, a Harvard-trained psychologist turned market researcher. It was less about program preference than a simple attempt to ascertain the number of radios in American homes, how much people listen, when people listen the most, and the like; programming was almost an afterthought. But the study was innovative in that it broke out the data based on geography, with categories such as "farm families." Starch concluded:

> Preferences for most of the different types of programs are practically the same on the part of farm, town, and city families. There are significant differences, however, with respect to several types of programs—semi-classical and classi-

cal music, and grand opera are preferred less by farm and small town families than by city families, whereas religious services, crops and market reports, and children's programs are preferred more by farm than by city families.[29]

An exhaustive study in 1929 by Archibald M. Crossley for the Association of National Advertisers Inc., drawing on a poll of radio editors east of the Rockies, six thousand personal interviews in twenty-five large cities, twelve hundred interviews in twelve other cities, and fifteen thousand interviews east of the Mississippi, revealed that, of the seventeen different programs named, most were musical (almost all popular music of various kinds) except for five. In this era, 33 percent of programs were produced by advertising agencies, 28 percent by the network for its sponsors, 20 percent by the sponsors themselves, and 19 percent by special program builders; these numbers gradually shifted toward the advertising agencies.[30]

In this same period, data were appearing that attempted to index listening preferences to income and age, such as these from a 1931 article by advertising man P. H. Pumphrey, who drew on a study commissioned by the Universal Broadcasting Company in Philadelphia. This study charted program types with income, revealing the unsurprising fact that high-income groups tended to prefer classical or "semi-classical" music over "Sacred" music or "Old-fashioned melodies," and that low-income groups overwhelmingly preferred dance music.[31] Pumphrey concluded that the popularity of dance music makes it the most desirable music for advertising (others had stated that it was youth who preferred dance music).[32] But good bands are very hard to find, Pumphrey wrote, and unless there is a "personality" such as early superstar Rudy Vallée, most programs could not be supplied. Thus, many advertisers found that the light classical or semipopular musical program, employing some "dance music, some musical comedy and light opera, some ballads, and occasionally some heavier music, is hailed by many as the golden mean."[33] This format "permits the development of a number of distinctive personalities," and Pumphrey continued by listing such programs, which "seem to have struck the least common denominator of popular taste, and appeal to everyone."[34]

Polling and audience research were to become even more important with a shift in the business model of the broadcasting industry. According to a historian of the N. W. Ayer agency, Ayer reversed the method by which advertising agencies worked. Before 1930, the strategy was to seek attractive programs and then attempt to find advertisers that would pay for them. But after the novelty and glamour of radio advertising wore off, advertising agencies realized that they had to begin with the client's needs and attempt to devise a program that would address them.[35] This shift, according to Stamps, required more "scientific" knowledge of the audience. Enter Archibald Crossley in 1929, who was asked by the American Association of Advertising Agencies and the Association of National Advertisers to head the new Cooperative Analysis of Broadcasters, which began rating program popularity in 1930. Crossley employed the "recall" method of learning what listeners preferred, which entailed calling them several days after a program had aired.

Learning how to attract a particular market segment became an increasingly important aspect of broadcast advertising as the 1930s progressed.[36] Listener polls attempted to be comprehensive both about programs and about the social class of the listener. A table published in *Broadcast Advertising* in 1930, for example, divided Boston listeners by occupations into three classes:

> Class A—8 per cent of the total—includes the families of merchants, professional men, executives, manufacturers, etc. Class B—73 per cent of the listeners interviewed—is made up of families of skilled and clerical workers, salesmen, city living farmers, retired, and small merchants. Class C—19 per cent—takes in the families of laborers, domestics, clerks, and non-employed.[37]

Polling, and the idea of attempting to capture a particular audience for a particular product with particular music, spelled the beginning of the end of the goodwill concept, also hastened by the onset of the Great Depression. Advertising agencies became bolder about incorporating advertising messages into the programs and targeting particular audiences. As *Fortune* magazine observed in September 1932, "The sponsors have shaken off all the old network inhibitions except the one about specifying prices during evening hours."[38]

Commodifying the Mass Audience

The National Broadcasting Company had originally conceived of programs as a means to sell hardware, since, because it was owned by the Radio Corporation of America, its main profits were realized through sales of radios and related equipment. But in 1932, government antitrust action forced the General Electric Company and the Westinghouse Electric and Manufacturing Company to relinquish their holdings in the Radio Corporation of America,

NBC's owner. Since General Electric and Westinghouse manufactured radio components, NBC lost this incentive.

But even before this, NBC had begun to shift its business model, thanks to competition from the Columbia Broadcasting System, which did not profit from radio sales. William Paley, the network's founder, understood what no one else did at the time—that selling what one would now call "content" was not the way to make money. This was old-think: if Tin Pan Alley music publishers sold songs, if publishers sold books, then broadcasters logically sold programs. Paley realized that what broadcasters really sold were audiences. That is, in a system in which programs were funded by viewers indirectly through advertising rather than directly through government subsidies as in Europe, the broadcaster's function was not to produce programs but to sell audiences to advertisers. The idea, as summarized succinctly by Dallas W. Smythe, is that advertisers purchase the anticipated attention of audiences of known demographic content who will attend to particular programs in predictable numbers at particular times in particular geographical markets.[39] Or, as Paley put it plainly in 1934,

> We start with the premise that the advertiser makes our 16 daily hours of radio service possible, just as the advertiser makes possible the daily newspaper and the national magazine. In order . . . to have something to sell this advertiser, we must render a very definite service to the radio audience. We must have listener attention—just as a newspaper must have reader circulation—before we can secure advertising revenue.
>
> This means the first problem of our business is to win an audience, hold an audience, interest an audience.[40]

Advertising agencies understood this perfectly well. As Roy Durstine wrote in 1930, "The public wants entertainment. The advertiser wants the public's attention and is willing to pay for it. Therefore let the advertiser provide the entertainment."[41]

Paley wrote in his autobiography that when he first acquired the majority share in United Independent Broadcasters, the original 1927 contract was a severe drain on the company's resources, for it obligated the network to purchase ten hours a week from each of its affiliates for fifty dollars an hour. The network was paying out about seven thousand dollars per week, regardless of whether it had sold time to sponsors to cover its expenses.[42] Paley's predecessor had devised a new contract, which required the stations to pay the network for sustaining programs that the network developed. But this system did not staunch the drain on resources, for the network didn't have that many sustaining programs in this period.

When Paley took over, he revised the contract again to make it more attractive to the network's affiliates. The sustaining programs would henceforth be free to affiliates, and the network would guarantee twenty hours of programming per week, pay the stations fifty dollars an hour for the commercial hours used, but the network wouldn't pay the stations for the first five hours of commercial programming time. The main change, however, was the crucial one: the network would have exclusive rights for network broadcasting through the affiliate, and affiliates would have to identify programs using the CBS name.[43] The affiliates agreed to the proposition in November 1928, and the fledgling network attracted more affiliates.

As *Fortune* magazine put it in 1935 in an analysis of the economics of broadcasting, "Falling down the rabbit hole of the broadcasting studio he is in a land of Mad Hatters and White Knights who sell time, an invisible commodity, to fictitious beings called corporations for the purpose of influencing an audience that no one can see."[44] This was the problem, as *Fortune* put it: Radio stations have to fill the air with sixteen hours of programming per day, from 8:00 a.m. to midnight (sometimes the networks would broadcast more). How? If, say, an independent station could cover three hours a day through advertising revenue, thirteen hours still remained. If the station got cheap and free talent and used prerecorded programs, it wouldn't cost that much (*Fortune* estimated it worked out to a talent cost per hour of just thirty-five dollars). Selling this airtime would generate significant revenue, but in the end, the independent station would pretty much break even unless it could manage to sell more than three hours per day.

Because of this risk, many independent stations elected to become part of a network, even though they had to give up their best evening hours, which they could have sold to local advertisers. In exchange, however, they received much better talent in the form of free sustaining programs provided by the network. Better talent brought greater prestige for the local station. With a network contract, local affiliates received prestige and security; the network received exclusive access to the affiliates' best evening time slots, which it could then guarantee to advertisers.[45]

Fortune provided a case study, a Cleveland radio station that derived 70 percent of its revenue from local advertisers and national advertising targeting that city. The affiliate's contract with CBS gave the affiliate

> an option on its time to the network, which may buy any hour it wants, even the choice evening hours. On the other hand, the network pays the affiliate something less than $100 an hour . . . for handling network commercial programs and at the same time sends out sustaining programs for the local station *to use free of charge* during those hours that have not been sold to advertisers.[46]

According to *Fortune*, "The motive for all Mr. Paley's toil has been to sell time. From 1929 to 1934 the number of hours Mr. Paley sold more than doubled."[47]

Paley later had the idea of enticing advertisers to purchase time on a greater number of affiliates, for in that period advertisers didn't always buy time on the entire range of affiliates. Paley realized that if advertisers didn't want the entire network, he could offer them a discount if they took the entire network. This would mean that the network-sponsored programs would be much more widely heard and raise the network's overall income.[48]

NBC, by contrast, charged its affiliates for sustaining programs, which gave them no incentive to air them, and it didn't reserve any hours for itself. This meant that local stations could run their own programs during the best time slots, which might have been desired by an NBC advertiser. NBC's comparative inability to guarantee audiences was discussed at a J. Walter Thompson Company staff meeting in 1931, in which a Mr. Spencer reported,

> N.B.C. is getting its network into better shape, and we hope that before very long they will have their stations lined up, either by purchase or by more firmly bound contracts so that we will know just what stations we are going to get when we put in an order for them. As you know, there are some stations on the network now that take a program or leave it, just as they like.[49]

Obviously, such a system was unsatisfactory to both advertisers and advertising agencies, but it was dominant until Paley's new contracts at CBS. NBC ultimately had to change its contracts, essentially duplicating CBS's.

A document in the NBC archives sheds some light on CBS's strategy in this period. Somehow (the memo attached to the report at NBC says, "A CBS program—how did NBC get it?"), NBC acquired a CBS publicity campaign report, dated 3 December 1931, for a program entitled *Music That Satisfies* with Nat Shilkret. After an introductory paragraph, the report states matter-of-factly, "The purpose of the campaign, in general, will be that of attracting listeners to the program rather than advertising the product. Columbia's publicity thus will center upon Nat Shilkret, conductor, and Alex Gray, Baritone soloist." Even though this program was sponsored by Liggett and Myers Tobacco Company, makers of Chesterfield cigarettes, the star of the show was to be Shilkret, not Chesterfield. This document mentions Columbia's "exploitation division," which was "assigned to the building up of artists in ways other than the dissemination of news and pictures designed primarily for radio pages." This division was essentially tasked with putting Shilkret or Gray in every conceivable venue for the publicizing of the show, including attempting to get one of the major railroads to name one of its new trains "The Chesterfield," the formal dedication of which would be attended by Gray and other cast members. The proposed publicity campaign was multipronged and extensive: placing stories in the radio press ("Columbia has taken the lead in offering tailor-made copy," it claimed); biographies of the stars to be distributed nationally, but also "localized," sent to "home town papers," stories not just of the stars but of the "production men and control engineer assigned to the program"; setting up interviews with the stars with radio editors at local papers; and "the fan mail received by the artists will be examined carefully for possible stories." "In short, the publicity department will put special emphasis upon Mr. Shilkret and Mr. Gray, but will attempt to cover the programs from every angle in a concerted effort to build an ever-increasing audience for 'Music That Satisfies.'"[50]

By 1933, as Stamps notes, both NBC and CBS saw that radio was primarily a sales medium.[51] Only fifteen years later, NBC could brag to a potential client, "Through what medium is it possible for an advertiser virtually to own a specific half-hour of millions of families' LIVES, with a week-after-week, month-after-month regularity?"[52]

Ears and Incomes

Learning more and more about audiences was not simply a way for broadcasters, advertising agencies, and advertisers to design programs that audiences might like; it was increasingly, as Paley grasped, a way to ascertain what kind of audience each program attracted in order to sell that demographic to advertisers.

In 1933, CBS published a study that tackled the question of income and listening preferences, *Vertical Study of Radio Ownership, 1930–1933*. The following year, it published *Markets in Radio Homes, by Income Levels and Price Levels*, and *Ears and Incomes*.[53] It hired Daniel Starch to attempt to discover how much of an audience a highbrow radio program might reach beyond its targeted audience. "Can a specific network program penetrate those upper income levels—in actual audience—as deeply as it does the lower? Even more deeply? And what about the income levels in between? Can it hold the three-room 'Smiths' while it wins the ten-room 'Smythes'?"[54]

To address this question, Starch examined the audiences for four different programs: *The March of Time*, a news program associated with *Time* magazine; *The Chesterfield Program*, a musical show featuring André Kostelantez and his orchestra and classical music guests; *The Philco Radio Program* with news commentaries by Boake Carter; and *The Fletcher's Castoria Program* with an orchestra led by Don Voorhees with classical music guests. Starch's research strategy was touted by CBS as more accurate than the ratings system used at the time, in which people were simply telephoned and queried about what program they were listening to at that moment. Starch's researchers went door-to-door to 7,490 homes across the country and asked specifically about each of the programs, in order to tackle "the question of the *whole job* which the *whole* advertising investment has done."[55] The income level of each family was coded as A (incomes over $5,000 per year), BB (from $3,000 to $5,000), B ($2,000 to $3,000), C ($1,000 to $2,000), or D (under $1,000). Income level was determined by the husband's occupation and the size and character of the home. It should be remembered that this was not a study that set out to find correlations between income group and radio listening preferences but rather one that was designed to see how far down the economic ladder highbrow programs penetrated, and whether or not an advertiser that aimed at an upper-income audience actually captured that audience. The CBS study concluded that it was possible to attract upper-income audiences as readily as those with lower incomes, and that programs designed to appeal to upper-income audiences could garner attention from lower-income listeners; and maintained that "even with a 'selective' program keyed to a selective audience, it is possible for an advertiser, in a few months of CBS broadcasting . . . to reach 2 out of 3 of all radio homes in all income levels, 36,000,000 listeners (while he reaches 3 out of 4 of all radio homes in the upper income levels)."[56]

A later study, by H. M. Beville Jr., research manager at NBC, further investigated the "social stratification of the radio audience," as his 1939 report was called. Beville, who used data from the Cooperative Analysis of Broadcasting, divided social class into four groups: over $5,000 (6.7 percent of the total sample), $3,000–$5,000 (13.3 percent), $2,000–$3,000 (26.7 percent), and under $2,000 (53.3 percent). Beville found that the link between income and interest in classical music was very strong; in the words of the foreword by the Princeton Radio Research Office, "When the audience of a serious musical program is analyzed, good music is shown to be the monopoly of the upper income classes. The audience decreases markedly with decreasing income."[57] Beville's data on this are clearer in a subsequent article, with data that generally trend downward from the most serious classical music to less, with the exception of a program featuring the Philadelphia Orchestra, but it's evident that this program was the highest rated, with 14.2 percent of its audience coming from the highest income group.[58]

Results

How did all this research play out? Money spent on radio advertising generally skyrocketed as broadcasters competed to hire the most attractive stars. The *Variety Radio Directory* wrote that in 1930, talent expenditures were about 30 percent of the total radio budget, but less than a decade later, the figures were much higher, varying from about 11 percent to 60 percent, though averaging around 40 percent.[59]

Greater pay combined with better data on audiences meant less freedom for performers. The renowned Russian violinist Jascha Heifetz wrote in the late 1930s of the difference between state-funded European broadcasters and those in America:

> In Europe an artist selects his material and submits it to the broadcasting station. If he intends to play the "Habañera" and someone else has just played it, he may be asked to substitute another number; but that is the most the station asks of him in the way of alteration. Anything further would be regarded as effrontery. Good manners alone forbid it; for the artist is an expert in his field and it is assumed that he knows his business.

In the United States the artist is shown into a luxurious suite and a contract is handed across the desk for his signature. Then he is asked: "What are you going to play?"

He mentions three or four pieces of music in which for weeks past he has been rigorously drilling himself.

"Oh, no," he is told. "They won't do at all."

"They won't?" he asks in bewilderment.

"We have to give the public what it wants, you see."

At this point Heifetz's hypothetical artist, whom he dubbed Petrov, wonders if the audience wants Petrov, and, if so, why not Petrov's pieces? He attempted to make the American radio representatives understand.

"Oh, now, you mustn't feel that way about it, Mr. Petrov," he is deftly placated. "You see, you don't know radio. We're radio experts; we know what the public wants."

Whereupon Petrov reflects a little wistfully that radio is barely fifteen years old. He has been pleasing the public for twenty, perhaps thirty years. He would not think of telling the technicians in the control booth how to adjust their dials. He would not think of telling the advertising expert at the desk how to prepare a layout. Yet no one has any compunction about telling him how to please the public with his music, the thing in which he has a special and expert proficiency.

Heifetz's concluding sentence was a strong condemnation of the commodification of the audience and the rationalized ways in which it was calculated in America: "I have played—quite recently—in Italy, Germany and Russia. I had to come to the United States to find a dictatorship."[60] Strong words in the late 1930s.

Programs were devised to appeal to what the audience wanted, usually divided demographically, and sponsors were pitched programs based on these demographics. For example, the World Broadcasting System Inc., based in New York City, a large producer of syndicated programs, employed a promotion department to generate documents outlining the programs it produced, documents that are quite revealing of the ways that this company and the networks conceptualized their audiences and the kinds of programming that a particular audience might respond to.

Broadcasters, sponsors, and advertisers worried endlessly (as they still do) over how best to reach an audience, and many of these debates focused on music. Phil Spitalny, who directed the *Hour of Charm* program, sponsored by General Electric, said in 1938:

> Experience showed that the vast majority of our people are music lovers at heart, provided they can be given music which means something to them. . . .
>
> To my mind, the answer is light music: melodic, rhythmic, well played tunes which will satisfy the ear and the emotions, without overtaxing an intellect which has not been trained so that it may grasp the beauties of the greater classics.[61]

This is the music of the masses, wrote Warren B. Dygert. But there is also music for the "classes," music with class appeal for those who know something about music. Dygert listed Ford's *Sunday Evening Hour* as a good example, a "radio program designed to select this limited but profitable audience."[62] But one couldn't go too far in presenting the classics, because, he says, "moderism [*sic*], *i.e.* extremism, is offensive to many listeners."[63]

The Fleischmann's Yeast Hour

> I've heard so much of Rudy Vallee that I think he's more wonderful than Bee-thoven's Sonatas.
>
> —Fan letter to the National Broadcasting Company, ca. 1937

Still, many national advertisers, then as now, wanted to attempt to reach as broad an audience as possible. One program that straddled the "classes and the masses" with great and long-lasting success was *The Fleischmann's Yeast Hour*, starring crooner Rudy Vallée, and I will spend some time discussing this program as a way of pulling together the various strands of argument in this chapter.

Vallée's was a variety show, one of the main ways that advertisers sought to cultivate a broad market: "Starting with the premise that radio is a 'mass' medium, advertisers have set out in assiduous pursuit of that will-o'-the-wisp, 'universal appeal,'" wrote one commentator in 1933.[64] And as two observers said in 1935,

Figure 2.1 Rudy Vallée, ca. 1930. (Author's collection.)

In order that his program may appeal to all classes of people and to all members of the family, the sponsor often tries to include within the same period a considerable variety of entertainment. Instead of turning to one program to listen to a comedian, another to hear a drama, a third to hear jazz, or a fourth to enjoy a symphony, we may turn to the Canyon Tobacco Hour and hear a little of everything. Perhaps no member of the family enjoys the whole hour, but the chances are that each will like a certain fraction of it. The variety program is the broadcaster's ingenious creation to appeal to the greatest number of people during one period.[65]

In many ways, *The Fleischmann's Yeast Hour* was an innovative and ingenious variety program. In a 1931 speech before the League of Advertising Women at the Advertising Club in New York City, Daniel P. Woolley, vice president of Standard Brands, Fleischmann's parent company, discussed the notion of "tempo" (a common word in radio advertising in this era)—that is, matching a product to a particular kind of program and entertainment—in the period before advertisers had much concrete knowledge of their audiences.[66] His main example was *The Fleischmann's Yeast Hour*. In those days, yeast was sold not simply for baking bread but for health, as a health supplement. So Fleischmann's yeast was marketed as more of a medicine than a foodstuff in this era, a difficult undertaking since its taste wasn't particularly appealing. Woolley's own words on the subject are worth quoting at length:

> Yeast for health is a very delicate subject to handle. It has much to do with good health, so when we started to look around for a radio program we said, "What is the audience we have to deal with?"
>
> We decided that, probably, now-a-days they wanted "It" more than anything else. Who had "It" the most of anybody we could find? We found a young crooner, Rudy Vallee, and we found the young ladies panting over him and even some of the old ladies. He also has a great many men admirers. So we engaged Rudy Vallee as the star of this great thing called Health. We wanted him to croon but also we wanted more in the program. We wanted athletics or robust health to play a part. We went through the list—Jack Dempsey and all. Finally we said, "Graham MacNamee [sic] as the noted sports announcer stands for sports!"[67]

("It" refers to sex appeal, the pronoun having been made famous by its attachment to movie star Clara Bow, the "It" girl.)

Woolley said that the company wanted to make sure it had a well-rounded program and so it should get some "ladies with deep and soulful voices and a soloist." Dr. R. E. Lee, head of the Fleischmann Health Research Department, was also included on the program to talk about health issues: "Now, I might tell you that that combination of MacNamee [sic] for virility, and Vallee for crooning, Dr. Lee to give the advice of the old family physician, plus a lady who sings, has been a very successful radio program."[68] It should be noted here that in this year, crooning was widely decried as an effeminate mode of singing, since the recently invented electrical microphone permitted singers to croon rather than belt, and so balancing Vallée with McNamee was an important consideration for Standard Brands.[69] Yet, as Roland Marchand has argued, this intimate form of singing became a way that advertisers and advertising agencies understood their relationship to their audiences, for intimacy and personalized address to audience members was a way both to sound modern and to attempt to reassure them in an era of increasing uncertainty and complexity.[70]

So, on 5 September 1929, J. Walter Thompson began producing and airing a program sponsored by Fleischmann's Yeast, with Vallée as the main attraction (example 2.1).[71] John Reber told his colleagues at a staff meeting on 26 August that the audition of the program went well. An "audition" was a hearing, in Reber's words, "merely a parading before you of the talent and of the general idea to be developed. We get it for nothing." Auditions were probably put on for sponsors to see before their program aired. Reber reported that the star was "really marvelous."[72]

Vallée did not enjoy much of a spotlight on his program at first. The early broadcasts featured Vallée mainly as bandleader, not as personality. The announcer, the renowned Graham McNamee, did virtually all of the talking, except for Dr. Lee, who told the listeners of the health benefits of ingesting three Fleischmann's yeast cakes per day. By the program that aired on 14 January 1932, the musical variety show format had started to solidify, reducing the announcer to little more than a commercial spokesman for the yeast; in the past, he had been the main speaker, as on most programs. But Vallée, who previously had only announced the numbers he was playing, began introducing the guests as well, at the behest of J. Walter Thompson. "This kind of personality opportunity became a JWT program characteristic," according to the brief, undated history of the program written by an anonymous employee of the company.[73] By the end of April 1932, Vallée told his listeners that he was both "announcing and directing" *Fleischmann's Yeast Hour*. Vallée says in his second autobiography that the show by 1932 had become "a program that was to discover and develop more personalities and stars than any radio show before or since."[74]

Vallée wasn't a trouble-free personality himself, however. At the height of his popularity in the summer of 1931, Vallée was the subject of a number of memos at NBC. He was causing consternation for "advertising anything and anybody," complained John F. Royal, director of programs, changing musical numbers at the last minute, and not having his programs cleared before broadcast, as was the norm.[75] Despite his employers' occasional misgivings, Vallée could behave this way because of his massive popularity as the first musical superstar in the new medium of radio—and one who was widely written about.[76] *The Fleischmann's Yeast Hour* remained on the air for over a decade, though as the practice of eating yeast for health waned, the program was rechristened *The Royal Gelatin Hour* in 1936 (Royal Gelatin was also owned by Standard Brands).[77]

Vallée continued to find work in radio because he was also thought to possess that quality most desired by advertisers—showmanship; William B. Benton, chairman of the board of the Benton and Bowles agency, called him "one of the greatest showmen in radio."[78] The audience might have been a commodity, but selling goods was no less important than the commodification of the audience. Vallée's first autobiography, written not long after he had started broadcasting (and just as his stint on the Fleischmann program was beginning), includes an entire chapter on showmanship. Vallée was more concerned with showmanship in live performance than on radio, though he admitted that showmanship on the radio was extremely difficult since the audience can't see the performers. He later offers a characterization of showmanship that approximates those promoted by radio writers and producers: "The arrangement of a well-balanced program with every number calculated to please someone in the average mixed audience—this is just as much an act of showmanship as is the presentation of the numbers."[79]

At the J. Walter Thompson staff meeting on 12 August 1930, George Faulkner, the writer of dramatic sketches for *The Fleischmann's Yeast Hour*, gave a presentation on showmanship in radio. He began by asking what a showman was, saying that the term had connotations of someone undignified, cheap; "it has a vaguely Semitic, Barnumish, Broadway air to it." This kind of showmanship is exploitation, said Faulkner. Showmanship in radio means the technique of show building, the craftsmanship of production. Showmanship in radio compelled people not only to listen but also to pay attention. Faulkner quoted an article from *Variety*: "One agency has as its radio slogan, 'while money will put a radio program on the air, only showmanship will put it in the ear.'" Faulkner elaborated on this problem:

> Radio has become to a much too large extent *background* music for the American home . . . a background for bridge or the evening paper or the evening meal or even for conversation. If you want an audience really to listen to an advertising appeal you must give that audience something which will catch and hold its attention . . . the audience must listen *actively*, not passively.[80]

The answer to this problem was "showmanship," which for the J. Walter Thompson Company in the early 1930s meant variety, unity, pace, punch, and, sometimes, humor.[81] William L. Bird Jr. has written of the conception of showmanship in this era, arguing that the term captured the business community's show business–ization of business.[82]

With the arrival of the variety show, advertisers, networks, and advertising agencies had found a way to appeal to the broadest audience possible, their main goal in this era, even as they were devising ever more sophisticated means of ascertaining information about their audiences. Demographic information began to drive the selection of programs, leading to the commodification of the audience as we now recognize it. Advertising agency workers were beginning to understand their power in creating meanings for goods, meanings that could be proffered to consumers in appealing musical packages, inviting them to consume even an unappetizing bar of yeast.

3

The Great Depression and the Rise of
the Radio Jingle

Consumption and the Great Depression

The onset of the Great Depression was one of the greatest crises in the history of capitalism and proved to be an
obstacle to the growing consumer culture in the United
States, though not a fatal one. The staff meeting minutes
at the J. Walter Thompson Company do not betray undue
panic or fear at the economic troubles in this era, and instead convey an impression of the giant agency biding its
time until happy days returned. Branching out into radio
advertising helped many agencies not only remain sol-
vent but grow. William Benton, cofounder of the Benton
and Bowles advertising agency in 1929, recalled later, "We
didn't know the Depression was going on. Except that our
clients' products were plummeting, and they were willing

to talk to us about new ideas. They wouldn't have let us in the door if times were good. So the Depression benefited me. My income doubled every year."[1] Nonetheless, many of the major advertising agencies before the Depression, which serviced major brands, suffered. Budgets were slashed, employees let go, expensive artists jettisoned for cheaper photographers.

Erik Barnouw writes that there was a near total blackout on discussions of current problems on the radio during the Depression and that there was very little news on the air; comedy shows reigned.[2] A memorandum dated 2 March 1933 from Bertha Brainard, head of programming at NBC, to various NBC employees said, "We have been instructed to delete absolutely all reference to bank failures and depression of any kind in our continuities starting immediately," and asked the recipient to pass this memo on to everyone involved in production.[3] Print advertising similarly carried on as though there were no trouble.[4]

Putting one's head in the sand—or the ether—seemed to help radio sales, for radio ownership continued to rise, though shakily, during the Depression. There was a slump during 1931–32, but sales increased again afterward, from $200 million in 1932 to $350 million in 1934.[5] Whereas in 1922, 0.2 percent of American households possessed a radio, nearly a quarter did by 1927; in 1930, the figure was 45.8 percent, and by 1940, over 80 percent.[6] In the 1930s, Americans spent 150 million hours per week at the movies, but they listened to nearly 1 billion hours of radio broadcasts. Typical winter evenings in 1938 saw 40 percent of American households listening to the radio.[7]

Even apart from the success of radio, consumption continued. Historian Gary Cross writes that Americans were reluctant to give up what they had come to enjoy in the 1920s, and if they couldn't afford certain things, they could still dream about them. Novelties of the 1920s such as radio became seen as necessities. Consumption continued through utilization of strategies such as installment purchasing, a practice begun in the 1920s; in 1932, roughly 60 percent of furniture, automobiles, and household appliances was bought this way.[8] Also, department stores began offering charge plans for consumers. Consumer loans for household goods more than doubled between 1933 and 1939.[9]

Advertising agencies, according to Jackson Lears, argued that advertising should increase during hard times, and, indeed, network revenue from radio advertising rose 316 percent between 1928 and 1934.[10] As indicated in a lead article in *Printers' Ink* in 1930, "Advertising helps to keep the masses dissatisfied with their mode of life, discontented with ugly things around them. Satisfied customers are not as profitable as discontented ones."[11]

Some thought that advertising could even help preserve American capitalism during this crisis, as opposed to Soviet-style socialism. A J. Walter Thompson publication called *A Primer of Capitalism*, published in 1937, said, "Under private capitalism, the *Consumer*, the *Citizen*, is boss. The consumer is the voter, the juror, the judge and the executioner."

> And he doesn't have to wait for election day to vote. He needn't wait for Court to convene before he hands down his verdict. The consumer "votes" each time he buys one article and rejects another—every day in every ward and precinct in the land. . . .
>
> In all history there has been nothing remotely like modern American business as a sensitive index to popular likes and dislikes. It is democracy plus.[12]

Because of the Depression, advertisers demanded more effective ads for less money, which thus resulted in more aggressive sales techniques, some of which, according to Lears, employed "carnivalesque tactics."[13] And Lears offers a 1938 quotation from the director of public relations for the Ford Motor Company: "Never before the advent of radio did advertising have such a golden opportunity to make an ass out of itself. Never before could advertising be so insistent and so unmannerly and so affront its audience."[14] *Fortune* magazine said in 1932 that before the Depression, "radio was polite. Radio was genteel. Radio was the guest in the home, not the salesman on the doorstep. . . . But some 18 further months of Depression have changed all that."[15] Many were affronted by jingles, which arose late in the Depression and which had roots in earlier, more, shall we say, carnivalesque, modes of selling such as the medicine show.

At the same time, there were some in this era who thought that certain aspects of advertising could be favorably compared to art, and that advertising could thus be a way of introducing Americans to higher forms of visual expression. Consumption was the vehicle of this introduction. One of the main proselytizers for this perspective, the influential adman Earnest Elmo Calkins, wrote in 1930 that the beauty and good taste in advertisements reached millions of people all the time, unlike art in a museum. A modern society needed to rely on advertising to uplift taste. It mattered not whether the art in an advertisement compared favorably to works by recognized artists, only that consumers' tastes were elevated. The art in advertisements could combat the ugliness of modern life:

> The important thing is whether there is enough beauty in these modern com-
> mercial designs to awaken some sense of taste in millions of minds with which
> they are bound to come into contact, and offset in some measure the ugliness
> and spiritual poverty of much of this modern machine environment. Few will
> ever see the painting, the statue or the print, and could not relate it to their lives
> if they did.[16]

And who is to bring these modern artworks to the public? Business. Only business can pay for it. Business "has the power to create beauty," but "not exotic beauty collected from the past and hung on the walls of museums, not even academic beauty, the works of modern artists hung on the walls of our homes, but beauty in our visual world, in our landscapes, our architecture and the tools and furniture with which we perform the operation of living."[17] I have never seen music mentioned in such grandiose terms in writings of this era. In fact, advertising's main contribution to music in this era was the jingle, far closer to the carnivalesque than the artistic. Yet the musical jingle proved to be an extraordinarily effective and long-lasting sales device.

Jingles: Introduction

Most people I know, upon learning the subject of this book, assumed it was about jingles, those snappy, catchy tunes used to sell goods. Dinner parties have turned into jingle memory contests, with people breaking out into song around the table. One friend asked, after an absence of some months, "Are you still jingling?" Barry Manilow recounted to me in an interview how, in a pe-riod early in his career, he was preparing to go on the road to promote his first album, which contained no hits. Knowing that he had better do something that the audience would know, he put together a medley of all the commer-cials he had done. When he performed the commercials medley, the audience loved it.[18]

Jingles, originally known as singing commercials, are indeed a major part of this book. They have a long and complicated history, deeply rooted in ear-lier practices of selling with and without sound (the *Oxford English Dictionary* traces the use of the term *jingle* to 1645).[19] This chapter, however, is concerned with the rise of the radio jingle before World War II, so I will keep largely to the radio jingle's more immediate precursors in verse, sheet music, and radio theme songs, regretfully treating in more cursory fashion earlier musical practices such as the street cry and medicine show.[20]

Musical Jingle Prehistory

Distant Precursors

Street cries, the shouted or sung advertisements by wandering merchants, have a long history that predates their first recordings in music notation in the thirteenth century in the *Montepellier Codex*, an important early collection of French polyphony—"Frese nouvele! Muere france!" ("Fresh strawberries! Nice blackberries!").[21] Other such treatments followed, in the work of major and minor composers from Clément Janequin in the sixteenth century (*Voulez ouyr les cris de Paris?* of 1530) to an aria from George Frideric Handel's opera *Serse* (1738), into the nineteenth and twentieth centuries.[22] Street cries caught composers' fancies, either for their perceived musical value or to provide a sense of verisimilitude in dramatic works.

Verse

But one of the most immediate precursors to the broadcast jingle of the 1940s and after with which most people are familiar was sales pitches in verse without music, sometimes called jingles. These became popular at the end of the nineteenth century, when they were frequently used in print advertising and placed in streetcars. Frank Presbrey, in his 1929 history of advertising in the United States, writes that the success of jingles in verse is attributable in part to the increased visibility of popular song in this era; "Probably in no other ten-year period have we had so many new songs that nearly everybody knew."[23] Presbrey traces the roots of the modern jingle in verse to one by Bret Harte for Sapolio soap from 1876 or 1877, which, in its brevity and memorability, set the tone for the modern jingles of the late nineteenth century and early twentieth:

> One Sabbath morn, as heavenward
> White Mountain tourists slowly spurred

> On every rock, to their dismay,
> They read that legend, always
> SAPOLIO[24]

In 1892, Procter and Gamble invented the (nonmusical) jingle contest. Presbrey writes that there was a large response from the public, and, monthly in 1893 and into 1894, the winning jingles were printed, with illustrations. The campaign that launched what Presbrey calls the "modern style in the great jingle period of modern American advertising" was for DeLong Hook and Eye, with jingles by Charles M. Snyder. Presbrey quotes an article from 1894 praising the campaign, and noting how the verses had infiltrated the memories of the public.[25]

> I come in sizes large and small
> I hold in calm or bluster weather.
> I fasten fabrics canvas tough
> And hook the finest lace together.

Some of the most famous advertising campaigns in American history were based on verse, which was frequently used to keep trade characters (such as Aunt Jemima) in the public's mind. Presbrey writes that one of the classics of the era was by James Kenneth Fraser for Spotless Town. The pictures in these advertisements showed "quaint architecture," with several happy characters of the exceptionally clean town praising the cause of its cleanliness, Sapolio. Presbrey says that these jingles become so successful that many readers eagerly anticipated them. References to Spotless Town became so common that the phrase turned into a synonym for "cleanliness, order and perfection." The popularity of the jingles was such that the soap manufacturer produced a play that incorporated the jingles, some of which included music. The play booklet included instructions for staging, and scenery and props were supplied by the soap manufacturer for one dollar. Presbrey writes that throughout the United States, many performances of this advertisement for Sapolio raised funds for good causes.[26]

The success of this campaign launched many more that included jingles. One of the most famous was Phoebe Snow, a trade character created by Earnest Elmo Calkins to represent the Lackawanna Railroad. Snow was concocted to tout the railroad's reliance on anthracite coal, which burned more cleanly than other coal, thus offering a cleaner ride so that travelers would not arrive at their destinations covered in soot. Snow was a New York socialite who traveled in white and whose travels and escapades were reported in verse, such as this:

> Phoebe says
> And Phoebe knows
> That Smoke and cinders
> Spoil good clothes
> 'Tis thus a pleasure
> And Delight
> To take the Road
> Of Anthracite.

Lackawanna used Phoebe Snow for nearly seventy years.[27]

Just as famous, though not as durable, was the trade character for Force breakfast cereal, dour Jim Dumps, whose disposition was greatly improved upon eating the cereal, which transformed him into Sunny Jim in an advertising campaign begun in 1902. The story of Sunny Jim was told in verses in advertisements:

> Jim Dumps was a most unfriendly man,
> Who lived his life on the hermit plan;
> In his gloomy way he'd gone through life,
> And made the most of woe and strife;
> Till Force one day was served to him
> Since then they've called him "Sunny Jim."

Signs for Burma-Shave on American roads beginning in 1927 offer another famous series of verse advertisements. A single line of verse would appear on each sign, which drivers would read consecutively as they traveled. The verses didn't always rhyme, and weren't always well written, but they proved memorable. Here's one from 1928:

> Every shaver
> Now can snore
> Six more minutes

> Than before
> By using
> Burma-Shave.[28]

By the end of this campaign in 1967, the musical jingle was well established, though advertising in verse has continued to have a life of its own.[29]

Perhaps these rhymes aren't as catchy as their musical cousins, but an author of an 1896 book on advertising confessed, "It is astonishing how some of the things that we think the silliest will stick in our minds for years."[30]

Sheet Music

Before the musical jingle, there were many ways that companies sought to put their goods before the public with music by publishing sheet music with advertisements for their product, a practice going back at least to the mid-nineteenth century; they would capitalize on popular songs that mentioned their product, such as "In My Merry Oldsmobile," from 1905, a song by Vincent P. Bryan and Gus Edwards (example 3.1), with the chorus

> Come away with me Lucille in my merry Oldsmobile
> Down the road of life we'll fly automo-bubbling you and I.
> To the church we'll swiftly steal, then our wedding bells will peal,
> You can go as far you like with me, in my merry Oldsmobile.

And they would adapt the lyrics of popular songs to suit their own purposes. Presbrey offers as an example the song "Harrigan, That's Me," from George M. Cohan's 1907 show *Fifty Miles from Boston.* Cohan's chorus

> H-A-double R-I—G-A-N spells Harrigan
> Proud of all the Irish blood that's in me
> Divil' a man can say a word agin' me
> H-A-double R-I—G-A-N you see
> Is a name that a shame never has been connected with
> Harrigan, that's me!

became

H-E-R-P-I—C-I-D-E spells Herpicide
That's the bloomin' stuff that makes your hair grow
Makes you look just like a human scarecrow.
H-E-R-P-I—C-I-D-E you see
First I rub it, then I scrub it, and I scrub it and I rub it,
Then there's HAIR AGAIN—on me.[31]

Advertisers would also commission songs in praise of their products, such as "Under the Anheuser Bush," a waltz by Harry von Tilzer and Andrew B. Sterling from 1903 (example 3.2).[32] The song's chorus is:

Come, come, come and make eyes with me
Under the Anheuser Bush
Come, come, drink some "Bud-wise" with me
Under the Anheuser Bush,
Hear the old German band [piano plays fragment of "Ach, du lieber
    Augustin"]
Just let me hold your hand Yah!
Do, do, come and have a stein or two,
Under the Anheuser Bush.

Such songs avoided hard-sell tactics, but their commercial intent was always clear. As in verse advertising, sheet music advertising continued after the rise of the singing commercial on the radio.

Radio, Advertising, and Music before World War II

Until 1938, advertisers spent more money on print than radio, and the broad advertising trends of this era are probably better tracked in print advertising than radio. Additionally, radio into the early 1930s was still a rather haphazard affair, though its novelty meant that it was in some ways Depression-proof, as we have seen, for the allure of this new technology was so strong that advertisers, and listeners, refused to go without. It is thus no accident that music, and specifically the jingle, as well as those songs that gave rise to it, were increasingly utilized in this period to sell goods—a hard-sell message could be sugarcoated with a catchy tune. And in this era, jingles were invariably happy and catchy. In the hundreds of jingles from this period that I have listened to, all conform to one of two stylistic types: relentlessly upbeat songs for adults, or relentlessly upbeat children's ditties for everyone.

Radio Theme Songs

In this era, many programs were paid for by sponsors, programs that were frequently produced by their advertising agencies (though there were some programs produced by the networks themselves). This meant that, at first, there was no need for a stand-alone commercial or jingle—the entire program served as an advertisement (as we saw in chapter 1), with, frequently, the sponsor's name in the title, or with musicians taking names that referred to sponsors. Some programs, however, employed theme songs that sound like jingles; these were the direct precursors to radio jingles. A well-known early example is the theme sung by the Happiness Boys (for Happiness Candy), "How Do You Do?," which was perhaps the first theme song in radio in 1924 (according to Ed. Rice, former writer at the J. Walter Thompson Company;[33] fig. 3.1; example 3.3).

> How do you do, everybody, how do you do?
> How do you do, everybody, how are you?
> We are here, we must confess, just to bring you happiness.
> Hope we'll please you more or less, how do you do?
>
> How do you do? How do you do?
> How do you doodle oodle oodle oodle oo?
> Billy Jones and Ernie Hare wish to say to you out there,
> How do you doodle oodle oodle oodle oo?

In 1929, when the Happiness Boys become the Interwoven Pair (representing Interwoven Socks), the song was retained but the lyrics changed (example 3.4):

> How do you do, everybody, how do you do?
> Gee, it's great to say hello to hello to all of you.
> I'm Billy Jones!
> I'm Ernie Hare!

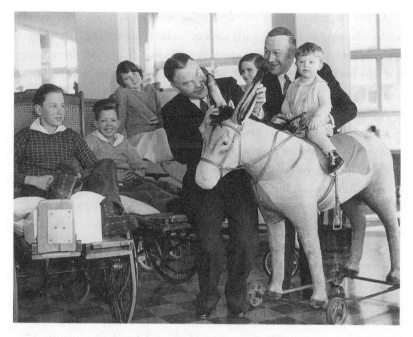

Figure 3.1 The Happiness Boys, 1920s. (Author's collection.)

We're the Interwoven Pair.

How do you doodle oodle oodle oodle oo?

Another early nationally broadcast jingle appeared on a program that began in 1931, and featured a song sung by Harry Frankel as "Singin' Sam, the Barbasol Man" (example 3.5).[34] According to the *New York Times*, the jingle was based on the tune of "Tammany," and the Barbasol Company obtained the rights and first aired it in the 1920s; it was the most popular singing commercial until it was dropped in the 1930s.[35] The show opened with:

Barbasol, Barbasol

No brush, no lather, no rub-in

Wet your razor, then begin.

Some programs employed specially written songs that incorporated the name of the program, and thus the product, such as the *JELL-O Program*, with Jack Benny, which began in the early 1930s (example 3.6), and whose song simply spelled out J-E-L-L-O.

As the Depression wore on, advertising agencies continued to become bolder, chipping away at the early ideal of "indirect advertising." They began to think that it was better to use specially composed, full-length theme songs that refer to the sponsor's product, as Warren B. Dygert wrote in 1939:

> A theme song is a better theme song when it is composed especially for the show. The use of a popular song, unless there are special lyrics which are sung at various points in the program, does not seem so effective as a specially composed song. Although original theme songs are not used for radio shows so much as formerly, the success of this type is proved by the successful sales of Tasteyeast [*sic*] and the resulting popularity of the theme song used on that radio program. Many requests for copies of the tune were received; some dance bands played it as the result of requests from dancing patrons.[36]

Dygert was quite right: if advertisers owned the copyright to the song, they could use it as they pleased. And they did: they would often print sheet music of their programs' theme songs and make them available at no charge to fans, as in the accompanying Tastyeast example (figs. 3.2 and 3.3; example 3.7); even with the rise of the jingle to prominence in 1940 and after, advertisers would still feature catchy theme songs and offer them to listeners.

Tastyeast provides an interesting example in that it employed radio early in its advertising existence. Herman S. Hettinger and Walter J. Neff (a professor of marketing and an advertising man, respectively) wrote that following unsuccessful newspaper campaigns in 1928 and 1929, the company turned to radio, and introduced, in January 1930, the Tastyeast Jesters, a vocal quartet, along with a comedian who told stories with a Swedish accent. The program was broadcast in the Boston-Springfield area. Tastyeast offered two of its yeast bars to any listener who wrote to the company, generating 720 letters after the first two broadcasts. By March of the same year, the company was receiving 3,000 letters per week and enjoyed near complete distribution in the area. It then shifted to a network broadcaster.[37]

"Tastyeast Is Tempting" was evidently a well-known tune, commented on by many, as in this 1931 letter contained in the NBC Archive:

> With regard to the use of theme songs, we find that a well written theme song is a very valuable asset to many radio hours. These not only serve as a reminder to listeners of the products which they represent, but they provide

Figure 3.2 "Tastyeast Is Tempting," front and back covers, early 1930s.

in some instances a means of making an advertisement announcement which is not only effective but quite inoffensive to listeners. For instance, the theme song of the "Tastyeast Jesters" is definitely a sales story, and it is at the same time a pleasant enough little jingle which is familiar to radio listeners everywhere.[38]

New York Times radio critic Orrin E. Dunlap Jr., writing in 1929, told of sponsored programs with theme songs that employ information about the product. One such song I have found is "Hurrah for the Wonder Bakers!," the theme song for Happy Wonder Bakers, the radio voices of Continental Bakery's Wonder Bread from 1929 to 1931 (fig. 3.4; example 3.8), with no chorus but with verses such as:

Figure 3.3 "Tastyeast Is Tempting," inner pages.

Yo-Ho! Yo-Ho! Yo-Ho! Yo-Ho!
We are the bakers who mix the dough
And bake the bread in an oven slow
And work for the Continental.

Dunlap thought that songs such as this overdid it. But,

there is a good opportunity lurking here for the gifted composer who can create an original radio tune, which if picked up and whistled or hummed by the
masses no matter where, will always be associated with a nationally advertised
product. If a boy whistles "Home Sweet Home" the tune is instantly recognized

Figure 3.4 "Hurrah for the Wonder Bakers!," sheet music cover, 1929.

as such and not as the tuneful name of a tooth paste, shaving cream, or breakfast food. For example, "Old Black Joe" would not be called the song of Palmolive.[39]

The Rise of the Radio Jingle

From these specially composed theme songs, as well as the precedents of advertising in verse and sheet music, it was a short leap to what was originally called the singing commercial. There was a structural problem, however, which was that before 1940, national broadcasters did not lease airtime in small increments, unlike today, when increments of time as small as fifteen seconds can be sold. Attempts were made to incorporate songs into various programs, though they were seldom freestanding jingles.

Most of what I have been able to discover about early jingles concerns national or regional programs; local stations' practices are harder to document and as a result have been less studied. But occasionally the national press would pick up on a local practice as an oddity worthy of reporting, which sheds light on the myriad practices before the rise of the national singing commercial, beginning late in 1939. Some believe that an NBC program in San Francisco, *The Women's Magazine of the Air*, with host Jolly Ben Walker, carried the first singing commercial, for Caswell's National Crest Coffee, sometime in the 1930s. The music is lost, but the lyrics are:

> Coffees and coffees have invaded the West,
> But of all of the brands, you'll find Caswell's the best.
> For good taste and flavor,
> You'll find it in favor.
> If you know your coffees,
> Buy National Crest.[40]

It is clear that local retailers used new lyrics set to existing music as sales devices before the rise of the national jingle. For example, the Symons Dry Goods Company, in Butte, Montana, aired in the early 1930s an evening program featuring "Powder River" Jack and Kitty Lee, a duet of cowboy singers. At the end of each program, "Powder River" Jack made up songs from the store's daily advertisements, such as this, sung to the tune of "O Susanna":

> Every week we sing a song next week we'll have one more
> For all you happy customers who come to Symons store
> To try and beat their bargains you would travel many miles
> Their dresses for your wardrobe have new color and new styles.
> Their values are remarkable, they're dainty and they're fine
> You buy your satin undies for a dollar forty-nine.
> Their toyland store of Hollywood is getting many calls
> And Mickey Mouse will greet you with the Shirley Temple dolls.

CHORUS

Oh Susanna your riding boots are neat
She bought them at the Symons store where prices can't be beat.
Now pencil down this little tip, don't lay it on the shelf
Oh—Give your man a Xmas gift like he would choose himself
The flannel robes, pajamas, gloves and sweaters are immense
And special fancy socks that sell, three pairs for fifty cents.
Pigskin gloves of quality one dollar ninety-five
And you'll be proud to wear them, just as sure as you're alive.
It's mighty nigh impossible as I said once before
To tell about these bargains that you'll find at Symons store.[41]

In Des Moines, the F. W. Fitch Company, manufacturers of Fitch's Dandruff Remover Shampoo and Fitch's Ideal Hair Tonic, sponsored a couple of programs in the mid-1930s that urged listeners to send in four-line original jingles (text only) along with a Fitch Shampoo cartoon. Five Bulova watches were given each week to the winners. For one program, the jingles were written to the tune of "Mary Had a Little Lamb" (though it's unclear if they were meant to be sung or if they were even sung on the air); the other program, which featured radio pioneer Wendell Hall, requested that jingles be set to the tune of his hit song "It Ain't Gonna Rain No Mo," and those jingles were sung.[42]

But, by and large, the path to the stand-alone jingle as a national phenomenon continued through theme songs to the use of songs selling goods that were embedded in programs. In 1936, Lehn and Fink, makers of Pebeco toothpaste and sponsors of the *Pebeco Hour* with Eddie Cantor, one of the biggest stars of the day and thought by many to be the best salesman on the air, broadcast a song praising the company's toothpaste. In order to solidify its success with this program, Lehn and Fink provided its distributors with a card for window displays that featured a picture of Cantor, a reminder of the program's broadcast time and network, pictures of Pebeco products and prices, and the toothpaste's jingle, music notation and all, entitled "The Cantor Cantata" (sung to the tune of "Schnitzelbank," a popular German drinking song of the late nineteenth and early twentieth centuries that is still occasionally heard). Reginald T. Townsend, an account executive at the advertising agency that produced the program, called this a "caroled commercial" and remarked that its popularity was so great "that thousands and thousands of requests

Figure 3.5 "The Cantor Cantata," 1936.

flooded his Hollywood headquarters and forced an encore. Before his season
ends it probably will be done many times more. Now it is called the 'Cantor
Cantata,' and has been printed on a comic broadside for nation-wide distribution" (fig. 3.5; example 3.9).[43] The "Cantor Cantata" was a bit of a gimmick,
however, and wasn't standard practice at the time on national programs.[44]

A few years later, in 1939, a daytime serial called *The Life and Love of Dr. Susan*, about a single woman doctor, employed jingles and was, according to Ed. Rice, the first program to do so. The announcer, Frank Luther, was also a singer,

> and we used to have him sing songs in the commercial. I think maybe they were the first jingles, commercial jingles. They weren't the kind of jingles we have now because we didn't repeat them over and over again like a Pepsi-Cola jingle, which was one of the early ones but each of the commercials had a little song in it that he would sing. Dick Leibert was the organist of the Radio City Music Hall and became the organist of *The Life and Love of Dr. Susan*, and we decided to have something a little different. Every other show had an organ, so we would use a new instrument called a Novachord. It was one of the first of the electronic keyboard instruments.[45]

The only recording I know of *The Life and Love of Dr. Susan* was made as a result of the National Archives requesting that station WJSV in Washington record its entire broadcast day, which was done on 21 September 1939.[46] The show opens, as Rice recalled, with an announcement followed by a song. The program concludes with another song that references several popular songs of the day: "The Trail of the Lonesome Pine" (with the chorus line "In the Blue Ridge Mountains of Virginia"), "By the Beautiful Ohio," "Carolina Moon," and "On the 10:10 (from Ten-Ten-Tennessee)" (examples 3.10 and 3.11).

The First Stand-Alone Jingles

Despite the clear existence of stand-alone jingles on local stations, radio scholars are generally agreed that a jingle for Wheaties breakfast cereal was the first freestanding jingle that wasn't simply pitching a local product (see fig. 3.6). On Christmas Eve, 1926, radio station WCCO in Minneapolis, owned by the Washburn Crosby Company, the precursor to General Mills, broadcast what consensus believes to be the first singing commercial. The station had marketed Washburn Crosby Company products before, but the secretary of the company, whose idea it had been to purchase the radio station, said that it was time to "find out what that radio station of ours is good for."[47]

The task was turned over to the first manager of the station, who devised a singing commercial, described by a historian of the company as "a model

Figure 3.6 The Wheaties Quartet, ca. 1926. (Courtesy of the General Mills Archives.)

of decorum, courtesy, and effectiveness. The Wheaties song did not threaten, intimidate, whisper to the snob, urge conspicuous waste, or commit any of the offenses against taste or truth of which many a later contribution to the literature has been guilty."[48] This commercial was sung by an amateur barbershop quartet—the Wheaties Quartet, naturally—consisting of an undertaker, a bailiff, a printer, and a businessman, each of whom received six dollars per week while the commercial was aired, an extravagant sum for unknown radio musicians in this era (example 3.12).[49] The rather lugubrious song employs the lyrics

> Have you tried Wheaties?
> They're whole wheat with all of the bran.
> Won't you try Wheaties?
> For wheat is the best food of man.
> They're crispy, and crunchy, the whole year through
> The kiddies never tire of them and neither will you

So just try Wheaties

The best breakfast food in the land.

When General Mills contemplated discontinuing Wheaties in 1929, the company's advertising manager pointed out that well over half of the total sales of Wheaties were occurring in the Minneapolis–St. Paul area, where the singing commercial had been heard for three years. "I believe," said a member of the advertising department, "that if the use of radio were extended to other territories these figures would be duplicated and that Wheaties need not be dropped."[50] The Wheaties Quartet, renamed the Gold Medal Fast Freight (Gold Medal is a brand of flour still manufactured by General Mills), was broadcast coast-to-coast, a rare event in this era, in a half-hour program of ballads and folk songs courtesy of the young Columbia Broadcasting System.[51] The Wheaties jingle is probably best known for its reuse as the theme song for the radio program *Jack Armstrong, All-American Boy*, which began in 1933, sponsored by Wheaties.

The Wheaties jingle was somewhat anomalous, since, as we have seen, most music and advertising practices until the end of the 1930s did not involve stand-alone jingles; the Wheaties jingle did not change the nature of using music in broadcast advertising. The jingle that did that, however, appeared in 1939 and was the first nationally broadcast freestanding singing commercial to transform broadcast advertising more generally. "Pepsi-Cola Hits the Spot" is one of the classics of the genre; *Advertising Age* listed this campaign as number 14 in the top 100 advertising campaigns ever, and it has been called "the most famous oral trademark of all time."[52] Pepsi used the jingle until 1958, when the price of Pepsi went up from a nickel, a low price emphasized in the song's lyrics.[53] The story of the jingle was recalled by Walter Mack, president of the company at the time, who said there was little money for advertising in this era of the company's history, so he therefore sought new and less expensive means of promoting the product such as skywriting. Pepsi had also begun a cartoon in 1939 featuring the Keystone Kops types "Pepsi" and "Pete" (pictured on the sheet music in fig. 3.7), who used the line "Twice as much for a nickel."[54]

Then, one day in 1939, two casually dressed young men came into Mack's office (having been recommended by an advertising agency) and played a demo of "Pepsi-Cola Hits the Spot" on a portable phonograph (example 3.13).

Figure 3.7 "Pepsi-Cola Hits the Spot," sheet music, front cover, 1940.

Mack writes that he had little use for radio advertising in this period, believing that people didn't pay attention to it. But "here was something different. It was amusing, entertaining, and catchy—although at the time I had no idea just *how* catchy—and it was short, just thirty seconds."[55] (Actually, the jingle began life as a fifteen-second version as part of a spoken commercial; the authors thought that it would take at least that long for an irritated listener to get up and turn off the radio.)[56] Mack offered the duo, Alan Bradley Kent and Austen Herbert Croom-Johnson (who went by Ginger Johnson; fig. 3.8), five hundred dollars up front, with the promise of another fifteen hundred dollars if the commercial was successful.[57] They sold the rights to the jingle to Pepsi-Cola early in 1940.[58]

Mack's advertising agency, Newell-Emmett, didn't support the jingle, believing it to be too soft-sell.[59] And Mack had a difficult time selling the commercial to NBC, which told him that it never sold advertising airtime in less than five-minute blocks. Mack tried CBS to no avail, but eventually located a small radio station in New Jersey that was desperate for cash and sold Mack thirty- and sixty-second spots. After two weeks, Pepsi sales in this listening area were up, so Mack's advertising agency bought more time on other stations in the area.[60] The jingle was becoming so popular that CBS and NBC relented and sold Mack the shorter time slots that he wanted, for fear (according to Mack) that advertisers would think they could operate without the networks.[61] "What made the jingle great, and what saved it from dying long ago," said the Pepsi-Cola account executive at Newell-Emmett, "was Mack's decision to play the song alone."[62] The early version of the jingle was so popular that the company fully orchestrated the song, hired a known band, and had recordings made, eventually receiving orders for over one hundred thousand discs for jukebox use;[63] over a million recordings were eventually released.[64] The song became the first freestanding jingle played from coast to coast by the networks; a letter from an NBC executive to Mack dated 13 March 1941 thanked Mack profusely for the order for the jingle to be aired over 135 stations.[65] "By 1941," Mack claimed, "that little jingle had been broadcast 296,426 times over 469 stations."[66] Mack was later to assert that he was "the first on the

Figure 3.8 Alan Bradley Kent and Austen Herbert Croom-Johnson, 1940s. (Author's collection.)

Figure 3.9 Alan Bradley Kent and Austen Herbert Croom-Johnson:
"Pepsi-Cola Hits the Spot," sheet music, 1940.

jingle."[67] In 1948, Mack installed a set of electronic chimes on top of Pepsi's Long Island City, New York, plant that played the first seven notes of the jingle every half hour.[68] A 1942 survey showed that the jingle was the best-known tune in America.[69] In 1944, the *New York Times* reported that the jingle had been played more than a million times, and was still being heard daily on 350 stations.[70] It was so popular it was translated into fifty-five languages.[71] And cover versions were released, such as a 1940s version with some lyrics changed, but much of Pepsi's jingle intact (example 3.14).

Pepsi and Pete were also featured in cartoon shorts advertising Pepsi (example 3.15). The lyrics that refer to "twelve full ounces" and the cost of a nickel refer to the standard practice in the era of selling soft drinks in six-ounce bottles, so Pepsi in this jingle was touting its product as being twice as much for the standard price; the *Magazine of Wall Street* noted that this fact was a major aspect of Pepsi's advertising.[72] During the Depression, twice as much for the same nickel was compelling. Emphasizing quantity in this way was part of the new vocabulary businesses began using in this period to attempt to reclaim leadership on economic issues from New Dealers, as William L. Bird Jr. has written.[73]

As so many jingle precursors were, the melody was derived from a preexisting tune, an eighteenth-century British folk song, "Do Ye Ken John Peel," that was already known in the United States.[74] The song was in the public domain and therefore royalty-free; for this reason, using public domain materials for jingles became a common strategy. Kent and Johnson also wrote that they chose this song because they "sensed how well suited it was to the light mood of a cola beverage."[75]

Later, after the war, the lyrics were changed, since advertising a low price in good times didn't work, according to Pepsi-Cola advertising executive Philip Hinerfeld.[76] When the amount of sugar used was reduced, the lyrics were re-tooled, and sung by Polly Bergen in the early 1950s:

> Pepsi-Cola's up to date,
> For modern folks who watch their weight.
> We made it light and dry for you,
> Refreshing without filling, too.[77]

Bergen also recorded a "barn dance" version of the music for a television commercial in the 1950s (example 3.16).

The success of the Pepsi jingle made Kent and Johnson's careers and helped lay the foundations of the postwar jingle business. In October 1940, *Life* magazine reported that Kent and Johnson were responsible for 90 percent of all one-minute spots.[78] Their minimum fee went to $2,500, and in one case they were able to "lease-lend" a soap powder song for a $20,000 retainer.[79] A 1948 article estimated that to broadcast Kent and Johnson's commercial music, advertisers and their agencies had spent roughly $200 million.[80] Their success, and that of later composers, meant that jingle composers could demand forces larger than a few singers or instrumentalists. Their jingle "Pillsbury's Pancake Serenade," for example, employed twenty-three brass instruments, a Hammond organ, and male voice, a size of ensemble that most classical composers in the United States in this period would have counted themselves lucky to have.[81]

Not everyone accepted jingles, however. Pepsi's jingle stimulated an efflorescence of such tunes, so much so that in only a few years, listeners were complaining; the *New York Times* radio station WQXR banned singing commercials early in 1944, stating that such commercials "were apt to create ill-will among listeners and ultimately work to the disadvantage of the advertiser."[82] (The "Pepsi-Cola Hits the Spot" jingle evaded WQXR's ban by being played on a celeste only, without vocals, and was heard three or four times per day that way;[83] a 1957 article in *Advertising Age* noted that instrumental versions of jingles could slip through WQXR's ban.)[84] A network executive later in 1944 complimented those "stations . . . in full possession of their senses, which refuse to accept the musical spots."[85] Nonetheless, the effectiveness of jingles—wrapping up a hard-sell pitch in a sugarcoated musical treat—ensured their survival, and, indeed, jingles became an important means of selling for decades.

The Heyday of the Jingle

> I would rather play Chiquita Banana and have my swimming pool than play Bach and starve.
>
> —Xavier Cugat, famous bandleader of the 1940s and 1950s

The popularity of the Pepsi jingle was such that jingle production companies began to form and to advertise their services, musicians got to work, and networks tried to drum up business; music wasn't produced by advertising agencies themselves as much as it had been in the past.[86] NBC made a pitch in 1948 to Borden, the dairy company, by saying, "Through what medium can your slogans become part of the American language? (Jell-O Again; Duz Does Everything; Pepsi-Cola Hits the Spot, etc.)."[87] There was even talk in the industry of jingle-playing faucets for soda fountains.[88] Such was the craze for jingles after the success of the Pepsi jingle that an entrepreneurial radio announcer in New York decided to write weather reports as jingles. He wrote sixty jingles on various weather conditions, recorded them, and sold them to radio stations—jingles with lyrics such as:

> Today's a day I'd really like to skip,
> For damp and nasty days, it is a pip!
> Outside we've got a mess of fog,
> It shouldn't happen to a dog,
> And I think the weather man's a darn old drip!

His company also branched out into time jingles:

> Oh Goodness Gracious! Sakes alive!
> Darned if the clock don't say it's five!
> Five o'clock, five o'clock, five o'clock.[89]

(As far as I can tell, recordings no longer exist, so one doesn't know what these jingles sounded like.)

Other jingles of the era registered the growing U.S. interest in far-off peoples and places, kindled in part by U.S. servicemen's time abroad. The most famous of these is the Chiquita Banana jingle, introduced in late in 1944, which was used for decades. It began as a one-minute commercial, arranged and recorded by Mack Shopnick (figs. 3.10 and 3.11; example 3.17). Disney also produced a commercial for theatrical use in 1947 (example 3.18).[90]

This jingle was declared "the undisputed No. 1 on the jingle-jangle hit parade" by *Time* magazine in 1945, and, according to the brand's website, was played 376 times a day on the radio; another source says that by November 1945, the jingle was being heard over 138 stations in the United States and over 24 stations in Canada;[91] by early 1946, it was heard on over 155 stations in the United States and 30 in Canada at least 15 times each week.[92] Various recorded versions were issued by famous musicians such as Xavier Cugat, Gene Krupa, Vincent Lopez, and Carmen Miranda, and nearly one million recordings were sold.[93] The popularity of this jingle was such that navy students at a midwestern college voted Chiquita Banana the girl they would "most like to get into a refrigerator with";[94] women workers at an aircraft manufacturing plant told a reporter for the company newspaper that they sang the song every morning; the jingle was used by the Famine Emergency Committee during World War II urging Americans to save fats, wheat, and oils by using fresh fruits and vegetables.[95]

On the *Alec Templeton Show* aired in New York City on 2 June 1946, the jingle was presented as a faux opera (Templeton was a Welsh composer and pianist), with maestro "Arturo Templitini," parodying the immensely famous conductor Arturo Toscanini. The announcer mimics the announcer for the Metropolitan Opera radio broadcasts, the music operaticizes the original jingle melody, and the words impart the same information as the jingle's lyrics (example 3.19).

The jingle began with "the idea of personifying the banana as a Latin-American girl who sings in a characteristic Calypso rhythm," according to a trade book.[96] But the United Fruit Company argued that the purpose of Chiquita Banana was not to sell bananas, which were in short supply during wartime, but to educate the public about them. What Chiquita sang, according to BBDO, the advertising agency that produced the jingle, was a hit tune made out of an educational story.[97]

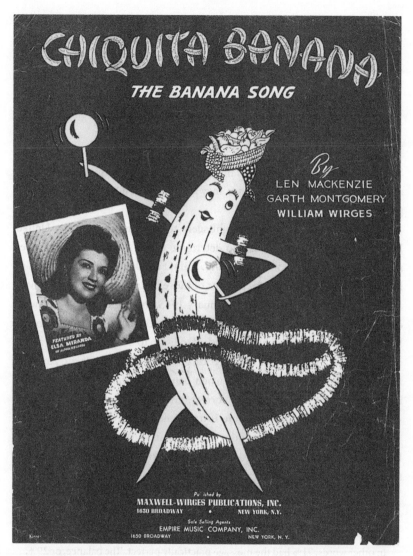

Figure 3.11 Chiquita Banana, sheet music cover, 1946. (Words and music by Garth Montgomery, Leonard Mackenzie, and William Wirges. Copyright © 1945 [renewed] by Music Sales Shawnee, a Division of Tom Cat Music Inc. International copyright secured. All rights reserved. Reprinted by permission.)

The war revealed a great deal as to the malnutrition prevalent in this country ... it seems pretty obvious that any food which people like and can be made to realize is good for them and their families, particularly the children, they will include in their "eating."

It is our belief that this educational radio effort properly carried out will result in the public realizing as it never has before the contribution its neighbors to the south of us have to make to the health and well being of the nation.

Our officials are also of the firm conviction that the only foundation on which an industry or business can be built to last is in the final analysis that it makes a sound contribution to people's needs. It is on the confident premise that bananas have such a contribution to make that this radio effort is undertaken.[98]

So the lyrics, as many still recall, informed listeners that brown spots on bananas are desirable, and that, since they are tropical fruits, they shouldn't be put in the refrigerator.

While the above statement might seem to be disingenuous, the United Fruit Company conducted tests to determine the ad's educational effectiveness. After a few weeks of broadcasting, BBDO conducted 500 interviews in Baltimore and learned that 90 percent of those interviewed knew Chiquita's advice about storing bananas.[99] In January 1945, the jingle was played twice over station WOLF in Syracuse, New York, a station that had never aired it before. A "panel of housewives" was asked to listen to the jingle and was asked questions about the content of the lyrics, generating 513 responses. Answers to the question "How do you tell when bananas are fully ripe?" generated responses that were 95.5 percent correct; answers to the question "Where should bananas never be kept" were 100 percent correct.[100]

In May, another test was conducted over station WMAL in Washington, DC. This time, listeners were asked to write out and send in the lyrics with a short letter saying what they had learned from the song. The results:

> 23 had the words letter-perfect; 21 had one error; 15 had two; 11 had three; 10 had four; and 12 had five. The errors were so slight as to be unimportant. In other words, 71% had the message practically perfect. The balance, or 29%, made six or more errors of omissions, spelling and punctuation . . . but *all* understood the message—and *all* were of the opinion that the song was catchy, pleasant, *and presented its story in a delightful and effective way.*[101]

United Fruit Company was able to conclude: "We are most happy over the fact that *we believe the child or adult who is not familiar with our jingle and its message is the exception and not the rule.*"[102]

As with many successful jingles, both the musical arrangement and the lyrics have been updated over time; the lyrics were last modernized in 1999 (example 3.20):

> I'm Chiquita Banana and I've come to say
> I offer good nutrition in a simple way
> When you eat a Chiquita you've done your part
> To give every single day a healthy start
> Underneath the crescent yellow
> You'll find vitamins and great taste
> With no fat, you just can't beat 'em
> You'll feel better when you eat 'em
> They're a gift from Mother Nature and a natural addition to your table
> For wholesome, healthy, pure bananas—look for Chiquita's label![103]

Jingles and Television in the Immediately Postwar Era

Jingles were receiving sufficient attention by the mid-1940s that specialists were beginning to offer taxonomies; Charles Hull Wolfe wrote that jingles fell into several classifications: prerecorded jingles could be a "chain break" type of only fifteen or twenty seconds (the Pepsi jingle was his example); other types were classified by length, down to a five-second recorded tag on live announcements. Live jingles included local program themes; brief musical identifications; fifteen- to twenty-second jingles used before or after commercial announcements; and longer jingles of fifty to seventy seconds.[104] Whether or not one accepts Wolfe's categorizations, it is clear that in less than a decade, the jingle had proliferated into a number of different usages.

Wolfe also noted the "new trend in one-minute jingles . . . toward the tune that follows the popular song format," and urged readers to adhere to this trend, in part because the public was used to it, and also because it had a built-in repetition of the main melody, which made it easier to remember; "Chiquita Banana" was an example.[105] And Wolfe listed four "advertising devices that are especially important in jingle lyrics":

(a) the "You appeal" that sings directly to the listener, as in Palmolive's "Oh, shavers, if you crave"; (b) the emotional appeal that talks to the heart rather

than to the mind, as in Colgate's "Don't take a chance on your romance";
(c) the testimonial, used largely in the "I" or "we" form by the singers themselves as in "I go for a man who wears an Adam Hat"; and (d) exactness, as in
"Just as Jell-O's six delicious locked-in flavors can't be beaten, so the proof of
Jell-O puddin's in the eatin.'"[106]

(This is the first time the question of emotional appeal has appeared in the
trade press with respect to music, a subject I will take up in the next chapter).

Wolfe also cautioned jingle composers to make sure they hadn't fallen into
any of the common pitfalls that beset bad jingles, including "voices [that]
lacked natural sincerity, happy exuberance, and good singing style."[107] "Happy
exuberance" often meant that jingles were composed in a style that was reminiscent of a musicalized nursery rhyme, whether or not the product was aimed
at children; one composer was blunt about this, saying that jingles must have
a gimmick, "a twist, something the kids will pick up, ape, chant or sing."[108]
Regardless of whether it was aimed at children, this sound was successful with
them; an article in *Nation* consulted a study by the Youth Research Institute
and noted that children quickly picked up jingles that they liked. "Even five-
year-olds sing beer commercials over and over again with gusto." Children
sing commercials throughout the day at no charge to the advertiser, with the
added benefit that "they are also much more difficult to turn off."[109]

Around the same time as the publication of Wolfe's how-to guide, a brief
interview in the *New Yorker* gave some additional insight into how advertising music worked in the immediately postwar era. The radio program director
would give the arranger percentages; a "sixty-forty jingle" was one that was
60 percent instrumental and 40 percent vocal. Advertising agencies determined the size of the instrumental group (based on budgets, one assumes),
which, according to this article, could run from a male quartet of singers to
a Ford commercial, "Bring Your Ford Back Home," which permitted the arranger, Mack Shopnick, twelve instrumentalists, sixteen singers, and a soloist.[110] Shopnick worked at home; recording was done in studios rented by the
advertising agency, which normally also hired the musicians, though sometimes Shopnick was expected to provide his own musicians, which he hired
from a regular pool "by calling them at their homes, by visiting certain bars,
and by standing on the sidewalk in front of 1265 Sixth Avenue, where Local
802 of the American Federation of Musicians has its headquarters."[111]

Television

The sound of jingles changed little with the advent of television, probably because advertising agencies' lack of understanding of television in its early years meant that radio practices continued. Adman Fairfax M. Cone said that the arrival of television was rocky, for nobody knew what to do with it. It proved not to be "radio with pictures," which was how it was first envisaged. Early television was "little more than vaudeville brought into the country's living rooms," he wrote.[112] Radio techniques didn't work.

Because of the ban on making recordings between 1942 and 1944 organized by the American Federation of Musicians (seeking a better deal with record companies—this is commonly known as the "Petrillo ban," named after the AFM president, James Petrillo), early television jingles were unaccompanied, or accompanied by instruments not recognized by the union, such as the ukulele, tiple (a steel-stringed instrument similar to the ukulele), Jew's harps, kazoos, children's xylophones, toy pianos, and sand blocks.[113] Austen Herbert Croom-Johnson described the permissible instruments as harmonicas, jawbones of asses, lutes, dulcimers, musical saws, lyres, and electric Jew's harps.[114] Singers would also imitate the sound of instruments: "Some of our people," said Robert Foreman of BBDO in 1950, "can dub in a bass fiddle by blowing a 'puck-puck-puck' sound close to the mike. There's one guy who does the snare drum, trumpet, and sax by breathing through his nose. He must be making a small fortune out of T.V. sound tracks."[115] In 1951, when the AFM temporarily banned the use of musicians in certain types of commercials, the jingle industry responded by employing whistling, hand clapping, and electronics.[116] Some of these techniques remained in the business.

Getting a jingle on the air in the early television era wasn't much different than in early radio. A *New Yorker* article described the process: Two young men entered the office of the vice president in charge of radio and television copy for the BBDO advertising agency, Robert Foreman:

"Let's have it," Foreman said.

The two men cleared their throats and, tapping out time, loudly sang a jingle in praise of Calso, a gasoline.

"It'll do," said Foreman. The two men departed.[117]

The jingle was sung to the tune of "Little Brown Jug," which satisfied Foreman for it was in the public domain and thus royalty-free.

Nursery-rhyme jingles continued, but there were jingles aimed at adults as well. Consolidated Cigar aired a spot in 1951 that featured a male and female soft-shoe routine, with Muriel, the animated lady cigar, asking, "Why don't you pick me up and smoke me sometime?" This Clio Award–winning commercial "annually received hundreds of requests for the commercial's music and lyrics from viewers wanting to dress up as the sexy cigar" (example 3.21).[118]

For the first few decades of their existence, jingles tended to track trends in popular music—with some lag time—though they were almost always unremittingly cheerful and upbeat, using happy tunes to sweeten the frequently bland information contained in the lyrics. They worked simply, by trying to create a positive affect around a particular product, occasionally promising something, whether suavity and attractiveness to women ("Brylcreem," music by John P. Atherton, words by Hanley Norins; example 3.22), or white teeth ("You'll Wonder Where the Yellow Went," for Pepsodent, by Don Williams, one of the first commercials aimed at the teenage audience, according to Lincoln Diamant; example 3.23).[119]

Fairfax M. Cone handled the campaign for Pepsodent and had little to say about the jingle, but the insider information is still telling. The problem the brand faced was that its main competitor, Colgate, was wintergreen flavored, which was more popular than Pepsodent's peppermint flavor. The equation of fresh breath / clean teeth was well established, and Cone thought that his company couldn't beat Colgate on the breath question. It found in a scrap pile the famous "You'll wonder where the yellow went" phrase, and rescued it for the campaign. Cone claimed:

> Nothing like this had happened since the early days of radio when the latest antics of Amos and Andy or the barbed wit of Bob Hope were reported and repeated as a part of the life of each day. The only difference was that this was strictly business. It was the first new approach to dentifrice advertising since Colgate had promised: It cleans your breath as it cleans your teeth.[120]

Cone said he gave the hastily put together jingle and newspaper ad the shortest introduction for a client he had ever given: he briefly introduced the recording with no explanation and asked simply for a yes or no from his clients.

When I played the record, and before I could unfold the newspaper advertisement, Bill Eastham ["the peppy Pepsodent marketing manager"] said, "How soon can you get it on the air?" He didn't wait for either [Milton] Mumford [president of Lever Bros.] or [Edward] Hicks [in charge of the Pepsodent division] to say anything, and when they did it was only to echo his question.[121]

Cone wrote that the success of the jingle was such that Harry Truman paraphrased the line—"You'll wonder where the voters went"—and Cone claimed that Pepsodent's sales doubled.[122] Elsewhere, he wrote that the Pepsodent campaign on the radio kept sales steady, while the introduction of Crest's new toothpaste resulted in drops in sales of other brands.[123]

The rise and success of jingles such as this occurred during the Great Depression, when advertisers and advertising agencies gradually abandoned the gingerliness with which they treated audiences at the beginning of the radio era: "Hard times meant a hard sell," writes Stephen Fox.[124] Jingles in this period, and after the conclusion of World War II, were uniformly happy, upbeat, and relentless, promoting not only particular commodities but also the continuation of consumer culture itself, which radio had played a powerful role in shaping in the 1920s. Alan Bradley Kent and Austen Herbert Croom-Johnson, cowriters of the landmark Pepsi jingle in 1939, wrote a decade later that jingles "should be a pleasing and intriguing form of sugar-coating the advertising pill," a musical strategy that would last for decades, until the next wave of heightened consumption practices began in the 1980s, the subject of later chapters.[125]

If you don't have an emotional hook, baby, you don't have
a prayer.

—Paul Stevens, *I Can Sell You Anything,* 1972

4

Music, Mood, and Television

The Use of Emotion in Advertising Music in the 1950s and 1960s

Introduction

One of the most striking aspects of early advertising music
and discourses around it was that affect or mood was almost never mentioned, even though emotional selling was
already an important aspect of print advertising from early
in the twentieth century, as historians of advertising have
shown.[1] Music was chosen for its ability to be evocative—
as peppy sounds for effervescent ginger ale, for example—
or cheery, to sell practically anything. Judging by the sound
of these jingles, affect was surely a consideration—dirges
were not employed to sell anything. But affect was largely
an unspoken concern. This, of course, makes sense, because
with radio one cannot see the product being sold: it had to
be animated with music, given a personality. After the rise

101

of television, the practice of imparting a personality to a product didn't disappear, but was joined by the now-ubiquitous strategy of using music for emotional manipulation, providing an affective underpinning for visuals.

While the postwar moment brought a number of important changes and strategies in the world of advertising, this chapter will focus on the question of emotion in music, since it continues to be central to how advertising music is conceptualized today; the following chapter will return to the history of the jingle, including its decline, to examine other shifts in the industry following World War II.

Heightened Consumption after World War II

The onset of the Cold War brought with it an increased sense of the importance of consumption as a civic duty that differentiated Americans from Soviets, but it did not vanquish the upbeat musical sales pitch in the form of the jingle. The Cold War, did, however, usher in a new strategy for the use of music in advertising and the promotion of new forms of American consumer culture. Lizabeth Cohen has written of two competing ideologies with respect to consumption in the twentieth century, the "citizen consumer," who consumed out of a sense of civic duty during the Depression and World War II, and the "purchaser consumer" of the same era, whose consumption was based more on self-interest. But after the war, she argues, another ideal emerged, that of the "purchaser as citizen" in a new "Consumer's Republic," in which consumers acting out of their personal desires could view themselves as acting in the public interest, helping to bring the country out of its Depression doldrums.[2]

Cohen writes vividly of the postwar moment after the initial boom in purchasing. What was to come next? Manufacturers made more products, and in a greater variety, including what were known in the industry as "parity products"—goods that were scarcely different from one another, giving the impression of a wealth of products in contrast to the few and standardized goods available under the previous regime of capitalism.[3] Obsolescence was planned, even accelerated.

American consumption reached new heights in this period, driven in large part by the advertising industry, which grew enormously in this era, finding new ways to sell by using psychology. In 1945, total billings of the ten largest agencies were $383,000,000; by 1960, billings had more than quadrupled, to $1,592,800,000.[4] Archival documents bear out the increased role assumed by advertising agencies. A J. Walter Thompson Company in-house publication from 1955 entitled *Huge New Markets* said:

> The attainment of new levels of prosperity will depend largely on our recog-
> nition that expanding *consumption* through *mass movements to better living
> standards* is the key to keeping our production and employment high—and is
> the key to a strong defense and a balanced budget.
>
> This is a challenge to marketing, because the change from a *production*
> economy, heavily influenced by government, to a *consumption* economy of in-
> dividual enterprise places the burden on selling, on finding needs and creating
> desires and on improving products or developing new products to meet these
> needs and potential desires.
>
> We have experienced the *miracle of production*—now, through the *magic of
> consumption*, we have the opportunity to keep our economy dynamic and grow-
> ing. The *magic of consumption* offers an opportunity for utilizing our increased
> productive ability in the positive form of a better standard of living.[5]

The document continues by citing statistics about federal expenditures and increasing consumption, then returns to exhortative mode, noting that American consumers' spending habits are difficult to change.

> There is the task of educating the American people to accept and work for
> the higher standard of living that their productive ability warrants. Selling
> and advertising can play a major part in the constructive urge to better living
> standards. And, as the standard of living advances along with productivity, the
> new and expanded markets thus created will have a *magical* influence on indus-
> trial growth and progress, on private financing and on increasing government
> revenues.[6]

It isn't necessary to point out the success of this approach, which, even after the onset of the Great Recession of the 2000s and 2010s, shows little sign of losing its adherents.

Motivation Research

The newfound interest in emotion in the 1950s was in part a product of the penchant for Freudianism and other psychological theories of the time, for psychoanalysis was on the rise, becoming commonplace among the urban middle classes.[7] Sherry B. Ortner has written of the Freudianism fad in the 1950s and the ways that it pervaded American culture, thematized in many forms of popular culture, in films such as *Forbidden Planet* from 1956, in which the threat proves to be not a creature but the id of the chief scientist. And there is Grace Metalious's novel *Peyton Place* from the same year, in which an important male character, whose father is dead, receives enemas every night from his mother and later turns out to be gay.

Despite the interest in Freud held by advertising agencies, introducing the idea of the utility of music as a mood manager to advertising was a slow process, for as many have observed, early television was conceptualized simply as "radio with pictures"; the transition from radio to television was slow and arduous. Yet the almost complete absence of discussions of mood and music in the early television era is still striking, since in the realm of film music, even before sound, mood was central.[8] What is noteworthy in the case of film versus radio is the distinction between them with respect to the question of affect, even though radio and film production became intertwined and interrelated early on.[9] Before World War II, there were occasional considerations of the question, though they were rare; even a 1935 volume entitled *The Psychology of Radio* confines itself largely to questions of audience preferences, which was what most publications were concerned with in this era, though near the end, the book included a brief meditation on music's ability to express "the basic feeling-tone—the mood, emotion, or desire—that underlies all experience."[10]

But such writings were unusual. Discussions of the importance of affect in radio do not enter mainstream advertising music discourse until the late 1950s (and by the 1990s became something of an academic subfield that I will discuss briefly below). In part, these early considerations were driven, I believe, not only by the advent of television but also by several other factors: the research of Ernest Dichter, whose ideas were further promoted by newspaper advertising man Pierre Martineau in a book published in 1957, and the critique of Dichter's work that appeared in the best seller *The Hidden Persuaders* by Vance Packard, also from 1957. The use of insights from psychology in advertising had a long history before Dichter (perhaps the most famous marker of the promise the industry felt that psychology offered was J. Walter Thompson Company's hiring of the well-known behavioral psychologist

John B. Watson in 1920), but it was Dichter's development of "motivation research" that marked a new era in the use of psychology in advertising.

Ernest Dichter (1907–91) earned a PhD in psychology from the University of Vienna and immigrated to New York City in 1938, where he worked for
five years under Paul Lazarsfeld, the pioneer in audience research, and later
founded the Institute for Motivational Research in 1946. Not without a flair
for self-promotion, Dichter became rather notorious when he concluded in a
study for Chrysler in 1939 that men viewed sedans as their wives but convertibles as mistresses; Dichter advised Chrysler to use convertibles in the show-
room window as bait to draw male customers in, a strategy that substantially
increased Chrysler's sedan sales.[11]

Another one of Dichter's arguments that illustrates his perspective concerned ice cream.

> Most ice cream advertising . . . strives to impress the public with the superior
> quality and flavor of one particular ice cream. These claims are augmented and
> illustrated with beautiful dishes of ice cream. To the advertiser the combination
> of copy and illustration adds up to good advertising. But is it enough—should
> not his goal be greater?
>
> A psychological study showed the "voluptuous" nature of ice cream to be
> one of its main appeals. In talking about ice cream, people commented: "You
> feel you can drown yourself in it," and "You want to get your whole mouth into
> it." Nothing, however, in the advertising produced the effect which this psycho-
> logical study showed they should have. The advertisements were not designed
> so as to satisfy people's desire for voluptuousness. Instead they created a feeling
> of neatness, an expectancy of sober enjoyment in eating X ice cream—all far
> removed from the emotionally loaded feelings most people have for ice cream.[12]

Not surprisingly, Dichter thought that the more quantitative kinds of approaches in other types of audience research were flawed.

> What struck me, coming from clinical psychology and psychoanalytic research,
> was that people were being asked through questionnaires why they were buying
> milk . . . and I just couldn't swallow that. It was almost comparable to asking
> people why they thought they were neurotic or to a physician asking a patient
> whatever disease he thought he had. I started fighting against that.[13]

To improve these superficial interviews, Dichter developed a technique he called "depth interviewing," which, he wrote, is "a procedure by which the respondent achieves an insight in to his own motivations. In other words, for the respondent it is a sort of introspective method." "In a depth interview," Dichter continued, "the interviewer attempts to bring about a full and spontaneous expression of attitudes from the respondent."[14] Elsewhere, Dichter described the depth interview as having been designed "to elicit the freest possible associations on the part of the respondent," as a way of determining "the *meaning* of the consumer's behavior rather than relying strictly upon her own explanation."[15] This and other techniques, some of which were more quantitative, could help the interviewer understand if people liked a certain brand of gum because it was fun ("bubble blowing") or because it evoked a feeling of aggressiveness ("tougher chewing").[16]

Dichter's influential ideas were popularized by Pierre Martineau, director of research and marketing for the *Chicago Tribune*, who was one of the first to proselytize for the importance of affect in advertising: "One of the great reawakenings of human thought has been occasioned by the rediscovery of feeling. For 300 years men have worshiped at the altar of Reason," he wrote.[17] Martineau believed that artists, as well as parents and salesmen, had always understood the importance of feelings in shaping human behavior, but rationality denied this.[18] Admitting that advertising practices already made much use of affective devices, Martineau said that affect had almost no presence in advertising theory, and that many of the affective qualities of ads were removed at the insistence of people on the business side because those on the creative side didn't have a way to articulate the importance of affect. But, he asserted, even the best sales techniques needed some sort of affective device to accompany them.[19] Martineau thus believed that the practices of advertising must change, making room for feeling and emotions.

Perhaps unsurprisingly, not everyone viewed positions such as Dichter's and Martineau's with favor. Vance Packard attacked Dichter in *The Hidden Persuaders*, believing that America had moved into a world of Big Brother, and that "the use of mass psychoanalysis to guide campaigns of persuasion has become the basis of a multimillion-dollar industry."[20] Successfully perceiving advertisers' and marketers' strategy, Packard argued that one of the reasons for the rise of "motivation research" was that the post–World War II glut of products on the market that weren't very different from one another—parity products—necessitated a different kind of advertising, one that didn't rely on logic or assumptions of the rational consumer. Betty Friedan also assailed Dichter in *The Feminine Mystique* for his culpability in attempting to interpellate women as housewives and mothers and convincing them that commodities could provide what they lacked in their lives.[21]

Music

It is not clear if musicians were participating in these debates, though surely some were familiar with Packard's best-selling book. Nonetheless, the idea of the utility of employing music for its affective qualities was slow to take hold in the world of advertising. Even in the late 1950s, advertising textbook authors were still discussing emotion in simplistic ways that show no greater degree of sophistication than the few prewar writings.[22] The only shift from the straightforwardly happy jingle in this era began around the same time that the United States entered World War II, when the march began to be used frequently as the basis for radio, and later television, jingles (example 4.1, "L-A-V-A," a jingle that was introduced on the CBS radio program *The FBI in Peace and War* in about 1944).[23] But most marches remained upbeat, whether selling cigarettes or breakfast cereal or razors (Gillette, "To Look Sharp," 1953, example 4.2, by Mahlon Merrick) or, especially, beer, obviously drawing on the German beer-drinking tradition ("My Beer Is Rheingold, the Dry Beer!," 1950s, example 4.3). Affectively, these examples are quite straightforward, but in their exhortative directness, they help make clear the combining of military and industrial interests that were coupled with the increasing pressure on Americans to conceptualize consumption as an important civic and patriotic duty during the Cold War. The martial nature of many jingles lasted almost as long as the form itself.

Nonetheless, advertising agencies were beginning, however feebly, to become more interested in the effectiveness of music used in advertising with respect to the question of emotion by the very late 1950s; a 1959 study revealed that music was used most when the advertising copy was motivational rather than informational.[24] A memorandum from the J. Walter Thompson Company the following year said that not much was known about the question of the effectiveness of music, but that "basically, it is felt that music . . . helps set and maintain the feel or mood of the commercial. It complements the copy and picture portion while acting as a unifying cohesive force. It gets under the viewers [sic] skin and helps make the commercial something more than just 'a commercial.'"[25] And an advertising practitioner urged his readers in 1961 to recognize the potential of music in commercials, pointing out how music in advertising could learn from the use of music in film and television. Like several publications in this era, this article mentioned Henry Mancini's theme music for the television program *Peter Gunn*: jazzy, dark, foreboding. The main argument the author forwards for the use of music in commercials concerns the service that music can provide in establishing mood.[26]

Yet sophisticated conceptions of music and emotion were slow in coming. In 1959, Beneficial Finance decided to employ music in its commercial; the "theory was that additional warmth and public understanding would be conveyed via the musical notes," according to an article in the trade press in 1962.[27] Phil Davis, a leading jingle composer in the 1950s and 1960s, was hired to make those notes, explaining his process thus:

> The lyrics and music of a service commercial, like Beneficial Finance, go beyond the literal.
>
> A man may have a pressing financial problem, which may or may not be in the forefront of his consciousness, but from which he basically seeks relief.
>
> Literally, this is a serious situation; yet, to write lugubrious lyrics or music would deepen the severity of the pressure. So the musical commercial producer does the inverse. He composes happy lyrics and music that suggest to the listener a possible happy solution to his problem.
>
> For example, interspersed between the voice of the announcer and the music of the commercial, you hear the following cheerful, optimistic lyrics: Call for money the minute you want it. . . .
>
> [The commercials] are written instrumentally to sound happy by the use of the celeste, orchestra bells, or bright, gay woodwinds—and nothing in a minor key.[28]

The article later reprints the jingle's lyrics, which were underlain by a "celeste background."

When the rise of rock 'n' roll in the 1950s threatened the livelihood of most Broadway composers, some entered the world of jingle composition. When these musicians, accustomed to writing music that engaged with listeners' emotions, encountered the affectively undeveloped world of jingles, there was a telling collision of the underlying ideologies of the two realms. Said Harold Rome in 1961, who wrote music for a Sanka commercial, "I can't get any emotion into Sanka coffee."[29] Affect was long a concern of these composers but still foreign to the world of advertising music in this period.

Two Mitches and a Roy: Leigh, Miller, and Eaton

The composer who, perhaps more than anyone else, helped broaden the emotionality of music used in advertising was Mitch Leigh (1928–), who formed Music Makers Inc. in 1957, which was emphatically not a jingle company (though it would please its clients that wanted one) but a company devoted to providing music that established the underlying mood of the commercial. Leigh, a former student of Paul Hindemith at the Yale School of Music, had impeccable credentials as a classical composer and also possessed strong ideas about the power of music to motivate, as well as the obsolescence of jingles. His bold pronouncements on the lack of usefulness of the jingle—an unsophisticated kind of music in his view, in part, I think, because of its affective one-dimensionality—helped him promote the idea that commercial music could be something more: "Jingles as we've known them for the past twenty-five years are dying. In fact they're dead right now and what is left is just the body cooling off," he said in 1960.[30] Elsewhere, Leigh compared his company's approach to the use of mood music in film. Today, this is the norm, but in the early 1960s, it was a novel idea.[31]

Using music for emotional purposes entered advertising practice through film, which, of course, had employed music to provide emotional underpinnings for decades. In advertising, using music this way was called "prescoring," referring to the fact that the instrumental music was recorded first, before the voice and visuals. Commercials began to be prescored in the late 1950s, and Leigh was a major proponent, for with prescoring, composers could tie moods with the visual with more nuance than was possible otherwise.[32] Leigh thought that music was the last of the arts to be used in marketing, but that, "in stimulating an emotional response to a product [music] can be advertising's most powerful instrument of communication," he said in 1966.[33] Leigh also said that he wanted to give clients "the most effective tool for producing emotions for remembering a product when you're in a supermarket crammed with different items."[34]

Other interviews with Leigh from the 1950s and 1960s make frequent reference to the importance of emotion in advertising. For him, the main question was, does the everyday person react emotionally to an ad?[35] In another

Figure 4.1 Mitch Leigh. (Courtesy of Mitch Leigh.)

interview, he said, "Music gives a product emotional memorability."[36] Leigh
said in a 1958 publication that his company called its approach "musical psychology," which referred to the "physical relationships of sounds, pitches, nu-
ances, rhythms, meters, melodies and harmonies" with which "we are able
to invade the unconscious of the viewer and affect his human sensibilities;
thereby setting him up for the commercials' 'haymaker.'"[37] In an interview, I
asked him about the role of emotion in music. He stated bluntly, "Emotion is
what advertising is," and, "I really honestly believe to this day that people buy
on the basis of emotion, they react to emotion." Leigh told me that his company was successful, he believed, because of the emotional selling of products:
"The one thing that remains totally emotional is music, and if it's used well . . .
we sold a lot of products."[38]

Leigh explained his compositional approach to commercial music in a
1959 *Wall Street Journal* interview with an example. A commercial for Ford
automobiles entitled "Backseat Blues" was designed to convey the impres-

sion that other cars were less roomy by employing images of people contort-
ing themselves getting in and out of these competing vehicles; Leigh's music
changed meter with them. "Each meter change gives the viewer an uncom-
fortable experience," he said, which, he thought, entered the subconscious
(example 4.4).[39] I have been able to hear the music to this commercial (but
not see the video), and the meter changes are quite audible. At the same time,
however, the affect of the commercial is relentlessly upbeat, in a vocal jazz
idiom of the era.[40]

Other commercials employed different techniques. A commercial for
Renault used French horns and timpani in a crescendo at the commercial's
end to leave listeners "with the impression of a spritely [sic] car with a peppy
getaway."[41] For an antacid commercial, Leigh's music opened with the sounds
of a calliope to communicate the madness of contemporary life, moving to
soothing music as the tablet took effect.[42]

While Leigh was probably the most vocal of proponents of the employment
of affect in advertising music in this era, he wasn't the only person advocating
more sophisticated approaches to music and emotion in advertising. Mitch
Miller, an influential figure in the commercial music world in this period as
head of A&R (artists and repertoire) at Columbia Records, wrote in 1956:

> I remember asking Rodgers and Hammerstein how they decided what to
> put to music, and what to leave as dialogue. And they replied that they used
> music and songs only when it became impossible to convey an emotional
> feeling by words alone. And the same should apply to music spots. If the mu-
> sic does not heighten the emotional impact of your message—better leave it
> spoken.[43]

And an article from April 1961 on Miller presented the idea of using emotion in music as an innovation.[44] Miller, like many in this period, believed that
music could serve a subliminal function in commercials. The example provided is for the 1959 Ford, which the company wanted to hype for its economy features. A trade press article wrote:

> The agency's writers felt that to do this, they would have to list all the major
> savings features. Given 60 seconds, only an announcer would be able to say all
> that had to be said. It couldn't be sung because getting all the nuts and bolts
> information into an effective and catchy song would be impossible.

Was this a problem music could solve? Because of a heavy emphasis on economy, the agency felt the image of the car as a quality item might suffer. Mr. Miller suggested they back the announcer with a Percy Faith arrangement of the Ford theme full of lush fiddles not ordinarily associated with a low-priced item. The result was a happy one for Ford sales and emphasized another Miller credo: "Words and music must be mated discriminately, or else you're going to end up with a mongrelized commercial."[45]

The other influential figure in advertising music who advocated the use of music for emotional purposes was Roy Eaton, a longtime vice president and music director at Benton and Bowles advertising agency, who, like Leigh and Miller, was a classically trained musician.[46] Eaton said in a 1963 article, "Music has an extremely potent emotional function in the sales impact of a commercial. The emotional impact of a commercial is a vital factor in its selling effectiveness."[47] And in an interview, he told me of a 1957 commercial for Kent cigarettes with the then-new micronite filter; in order to convey a feeling of newness, he used modern jazz in the commercial.[48] An advertisement for instant Yuban Coffee was thought to require modern sound since instant coffee was a fairly new product, so an arrangement of the original theme was made, this time with "modern chord progressions," resulting in "a changed harmonic setting, a modern difference."[49]

In 1960, *Television Magazine* argued that as broadcast advertising had become more sophisticated, so, too, had sponsors and their tastes in music, which was increasingly judged by feeling more than anything else.[50] Discussions with Eaton revealed that commercials' factual information didn't require the use of music for affective purposes. Some of the rationales for using the affective properties of music didn't always make sense, as in this trade report from 1960 on Yuban Coffee that Eaton worked on: "With General Foods' Yuban Coffee . . . where the selling story is quality resulting from the blending process (aged coffee beans), an emotional build-up is called for—and accomplished with orchestration and vocal theme ('*deep, dark, delicious Yuban*')."[51]

This article about Eaton provides several useful examples, for it points out the differing conceptions of the use of music in this era. One example was for Prell shampoo, which showed a sexy woman using the product; the copy employed only 44 words (we are informed that 150 is the norm for a sixty-second commercial). Eaton

Figure 4.2 Roy Eaton. (Courtesy of Roy Eaton; photo by Ken Howard.)

went to a musical style similar to [Maurice] Ravel for two arrangements: one made use of two flamenco guitars, the other used ten instruments, including French horns, trumpet, violin, harp, flute and drums. Human voices were also used in the latter arrangement for some of the copy phrasing. The overall effect is as sweepingly sensuous and pleasurable as the core of the Prell message.[52]

The other example was for Zest soap, which "also reflects emotional personal product involvement"; the commercial showed a mother and small daughter being caught in the rain. The task for this commercial, according to the article's author, "was to evoke reminiscence of the clean, fresh feeling of rain to a child and translate this into the type of physical sensation Zest will give to an adult." Eaton's solution was to concoct what he called "'a one-minute Peter and the Wolf'"—that is, a more descriptive kind of musical treatment.

Orchestration was for ten instruments—chime effect for rain, violins for sweep, cymbal and woodwinds. In translating character to musical instrument (to give each character a representative musical "image" or "voice"), the daughter was represented by a flute (lightheartedness), the mother by an oboe (maturity).[53]

The Maturation of a Strategy

After Leigh, Miller, and Eaton in the late 1950s and early 1960s, the emotionality believed to be implicit in music was employed, and referred to, with increasing frequency, in part, it was thought, because of the growing sophistication of audiences. Late in 1963, the New York Times printed an article on the "new wave" of jingles, noting their continuing popularity: "Ad music is in. Way in." The author noted the new trend toward the increasing sophistication of their sound ("Musical cognoscenti say they hear strains of Busse and Debussy in them"), and compared them to New Wave cinema in their "honesty, intimacy, simplicity, an effort to say more with less, and above all, an attempt to evoke, not provoke, the viewer's sensibilities." The main exemplar in this article was Granville (Sascha) Burland, proprietor of C/Hear Services Inc. in New York City. Burland thought, as many did in this era, that there was too much "clutter" on the air, which rendered advertising copy meaningless, and he had nothing but contempt for hard-sell tactics, what he termed "highbutton shoe thinking."

> We're trying to create a new atmosphere through music—not merely jingles, but to evoke moods, color through original jazz and sounds around us. For years ad music was played on an organ or celesta and it sounded like "Three Blind Mice." With the tremendous amount of creative talent coming into this field, we're changing all that.[54]

Elsewhere, Burland articulated some ideas with respect to affect, matching instrumentation, rhythm, style, and more to create an underlying mood for the commercial.

> The possibilities of applying music to ads is [sic] endless. Take a bread ad. Bread is to enjoy, not to safeguard your health. So we'll compose a flute passage and perhaps some rhythm and strings and come up with a message that will be

giddy, such as "Carroway [*sic*] seeds are better than vitamins." If it's a gasoline spot, we'll give it a jazz orchestration with 35 musicians because you want a "go" feeling. To achieve a sense of dignity or stature we'll use French horns. For excitement, it's brass and polyrhythms. If we want to communicate the sensual delights of travel, we might abstract the folk music of the region to give the audience the feel of the place.[55]

Burland here gave evidence that the advertising musician was beginning to think of his music as did film music composers, though, as we shall see, the conceptualizations of affect continued to become refined. This kind of language, reflecting the growing influence of film music techniques, was also part of the much-vaunted "Creative Revolution" in advertising in the 1960s, when creativity in advertising was given more of a free rein than in previous eras.

By the late 1960s, it appears to have been normal for musicians to discuss mood with copywriters or others involved in the production of ads.[56] Questions about mood are largely absent from the trade press by this time, for they had been normalized—people in the industry were talking about music and mood all the time, no longer simply advocating for the use of music to provide mood. It was thus probably inevitable that advertising agencies began to think in terms of writing songs for advertisements that could capture a desired mood. In 1974, a commercial entitled "Sweet Memories" for Kodak was described in the trade press employing a kind of nuance that people were talking about with respect to selling.

The song itself is really the mainspring of the piece. It's like the clockwork mechanism in the center of a fantastically complex clock—motivating the ebb and flow of feelings and images that run through the film. There are three basic elements in the film: the song, the woman and the place. They are what you remember, what stays with you.

The interesting thing about the making of Sweet Memories was that it involved filming a song. Everything else kind of dovetailed with that original idea. And it was not an easy kind of song to film. It had to do with capturing a feeling, a feeling of evanescing reality, turning into bittersweet memory. The other interesting thing about it was that it did all this in such a way as to make the end product of commercial value. In other words, it sold the product. It made you think nice thoughts about Kodak, and believe that Kodak has a unique way of keeping you and your memories together.[57]

Commercials such as this, described in sophisticated language of affect ("evanescing reality," "bittersweet memory"), were leading to a shift in the production of advertising music: music and the mood or moods it was thought to
evoke could drive the production of commercials.

Heartsounds

In 1975, when McDonald's decided that it was unhappy with the famous "You
Deserve a Break Today" commercial, its advertising agency found Ginny Redington, a jingle singer and composer who had written some notable jingles in
the past. She wrote a new jingle with lyrics by the advertising agency's copywriter, Keith Reinhard, entitled "You! You're the One!" Reportedly dressed in
jeans, she auditioned the song before the advertising agency suits, who asked
her to record the song for use in the commercials. The recording was matched
with film showing happy working-class families eating at McDonald's (examples 4.5 and 4.6). The advertising agency wanted to test the commercial,
and concluded that the song was memorable. It then rented the Civic Opera
House in Chicago to pitch the commercial to McDonald's executives, who
decided to keep the account at the agency, after having threatened to take it
elsewhere.[58]

The rescue of the account by a song became the talk of Madison Avenue.
Time magazine called the jingle the "quintessential 'me'-decade song," which
concludes with the tagline "We do it all for you."[59] As a result of the success
of this song, other agencies began to use music more frequently in their commercials, so that by the late 1970s and early 1980s, many commercials employed a song that made a direct emotional appeal in a strategy referred to by
some as "heartsounds." Many such songs addressed listeners explicitly, as in
Redington's for McDonald's.[60] Talk of emotion was on the rise in the industry.[61] Major campaigns with music that were launched following "You! You're
the One!" were the army's "Be All You Can Be" (example 4.7, music by Jake
Holmes); "Good to the Last Drop Feeling," developed by Maxwell House
with Ray Charles; and "We Bring Good Things to Life" for General Electric,
by Thomas McFaul and David Lucas.[62]

With the triumph of the "heartsounds" strategy, composers began to have
to be "chameleons with a feeling for the musical sound of a mood," said one
composer in 1976.[63] A 1977 overview of the work of advertising composers
noted that the composer had the difficult task of setting the mood in a com-

mercial in a matter of seconds, which meant that composers had to possess varied musical backgrounds so that they could call upon different musics to evoke or support the mood in a commercial.[64]

Perhaps the quintessential heartsounds commercial actually employed a heartbeat-like sound in a mid- to late 1980s Chevrolet campaign called "Heartbeat of America." Chevrolet's advertising agency auditioned over a hundred songs before choosing one, by Robin Batteau, a songwriter and singer. Batteau wanted listeners to associate Chevrolet with the birth of rock 'n' roll, and described the music as beginning with a folklike sound, moving to Motown, and then ending with rock (example 4.8).[65] The music also employed synthesized heartbeat sounds. A New York City advertising music producer, who was not involved with this commercial, said that this music "has a wonderful sense of freedom; a fun quality that's very loose, undisciplined; it sounds like real rock 'n' roll instead of being contrived."[66] *Advertising Age* reported that consumers wanted to know where they could buy the music, and a record release was considered.[67] *Advertising Age* wrote that the campaign identified the aspirations of Chevrolet with those of Americans instead of attempting to encourage viewers to identify with Chevrolet. The executive vice president–creative director for Chevrolet at the automaker's advertising agency said that the mission statement for the campaign, forged in Ronald Reagan's America during a period of increased nationalism, "demands that Chevrolet stand for America and for Americans, that it be the supplier of excitement and dreams for all of us who can't afford Ferraris and Maseratis."[68]

An article from 1981 discussed the rise of heartsounds and quoted several composers on the sound; one, Tom Dawes, who authored such music, said, "It's a time for emotion. Tear-jerking stuff sells today. It's not enough to just get consumers to understand in a commercial. They have to *feel*, too." Another composer, Mike Uris, agreed. "You can tell, tell, tell viewers until you're blue in the face," he said, "but it doesn't matter unless they're touched. You can't influence purchase decisions unless you touch the consumer—and I'm convinced that in a majority of cases, music 'emotionalizes' your selling proposition."[69]

Music and Advertising in an Era of Heightened Consumption

The rise to dominance of the thirty-second commercial in the late 1960s meant there was less music scoring, but this didn't hurt the jingle part of the business, for the increased federal regulation of advertising copy meant that music had to work harder in commercials. Strengthened restrictions on claims that could be made in advertising copy in this era meant that less could be said about products, putting more of a burden on music and other means of nonverbal communication.[70]

And it was inevitable that surveys about the use of music began to reflect the relatively new interest in emotion. A music production house conducted a survey of clients in the late 1970s and offered the results shown in table 4.1 to readers of *Advertising Age*.

The rationalization of the benefits of using music for emotional purposes took many forms. A 1980 article included a little chart of the emotional benefits that music could produce with various household products (table 4.2).

In the early 1980s, perhaps as a result of the renewed emphasis on consumption in American culture, due in part to the efforts of Ronald Reagan and other conservatives to promote consumption as a necessity of citizenship, there was an uptick on questions of mood as a means to sell more goods.

Table 4.1 What they think of commercial music, 1978

Music can create a strong emotional environment in which to deliver your message	23.6%
Music can emphasize visuals and copy points	18.9%
Each time your jingle is remembered, hummed or sung, a "free" advertising registration is made	16.5%
Because music can elicit an involuntary emotional response, it can help overcome a listener's inclination to turn off the ad message	15.1%
By functioning as a sort of connective tissue, music can pull the spot together	14.5%
Music makes the message more palatable by entertaining the listener	11.4%

Source: Norm Richards, "Hints to Make Commercial Music Sing," *Advertising Age*, 23 January 1978, 54.

Table 4.2 Emotional benefit added by music for various products

Product	Product benefit	Emotional benefit
Diapers	Dryness	"I'm good to my baby"
Vegetables	Taste, nutrition	"I'm good to my family"
Dog food	Taste, nutrition	"I'm good to my dog"
Toothpaste	No cavities	"I'm good to my children"
Mouthwash	Fresh breath	"I'm good to my friends"

Source: Edward Vick and Hal Grant, "How to Sell with Music," *Art Direction*, May 1980, 67.

(I will discuss the rise of a new wave of consumption in the 1980s in chapter 7.) A 1982 article by the vice president and associate research director at Young and Rubicam shows the sophistication with which the topic of music and emotion was being discussed by people in the industry in this era, beginning by acknowledging the importance of music in commercials—"Music is the catalyst of advertising." The author, Sidney Hecker, wrote that good jingles "have a clearly defined objective," which he characterized as eliciting the appropriate feelings; good jingles "offer the listener a *reward*, in the sense of particular *emotional feelings*"; and "these executions clearly exemplify a brand personality." Hecker's article is all about the importance of music in imparting feelings to commercials: "Good composers can develop moods that range from dreamy, tender and soothing to bright, cheerful, joyous, to exciting and exhilarating, to triumphant, majestic, and even spiritual." He continued, "Here is the power to *move* the listener, to turn him or her in a desired direction, to create empathy or rapport with our characters and with our brand, to augment or become part of the brand personality."[71]

Additionally, with the advent of the fifteen-second commercial in the mid-1980s, there was some discussion of using music for mood purposes rather than jingles, since the short period of time didn't allow for a melody that could be developed. Suzanne Ciani, the renowned composer of electronic music in commercials, said that her way of dealing with the shorter commercials was to use music to aim always to express mood. Ciani saw her role in these sorts of commercials as "painting the sound."[72]

The increased use of music was accompanied by an increase in its detractors, however; advertising legend David Ogilvy's famous line—"If you have nothing to say, sing it"[73]—is mentioned in many trade press articles in this period, though most who defended the use of music referred to the changing landscape of the business. Composers understood their task in this era as attempting to inflect or create minor differences among parity products.[74] This point was reinforced in another publication of the era, using the example of Burger King and McDonald's. Since their products are much the same,

> jingle writers ... find themselves in the business of influencing trivial decisions: it simply makes no difference which hamburger one buys. One technique widely used to deal with this problem is to sell not the product, but various intangibles that can be associated with the product: sex, status, excitement,

Table 4.3 Sample printout from the Soper MusicSelector software package, 1982

MOOD: GRAND	STYLE: ORCHESTRAL
TIME: 3:00	EXACT TIME: 3:03
TEMPO: MED FST/160	GROUP SIZE: LRG
INSTRU: RHY, STR, BRS, WNS, HRP, XYL, VIB, PER	
KEY SIGN: D	
TITLE: CORPORATE FANFARE	
COMMENTS:	
CAT NO: 42B-4	

Source: Carol Deistler, "Tops with the Pops," Audio-Visual Communications, March 1982, 24.

or Anita Bryant. Music has been found to be very effective in increasing these associations."[75]

One way to acquire an understanding of just how important the question of mood had become by the 1980s is by examining library music, which is music composed to be stockpiled, waiting to be used commercially.[76] Music libraries have long catalogued their music by mood, as well as style and other information. A 1982 article that discussed a computer software application that allowed users to search for music in a database included a sample printout resulting from a search for a three-minute track with a "grand" mood by a large orchestra (table 4.3). Only one mood category is indexed here, even though the landscape of moods was increasing in this period.

Another sign of the increasing hold the idea of mood had on the commercial music industry was the rise in the 1980s of scholarly publications that explore connections between mood and music. With titles such as "Music, Mood, and Marketing," and published in such periodicals as the *Journal of Marketing* and the *Journal of Consumer Research*, these articles are designed to aid advertisers and marketers. They are, from my perspective as an interpretive social scientist, much too scientistic to be of more than ethnographic interest, serving to point out how established the connection of music and mood had become in the advertising and marketing industry.[77] One advertising textbook mined some of this literature on music and mood to produce a chart that simplistically links (for example) "sad" music to the minor mode, slow tempo, low in register, of "firm" rhythm (which is meaningless to musicians), consonant harmony, and of medium volume.[78]

Emotion as a Selling Point

By the 1980s, composers were routinely touting the emotional effects that they thought their music could deliver. "Music enables you to emotionalize your product and its benefits: your entire selling proposition. Through music, you are selling from the heart, to the heart," wrote one commentator in the trade press in 1983, concluding, "Music hath charms to soothe the savage breast, and sell a lot of soft drinks."[79]

The music and mood ideology became so influential that it began to infiltrate demographic considerations. A good example is recounted in a 1981 article concerning Bon Jour Jeans, an account belonging to Backer and Spielvogel. According to Bill Backer, "Blue jeans should be fun to wear, so a commercial for blue jeans should be fun to watch." He thus worked to transform the image of the product from harsh "New Wave / punk" to soft "continental/ romantic" by using Jacques Brel–type love songs. "Our research indicated that this kind of musical approach could help build Bon Jour's franchise most quickly," Backer said.[80]

A few years later, *Advertising Age* began an article in late 1987 thus: "Emotion—defined as 'any strong manifestation or disturbance of the conscious or unconscious mind' (Encyclopaedia Britannica)—is what sells everything from diapers to diamonds in this country." This preceded an interview and profile of composer/lyricist Joe Lubinsky of Hicklin Lubinsky Company or HLC Music in Hollywood. "Prime emotions are what make great advertising," said Lubinsky, and, "great emotion works forever." Lubinsky, like others in this period, began to speak in greater detail about how composers attempted to employ emotions in their commercials. "I have a tremendous concern that whatever I produce for my clients has some sort of emotional hook to it— something that will stay with the consumer. Emotional times are what you remember most in your life."[81]

Music and Mood Today

Music and mood have become the main language by which people in music production companies and their clients in the advertising industry communicate, especially when clients aren't familiar with musical terminology, which can be frustrating for musicians. As Fritz Doddy, creative director at Elias Arts in New York City, told me:

So we get together and figure out—my sad is your sad, and your blue is my
blue, my fast is your fast . . . so we have some sort of understanding that, "Well
we don't want the spot to be melancholy, we want it to be bittersweet"—so
we're dealing in very subtle shades. "We want it to be a bossa nova, we want it to
be a tango, we want it to be heavy metal"—so we define some very broad genre
and mood parameters for a project.[82]

Again, the practices of library music composers shed light on the question
of music and mood in advertising. An interview I had with such a composer,
Andrew Knox, covered the question of mood in some detail. Library composers, perhaps even more than composers in music production houses, deal with
questions of mood on a daily basis, for they not only compose music to fill
niches in their libraries but they also write prose that describes their music so
that it can be searched in vast databases.

Adjectives—they try to give me as many adjectives as possible, and most of the
time they're not musically inclined, and they don't know what to say. "So, we
want it to be more yellow, or more blue. . . ." You have to start to learn the different adjectives that people use and then kind of interpret that into music. "Okay,
I want something that's simple and sad, but not over the top." So maybe we go
for an oboe kind of a sound rather than a violin, because a violin seems too sad-
sounding. So maybe a light flute or solo piano might do that. So . . . you get to
interpret, which is kind of fun for me to interpret their feelings, or their words,
into music.

One of the skills a library composer must have, Knox told me, is to be able
to describe music vividly in a single sentence. The goal is to characterize the
tracks so pithily that they can appear in his company's extremely sophisticated
search engine.

The whole idea with these descriptions is to try to sell the client on actually
listening to this track, 'cause once they listen to it, then they have their own
idea. But . . . you have to figure out, "Okay, what can I say that talks about this
piece of music but then also will let the client buy enough to even put it in the
CD player?" The other thing that you think about when you're describing your
music is now, in the world of technology, . . . we have computer programs that
you can search for music by descriptive words.

[*Typing*] "Sad," "orchestral," it's like doing a Google search. . . . And, let's see, 1,194 tracks came up with that. Now I'm sure there's more than that many, I'm sure there's more than that many, but those are all the ones that have "sad" "orchestral" in the description.[83]

The solution is what Knox calls the "shotgun," whereby he provides a variety of selections and hopes that one fits the client's needs.

Record labels similarly employ mood descriptors to classify their music to make it searchable by music supervisors, advertising agencies, and others for their use in broadcasting. In the mid-2000s, Sony Music offered a website called SonyMusicFinder to aid potential licensors of its music, offering seventy-one adjectives referring to affect (table 4.4). The sheer number of these terms as well as their subtlety provides a good example of just how refined this contemporary discourse of mood has become in the realm of commercial music today. It has to be—this is the primary means that consumers are interpellated as consumers, addressed by sounds at an emotional

Table 4.4 "Mood List" from SonyMusicFinder

aggressive	detached	melancholy	rowdy
amiable/good-natured	druggy	nocturnal	sensual
angry	earnest	organic	sentimental
angst-ridden	earthy	party/celebratory	sexual
autumnal	eerie	passionate	silly
bitter	elegant	playful	soothing
bleak	exuberant	poignant	sophisticated
boisterous	fun	provocative	springlike
brash	gentle	quirky	stylish
brooding	hostile	rambunctious	summery
campy	innocent	raucous	tense/anxious
carefree	intimate	rebellious	theatrical
cathartic	ironic	reckless	thuggish
cerebral	joyous	refined/mannered	visceral
cheerful	laid-back/mellow	reserved	volatile
confident	light	reverent	whimsical
confrontational	literate	rollicking	wry
cynical/sarcastic	manic	rousing	

Source: http://www.sonymusicfinder.com. This now-inactive URL was operational in the late 1990s and early 2000s.

level that advertisers and ad agencies hope will encourage them to purchase goods.

Since the late 1970s, the ideology of affect has become so deeply ingrained in the culture of the production of advertising music that composers routinely refer to music's almost magical powers to influence consumers, speaking in matter-of-fact terms far from either Dichter's psychologism or the scientism of later authors: this has become a central ideology that is repeatedly articulated by many in the field. For example, Phil Dusenberry, former chairman of BBDO, wrote in 2005, "Emotion is how a branding relationship begins."[84] Commercial music composers who have had occasion to write something about the efficacy of music in advertising nearly always refer to the idea that music will help consumers remember the product, even, or especially, at the point of purchase, and that the mechanism for this is emotion. One jingle composer wrote, "Music moves people emotionally . . . [and] hopefully puts them in a frame of mind to buy a specific product."[85] And another believed that music's "messages sneak into our brains and cause us to act in certain ways. We buy products and services and may not even know why. We have been influenced by these creative messages and we respond often in spite of our better judgment."[86] A composer/owner of a music production company said in 1979:

Psychologists . . . tell us that most of our decisions are made on a subconscious, emotional level. . . . [Thus], we should be trying to reach [consumers] on those same emotional levels. If being easy to remember ["memorability" being a buzzword in this era] is a function of intellectual activity, *it's possible for the consumer to remember your commercial consciously, but not have it count as a factor in his emotional decision of whether to buy your product or service.* . . .

And that, I firmly believe, is music's main value as a marketing tool—*its ability to cut through all the intellectual irrelevancies, and affect someone right in the gut, where brand preferences are often determined, and most buying decisions are made.*[87]

In the fifty years since the advent of discourses about mood in music, it has been used, sometimes with great effectiveness, to support the postwar rise in consumption through the 1950s to its heightened importance in the 1980s, becoming indispensable in creating apparent differences between parity products, whether hamburgers or soft drinks. Coming in on the fashion for Freud in the 1950s, the use of music to create and manage mood in commercials has survived to the present, now with complex languages of affect—languages that can sometimes be vague and vexing for musicians dealing with nonmusicians. Today, not only is a language of affect dominant in the industry, it has its own rarefied and scientized language authored by academics and industry workers, which has continued to be employed during the Great Recession and afterward. The "magic of consumption" described by J. Walter Thompson in the 1950s is now driven in part by the emotionality of music.

[A jingle is] a piece of music that's not quite long enough . . .
sounds like someone else, but not close enough to someone
else to get you sued . . . uses one or two words too often,
makes a lot of money for a very few people . . . and goes up
at the end.
                              —Composer Doug Katsaros, 1988

Could this guy [Mozart] Do Jingles? Are you kidding, *A Little
Night Music* had "beer commercial" written all over it.
                    —Look & Company advertisement, 1992

5

The Standardization of Jingle
Production in the 1950s and After

Introduction

This chapter takes up where chapter 3 left off, with the history of the jingle, beginning in the immediate postwar era.
I recommence here not because it makes sense in terms of
changes in musical production but because of the historical
turn toward heightened consumption practices discussed
in the previous chapter: jingles continued to be the musical workhorses of the advertising industry in the postwar
phase of American consumption. This wave of heightened
consumption was driven by changes in American capitalism in this period, in which the increased emphasis on the
mass market discussed in the previous chapter resulted in
increased standardization of production as well as of products, a consequence of a new cycle of expanded reproduc-

tion in this era that was spurred by the expansion of the means of production sector, as Tom Kemp writes.[1] But with changes in the means of production, new products differed little from those manufactured before World War II. This is as true of automobiles as cultural products, whether films in the studio system in Hollywood, or jingles.

In the postwar period, the business of jingle production grew. And as it grew, the occupation of the advertising music composer became increasingly professionalized. The legendary adman and musician Bill Backer told me that when he first got into the business in the 1950s, it wasn't clear what to charge for jingles.[2] But in the course of that decade, the advertising music business became increasingly regularized and professionalized as it became more of a part of the massive and growing apparatus for creating and promoting consumption in the postwar era. Such was the voracity of capitalism in this period that composers outside the realm of advertising found themselves increasingly drawn into it. While still sensitive to trends in popular music, the jingle ultimately achieved its own sound, which was dubbed the "Madison Avenue Choir" by industry insiders. Ironically, however, the achievement of this sound spelled the beginning of the end of the jingle, for almost as soon as it appeared, many in the industry began to view the sound, and the jingle itself, as old-fashioned and as too transparent a selling device to be effective in a media world increasingly influenced by baby boomers and young people.

Increasing Professionalization

From Broadway to Broadcast

The commissioning of original music for commercials took off in the mid-1950s in radio advertising. The use of music more generally was sharply on the rise in this period. In 1955, only 5 percent of TV commercials featured original music, but by 1960, about 85 percent employed music. Also by the late 1950s, independent firms made most jingles, instead of their being produced by advertising agencies in-house, as was the norm before; a 1959 survey showed that only about 20 percent of advertising agencies produced their own jingles.[3] Agencies frequently employed outsiders to work on their jingles for arranging and production. As one music producer put it in 1960, "Agencies do not retain these men to make money on jingles, but for a measure of insurance; with the amount of sweat that's been put into the tune, they want to own it lock, stock, and barrel."[4]

Jingle writers became more professional, coaxing into their ranks some major composers from Broadway, who found it increasingly difficult to earn a living after the rise of rock 'n' roll. Richard Adler, of *Pajama Game* fame, told *Time* magazine in 1961 that he had been approached many times to write a jingle, but, "I finally decided 'Why the hell not?' Rock 'n' roll was eating up all the air time anyway, and I was offered a good big piece of money."[5] "At first I was ashamed of writing jingles," he said elsewhere. "Then when I saw it catching on I saw what a jerk I was. Now I'm happy to be identified with them." Adler and other erstwhile Broadway composers, however, tended to prefer the term "advertising musical."[6]

And Broadway composer Frank Loesser started his own firm in 1957, Frank Music Corp. According to his daughter, Susan Loesser:

> During lunch one day with an executive at Young and Rubicam, the subject of commercial jingles came up. "Jesus! What do you pay for that crap?" my father said. "I could provide you with writers who would knock your socks off, and you'd be paying them less than you pay those schlemiels you've got now— they're already working for me." A deal was struck. As Herb Eiseman [the company's general manager] remembers it, "Everyone was happy. We were able to deliver writers to the agency at a price much lower than they had been paying. The writers were happy because they were getting ASCAP [American Society of Composers, Authors, and Publishers, which collects fees] performance income, we were giving them more assignments, and they were attracting attention." FMC produced jingles for Sunkist Lemonade, Halo Shampoo, Newport Filter Cigarettes ("A hint of mint makes the difference"), Sanka Aroma Roast, and various (and very local) beers. My father just enjoyed it to tears.[7]

Loesser's firm included on its roster composers Hoagy Carmichael, Vernon Duke, and Harold Rome, as well as lyricist Ogden Nash.[8]

Time reported in the late 1950s that the J. Walter Thompson Company consulted experts for spotting potential hits so that they could be used in commercials. Many Broadway composers liked recycling their songs as jingles; it could give their songs a boost, and they could make money. Cole Porter leased his "It's De-Lovely" to De Soto, for example.[9] And even before Frank Loesser formed his firm, Ford made use of one of the hit songs from his musical *The Most Happy Fella* (1956), "Standin' on the Corner," whose lyrics "watchin' all the girls go by" were changed to "watchin' all the Fords go by," a very success-ful jingle (other lyrics were changed as well; example 5.1).[10] Loesser also gave White Owl Cigars the title song of his musical *Most Happy Fella* for a filmed commercial, which employed the six principals of the Broadway cast. "The result," said *Time*, "sold not only White Owls but tickets to the show."[11] There were, however, some who refused. A 1959 article told the story of Alan J. Lerner selling the rights to a song from *My Fair Lady* to the J. Walter Thomp-son Company for ten thousand dollars. His partner, Fritz Loewe, asked Lerner to purchase the rights back; Ford, the advertiser, refused to take the money but canceled the commercial.[12]

Some insight into how these deals with Broadway composers worked is revealed in a 1958 letter in the J. Walter Thompson Company Archive. A com-pany official met with composer Meredith Willson, at that point at the peak of his fame (*The Music Man* had opened on Broadway the previous year), to discuss the prospect of writing music for a commercial. The company's pitch was reported in a letter to an employee at J. Walter Thompson.

Doing a Commercial

If the maestro involves himself it will be with intensity—in talent and in money. The fact that he's got loads of both does not diminish his interest in either. In this attitude he has my blessings and, I must say, my envy (on both counts!)

His opening gambit to my dissertation on the proposal to create a commer-cial sound/jingle/song/effect was quite evasive: "I want a $5,000 guarantee."

He would then want to spend a day with you (or your representative) to gather all the facts one hoped to get into the effort. If he felt he couldn't do it to his satisfaction, the deal would be cancelled. If he felt he could do it to his satisfaction he would want this $5,000 guarantee paid him in 1960, plus the usual residuals.[13]

Adjusted for inflation, that five thousand dollars is nearly thirty-seven thou-sand dollars as of this writing, giving a sense of the figures the advertising in-dustry was willing to pay for top talent in that era. (The file contains no record of Willson having accepted the deal.)

Another effect of the entry of Broadway composers into the realm of jin-gle composers was that by the early 1960s, the effort to raise the quality of jingles—and, not inconsequentially, the standing of composers—continued. According to one, "A small minority still feels that there is no difference between a person who sells ten-penny nails in a hardware store and a composer-arranger. But this minority is dwindling. The trend is toward a constantly improving use of music on the part of ad agencies."[14]

Fashioning Jingles

The success of some jingles meant that there were soon endless discussions on how to write them, how to choose music, and more; the trade press started to write about them as more than ephemeral phenomena or gimmicks, and advertising textbooks began to consider them, sometimes at length.

One such textbook held that, because of the paramount importance of words in jingles, which convey the advertiser's message, "fast rhythms," favored by youth, don't usually work. The authors told of the difficulty jingle singers had with the name of Schlitz beer ("that orally elusive brand name") until the director had the singers make the word two syllables—"Shuh-litz." "Clarity of diction," the authors concluded, "is the reason many advertisers prefer to hear one singer rather than several in their jingles."[15] Diction, and the sales message, were of great concern in the industry, and advertising textbooks from the era contain many a warning about singers. "When featuring a jingle, five or six voices are not always necessary. In some cases, groups of singers are carried away by their own harmony and fail to register clearly and audibly the important selling points of the project."[16] A 1956 memo at the J. Walter Thompson Company made several suggestions: that someone "translate" the words while they were being sung, a "singing-talking duet." Another suggestion was to have the singer and speaker enunciating the same words simultaneously, or, the executive continued, "have the words spoken very rapidly just before they are sung."[17] Singers with impeccable diction could be handsomely rewarded. One author wrote that a vocal quartet, the J's with Jamie, possessed diction "that makes poets out of admen," one of whom said, "Their words seem to be coming from a foot outside of their mouths in a kind of bas-relief."[18]

Composers could emphasize words also. Joey Levine, composer of many well-known commercials from the 1970s and after, told me of studying some recordings of jingles by Steve Karmen, known as "the King of the Jingle" in that era.

So he gave me his reels and I kind of really went home and studied it, and what I picked up most from him was the way he'd accentuate the main lines. That he would punctuate them. He would do pauses, and he would do tympani hits . . . so that the words that came out, the phrases, really stood out, and I learned a lesson from that. Just listening, I said, "Ah." So when I wrote "You Asked for It, You Got It," I wrote it, because it was kind of—[*sings*] "You-oo asked for it, you got it, Toyota." You know, it was like the accentuation of the word *you*.[19]

While words dominated, they were not the only concern. Robert Swanson, who studied with the well-known composition teacher Joseph Schillinger, had a formula for the successful jingle:

(1) Figure out the best way to get the message across in the shortest possible way. (2) Put the words together in a simple rhyming pattern. (3) The melody must be simple and memorable, never intricate. (4) If these basics have been accomplished, you can now go ahead and elaborate all you wish in the production of the commercial.

Said Swanson, "The desired effect is to catch the listener on a musical fish hook, dangle him in mid-air, and seduce him into buying the client's product or services."[20] But there was no consensus in this era about jingle composition.[21]

The types of commercials solidified in this period. According to a jingle composer and guidebook author, there was "the thematic," which is what he called more recent radio concepts in which the song has nothing to do with the product; his examples included the instrumental pieces "Music to Watch Girls By" (for Diet Pepsi in 1966 and 1967, which sold over a million copies and was covered many times;[22] example 5.2) and "No Matter What Shape Your Stomach's In" (for Alka Seltzer in 1965; example 6.21).[23] And there was "the hit song," a type written in the style of, or intended to be, a hit song but in which the words mention the product or service, such as "I'd Like to Teach the World to Sing" (for Coca-Cola in 1971; example 6.19).[24]

Specialty Singers

Just as jingle houses sprang up, so did specialists in jingle performance, especially singers. Some of them parlayed jingle experience into mainstream success as popular singers, with Barry Manilow perhaps the most famous

Figure 5.1 Linda November. (Courtesy of Linda November.)

example (he also wrote some memorable jingles); there were plenty of other now-famous musicians who began in jingles but tend not to remind listeners of that fact, unlike Manilow. Jingle composers and producers I spoke to dropped many a name, from Herbie Hancock to Carly Simon. In the 1960s, rock bands could be introduced to the public as jingle musicians first, according to Brian Albano, a musician I interviewed; the idea was to get them accustomed to studio work before going into the studio to make a recording as a band.[25]

Jingle singers had to be able to appear and perform with little or no rehearsal—singers were expected to show up and sing. Reading music was a necessity according to some, like Linda November, dubbed "the Queen of the Jingle" by *New York* magazine in 1979.[26] For singers and instrumentalists, it was an attractive way of making a living and escaping the grueling life of constant touring normal for musicians appearing in public.

Jingle singers are usually the best remunerated of all advertising musicians, for they are protected by powerful unions, the Screen Actors Guild (SAG) and the American Federation of Television and Radio Artists (AFTRA).

Jingle singers could make quite a bit of money in this era; the hottest singers could make $10,000, even $25,000 per disc in the 1960s. The J's with Jamie, for example, earned about $250,000 per year (they also had a brief burst of fame and recorded an LP for Columbia in 1963, which employed their signature sound).[27] Linda November told me that forty minutes of work on a jingle in the 1960s that aired on network radio netted her $18,000 in her first paycheck; this was the first of over twenty-two thousand commercials she recorded as one of the most sought-after jingle singers in the business.[28] Jingle singers could make so much money that one, Janie Fricke, told me that when Columbia Records approached her with a contract, she seriously considered turning it down since she was doing so well as a jingle singer, though she eventually left to pursue a career in country music.[29]

November, who was the singer for the famous "Meow, Meow, Meow, Meow" commercial from 1976 (example 5.3), told me in an interview what a recording session was like in this period for top jingle singers.

> I'll never forget that when we did it . . . Tommy McFaul, who wrote it for Lucas, McFaul, said, "We are not showing you the film yet." I said, "Oh, c'mon! I wanna!" . . . and he said, "No, no, no, no." So . . . the group sang the underscore. . . . it's very hip, it's a great little piece. And then they just gave it to me [*sings "meow, meow, meow"*] and I did it, I laid it down in a second, and I said, "Yeah I take it, Tom, you want it breathy?" . . . and he said, "No, yeah, just do your Linda November, that's what I want, I want that wonderful quality that you have up there."
>
> So then before they let me see it, they said, "We're not happy with the last shot where the cat licks her chops and she says 'Meow.' So we would like you to look at it. . . . " So I had to look at the footage, and they finally found a piece of footage that they liked, this last piece, which is wonderful, when she licks her chops, she went "Meow." And on the third take . . . I got it and they went, "Perfect! Come in," they handed me a glass of champagne, I said, "I have six more jobs"; he says, "I don't care; we want you to have a glass of champagne. . . . "
>
> They synced the thing up . . . and played it and all of—we just burst into tears, it was the most darling, plaintive [song].[30]

Making Songs: The Advertising Industry Meets the Music Industry

In the postwar era, the music and advertising industries were beginning to move closer together, a trend that continues to the present. Mitch Miller, who was the head of A&R (artists and repertoire) at Columbia Records beginning in 1950, addressed the American Association of Advertising Agencies in 1956 on the subject of jingles. He raised the importance of sounding like the popular music of the day, for "music spots are competing with hit records for the listeners' ear—therefore—an appealing spot must have all the appeal of a good pop record." Good jingles, then, must possess the same characteristics as a pop song: mainly, they can never be uninteresting but must also be "simple—and yet have enough color, performance and humor not to be dull."[31] Miller also said commercials with music must have a personality, which is often sacrificed in the making of a music commercial since composers and musicians have to please so many masters, from advertising agency personnel to their clients.[32]

A 1961 story on Miller said that he made his first foray into advertising music in 1955 when he was contacted by an executive at the J. Walter Thompson Company, which had been using cover versions of popular songs to sell Ford automobiles with little success. Miller realized that music could have been employed as a means to break up the commercial message.[33] Miller also introduced the concept of having known singers such as Frankie Laine and Rosemary Clooney sing commercial parodies of existing popular songs, since it would aid their careers in a variety of ways: greater exposure and promotion of their recordings.[34] Miller was also credited with lowering the price of licensing a song from a publisher, since the exposure publishers received was so profitable.

Rosemary Clooney and "This Ole House" for Ford

The story of a song popularized by Clooney provides a good example of how ingenious advertising agencies, clients, and musicians such as Miller could be in using popular music to sell products in this era. Clooney, a big star in the 1950s, had recorded a version for Ford of "Come on 'a My House," which had generated an enthusiastic response. So in 1954, Miller's assistance was sought in choosing another song that could be used in a similar fashion. "This Ole House" by Stuart Hamblen was selected. Two J. Walter Thompson Company employees wrote a Ford version of the lyrics, which were recorded by Clooney. The noncommercial version was released, and charted at number 1, and then a version with the Ford lyrics with the same backup as the original.

Sponsor magazine perused the J. Walter Thompson Company files to chronicle the rise of this commercial, revealing its genesis.[35] It is clear that the idea to use Clooney appeared early in the song's development. Robert V. Ballin, head of Ford radio-TV programming at J. Walter Thompson, wrote to the Thompson Company on 18 May 1954 and responded enthusiastically to the question of employing Clooney, indicating more generally that "we have felt that the technique of tying in with a popular number, either current or revival, gives us plus values that are unbeatable, even if not precisely measurable."[36] Then a snag emerged: stars were becoming chary of associating themselves too closely with particular products for fear of being denied guest appearances on programs sponsored by competing advertisers. But, according to Joe Stone, the Ford Group copy head, "Mitch Miller of Columbia Records is going to talk with Ed Sullivan. As head of the popular record division of that outfit, he is naturally interested in seeing us make a deal with his top recording star. He is certain that such an arrangement means a big lift for the song parodied [i.e., the Ford commercial version of "This Ole House"].[37]

For various reasons, the potential problem was avoided, and a song selected. A letter from 7 August 1954 informed the client that Stone and Miller had "turned up a tune, 'This Ole House,' that is back-to-back with 'Hey There' which is now going well." But the latter tune wasn't deemed suitable to be turned into a commercial; it was "too slow for a commercial which has to make as many points as Ford copy must." They thought "This Ole House" was extremely promising, however:

> Musically, it appears perfect for commercial exploitation; it is fast, lively and novelty in character. And the Rosemary Clooney rendition of the number is tops. Joe and Mitch admit that there is no way to guarantee these things, but they feel rather strongly that this song has hit possibilities, and that these will be achieved by the time our version hits the air.[38]

Another letter with the same date announced that the deal was set: Clooney would record several versions. The price was high (and not disclosed) but was thought to be worth it. The composer was located, the broadcast deal struck. The commercial was recorded at the end of September 1954; Ford dealers wanted to broadcast it as early as 26 October. A rough demo was sent to the client at the end of August, in several versions for him to choose from. Six were offered, and, unsurprisingly, Clooney's "This Ole House" was the favorite (it's not clear what the others were). The client thought, "It is going to do a big job," and agreed with Miller's recommendation to use "exactly the same quartet and orchestra. Part of the success in the performance of the original is doubt-less due to the unique combination of talent and arrangement, and we might do well to duplicate it."[39] The song was evidently recorded in different styles, common in this era as a means of using the same melody to appeal to different groups, for a letter reporting on the recording session said, "One of the tunes was changed from a cowboy beat to a mombo [sic]," at Miller's suggestion, an attempt to cash in on the popularity of "Latin" music in this period.[40] Some delays in Clooney's recording contribution ensued, but the song was recorded. Several sighs of relief were written, concluding with a letter from W. Eldon "Hap" Hazard, J. Walter Thompson radio-TV representative on Ford, Detroit, that included a quotation from a Kansas Ford district committee that said, "In our opinion the most exciting part of the campaign is Rosemary Clooney singing 'This Ole House.' We consider it the best musical commercial we have ever had and the finest to appear to date in the automobile field."[41]

This spot was the beginning of a string of successful commercials produced for Ford and other clients by the J. Walter Thompson Company, described by the vice president and copy group head thus: "We just spot potential hits and hitch-hike our way to the top."[42] (This person was in charge of this initia-tive because J. Walter Thompson staff wrote new lyrics for the existing songs, promoting Fords.)

Kodak: "Turn Around"

In the 1960s, it was fairly normal for an advertising agency to find a song that it felt was right to promote a particular product, and then attempt to get a known singer to sing it. In the early 1960s, the J. Walter Thompson Company campaign for the Eastman Kodak Company called "Turn Around" featured an existing song (by Malvina Reynolds, Allen Greene, and Harry Belafonte) with that title. An agency copywriter heard the song "Turn Around" on a Be-lafonte record and noticed the lyrics, which refer to a little girl growing up: "Turn around and you're two / Turn around and you're four." The copywriter thought that the lyrics would go well with a Kodak commercial promoting photography. It proved to be easy to find photographs to go in the commer-cial, since some had been provided by a California doctor, documenting his daughter's passage from childhood to motherhood, and had been obtained by the agency for a print advertisement that had never been run.

J. Walter Thompson and Kodak liked the resulting commercial, but Belafonte, who owned the rights to the song, had to be convinced that such a usage of his music was acceptable; the agency was able to convince his company that the song would be used tastefully, so a version of the song for the commercial was recorded by guitarist Tony Mattola and singer Paul Arnold (example 5.4).[43]

This campaign was hugely successful, and generated significant fan mail to Kodak; some of the received letters were retained by the Thompson Company, which later claimed, "In one year, Kodak received more letters of praise . . . than *all* the letters of complaint about *all* commercials received that year by the FCC."[44] "Thank you so much for the best television commercial I have seen in a long time," wrote one viewer, going on to praise the commercial's taste, and inquiring when it would be aired again. Another described the music as "enchanting," saying that the commercial was "a joy to watch and listen to." Yet another letter writer said that the commercial was "the finest I have ever seen."[45] Jack O'Brian of the *New York Journal-American* described the commercial as "warm, simple, lovely and unexpectedly fine hearthside huckstering."[46] Kodak said in *Kodak Dealer News* that the commercial "caused a boom in records and sheet music for the background theme. One tele-watcher pleaded, 'Please let us know if it's been recorded . . . being in the record and sheet music business, we get lots of inquiries about it.'"[47]

The Madison Avenue Choir

Despite the success of some commercials, however, most advertising music in this era was becoming increasingly homogenous and similar in sound. A style of music emerged in the postwar era that sounded like nothing else, which was commonly referred to as a jingle that employed the "Madison Avenue Choir." These jingles drew on popular music styles and sounds, but were nonetheless unique: they were always upbeat, contained crisply enunciated vocals that were usually sung by a group, or a group interacting with a soloist. A composer of jingles said in 1976, "Up to now, original music had its share in tv commercials, but mainly they were influenced by what the record industry was doing. Now, because of the quality of music available to the agencies, the music is developing a style and dignity of its own."[48] Jingles offer positive affect as well as lyrical information about products, and use particular musical signs to convey this positive affect.

The rise of this sound was due in part to economic factors. Steve Karmen, a major figure in advertising music in the 1970s and 1980s, wrote that evolution of multitrack tape recorders from four to more in the mid-1970s meant that what was once recorded live could be assembled piecemeal. New multitrack tape recorders also meant that vocals could be doubled (that is, the same singer could record one part and then record another), and doubling, said Karmen, "became the rage,"[49] in part because of the sound, but also because, as we have seen, singers' contracts were more lucrative than for any other musician in the studio, including the composer—it was cheaper to hire one or a few singers to sing multiple parts.[50]

Some in the industry believe that multitracking led to the increased homogeneity of the jingle sound. Norm Richards, composer and owner of a jingle house in New York, wrote in 1979 that jingles had become so standardized that

> a composite profile of your next jingle can be drawn up now, with a reasonable probability of being accurate. Chances are good that it will utilize males and females singing the client's name in full harmony before the announcer's message and at the end. . . . The 30-second spot will be bright, up-tempo, having a pop, disco, rock, country and western or middle-of-the-road style and have a rhythm section with prominent guitar(s), and maybe some trumpets.[51]

Another article in a trade magazine complained about the advent of the "Boring Middle-of-the-Road Jingle."

> No one claims to be its mother or father, but many are its silent and devious practitioners. They use very few chords and many singers and musicians; they use the same ways of resolving songs over and over again, and they leave bored Woman and Man to the point that only nine out of the top twenty-five commercials of 1983 . . . are musical.[52]

A vice president and art supervisor for Doyle Dane Bernbach said in 1984, "What I hear from many music companies are similar sounds. Music has become middle of the road and anonymous. If someone does something successful it's copied. People tend to go with something that's already established." This observer also noted that soft drinks, automobiles, and airlines alike were using similar sounds, all of which employ an "anthem-like feel which is soulless and almost bubble-gum." He thought that the problem was in the creative process, which was not hospitable to new sounds, and the fact, commented on by many observers in the industry over many decades, that musicians weren't brought into the process of devising a commercial until late in the game.[53] Another author wrote that in the late 1970s, "the solo voice is de-emphasized in favor of the large, anonymous choral effect. The attempt is no longer to link the product to a specific singer, but to bathe the listener in a sea of friendly voices."[54]

This, then, for better or worse, was the sound of the Madison Avenue Choir jingle: 1950s and 1960s big-band-style music with a chorus, or sometimes a vocalist backed by a chorus. For this sound, advertising composers employed a vocal ensemble to make a chorus of approbation for the advertised product in a kind of secularized gospel music style (and it is perhaps no accident that advertising executives frequently referred to commercial songs as "anthems" in the 1970s and 1980s).[55] A Burger King jingle by Jake Holmes from 1981, for example, employs a soloist and chorus format and ends with a plagal cadence, the same as in a hymn on the word *amen* (example 5.5). The "informational" content of this commercial is left to a male soloist, as though he were the religious leader imparting timeless truths, while the chorus chimes in with more emotional, even ecstatic, music. The Madison Avenue Choir sound was a pinnacle of advertising music, but quickly this zenith became its nadir: the more advertisements sounded like advertisements, the more objectionable many found them to be as the baby boomers came to power in the industry in the 1980s and 1990s, as I will discuss in later chapters.

Detractors, Complaints, Decline

This industrially produced, homogenous sound contributed to the decline of the jingle in the 1990s, though some in and out of the industry had assailed jingles for decades.[56] As the advertising music business became increasingly industrialized and rationalized in the Weberian sense, and populated more and more by organization men throughout the 1950s and into the 1960s, the means of assessing its effectiveness also became increasingly rationalized and scientistic; jingles weren't just homogenous in sound, but were brought into the rationalized and bureaucratized world of midcentury American capitalism. The modes of polling described in chapter 2, however, became increasingly sophisticated and expensive. One study, published in 1950, is fairly straightforward, concluding that jingles effected the highest level of memorability after two months compared to other kinds of commercials.[57]

Later polls and studies were more sophisticated. A 1958 memo in the J. Walter Thompson Company Archive noted that 88 commercials out of a survey of 350 "contained some jingle material." The research corporation it hired determined that commercials with jingles were slightly less effective than those without jingles. The research also determined, however, that *"effectiveness varied with the amount of time devoted to jingle,"* and concluded that *"(a) Just a little jingle is usually not enough to have much impact, and is apt simply to distract; (b) A commercial that is mostly jingle may be entertaining, but not leave much time for serious sell or meaningful demonstration."*[58] Only a few years later, however, Schwerin Research Corporation concluded, "Jingle melodies and background music are certainly desirable commercial elements," for they make television "less strident, more palatable." Commercials with music are more liked than those without, but not necessarily more effective, they claimed.[59] Subsequent studies, of which there are many, varied as these do, and did little to support jingle's advocates or vanquish its opponents.[60]

Despite whatever data the surveys produced as well as other fears, agencies continued to push jingles, to a point, using the kind of unscientized, impressionistic mode of argumentation common among creative personnel in the industry when combating facts and figures beloved of those on the business side. Robert T. Colwell of the Thompson Company said in a speech in 1965:

> There is a warm welcome for jingles that are bright and ingenious musically and lyrically.
>
> Moreover, jingles are durable. A good song will not wear out its welcome as fast as the little drama whose ending surprises us the first time. People who tire of repetition in other types of advertising feel just the other way about their favorite words and music in advertising. They like to sing them, not just once but over and over. Familiarity breeds popularity.[61]

Or so it was hoped. This is one of the most frequently articulated justifications of jingles, still used today.[62]

But by the 1980s, jingles began to be seen by many as too obvious a selling device, too hard-sell. Those employing the Madison Avenue Choir sound, which had grown out of 1950s mainstream popular music, no longer sounded like any other music, exposing their function. A 1990 report by an advertising music composer to the J. Walter Thompson Company office in Chicago addressed the question of the death of the jingle, saying that jingles weren't dying, "but they've been beat up pretty badly" for, among other things, being "phony and insincere," unable to sound like anything other than something that was industrially produced. The recommendations included: jingles should sound like good records, not "jingles," and that lyrics should be sincere, real, and warm.[63] The quality of sincerity was coming to be paramount. Chris Wall, an executive creative director at Ogilvy and Mather Worldwide, reflecting on the waning popularity of the jingle, said in 1999 that the jingle represented "everything that's wrong, dishonest and insincere" about advertising."[64] The perceptions of "dishonesty" and insincerity were a result of the jingle's role having become increasingly obvious. The jingle by the 1990s had become tainted by the selling process.

The public's and advertising industry's shifting views on the jingle were actually tackled in a few television commercials from the 2000s, ads aimed at the jingle and its formulaic, hard-sell associations. A good example is Nabisco's Crispy Thins ad from 2002, in which the music generally signifies folk authenticity in music, for the musician is a lone woman with an acoustic guitar who sings in an intonation-challenged, warbly voice to an advertising agency boss and two underlings. But even this authenticity is tarnished, its effectiveness diminished. The boss rejects the jingle and instead offers a kind of straightforward description of the product, a mode of advertising, that, incidentally, ad agencies had eschewed for decades in favor of ads that depicted goods as part of a desirable lifestyle. The language of sales has been presented as refreshingly direct through its juxtaposition with the suspect jingle, now so discredited that all the folk music signifiers of authenticity that can be crammed into a few seconds of music are rejected. Interestingly, though, the jingle concludes the ad, still poking fun at its hard-sell past (example 5.6). In this ad, the jingle music is a sign of the hackneyed hard sell. What this ad accomplishes is a kind of cleansing of the language of sales: the jingle is so obviously a jingle, so obviously a sales mechanism, that it is constructed as false. The boss's plain speaking is thus rehabilitated after the opening jingle—it's straight talk, removed from the realm of selling.

Around the same time as this commercial, IBM aired a few commercials that also lampooned the jingle for being old-fashioned and insincere. "Hip

Hop Guys" shows two young African Americans in a room full of suits, being questioned about using their music to help this fictitious computer company improve relations with its customers. Music is made to be useless in this endeavor—the whole point, the ad seems to say, is that products and services should be of high quality. And yet, this commercial ends with a jingle, though obviously not one that would have been written by the hip-hop musicians, and is more in the now-outmoded Madison Avenue Choir style, as if to emphasize the complicity of music with sales (example 5.7). This ad is similar to the Crispy Thins commercial in that music is tried out and rejected (in this case not even heard), in favor of plain speech. This IBM ad is also poking fun at a spate of commercials in the last decade or so that use hip, underground music (though rarely hip-hop) for selling, as advertisers try to attract youth audiences for their products (see chapter 8). A different IBM commercial, from the same year and entitled "The Rockers," depicts aging rock musicians who are expected to perform the same service (example 5.8). The taint of the jingle was so strong in these ads that IBM took them off the air. A representative from IBM told me that the company had tested the commercial and found that "frankly, it didn't do too well. People thought the jingle was kind of silly and not really appropriate for IBM, which is one of the reasons why we haven't done any jingles for a long time."[65]

In the mid-2000s, two commercials for Snickers candy bars also parodied the jingle. "Happy Peanut Song" makes fun of the innocence of jingles past with sweet music and naïve lyrics (example 5.9). The object of these commercials' parodies is complex—the old-fashioned hard sell wrapped in a sweet package, the faux sincerity thought to be characteristic of jingles, the idea that music could make a weak product seem better. But they also parody the sound of capitalism itself, a sound that was designed for selling and nothing else, and was thought to have outlived its usefulness.

In addition to perceptions of its insincerity, the jingle also fell out of fashion in part because of changing demographics in the advertising industry, which became increasingly youth-oriented and therefore attentive to youth music and, later, music associated with the baby boom (chapters 6 and 7). The jingle's demise was precipitated by still other factors, such as the rise of the fifteen-second commercial in the 1980s, which made it more difficult to devise an ad with a memorable jingle, so music went more into the background. Additionally, what people in the industry are calling the "convergence of content and commerce"—that is, the growing symbiotic relationship between the production of popular culture and advertising (chapter 8)—has edged out the jingle as real songs become increasingly common in advertising.

Also, a massive shift from acoustic to digital sound production in the 1980s and early 1990s meant that many musicians who were slow to adapt found themselves unemployed. Younger musicians from the world of rock who did know how to use these technologies began competing for jingle jobs and were not union members, which meant they could charge less; they were also not in the jingle business and had no allegiance to the way things had been done.[66] Many people I interviewed who had been in the business during this shift described it as one of the biggest changes they witnessed in the industry; one such veteran said that these older studio musicians hated the new technologies.[67] Composer Steve Karmen wrote of how MIDI (Musical Instrument Digital Interface, introduced in the early 1980s, which standardized the way that computers and electronic musical technologies communicated with each other) put advertising musicians out of work, since a single machine could produce many sounds. Only the jingle singer has survived, Karmen said;[68] but not very many years later, jingle singers were almost gone as well. As Karmen said, one the signs that convinced him it was time to leave the jingle business was when a client told him that his twelve-year-old son used the same synthesizer.[69] When the person hailed as "the King of the Jingle" for the better part of two decades decided to leave the business, as Karmen did in the early 1990s, it is clear that an era had ended.[70]

To conclude this chapter, let me return to the question of insincerity. The decline of the jingle spoke to desires for the authentic, the sincere, in this era. Jingles, perhaps the quintessential sounds of capitalism, couldn't compete with rock and pop songs, which were being increasingly employed in commercials (as I will discuss in the following chapter) and which were thought to be ideologically purer and more authentic. Steve Karmen wrote that a music director with many years of experience told him,

> "Today, advertisers don't want a jingle, they want a song. Jingles, meaning an original happy melody written about a product or service that extols the benefits, qualities, and excitement that come from owning or using that product, are no longer considered *honest*. The world has changed. We have to be more honest in our advertising. More real. We use music that is real because the best ads are real. Pop songs are real. They reach the young market. Jingles do not."[71]

With this, we are in the realm of what some have called the postmodern, a world awash in goods—and pretty advertisements for them—to the extent that what is "real" or "original" or "authentic" has become increasingly difficult to discern. Theorists of postmodernity argue that the world by the 1980s or perhaps sooner had become a mass of signifiers ungrounded in history or any meaning other than those on the surface, and thus concepts such as authenticity or the "real" become mobilized in attempts to rescue fragments of an objective reality no longer easily discernible. As Jean Baudrillard writes, "When the real is no longer what it used to be . . . there is a proliferation of myths of origin and designs of reality; of second-hand truth, objectivity and authenticity."[72]

Pop songs, of course, are no more—or less—"real" than jingles: they were made and performed by some of the same people, and there was a considerable overlap in styles by this period. It's possible to make the same case for popular songs and jingles that Baudrillard famously made about Disneyland: the theme park is taken as a fantasy world because of its obvious fabrication as opposed to the real world surrounding it, but it is that very artifice that characterizes the "real" world today.[73] Jingles, particularly those that employed the Madison Avenue Choir sound, had come to be seen as artificial and as mass produced as the commodities they purveyed in this era, but, of course, they serve to point out the way things really are in a world in which commodities, advertising, and consumption play even greater roles in people's lives than they ever had before.

It went from suits and short hair to jeans and long hair. It was just like us, only they were older. But they were just like us—they were trying to be hip.

—Musician Ron Dante on the transformation of the advertising industry in the 1960s, interview by author, 2009

Jingles are not meant to be hip, but to sell products.

—Jingle composer Ron Lockhart, 1979[1]

6

The Discovery of Youth in the 1960s

Introduction

Even though it seems that everything moves at a breathless pace in the advertising industry, major trends in fact take quite some time to gather steam. The industry is too huge, and too beholden to clients' wishes, to make drastic changes happen quickly. Thus, even with the "discovery" of the youth market in the 1950s by the recording and other industries, it wasn't until well into the 1960s that this started to influence the production of commercials, which began to emphasize the hip and the cool, an ideology that has come to suffuse the industry.

With this discovery of the youth market and its culture in the 1960s, the advertising industry had found one of its most potent strategies for selling commodities, appealing to the youth market, first as youth in the 1960s, then as aging baby boomers. The ideology of the importance of youth and its tastes influenced not only the production of advertisements but advertising culture itself, as the epigraph by Ron Dante above shows. In other words, the field of cultural production of advertising is powerfully shaped by ideas associated with youth and the counterculture, the hip and the cool.

As this chapter will show, by the late 1960s, capitalism, at least in the realm of advertising and marketing, had already begun to attempt to address youth culture on its own terms. Sometimes the music that was used bore little resemblance to rock music as we understand it today, but it didn't take long for rock and popular musicians to make commercials and hawk products aimed at youth and those who aspired to stay young, such as baby boomers, sometimes with spectacular success. Rather than capitalism being simply reactive or appropriative, it was, in this particular historical moment, proactive, attempting to make the consumption of goods more palatable by adapting youth music and other hip and cool aspects of youth culture in order to sell goods. What one might call "gray-flannel" capitalism had given way to blue-jeans capitalism, as Dante's observation implies. This happened so quickly, and so decisively, that many people in advertising agencies were unprepared for the shift, as I will show. But the change did occur, and has become a deep and seemingly irrevocable part of the world of advertising and American culture more generally.

Adapting Songs

The growing recognition of the youth market and the important role that music played in this group made it difficult for some composers of advertising music to resist attempting to make commercial music sound less like commercial music. One of the ways that audiences for commercials—especially youth audiences—were increasingly cultivated was by eschewing the jingle and attempting to offer a "real" song. And some commercials slowly began to track more closely popular songs of the day. In the era when workers in the advertising industry were increasingly worrying about "clutter" on the airwaves, some thought that making jingles compete with popular songs might help the cause of advertisers.

In 1960, the Kingston Trio, at the height of its popularity, struck a deal with 7UP to sell a recording called *Cool Cargo*, containing four of its songs, including its hit "Tom Dooley," for fifty cents and a coupon from 7UP dealers; the trio's agreement also included appearing in commercials for the drink.[2] A commercial from 1960—probably the first in this campaign—opens with a presentation about why the trio is making commercials. It is an astonishing four-minute production that rationalizes its pitching for 7UP, presents one of its songs with 7UP–ized lyrics, and then moves into another of its numbers, also with lyrics selling 7UP (example 6.1).

This strategy was slow to catch on, however, for advertisers and marketers had little idea of, or perhaps little sympathy for, the sounds associated with youth. In the summer of 1962, for example, Ford aired a summer replacement program called *The Lively Ones*, described by *Advertising Age* as "a mood-music color stanza," hosted by singer Vic Damone with stars such as Peggy Lee, Dave Brubeck, Gene Krupa, and Stan Kenton, none of whom would be appealing to most youth of the era, the majority of whom had long been fans of rock 'n' roll. This program was evidently a television version of Ford's then-current campaign "about those go-go-go young people, who have fun living and laughing it up—and getting there, of course, in a Ford," wrote *Advertising Age*.[3]

But brands continued to attempt to target youth. Perhaps nowhere was the strategy of using popular music sounds or songs to appeal to youth clearer than in the long-standing battle between Coca-Cola and Pepsi-Cola for supremacy in the soft drink market in the 1960s and after. The battle for youth in the so-called cola wars was initiated by BBDO's chairman, Tom Dillon, who wrote a "white paper" in 1960 about Pepsi advertising, admitting that Pepsi was a parity product (i.e., not really different from any other cola), and that it would make more sense for advertising to place a greater focus on the consumer—whose age, he thought, was about twenty-three—than on the product in commercials.[4] Since, as a Pepsi executive noted, "Teenagers consume soft drinks far in excess of their weight in the population,"[5] a new campaign called "Pepsi. For Those Who Think Young" was devised in 1960.[6] A vice president at BBDO said that this campaign was meant to differentiate Pepsi from Coca-Cola, "a drink for people who are out of step, out of touch, out of date."[7] Alan Pottasch, senior VP–creative services at Pepsi, said, "The concept began, with 'for those who think young.' It became a question of labeling that group we were after." Pottasch claimed that the Pepsi generation was "everyone with a young view of things. . . . The Pepsi generation is a special breed of people—not an age group—that believes in living life to its fullest."[8] "Today, all America thinks

young," said Philip Hinerfeld, Pepsi's vice president for advertising, in justifying the campaign. "Less than three weeks ago," he said, "America inaugurated
the youngest elected President its history. The average age of his cabinet is also
the youngest ever. Why, at Pepsi-Cola Co., the average of our top management
team is under 46 years of age."[9]

For this campaign, a 1928 song called "Makin' Whoopee!" was resurrected,
with new lyrics sung by Joanie Sommers, a young singer.[10] The arrangement
was scarcely different from the previous Pepsi song, "Be Sociable"—light,
jazzy, unchallenging—which had begun airing in the spring of 1958.[11] Special
lyrics were written to appeal to local markets, such as New Orleans ("From
Mardi Gras to Sugar Bowl / Cook southern-style to cook Creole") and Long
Island ("From Hampton Shores to Oyster Bay / The tide has turned the Pepsi
way"; example 6.2).[12] Tom Dillon said that if his company missed its target
audience of young people (who in fact probably wouldn't have recognized a
popular song from their grandparents' generation), other people might at least
recognize the music; and it would appeal to the all-important bottlers (who
must always be brought on board any advertising campaign, in part to ap-
prove it and in part because they pay a portion of the media-placement bills;
Dillon characterized Pepsi-Cola as "a marketing company on behalf of their
bottlers").[13]

Philip Hinerfeld, Pepsi's vice president in charge of advertising, said that
this commercial tested well: "Research in several markets indicates it has a
high degree of memorability and listeners associate it with 'young, successful people.'"[14] Teenagers continued to be part of the market, and Pepsi's radio
advertising was going to include local commercials noting teenagers' accom-
plishments, wishing them happy birthday, and more.[15]

This commercial marked the first salvo in the battle over youth in the long-
running cola wars, as smaller, upstart Pepsi sought to challenge the supremacy
of Coca-Cola. I will not go into great detail about the cola wars and youth
culture, since that has been well documented by Thomas Frank.[16] But I will
devote comparatively more time to the music used. Coca-Cola's response
to Pepsi's "Think Young" campaign was "Things Go Better with Coca-Cola,"
beginning in 1963 with an ad featuring the Limeliters, which *Advertising Age*
said "revolutionized jingles forever" because it wasn't a jingle, it was a song, or,
as the magazine wrote, the "first 'song-form' commercial, geared to the Top
40 radio and rock 'n' roll market" (example 6.3).[17] The magazine quoted Bill
Backer, who was music director at McCann-Erickson at the time: "Our idea

was to write minor hits that used Coke in the same way as the old hit 'Rum & Coca-Cola' did."[18] The campaign's goal with this song, according to the senior vice president at McCann-Erickson, Atlanta, was to "be 'in' without getting 'way out'"—that is, alienating older viewers; he noted that young adults were the main targets of the commercial.[19]

But it wasn't easy, for most major brands were leery of rock music in this period. Backer said that "we had a hard time convincing them that people who listened to rock 'n' roll weren't devil worshippers."[20] Elsewhere, Backer observed, "Rock music was considered dirty and low-class."[21] Both comments speak to advertisers' reluctance to have anything to do with African American musics in this period. Jingle composer and singer Anne Phillips told me that she had visions of one executive on his knees before his bosses pleading with them to let them record popular musicians before Coca-Cola did.[22] This was probably Hilary Lipsitz at BBDO, who recounted in similar terms the difficulties he had with his superiors over the question of hiring Diana Ross and the Supremes for a Pepsi commercial, with his bosses telling him that "that kind of music is never going to make it"; an agreement had been made, but the bosses demurred, and so the Supremes recorded for Coke. This changed attitudes at Pepsi, which immediately permitted Lipsitz to engage the Four Tops.[23]

Advertising Age reported that thirty-five musicians sang songs with the tagline "Things go better with Coca-Cola," from Petula Clark (example 6.4) to Ray Charles (example 6.5) to Aretha Franklin (example 6.6) and the Fifth Dimension (example 6.7), in an attempt to blanket the market.[24] Coca-Cola's vice president and brand manager said about this campaign and the many versions of the jingle that were produced with various well-known singers, "The name singer series has performed in much the manner we hoped it would. It's a smashing hit with the target audience." And, "It injects product action where the action is . . . in this growing under-25 soft drink market."[25]

Pepsi responded with the "Think Young" campaign, launched in late 1963, followed by its new song "Come Alive" in the autumn of 1964. BBDO chairman Tom Dillon said the campaign was trying to be on the "cutting edge of social movements."[26] Philip Hinerfeld said that the whole country was "going beyond thinking young, it was acting young. So we put our name on this time, we called it the Pepsi Generation."[27] John Bergin, who worked on the Pepsi account at BBDO, recounted that the campaign was definitely aimed at youth, and that they at BBDO realized that there were millions of "war babies" who were at the right age to begin drinking cola. But nobody came to the creative department and told its people what to do; they were operating in the dark, he said, with very little research or information. Pepsi, for its part, thought that the average age of its consumer was twenty-eight.[28]

The plan was to make Pepsi a part of a youth-oriented lifestyle; Allen Rosenshine, later the head of BBDO, said that "youth" was "attitudinal rather than chronological" in these commercials.[29] According to Dillon, "We are in fact kind of creating a little daydream in which you are a participant." To do this, BBDO felt it had to move beyond jingles. Dillon said, "The Pepsi thing got music out of what you might call the 'pure jingle stage.' By and large, stuff before that was kind of simple-minded music. It was kind of doggerel, and . . . frequently written from things in the public domain. And it wasn't all that much 'composition' for television; people weren't really doing that."[30]

So, in September 1964, Pepsi launched its "Come Alive! You're in the Pepsi Generation" song, written by Sid Ramin, which was initially planned to be a short-term campaign in the month of August 1964 and on radio only;[31] Thomas Frank says that commercials in this campaign were Pepsi's first that employed television.[32] Louis and Yazijian observe that this "generation" was young, pristine, unaffected by the Vietnam War, and report that the campaign became a "national idiom," and was commented on extensively in the popular press.[33] Frank writes, however, drawing on an *Advertising Age* article, that the campaign was broad enough to communicate an ideology more than inter-pellate a particular demographic group: it was, in part, about hipness versus Coke's squarer image, individuality versus conformity (example 6.8).[34]

But nothing about Ramin's music seems designed to appeal to youth (before entering the advertising music business, Ramin had worked as an arranger on the *Texaco Star Theatre* starring Milton Berle[35]): the music was conceptualized as a big band song, and there is a full swing orchestra with choirs of horns and saxophones and a jazzy flute. Ramin, who was given the lyric and asked to compose a song to it, thought it should be "rather fanfaric" and "heraldic," so he wrote the opening three-note gesture. (Ramin also used terms like *bold, big, confident,* and *almost commanding* to describe the opening of his composition.) But he knew who the singer was, that she was young, and that the youth audience was directly addressed: "Come Alive! You're in the Pepsi Generation," sung again by Joanie Sommers. Ramin didn't think a rock version was ever recorded, though he thought a popular vocal group sang it.[36] Tom Anderson, musical director at BBDO, said that in "Come Alive," the company had, for the first time, an "emotional campaign." It knew the campaign had to reach people's emotions, and television was the best medium with which to do so.[37] According to John Bergin, Don Kendall, the CEO of Pepsi at the time, was moved to tears the first time he heard the song.[38]

In launching this campaign, Philip Hinerfeld, Pepsi's advertising vice president, stressed the "action nature" of the commercials, which showed young people on the move.[39] This contrasts, as Thomas Frank observes, with the "Things Go Better with Coke" commercials, which represented the "the drink of workplace order," organization cola.[40] Frank draws on Jackson Lears's characterization of American advertising as alternating between depicting images of carnival and those of "personal efficiency," and places the Pepsi commercials in the former category and Coke's in the latter.[41] It seems to me, though, that the commercials represent the long-standing tension in the industry between soft and hard sell, or lifestyle marketing, in its naissance in commercials such as these, versus older "reason why" advertising.

Pepsi's next campaign departed from its normal strategy of identifying its product with a model consumer and instead touted the product itself. This was the "Taste That Beats the Others Cold / Pepsi Pours It On" campaign of 1967–69, whose two taglines were the products of two different advertising agency efforts that were combined.[42] Lipsitz, who was involved with the campaign, said that BBDO didn't want to change to this campaign but its client gave it no choice.[43] Many at Pepsi and BBDO saw this campaign as an aberration, a move away from the youth theme, and it didn't last long.[44] But if one views the commercials, they were clearly aimed at youth audiences; two I have seen were both filmed in recording studios, showing singers (the Turtles in one case, example 6.9; the Four Tops in another ad, example 6.10) and instrumentalists grooving to Anne Phillips's music.

Pepsi's campaign from 1969, "You've Got a Lot to Live, and Pepsi's Got a Lot to Give," was directed both at the current youth market as well as at the earlier one that the company had originally targeted.[45] Allen Rosenshine said that "You've Got a Lot to Live" became a hallmark of Pepsi advertising because of its scope and grandeur, and camera techniques that gave "glimpses of people at their moments of spiritual best," "coupled with the music itself, a truly soaring, uplifting, musical treatment, which then became a pattern for treatments to follow." Earlier jingles (by Ramin), Rosenshine thought, were still slogans set to music. "This was the first . . . major expression of spirit through song," he said; subsequent Pepsi campaigns were just reiterations of this song.[46] Rosenshine claimed that "You've Got a Lot to Live" and later

Figure 6.1 Anne Phillips. (Courtesy of Anne Phillips; photo by Judy Kirtley.)

songs linked Pepsi to "things that go beyond bubbly, good-tasting refreshing flavored liquid." "There is a Pepsi spirit one could catch." "From 'Live/Give' on there was a certain Pepsiness, a Pepsi way, a Pepsi attitude, a Pepsi point of view.... This is what we tried to purvey."[47]

Several people involved with the campaign noted the turmoil of the 1960s and suggested that comparing the first commercials from the early 1960s with those in the "You've Got a Lot to Live" campaign shows how much the country had changed; and music had changed—the Beatles had profoundly influenced the world of popular music, including advertising music—after the first commercials.[48] John Bergin said that because of the unrest of the 1960s, Pepsi wanted to be the voice of something optimistic, telling young people that "we're on your side." Bergin said that the campaign generated incredible letters, even from people who wrote that they were about to attempt suicide but stopped upon hearing the song. The commercial was an adult voice speaking to younger people, he thought. "I think the greatest thing Pepsi-Cola ever did, was make Pepsi the official drink . . . of young America. And the reason why it was a good idea was that there were so damn many of them."[49]

The jingle was a powerful song by Joe Brooks (later famous for writing the

1970s megahit "You Light Up My Life"), described by the company president as "gospel rock"[50] and by Pepsi elsewhere as "jubilation rock."[51] These characterizations are apt enough and sufficient to point out yet again that, while youth and the counterculture were both being referenced and targeted in this commercial, the music was pop-oriented and slow (example 6.11). Frank writes that someone who had been in tune with the hippie movement conceptualized the original idea for this commercial, but Pepsi did not want to risk alienating part of its audience and so opted for a more mainstream approach. Pepsi described this music to its bottlers thus:

> Exciting new groups doing out-of-sight new things to, and for, music. It's youth's bag and Pepsi-Cola is in it. With a song composed for the "now" sound. With lyrics that make this generation's "thing" our "thing" like never before.
>
> There's a whole new way of livin' and Pepsi's supplyin' the background music. . . .
>
> It's a radio package that obliterates the generation gap and communicates like a guru.[52]

In 1970, the music was recorded by a number of different artists, including Johnny Cash (example 6.12), B. B. King (example 6.13), Odetta (example 6.14), Tammy Wynette (example 6.15), and Three Dog Night (example 6.16); a three-LP set was produced for radio use with these and other different versions. Pepsi's message on the back of the box reads like a Hollywood script depicting the beliefs of the counterculture:

> You've got a lot to live.
>
> Pepsi's got a lot to give.
>
> Listen. There's war and hate and hunger in the world. There's fear and suspicion and suffering.
>
> But listen. There's also love. And the greatest generation of young American in history. Theirs is a "whole new way of living." New, and sometimes jarring, but filled with love and hope and joy.
>
> Just listen. You can hear the sounds of change. Of a happier, more peaceful world that's coming, maybe tomorrow, the day after for sure.
>
> Listen. We're not in the philosophy business, we sell soft drinks. We're out to make a profit, but that's not our only goal. If we can help remind America that

things are getting better, *all* of us will profit. These are commercials for Pepsi, but the message belongs to us all.

So listen.

The lyrics of Joe Brooks's song follow:

There's a whole new way of living,
Pepsi helps supply the drive.
It's got a lot to give to whose who like to live,
'cause Pepsi helps 'em come alive.
It's the Pepsi generation,
comin' at ya, goin' strong.
Put yourself behind a Pepsi.
If you're livin', you belong.
You've got a lot to live,
And Pepsi's got a lot to give.
You've got a lot to live,
And Pepsi's got a lot to give.[53]

For 1971, still more versions were recorded, described by Pepsi as pop, country and western, and soul, with artists such as B. J. Thomas (example 6.17) and Roberta Flack (example 6.18) and others. The inside of the double album contains a message about the jingle: "Pepsi's back big. With the big 'now' sound, the big 'now' song that talks straight to the heart of young America." And there are vignettes of the musicians that describe them employing terms from the jingle: the Ides of March "come on strong" with their rock sound; B. B. King influenced a "whole new generation" of musicians.[54] BBDO chairman Rosenshine recounted in 1984 that this song, and all of the Pepsi songs since the beginning of the "Think Young" campaign, were re-creating and updating the same attitude sociologically, with a social relevance, making sure Pepsi "was in tune with what people felt was important to them." Also, Rosenshine said, Pepsi had to be sure to please its bottlers, who didn't want to hear the same song for twenty years, but they understood that the campaign was being updated sociologically, not changing strategy.[55]

But perhaps the most celebrated of all these commercials in the musical cola wars of the 1960s and 1970s was one for Coca-Cola called "Hilltop" from 1971 (example 6.19), which is better known by the song it used by Billy Davis and Roger Cook, entitled "I'd Like to Teach the World to Sing" (Bill Backer provided the line "I'd like to buy the world a Coke and keep it company").[56]

> I'd like to buy the world a home and furnish it with love
> Grow apple trees and honeybees and snow-white turtledoves.
> I'd like to teach the world to sing in perfect harmony
> I'd like to buy the world a Coke and keep it company.
> That's the real thing.

Backer told me, as did so many people I interviewed, that in that era, budgets were pretty much unlimited, so creative workers could do whatever they wanted.[57] In this case, as Backer wrote, they wanted the commercial to "try to be the voice of the times—the end of the sixties."[58] He said to me:

> When I did the Coca-Cola music, I just had a budget. I could write, and they wanted to have me do as many versions as they wanted. . . . After "Teach the World to Sing" came along, and everybody wanted another, I said, "Those things don't happen. . . ." I said, "Let's do an album complex. We'll go to any groups that we think, of singers that we want, and record three, four, or five if we want to. And . . . maybe a single would come out, and maybe it wouldn't. But I guarantee every time we have to write, we'll try for one."[59]

The commercial cost about $225,000 (over $12 million today).[60]
Backer also told me that while it is difficult to know just how much a commercial can affect sales of soft drinks, the commercial did benefit the product.

> The year that "Teach the World" became a song, I remember seeing presentations of what that did to brand identity. . . . It's very difficult to attach the big products to any direct sales, because one like Coca-Cola, hot weather and marketing price add [so much], and even what the competition is doing, has so much to do with it, so you never can really be sure. But you can test brand identity and reason to buy and that kind of stuff. And those kinds of commercials did those products a lot of good.[61]

Coca-Cola received many requests for lyrics, and gave away free copies of the music in manuscript. One teacher wrote to the company saying that she wanted to write a play based on the commercial's theme.[62] A press report on the commercial tells of an advertising executive who, desiring to demonstrate the power of mass communications, asked his audience to stand for the "World's National Anthem," then played the Coca-Cola song.[63] The song was re-re-recorded by the original singers, the New Seekers, in a commercial version, and several cover versions appeared as well, some of which enjoyed brisk sales.[64]

This commercial outdoes Pepsi's in its presentation of squeaky-clean youth, but was more multicultural: it wasn't just representing American youth culture, but the international student movement more generally. Stolid Coke had jumped on the youth bandwagon as well.[65]

Youth and the Counterculture

Clearly, some of these soft drink campaigns, particularly those by Pepsi, were aimed at capturing the youth demographic, in part by representing youth in commercials, but also by drawing on sounds and other signs calculated to resonate with youth. Probably everyone is familiar with this strategy, which Thomas Frank has called the "conquest of cool" in his exceptionally useful book on the subject that chronicles how the advertising industry since the 1960s has attempted to locate the hip and the cool in order to harness these properties for selling.[66] There was also a growing sense that youth were easier to market to; as one textbook put it in 1983, "Desires of young people are more plastic than those of older persons, and it is easier to establish new habits of consumption among these groups."[67]

These colas, as Frank points out, were ahead of their time in their cultivation of the youth market and representations of youth. Most advertisers and their agencies were still grappling with how to deal with the youth question in the early 1960s (which was, culturally, still the 1950s) and well into the middle of that decade. In 1965, for example, J. Walter Thompson president Dan Seymour talked about the ever-increasing rate of change in contemporary culture, with special reference to music.

The most significant component in the new world of sound is music. Music— like visual communications—responds to the needs and pressures of our society. It is a litmus paper by which we can gauge what is happening to all of us. And something *has* happened to us over the last ten years. Our traditional reluctance to accept new ideas in sound, to depend on what has gone before, has been replaced by a spirit of diversity and exploration. Today, one's ears are hearing music that is far more subtle and sophisticated, even when it's shattering the ear drums.[68]

Seymour doesn't say so, but, clearly, he is expounding on a theme that, with all of the fast changes going on in the culture, advertising must keep up.

Two years later, Seymour discoursed on the fragmentation of the radio audience in the late 1960s, maintaining that with the ubiquity of radio, there were about a dozen different audiences. He dramatized this fragmentation with a takeoff on the old *Aldrich Family* radio program (first broadcast in 1939 and on which he had been an announcer). How were advertisers and advertising agencies to reach today's diversified audience? For youth, you need "Hulking Henry Aldrich." (I don't know what audio he played but am certainly curious.) Seymour played musical examples for several different audience groups, including the "post–teeny bopper / pre–jet set" audience and "the affluent, intellectual elite," which doesn't like any form of popular music.[69]

Seymour's and others' sensitivity to the use of rock and pop musics didn't mean that major advertisers were adopting popular music with alacrity—they weren't. Clients were skittish, and advertisers and agencies still believed in a kind of mass campaign, as Seymour's speech indicated, which meant that a variety show format was still used. When he pitched a new television show before the Distributor Sales Meeting of RCA in Indianapolis, he said:

And when we're appealing to such a broad group . . . people of every age and every income level . . . people with many different interests, many different enthusiasms . . . it is essential that we structure a program of the broadest possible appeal, but with attractions for every part of our swinging society.

Who might that be? Perry Como, who was sure to appeal to the different groups that RCA would want to target.

Surrounding Perry are some of the newest, most exciting and most popular acts in this sometimes perplexing entertainment world of 1967. They're the last word in what's "In" right now, this autumn.

Maybe you and I don't "dig" all of them, but they're the pied pipers who excite the record buyers . . . the young marrieds shopping for Color TV . . . the stereo buffs . . . and the college crowd that are the RCA customers of today and tomorrow.

It's just possible some people might think Jefferson Airplane is something akin to the Ford Tri-Motor [an airplane produced in the 1920s and 1930s]. But if you read TIME magazine a month or so ago, or have been watching pop record sales, you know that Jefferson Airplane is the hottest personal appearance group of our current times. It's five fellows and a girl with a particular beat and unique sound that has kept their latest RCA album at the top of the Variety best-seller list for the last twenty-four weeks. . . .

In this constantly changing world of ours, the craze of a year ago oftentimes is just a memory today. The men in our TV department, whose job it is to know what people are reacting to right now as well as what will excite them six months from now, tell us that the emerging new sound is a special kind of South American beat, and its prophets are Sergio Mendes and Brazil '66. So they'll be with Perry, too.[70]

The year 1967 appears to mark the point at which the potential of capitalizing on youth culture had become an unstoppable trend, though music associated with youth had been finding its way into advertising for some time. Fairfax M. Cone, writing of trends in October of 1967, said:

1967 . . . is the year of the discovery of youth.

What is youth?

Youth is riding tandem on a Honda motorcycle or walking the streets with a transistor radio. Youth is playing a guitar, drinking Coke, eating pizza. Youth is long hair and mini-skirts, white lipstick and Clearasil.

Youth is a wonderful time to be alive.

Also, for the caterers of the above, and such incidental items as portable phonographs and records, panty stockings, false eyelashes, dark glasses, sandals, sarapes, and the paperback editions of the great authors—including William Burroughs—youth is very good business.

Cone is rather skeptical of the apparent fad for youth, and points out that demographics show that, while people under twenty-five were nearly half the population in 1965, very few were heads of households and therefore not likely to be purchasing expensive goods.[71]

Cone's caveat did little to dampen interest in cultivating the youth market. Because of the newfound interest in it, advertising agencies had to educate themselves and their clients (and potential clients) about the importance of youth, sometimes, as Frank shows, with unintended comical effect, at least for today's readers. One person, who owned a music production company in this era, told me of how he would be hired to go around to advertising agencies in the 1960s to lecture on popular music, with titles such as "Who Are the Beatles?" A 1967 trade press article noted the importance of knowing the difference between the "Motown Sound" and the "New York Sound," "and wouldn't think of trying to get the 'Nashville Sound' on a commercial by recording the spot in San Francisco. These days both creative and media people at agencies must know what kind of musical spot will trigger a positive response among various demographic groups for the product or service advertised and which tv program and radio stations to slot the spots."[72] In the summer of 1970, *Advertising Age* magazine held a workshop that showcased different rock acts to educate advertisers about different kinds of music. The groups were Greenwood County Farm (described as "big band rock"), Hardy Boys ("bubble gum rock"), Mason Proffit ("western rock"), Rotary Connection ("acid rock"), Shadows of Knight ("hard rock"), and Soul Experience ("Afro-electric rock"). Various experts were on hand to "dissect the youth world."[73]

And some people in advertising in this period even solicited youth input. A story in a trade journal in 1965 of a Raleigh, North Carolina, department store chronicled the work of the advertising manager, Marilyn Holder, who wanted a jingle but didn't want to commission it from a traditional jingle house, believing, "That just wasn't *us*." But through her local television station, she found herself in a jingle house in Chicago, where a local jazz group and a male and female vocalist recorded the jingle. Returning to Raleigh, Holder immediately auditioned the jingle by humming it before the department store's "advisory panel" of twelve high school seniors. "This youth-market thing," Holder said, "you can't underestimate that."[74]

Chico Hamilton, an African American advertising musician, when asked in 1975 how he composed new music that appealed to large audiences, replied:

There are no new sounds . . . at least not until they invent new instruments. The best sounds come from the streets . . . from young people. To compose for them I have to keep contemporary. I do concerts in New York City grade schools— the seven-year-olds love our stuff . . . we don't play down to them. The only way to understand young people, teens especially, is to put yourself in their bag.[75]

The Sounds of Youth?

The "discovery" of youth (Cone's skepticism seems rather quaint at this point) did not mean that rock music found its way into commercials immediately, as we have seen. Infatuation with youth did not necessarily mean that rock music was employed in commercials, though rock sounds sometimes were. What was described as being rock (or rocklike) in this era sounds quite watered-down today. Nonetheless, youth and the counterculture could be successfully addressed through lyrics and images, if not sound, as Coke's and Pepsi's successes demonstrate.

It must remembered just how radical this music was, not only to general audiences of the 1950s and 1960s, but perhaps especially to advertisers and advertising agencies, who constantly had to be wary of offending potential customers. Rock music was treated in an extremely gingerly fashion, and made inroads into the production of advertising music only slowly.

The first mention I can find in the trade press of a rock band used to sell a product is in 1964, the "Wet and Wild" series for 7Up, which I have been unable to view or hear.[76] Another early one was for Yardley Black Label aftershave from 1966 featuring an upbeat song with pastoral and active scenes in which members of the Monkees sang "Some guys have it, some guys never will" (example 6.20).

Far more common than featuring bands in commercials was the slow incorporation of sounds associated with rock music into commercials with music that had been written by professional jingle composers. A commercial for Alka-Seltzer in 1964 (example 6.21) resulted in a pop song, "No Matter What Shape," by the T-Bones (the title for the commercial was "No Matter What Shape Your Stomach's In"). The composer, Sascha Burland, said that the advertising agency wanted nothing but stomachs on film,

> so I figured out a relaxed rock 'n' roll concept, done in a humorous way. As I sense it, the ad really was an episodic movie, but I felt that the musical theme had to unify a group of largely divergent frames. It was the theme that led later into the popular recording. It had a kind of "now-it's-happening" feeling, which I guess is why it took off as a pop hit. We used our own version of the "Mersey Sound," which had done so well for the Beatles. However, the factor that really established it as part of the popular music scene was the counterline. It had a Bob Dylan harmonica sound done by "Toots" Thielmans [the leading jazz harmonica player], backed by Fender bass, guitar and drums.[77]

Other insiders tell a somewhat different story about this commercial: Burland's music was thought to sound too contemporary, too sexy, and the music was toned down.[78] Diluted or not, the instrumental tune was so popular that it was released on a recording by the T-Bones and climbed to number 3 on the national charts for twelve weeks, selling over a million copies.[79] One industry insider wrote that the spot's creator estimated that the commercial "played on over $20 million worth of network air time."[80]

Also in 1964, the "Teaberry Shuffle," based on the "Mexican Shuffle" recorded by Herb Alpert and his Tijuana Brass, for Teaberry chewing gum was successful (example 6.22). Several commercials utilized it, showing people from a variety of age groups kicking up their heels to the music. Later, a 1969 commercial for Crocker Bank with lyrics and music by Paul Williams and Roger Nichols was made famous by the Carpenters as "We've Only Just Begun" (example 6.23).[81]

Composers' discourses about the creeping influence of rock music—with the approval of reluctant clients—is illustrative of how established advertising musicians coped with rock, and the hip and the cool. Steve Karmen, for example, on the "When You Say Budweiser, You've Said It All" jingle of 1970, offered a lesson on the importance of finding "unique audio" for the lyric (example 6.24).

> For the first arrangement of "When You Say Budweiser, You've Said It All," I sought a new musical sound, at least one that was not being used by other beers of the day. . . .
>   To try and stand out in this crowd, I chose to begin my Budweiser song with a rhythm section of a tuba (playing downbeats) and three trumpets (playing offbeats). The tuba is a traditional beer-hall instrument, but it is used infrequently because of its Germanic um-pah-pah sound (not hip for the hip beer drinker). But as the basis for a rock and roll track, the tuba proved to be a unique and perfect bottom for the orchestra. As soon as the commercials began, even before the lyric, the consumer recognized it as the sound of Budweiser.[82]

Writing in 1980, Michael J. Arlen offered a description of a recording by Phoebe Snow for an AT&T radio commercial; the song had already been recorded by Roberta Flack and Ray Charles; José Feliciano, Tammy Wynette, and Paul Williams were scheduled to record it, and a different arrangement

Figure 6.2 Steve Karmen. (Courtesy of Steve Karmen.)

of the "Reach Out and Touch Someone" theme had been written for each of them. David Lucas and Thomas McFaul wrote a song from the slogan, which was turned into more variations for television commercials. Arlen described the recording studio and session, which was attended by a freelance song-writer and arranger who had arranged the "Reach Out" version for Snow. In charge was the chief musical consultant for the N. W. Ayer agency, which was producing the commercial.[83] Arlen interviewed Bill Eaton, the arranger of the "Reach Out" music for Phoebe Snow's radio version:

> I took the original David Lucas score and mulled it around in my head until I
> reached a point of view. What I wanted was something with a rock beat—but
> not too much of a rock beat—and also with a hint of disco. . . . When I do a
> commercial, I have to accept the responsibility for making it stylistically right
> for the artist, and for making it unique in such a way that the artist can convey
> his own personality. My work is close to popular, of course, but it's not the same
> as popular.[84]

The caution with which advertisers handled rock music ("Rock was treated like a diseased person," recalled one industry veteran in 1989[85]), and their general ignorance of popular music, continued for many years. Artie Schroeck, a composer and arranger in the business at its heyday, told me about writing promotional music for ABC in the early 1980s. He had written a song for the network that won a Clio Award in 1982.

> The following year . . . they wrote another lyric, and they wanted to use "Alexander's Ragtime Band" [a song composed in 1911]—[*sings*] "C'mon along, c'mon along with ABC."
> And at the time Irving Berlin was still alive, and he didn't want anybody to do his song—they asked him one time, they wanted to put out a whole book of all his songs. . . . And he said, "Naw, I don't want anybody to sing my songs anymore." . . . So . . . they wouldn't let us do "Alexander's Ragtime Band," so I wrote another song. . . . I wrote a song on the order of "Alexander's Ragtime Band." And I brought another [more contemporary] song in . . . and they ended up taking the more contemporary song. . . . [*sings*] "Come on along with ABC, we're reachin' out for you and me."

By "more contemporary," ABC meant more rock 'n' roll, Schroeck told me.[86] These anecdotes demonstrate just how much slippage there could be between sounds as conceptualized by advertisers and as heard by musicians and fans. By the mid-1970s, everyone knew the importance of sounding up to date in order to continue to appeal to the youth market, but this still meant different things to different people. Different clients had different sounds in mind, not all of them contemporary, even if they desired to capture the youth market.

Baby Boomers and Nostalgia

> Baby boomers, the size of the baby boomer market and the money that baby boomers have, they're like a gorilla, an eight hundred–pound gorilla. They control the music tastes of a lot of clients.
>
> —Hunter Murtaugh, interview by author, October 2009

The attempts to attract the youth and baby boomer markets grew more intense throughout the late 1970s and after. In 1976, a company called RockBill was founded in New York City, whose purpose was to promote rock acts to corporations for potential sponsorship in a slick magazine. Shaped and modeled after *Playbill*, *RockBill* eschewed hard sell about bands and featured short articles, interviews, and informational bits about various bands and musicians. *RockBill's* free distribution was assured through contractual agreement between musicians' management and their concert promoters, so between one hundred thousand and two hundred thousand copies were printed for each band's tour.[87] Jay Coleman, RockBill's president and founder, helped negotiate some major deals, linking the Rolling Stones and Jovan, the fragrance company, and Julio Iglesias with Coca-Cola.[88]

In late summer of 1985, Warner Special Products contacted all New York advertising agencies billing more than twenty-five million dollars annually with information on the benefits of using original recordings in advertising. Phase one of this direct mail campaign included a "How to Make a Commercial Rock" packet that included a disc touting the use of original recordings, and a mail-in card to request a free cassette entitled *Fortyfive Ways to Make Your Commercial Rock*. The next phase involved a national direct mail campaign as well as placing ads in trade publications.[89]

In the fall of 1986, *Marketing through Music* began publication as a monthly newsletter published by *Rolling Stone*. Its mission, like *RockBill's*, was, as its title suggests, to promote music for commercial uses. The magazine's publisher wrote in an introductory letter that the purpose of the newsletter was to "encourage marriages between music and non-music marketers."[90] For an annual subscription fee of fifty dollars, this newsletter helped bring together marketing, advertising, and music executives. The newsletter was a booster for the use of music in advertising, containing stories about advertising campaigns that used music in prominent ways, statistics about revenue derived for corporately sponsored acts, and more. *Marketing through Music* ceased publication after three years. But its mission was realized; sponsorship amounted to hundreds of millions a year by the mid-1990s, according to Jay Coleman of RockBill; some national brands sponsored dozens of bands.[91] All of these efforts resulted in vastly more spending on marketing and music; in 1981, roughly two million dollars was spent on music marketing; by 1984, the figure was over twenty million dollars.[92]

Even as baby boomers aged, they continued to be targeted by marketers (as they still are); one composer said, "The baby-boomers are a musical generation, no doubt about it. They have made music the language, the idiom of the country. As a result, almost everyone has musical ears today—we're a music-crazy nation."[93] An article in 1980 noted that the target audience was frequently "war babies," who liked the Beach Boys and James Taylor.[94]

The emphasis on adapting for and attracting baby boomers and younger generations of youth resulted in more and more music being used in commercials in the 1970s and 1980s, perhaps also as a result of the publications just mentioned. In 1979, 60 percent of all television commercials had music, but a little less than 50 percent employed jingles as the main music; as usual, the parity products of beer and fast-food jingles dominated.[95] An article in 1980 said that 70 percent of all commercials had music;[96] another article in 1981 reported a figure of 80 percent.[97] In 1984, many people in the industry were noting that business was booming; one person reported using music more than twice as much as just two years previously.[98] Music houses were also on the rise; an article from early 1984 reported that one music house owner thought that the number of music houses had increased at least tenfold in the previous fifteen years.[99]

It was the film *The Big Chill* (1983) that alerted the business world to the potential of baby boomer consumers' nostalgia, including nostalgia for music; advertisers learned to use popular music from the 1960s in commercials from this and other films. An art director at BBDO in early 1987, referring to the "baby boom syndrome," said:

> There is a huge market of people out there who grew up on music from the Temptations to the Rolling Stones to the Moody Blues. Music is part of their lives. These are people with money in their pockets, who are willing and capable of buying just about anything that is offered. That is why you see so much music being used and for the most part used effectively. The audience is more sophisticated, and consumers don't want to be hard-sold. The music method is one that appeals to them; it is easier for them to relate to.[100]

According to Hunter Murtaugh, who was vice president of Young and Rubicam and director of music production in the mid-1980s:

> It's an idea whose time has come. The people of the '60s are grown up. They have money, jobs and new consumer needs. Ads have to reach them. To connect the car with the consumer, the music takes them back to when they

learned to drive and what cars meant to them. Everybody has slammed the door to a car, put their foot on the gas and felt free. It hits everybody.[101]

Murtaugh also discussed this in our interview.

[It's] 2009 right now. You're perfectly hip to walk into a client meeting and say, "Got a great idea. You need a piece of music from forty years ago. Richie Havens. This is a great American spirit, it's . . . great." But in 1980, if you'd walked into a room and said, "I've got a great idea for you. Glenn Miller, forty years ago, still a great hit." . . . The same forty years, people would laugh you out of the room. They would say, "Hey, Hunter, it's 1980, what are you talking about, forty years—Glenn Miller, that's like a thousand years ago!"[102]

An early campaign that made use of rock music to attract nostalgic baby boomers was for Ford's Lincoln-Mercury Division in 1984, which employed seventeen classic rock hits underlying "witty mini-scenarios of baby-boomer life-styles." Known to industry insiders as the "*Big Chill* campaign," it targeted potential buyers with a common denominator of rock music, according to the company's market research, an attempt to dispel the carmaker's image as a brand for older people. Lincoln-Mercury's advertising manager said, "Regardless of background, the music of the '60s created positive feelings of the time—college, the prosperous country, boyfriend-girlfriend."[103] He said elsewhere that the company used popular music from the 1960s so that its audience would understand it, and that Lincoln-Mercury understood its audience.[104]

According to the creative director at the advertising agency that produced the commercials, "The music makes younger viewers feel that Lincoln-Mercury understands them. It recalls their adolescence, the most exciting time of their life and it transfers some of those good feelings to Lincoln-Mercury."[105] The advertising agency conducted research before and after the commercials were made, and determined that the first commercial, with "Ain't No Mountain High Enough," engendered a "remarkably deep and complex" effect in the audience. "Research showed that they were reading a variety of positive things into the spot, recalling all kinds of wonderful moments from their college days, and attributing those moments to the brand name Mercury."[106]

The research done by the automobile company's advertising agency determined that its target audience didn't want the lyrics of the music tampered with (in other words, tailored to sell the product), so the original musicians re-recorded their hits for the advertisements (though in the case of the Beatles, the agency employed a soundalike group, a fairly common strategy in this period, and the spot was produced by Beatles producer George Martin). Sometimes, performers would appear in commercials featuring their music. The four spots that were produced presented, according to an article in the trade press, images designed to appeal to baby boomers, and borrowed their titles from the songs they employed: "Born to Be Wild," "Ain't No Mountain High Enough," "Mama Said," and "Wouldn't It Be Nice." Market share increased from 5.5 percent to 6.5 percent.[107]

The Ford Motor Company issued a press release in the summer of 1985 trumpeting the usage of a cover, or remake, of the Beatles' "Help!" in a commercial as part of this campaign:

> Lincoln-Mercury Division is using Beatles music from the 1960s to appeal directly to the "baby boom" market. This is the first time a commercial has used music by the world's most famous rock group.
>
> Lincoln-Mercury Division is currently airing a commercial for its automobiles which features the song "Help!," the title song from a 1965 Beatles movie. The commercial is one of four being used to promote Mercury cars, all of which feature hit music of the '60s and '70s. Howard Guard, who directed the Mercury commercial, also directed the musical sequences in the movie "Help!"
>
> Lincoln-Mercury Advertising Manager Tom Ryan says the commercials are part of an overall effort to increase Mercury's appeal to younger buyers.[108]

The company's research indicated that music from the 1960s and 1970s would help reach the market of twenty-five- to forty-year-olds that the company was targeting, particularly if the music hadn't been tampered with. "We realized that this music is very important to our audience," Ryan said. "We didn't want to do anything to alter its basic integrity." The company thus employed original lyrics, and used the same recording studio and engineers who produced the originals. Ryan believed that the commercials had been effective; the average age of the Mercury Cougar buyer was forty-four in 1983 but dropped to thirty-five as a result of this campaign.[109] This campaign was the first of its kind, spawning many imitators, and was the main initiative to impress upon the advertising industry the potential sales to be gained from licensing existing rock music (to be discussed in chapter 7).

A later campaign for Lincoln-Mercury featured megastar Rod Stewart to sell not just a single car but the brand itself. "When consumers hear Rod Stewart's unique voice, no matter what the song, they'll immediately know that it's a Lincoln-Mercury spot," said the advertising manager of Lincoln-Mercury. Predictably, the target was baby boomers:

> We are trying to reach people born between 1946 and 1964. That's the heart
> of the baby boom, a huge segment with purchasing power that is continually
> rising. We think that there is no better way to reach them than through music.
> Rock is an extremely strong emotional connection for that group. Buying a car
> is a decision that is also very much influenced by emotions. That's why music is
> a very powerful marketing tool for us.[110]

Lincoln-Mercury tested Stewart with audiences, who liked his music even if they couldn't identify him. Stewart re-recorded four of his biggest hits for the campaign.

According to one trade report, a major reason that rock stars and commercials began to appear together was that "both the music and the medium have a respectability they didn't have in the 1960s and 1970s, when rock stars resisted commercial endorsements and few companies wanted them as spokesmen."[111] In other words, as a different author put it, "rock music lost its countercultural status."[112]

In October 1987, *Marketing through Music* reported on a book called *Youthtrends™: Capturing the $200 Billion Youth Market* by Lawrence Hamdan and Lawrence Graham, who described a generation after the boomers they call the "Fun Loving Youth en Route to Success," or "F.L.Y.E.R.S."[113] Author Graham told *Marketing through Music*, "Music can quickly provide an image for your product. A company can make the most outdated product seem current by using current music." The book's authors said that the most successful recent campaign was Pontiac Fiero's sponsorship of the 1984–85 Daryl Hall and John Oates tour, and argued that the success of this sponsorship wasn't just the music, but more how Pontiac carried it out. The promotion was so good because Pontiac covered so many different angles. They made sure that the tie-in was not just at the concerts—where they had pictures of Pontiacs and other promotional materials—but that they had actual record albums—with Hall & Oates posing next to a Pontiac Fiero, and they had ticket giveaways and contests at the showrooms—in the neighborhoods where young people go to look at cars.[114]

Later, New Age music was employed to attract the same baby boom consumers, and was first noticed in a trade publication in 1987. A Lincoln-Mercury campaign, departing from its successful *"Big Chill"* strategy, turned instead to New Age music. Two English musician/producers were hired to write five original New Age pieces for use in commercials in 1988, electronic works that were more closely related to classical music than rock, according to *Marketing through Music*. The Lincoln-Mercury Division general marketing manager said, "This new genre of music has become quite popular, particularly among younger, more affluent buyers. We believe this music will succeed in creating a contemporary image and help us attract the 25–44 year-old group [in other words, those born between 1943 and 1962—still primarily baby boomers]— the primary target for the Mercury brand."[115]

Another article on New Age appeared in *Marketing through Music* in May 1988, and noticed, "A new buzz word is being bandied about more and more in music marketing circles these days. That buzz word is 'new age,' and corporations targeting an upscale, sophisticated demographic view new age aficionados as a particularly attractive audience." The article mentioned usages of the music by Lincoln-Mercury and Hitachi, which sponsored Kitaro's North American debut tour (which it reported on in November 1987[116]). A management company specializing in the music was formed in Oakland, California; its president said, "The horizons for utilization of this kind of instrumental music in film, video, merchandising and marketing campaigns are vast and untapped."[117] *Marketing through Music*'s "M.T.M. Datafax" feature presented data on New Age listenership in the March 1989 issue. The broadest listenership was listeners under the age of forty-four: "Belying the misconception that new age music attracts an older demographic, this month's DATAFAX shows that the genre's appeal actually drops off after age 45!"[118] And an article in *American Demographics* from the late 1980s noted that pop and New Age music "had the most universal appeal."[119]

One of the reasons that rock and other musics liked by baby boomers could appear in commercials was because boomers had begun to ascend to positions of power in the advertising world in the 1980s and 1990s, and they had no compunction about using music from their youth in commercials. One industry insider said:

> There are a lot of people in advertising who grew up in with rock 'n' roll. So you see a lot of old rock 'n' roll songs creeping in, and a lot of current ones as well. We live in an age where middle adults—people under 50—were young enough to have been into rock 'n' roll. I think there's a real identification there: there's a sense of youth about yourself. I think there's a real value to it. Even if a song doesn't tie into the product exactly, there's a certain emotional pull.[120]

The baby boomers' rise to positions of power in the advertising industry by the mid-1980s was noticed and commented on by people in the industry. No longer were they simply the targets of marketing—they could be the targeters. Spencer Michlin, a leading jingle composer of the 1970s and 1980s, noted the increasing number of styles available to jingle composers, and how demographics brought a change to jingle styles: "The baby boom bulge—I'm part of it—was raised on rock 'n' roll. When I started business, clients were afraid of it . . . didn't want to turn off the older people. Now the older people are us. The clients are us. If you listen to almost any commercial now . . . you hear a good beat."[121] Kendall Marsh of Mental Music Productions said, "The baby boomer generation grew up with this music. Ad execs are in love with it, so they want to see their products associated with it. . . . You don't have to say anything else. You're associating yourself with a product which has a resonance with this tune. You're buying into a lifestyle."[122]

New Music

RockBill, Marketing through Music, and other ever-increasing efforts to attract youth and baby boomers meant that that the distance between some advertising music and popular music began to diminish in the 1980s. Susan Hamilton, of the music house Hamilton, Buskin and Batteau in New York City, said in 1990, "There used to be such a *gap* between records and music for commercials. Jingles used to be pale, watered-down derivatives of hit records. Now commercials are as innovative, and the onus is gone. I mean, celebrity

Figure 6.3 George Martin, Susan Hamilton, and Bernie Drayton, 1972. (Courtesy of Susan Hamilton.)

talent—the most amazing people are doing jingles!"[123] In our interview, she mentioned Leontyne Price, Michael Jackson, and Elton John, among others.[124]

In the early 1980s, a trend away from the jingle continued, in an effort to make commercials sound more like real songs. The shift was described in the trade press thus: "Today the jingle is conceived of more as a song with copy integrated within the melody and rhythm, rather than music which supports strong copy."[125] Producer Bernie Drayton (fig. 6.3), of the music house HEA, said in 1984:

> In the early '70s, things got very myopic in the music business. Everyone wanted to have their music sound like a jingle. Since then the jingle has evolved into a song with a contemporary feel. Basically our policy is to stay away from derivative music. . . .
>
> It has to be believable, and feel good. If we have to take a line out of the copy to make it flow, then that's what we do. It makes things more alive, more real. In general jingles don't relate to the real world, whereas a real song does. . . . In the last five years, the jingle has peaked. In some of the longer formats we do, such as radio spots, we actually do "real" music.
>
> Although commercials always lag behind popular music, our time gap is pretty close. Our writers are producing the real stuff.[126]

A firm in New York that mainly produced theme songs for television branched out into the jingle business, describing its work in that arena as writing "un-jingles," approaching each commercial as a little film. It attributes audiences' increased sophistication to MTV (which had begun broadcasting in 1981; see chapter 7) and a general tolerance for different musical styles. For the firm, this meant using a softer-sell approach. Commercials were coming to be seen as entertainment in their own right, not just selling instruments. The popularity of MTV was such that advertising agencies were beginning to seek out musicians with backgrounds in the entertainment industry. The advent of stereo TV was important to these composers, for they saw this technological innovation as a boon to their creativity.[127]

The "un-jingle" approach caught on. A 1983 article wrote of the abilities of country/pop singer Janie Fricke, who recorded many well-known commercials. One, for Busch beer, was so successful that the advertising agency's copy director said that the commercial was successful because it became "a Janie Fricke Busch beer spot rather than a Busch beer spot with Janie Fricke. She lent her originality to it."[128] In other words, it transcended the lowly status of being a jingle and became a song.

In the mid-1980s, a commercial for Löwenbräu beer featured music by Bob Rans of Tullio/Rans, who was chosen "because he was heavily into records—not commercials. We wanted a noncommercial, nonjingly sound—an original sound with international appeal compatible with the brand image." *Advertising Age* reported that the style was "techno-rap."[129] A late 1980s interview with Stu Kuby, senior vice president–director of music production at an advertising agency in New York City, who "discovered" Whitney Houston for a Diet Coke commercial, reported that Kuby thought it important to try to take somebody who wasn't well known but on the rise for use in commercials, believing it to be useful to offer a musician, whether known or unknown, the opportunity to shape a new song rather than covering an existing one.

> Most agencies will take an existing song and maybe rerecord it. But they're taking a record that already exists and using it for their purposes; they're not commissioning that person to create a new piece of music for them. Eric Clapton, Phil Collins, people like that, there they are on the screen singing, but it's not a new piece of music; it's a record they've already done. They're lending the music they've already created.[130]

When seeking to hire a well-known musician, Kuby believed that it was necessary to find someone who cared about the product, not someone who simply
picked up a check. Kuby and his colleagues found new musicians by employing people to go to clubs and listen to a good deal of music. Seeking out new
musicians this way, seeking the hip and the cool, was to become one of the
most potent ideologies in the world of advertising, active to this day.

New Capitalism

This adoption of the hip and the cool marks a new strategy in postwar capitalism, as Luc Boltanski and Ève Chiapello have written. They argue in *The
New Spirit of Capitalism* that critiques of capitalism, which they label as
"social" (a set of critiques that emerged during the Great Depression about
capitalism's unfairness) and "artistic" (critiques from the 1960s counterculture about capitalism's inauthenticity), play a role of a "motor in changes in
the spirit of capitalism."[131] It is the "artistic" critique that interests me here,
since this is linked both ideologically and chronologically to the counterculture and the later (and continuing) infatuation with the hip and the cool. This
critique has its roots in "a bohemian lifestyle" whose progenitor was Baude-
laire and the dandy, a critique that rejects disenchantment, inauthenticity,
the loss of a sense of beauty resulting from "standardization and generalized
commodification."[132] Boltanski and Chiapello place the artistic critique in the
late 1960s, epitomized in the events of 1968, the artistic critique having been
taken on board by students around the world.

   In the post–World War II era, they say, capitalism "offered itself both as
a way of achieving self-fulfillment by engaging in [it], and as a path of liberation from capitalism itself, from what was oppressive about its earlier
creations."[133] Consumption, which has been much discussed as a kind of pal-
liative, was one such path, but also advertisements—especially those with
music—offer emotional bribes, even emotional rewards. And aesthetic ones
as well, since, as is often remarked, some advertisements are better than the
programs they interrupt. Boltanski and Chiapello write of the "'privatization
of cultural consumption' made possible by the rapidly developing cultural
industries . . . as a form of liberation via the commodity."[134] They also say that
they take seriously capitalism's penchant for commodifying desire, though I
would express this in a less psychologistic way and instead refer to the ques-

tion of the emotionalization of advertising through the use of music articulated in chapter 4.

Boltanski and Chiapello write that goods, in order to be considered "authentic," had to draw on something from outside the commodity sphere, commodifying the authentic.[135] In this realm of advertising, the strategy since the 1960s has clearly been to seek what Boltanski and Chiapello call "sources of authenticity" in the practices of youth, in particular their musical tastes. As an advertising agency worker told Joyce Kurpiers when selecting music for a commercial, youth "are burned out on big, oversold stuff—they value authenticity."[136] In the 1960s, the decade that witnessed the rise of the infatuation with youth and the hip and the cool, one of the ways of being hip was to critique the commercial, consumption-oriented culture of the 1950s by characterizing it as inauthentic; this was the grounds on which the baby boomer generation in the advertising industry phased out the jingle, as discussed in chapter 5.

Boltanski and Chiapello trace the last incarnation of this "artistic critique" of capitalism to 1968, but, as we have seen, the advertising industry had begun to co-opt the youth culture critique of capitalism before then; adman Fairfax M. Cone said 1967 was the year of the youth, and, even though this co-optation was slow, it doesn't conform to Boltanski and Chiapello's chronology.[137] Nonetheless, I would be reluctant to swing the pendulum all the way back to Thomas Frank's view of things, that the advertising industry's "conquest of cool" was a conscious and deliberate conquest.[138] It was, partly, but it was also part of a broader shift in American and other nascent postindustrial cultures. The advertising industry is not "outside" of culture at large, it is part of it. What some people in the advertising industry believed in the 1960s, especially those who were part of the so-called Creative Revolution, was largely congruent with the youth culture of that period; each, as Stephen Fox observed, lacked a historical memory, disliked authority, and was visually oriented.[139] I would thus favor a more dynamic interpretation of the workings of the advertising industry, and American culture more generally: The advertising industry co-opted youth and the counterculture as much as it was shaped by them. And the result was an ever-increasing infiltration of capitalism into everyday life, introduced, in part, by the use of music entering people's ears, bodies, and minds.

Capitalism's response to this "artistic critique" was to internalize it, Boltanski and Chiapello write. "This recuperation took the form of a commodification—that is to say, the transformation into 'products,' allocated a price and hence exchangeable on a market, of goods and practices that in a different state of affairs remained outside the commodity sphere."[140] That is to say, the hip and the cool, once outside of the commodity sphere, at least to some extent, have been increasingly drawn into it.

It's all branding and lifestyle, just trying to get people to buy
into, you know, "This is the soundtrack to your life, and this
is the cosmetic that's gonna go with it and make you feel a
complete whole."

—Composer Andy Bloch, Human Worldwide,
interview by author, 20 April 2004

Music is identity!
—Sam Michaelson, advertising agency
vice president, director for radio buying, 1986

7

Consumption, Corporatization, and
Youth in the 1980s

Introduction

Despite the growing awareness of the importance of
youth culture, whether in its baby boom incarnation or
subsequent iterations, few publications mention demographic information in discussions of music before the
early 1980s, even though advertising agencies continued
to commission studies, some of which were quite detailed.
But interest in demographics and music grew in the late
1970s and beyond, as advertising agencies increasingly
targeted consumers based on their tastes, their lifestyles,
income, and much more. At the same time, the rise of
MTV meant that music was permeating American culture ever more, helping propel some musicians to super-

stardom that advertisers and advertising agencies were anxious to harness for their own ends.

Consumption, Lifestyles, Segments

In the 1980s, a new wave of consumption ideologies heightened most Americans' already strong consumption practices, newly invigorated by Ronald Reagan's sacralization of consumption in this era, as George Lipsitz has written.[1] (I have discussed the new wave of consumption in the 1980s elsewhere and need not do more than recapitulate it here.)[2] Reagan's and others' emphasis on consumption helped shape a culture in which consumption increasingly became part of everyday life, even as a form of leisure. Slogans from the era help recapture this ethos: "Shop 'til you drop," "When the going gets tough, the tough go shopping." Additionally, with the rise of the World Wide Web in the 1990s, it became easy to purchase goods online, which meant that one could shop at times and places where consumption was impossible before. By the 1990s, the average American consumed twice as many goods and services as in 1950, and the average new home of today was twice as large as the average house constructed after World War II so as to hold all of its owners' possessions.[3]

Heightened consumption in this era became a way to realize one's identity, an ideology, and strategy, that arose in the post–World War II era.[4] Consumption increasingly became not just a leisure activity but also a means of self-definition, self-creation. Wearing particular clothes, sporting a particular haircut, listening to a particular kind of music rather than another—these and many other modes of consumption and self-representation became important ways for many Americans to fashion their selves.

The new increase in consumption was driven not only by political ideology but also by technological innovations such as the Universal Product Code (UPC), or bar code, which first came into widespread usage in the mid-1970s, and which allowed retailers to track with great precision who was purchasing what, where, and when. One of my interlocutors, Scott Elias of Elias Arts (one of the biggest music production companies in New York and Los Angeles at the time of the interview in 2004), said that the utilization of the UPC was one of the two main innovations he had seen in the industry in his decades in it (MTV was the other).

When I first got involved in advertising, the agencies had a very important role to play in the marketing and the research, the design and development, not only of advertising, but in the marketing efforts. . . . What I think fundamentally changed was that now retailers . . . could have such a powerful impact, not only in America, but potentially even globally, that they could have so much data about any product, it could be a Gillette razor, it could be a consumer.[5]

Audience measurement had becoming increasingly refined since its inception in the 1920s, but an important breakthrough occurred after the rise of the UPC with the adoption of the People Meter by Nielsen in 1987. This device, attached to televisions of four thousand American homes (up from an earlier sample size of fourteen hundred), doesn't simply track which programs are watched but allows individual users to indicate that it is they who are watching. If big sister were watching, she pressed her button on the People Meter corresponding with her profile with Nielsen; if little brother were watching, he pressed his button. The data thus generated were much more specific about the tastes of individual viewers, not just those of an undifferentiated household.

Another effect of these developments was that niche markets were cultivated even more assiduously than before in an effort to increase profits, since profits began to matter more than the quality of the advertising agency's work in this era. One worker in the industry described what the process was like during this period.

> The process of developing a musical image, or jingle, for an advertiser or broadcaster usually follows a similar course. A detailed consultation with the client takes place initially to establish the primary goals and objectives. This process also includes developing a profile of the client's potential customer from the information given, which in turn helps to dictate the musical style, delivery and lyrics best suited to strike the responsive chord.
>
> The depth to which this profile is taken has grown measurably in the past decade. Once the development of a musical theme or concept was almost entirely dependent on the character of the product or service to be advertised. But recently a shift in emphasis has altered the positioning and presentation of such things.[6]

New businesses sprang up that specialized in bringing music and marketers together. Gerry Dolezar, president of a company called Radio Kings, described his role in 1987: "I'm basically a buffer between artists and agencies. I bring them together in combinations that are appropriate for each campaign." The trick, however, was to try to keep so abreast of trends that artists could be hired at affordable prices before they became popular and thus prohibitively expensive.[7]

This new segmentation of markets provided, and necessitated, ever more refined demographic data.[8] People were analyzed with a new "science" called "psychographics," a kind of psychological profiling of demographic groups. Now, demographic data could be used to target youth and others in increasingly sophisticated ways, frequently through music. Perhaps the most influential scheme in this era was the "values and lifestyles" or VALS 1 typology, developed by a think tank called SRI International in the early 1980s.[9] According to SRI, the VALS 1 typology comprises nine different types of consumers, divided into three groups: Need-Driven, Outer-Directed, and Inner-Directed. Need-Drivens are the "farthest removed from the cultural mainstream" of the nine lifestyles, and the "least flexible psychologically and least aware of the events of our times."[10] Need-Drivens include "Survivors," who are old and poor; and "Sustainers," who are living on the edge of poverty. The Outer-Directed groups contain Middle America; generally, people in the Outer-Directed groups "respond intensely to signals, real or fancied, from others" and "conduct themselves in accord with what they think others will think."[11] The Inner-Directed groups (the term is derived from the noted Harvard sociologist David Riesman, we are told) are motivated by internal forces; they are sensitive to their feelings.[12] Outer-Directeds include "Belongers," who are conventional; "Emulators," who are youthful and ambitious; and "Achievers," who are middle-aged and prosperous. Inner-Directeds include the "I-Am-Me" lifestyle, which is people in a transitional state who are young and narcissistic; the "Experiential" lifestyle, youthful people who are in search of experience; and the "Societally Conscious" lifestyle, which is mission oriented and mature.[13]

Advertising agencies and marketers were well aware of the usages of music in the psychographics era. A president of a music marketing agency wrote in *Advertising Age* in 1985 that since psychographics helped advertisers become part of a person's lifestyle, and that, since "the consumer's values and fantasies are embodied in their favorite artists," the use of music could help advertisers transfer a consumer's loyalty from the musician to the sponsor or product.[14] A 1985 trade press report noted how obsessed the advertising industry was with market segmentation, quoting a composer who said, "The great thing about music is that it breaks things out demographically. You can really nail the prospects depending on the music played; it's a great advertising and marketing tool."[15] A 1988 report in *Advertising Age* summarized the state of the business well:

> The genius of music marketing stems from the knowledge that each performer—like each product—appeals to a particular niche audience. By properly identifying the characteristics of its target consumer, and then correlating that profile with the fans of potential music celebrity endorsers, savvy advertisers are able to tap into the relationship that exists between a group and its followers. The marketing-through-music concept is so effective at converting band loyalty into brand loyalty that it has been extended from traditional youth-oriented product categories—fast food, fashions and fragrances—to non-traditional segments such as cameras, cars and even cat food.

The article went on to note the fit between particular goods and services, target audiences, and music (Frank Sinatra singing for Holiday Inn, Pat and Shirley Boone for the Recreational Vehicle Industry Association, and many more).[16] And the article referenced the newfound success that old songs can have once they are introduced to new audiences through their use in commercials; Sam Cooke's "Wonderful World," for example, charted higher after its use in a Levi's commercial than it did in its previous release some twenty-five years earlier. *Advertising Age* concluded with a useful summary, from marketers' perspective, of the benefits of marketing through music and how music was being used to target specific social groups:

> We're seeing the ascendance of a new marketing tradition. It's one that combines nostalgia, music and musical personalities—some of whom are finding a new generation of appreciative audiences—with products in a way that strikes a powerful, resonating chord in today's marketplace.[17]

Race, Class, and Ethnicity

Ethnic groups began to be increasingly marketed to as well in this period, in part because of the rise of minority-owned advertising agencies. Bernie Drayton told me of how he was hired by Herman Edel in the 1960s but was deliberately prevented from working commercials that might have employed African American music, for it would make him "'the black guy that does all the black stuff.'" But, "then the eighties came and the advent of African-American advertising agencies really bourgeoned. And by this time I was an established guy, I didn't have anything to prove, and so I jumped right on that."[18]

Hilary Lipsitz of BBDO, which produced many Pepsi-Cola commercials with music, recounted how his company never made a black-music commercial for black radio stations—it made youth-market commercials for youth-market stations: rock 'n' roll, top 40, black and white. He said that black players couldn't play on commercials in that era (though it's not clear why), so Lipsitz sought to change that with the commercials he produced for Pepsi. Quincy Jones recorded his second commercial ever for Pepsi's "Come Alive" campaign, and BBDO filmed black groups in the mid-1960s such as the Four Tops.[19]

A late 1970s article in the trade press described how advertising agencies attempted to reach African American audiences through music. One agency had developed a melody to sell a soft drink, which was described thus: "We used very little rhythm and a lot of shimmering high-end tonality; bell tree, orchestra bells, car keys, triangle, electric keyboards and violins and a single female vocalist." Evidently, it was thought that a different tack was needed for the African American audience:

> For the black exposition of the same melody we studied the playlists of black radio stations in the major markets and let this information dictate our orchestration and arrangements. There should be no confusing this music with that of any other soft drink. And the care taken to provide customized music for different groups should reflect well on our client's product.[20]

The same author recounted how his company located Cuban and Puerto Rican musicians in New York City for a client who wanted to reach that market, but needed to travel to Los Angeles to record "Chicano versions" of the music. "We knew we were in the right place when the lead singer introduced himself as 'Willie G. of the Southern California Dukes' and asked if our music was going to be salsa or lowrider. It makes musical and advertising sense to have people in the subculture speak to the subculture."[21]

Composer Chico O'Farrill spoke in a 1984 article of the growing influence of American popular musics on various Latin musics and vice versa, so that a new generic sound was emerging, a sound that he employed to reach the Hispanic market, though he had been writing music for major Hispanic advertising agencies for a decade.[22]

There were also periodic attempts to market to working-class and/or rural viewers and listeners; the trade press includes occasional articles throughout the 1950s and after on the rise of country music in advertising.[23] But such attempts never really caught on at the national level. Country music or musics associated with nonwhite ethnic groups are frequently used, but chosen for their efficacy in marketing a particular product in a particular way, not as part of a more general series of campaigns.

The Influence of MTV

Market segmentation in the 1980s was greatly aided by the rise of cable television, which had been devised after World War II for Americans living in rural areas too remote from a broadcast signal, but which really took off in the 1980s for many Americans. One of the earliest and most successful of all the early cable channels was MTV, a cable television station that plays videos of popular songs. It debuted on 1 August 1981, but it wasn't until the mid-1980s that the advertising trade press was reporting on its influence on commercials—the Madison Avenue Choir sound was beginning to give way to MTV's world of spectacle and fantasy. And, not coincidentally, MTV helped make rock music more palatable to advertisers.

The influence of MTV can't be overstated since it ushered in a new, fast-paced visual language to accompany music. The music itself, commonly thought of as an accompaniment to visuals, was now driving the production of visuals, which had a tremendous impact on the production of commercials as music video directors shot commercials. Scott Elias described the effect of MTV as having taught listeners that music can be accompanied by visuals in meaningful ways: "I think that now visuals and music or sound or a sound track, always are associated with an image. And if you see an image, and it's a filmic or cinematic image, I think we always in our head dream up a sound track. That sort of socialization is now something that we sort of take for granted."[24] The visual language of MTV was so novel that it featured prominently in many scholars' theorizations of postmodern culture in this period.[25]

Examples of the influence of MTV on advertising include a commercial from the 1980s for Edge shaving gel that shows a young man floating out of bed into the bathroom, where he shaves with Edge when a beautiful woman appears in the doorway. By the next scene, they are gone, the camera showing only the water left running in the sink. According to the senior vice president= account director of the advertising agency that produced the commercial, "We wanted to create a fantasy experience the way MTV does. We want young men to think of our product as high-tech, high-performance in the same way that they think of cars and stereos."[26]

This article didn't say so explicitly, but it seems to be the beginning of the shift away from older modes of advertising that made clear pitches, sometimes with jingles. One agency executive showed his colleagues some European commercials, all of which had "strong visuals, dramatic music and only a little copy." The article also noted the trend toward making commercials that seem like little programs instead of commercials; according to one executive, "Everyone is so tired of commercials that it's become incumbent upon advertisers to reach out and capture viewers by making them think they're watching a program. Once you do that, you slip in a product message at the end."[27]

MTV also helped to contribute to an aestheticization of advertising. Many in the advertising industry felt that commercials could be creative expressions in and of themselves, just as an MTV video was a creative expression, even though, of course, it was in essence a commercial for a song, an album, a band, and a record label. Since many video directors worked in MTV and vice versa, it was inevitable that MTV video techniques found their way to the production of commercials. MTV-influenced commercials became known as "atmospheric advertising," commercials featuring audio and visuals eschewing the hard sell.[28] A late 1980s assessment in *Advertising Age* of the influence of MTV on commercials said, "The videos' quick cuts, pulsing beats and high energy would change the look and feel of TV programming, commercials and motion pictures forever," to the extent that "it's almost hard to tell one from the other," according to MTV's senior vice president=creative director. A commercial director thought this influence was negative, for "the techniques become the message."[29]

The substance of commercials changed as well. Honda aired some commercials in 1984 featuring popular musicians that were directly influenced by MTV in their use of bright colors and a new style of graphics. The commercials were for motor scooters and were deliberately targeted at young people, making no mention of anything technical about the scooters. A senior advertising specialist for Honda said, "It's not a product commercial at all. It's more a portrayal of a sense of style and panache." Not surprisingly, the commercials were aired on MTV.[30]

A Levi's 501 Blues campaign from the mid-1980s employed many famous musicians, such as Jerry Garcia. The ad agency's executive producer said, "We let the artists be themselves. It's not unlike the instruction we give the people appearing in the ads, which is 'just be yourself and we'll film.' We tell the musicians to do what *they* do, not what they think we want them to do."[31] Artists were allowed to do whatever they wanted, though they had to mention Levi's 501 jeans, and the phrases "shrink-to-fit" and "button-fly." And, according to a press release, "no jingles."[32] A Levi's executive said that the reason it hired famous musicians "is to pull from them the kind of music that they normally do. One interesting thing is that we do the music first. Before we even run the camera, we've got our musical tracks together. We basically shoot to the music," showing the influence of MTV.[33] *Marketing through Music* reported that this campaign raised sales by 50 percent.[34]

Pepsi Again

And MTV helped propel Michael Jackson to superstardom, which brought him to the attention of advertisers. Doubtless the most celebrated early examples of the convergence of popular music and advertising occurred when Pepsi paid Michael Jackson a reported five million dollars to appear in TV commercials in 1984. This was reputed to be the largest celebrity endorsement ever, which transformed the world of music and marketing. John Sculley, president of Pepsi, said in 1980, "We haven't really changed our advertising—the Pepsi generation—in 18 years," for "we think we articulate a life style that large groups of Americans can aspire to."[35] Allen Rosenshine, worldwide CEO of BBDO, which produced the Jackson commercials, wrote that "The Pepsi Generation" had been very successful but Coke was making inroads.[36]

In the midst of devising this campaign, Rosenshine said in an interview that he didn't think there was a real "Pepsi style" out in the world, "there never is." "There are attitudes and styles which we wish to make signals of, or synonymous with, the brand. Advertising and brands don't really create style. They take styles that exist, hopefully at the forefront . . . and try to make [them] the property, proprietarily owned by a brand."[37] He wanted to make the drink a badge that said, "If I drink this, I have a certain style."[38]

Rosenshine also said that "Choice of a New Generation" marked a turning point in 1984 because BBDO changed the advertising and the advertising's way of reaching the consumer in terms of both tools and strategies. Michael Jackson possessed "all-age, all-family appeal." The commercials' strategy was devised before Jackson was engaged, and he was hired because he fit that strategy. The target audience, he said, was twelve to twenty-four. "What characterizes those people that we can own, lifestyle-istically?" "We want to offer them the sign of 'we're a step ahead, we're a little snappier, we're a little wittier, we're a little cleverer, we're a little out front.'" "If you want to be that," he said, "you can't not be in music." Continuing, he said:

> You can't ignore the world of music if you wish to be the badge of the leading edge of youth, because youth is into music. And that is part of their leading edge, they express themselves through music, they live through music; MTV is not an isolated phenomenon. So if we're going to be leading edge, we have to be in music.

Pepsi thought that Jackson wouldn't alienate older viewers, that, in fact, older viewers liked Jackson because he made them feel a little like kids, and that's what Rosenshine desired: he wanted older people to think of themselves as being part of the new generation when they drink a Pepsi or think of Pepsi.[39]

Jackson's association with Pepsi began when Roger Enrico, head of Pepsi, was approached by Jay Coleman, founder and president of RockBill (a company that specialized in bringing musicians and corporations together, which was begun in the mid-1970s and which published a magazine of the same name, as discussed in the previous chapter). Jackson's representatives had approached Coleman seeking tour sponsorship. Coleman said, "The obvious place to take Michael is to a soft drink company. Cars, liquor—for a dreamy, clean-living kid like Michael, these make no sense. He needs a product that's soft, cuddly, harmless, and fun. And that's soda."[40]

Pepsi and advertising agency executives weren't sure what they were getting, despite the massive success of Jackson's *Thriller*, released in 1982. Enrico wrote that Jackson's music videos that Coleman used in his pitch were the first ones he had ever seen, but he found Jackson's dancing so captivating that he thought the videos would be compelling with the sound off. "He's magic. We've got to sign him," wrote Enrico.[41] Enrico balked at the five-million-dollar price tag, but Don King, Jackson's manager, held out successfully. Enrico's boss, head of PepsiCo's Worldwide Beverage Group, was not happy. "Look, do you have a record or *something* this guy has done? I'd like to listen to it over the weekend and see what we're buying for five million dollars," recounted Enrico, emphasizing yet again the frequent disjuncture between popular culture and the rarefied world of advertising.[42] But the deal was signed.

"Billie Jean" (example 7.1) features Jackson look-alikes, including a young boy, who bumps into the real Jackson in the course of the real commercial. The original lyrics were altered to contain Pepsi content, revisiting the generation theme with lines such as "You're a whole new generation."

Enrico claimed that after the release of these commercials, 97 percent of the American public saw them at least a dozen times in the space of a year, pushing sales to new levels.[43] As a result, Phil Dusenberry, chairman of BBDO, said, "Awareness of Pepsi's advertising went up 24% . . . [and] recall scores doubled the category norm. Nielsen shares increased a whopping two points in twelve months; that's $250 million a point."[44]

Pepsi engaged Jackson again in 1987 for more commercials for a reported fee of fifteen million dollars (though Enrico said that the contract prohibited him from mentioning a figure but claimed it was considerably less).[45] *Marketing through Music* called this arrangement "the most far-reaching and lucrative music marketing deal ever between a corporation and a performing artist."[46] Pepsi was put on the defensive about Jackson's popularity, which some thought had waned since the first commercials in 1984; Enrico himself wondered if Jackson could possibly be as hot in 1987 as he was in 1984.[47] But an anonymous Pepsi insider said, "We expect him to be a trendsetter again. A lot of people say he's through; we are convinced that he's still hot."[48]

Enrico told *Advertising Age* that the second deal wasn't just a celebrity endorsement, but it was rather a "relationship," and that the cost of the deal was "the most money paid for any relationship of this kind." Jackson was slated to act as a "creative consultant" to Pepsi and perhaps direct a commercial; his first song written for Pepsi would be included on his next album. The contract did not require Jackson to hold, drink, or come into contact with Pepsi, something that Jackson had received criticism for in the first campaign.[49] Enrico insisted that such deals nonetheless paid dividends; the company said that sales rose 8 percent within thirty days after the last campaign. Enrico claimed that the Pepsi commercials would be zap-proof, referring to users' ability to mute commercials with remote control technologies that were becoming increasingly common in this era.[50]

The new deal included Jackson's writing original music for two new commercials. The broadcast of the new commercials was delayed to coincide with the release of Jackson's new album post-*Thriller*, *Bad*.[51] Pepsi's marketing was closely tied to Jackson's album. The series of commercials consisted of four spots, the premiere of which was delayed, however, because the release of *Bad* was behind schedule. A trade press report said that the campaign marked a number of precedents in the industry: The campaign featured the song that was expected to be the album's biggest, and it was "unusual to buy the rights for a TV commercial before the song ha[d] proved itself on the charts"; the song was purchased as part of the overall deal with Jackson. Additionally, the two commercials cost two million dollars to produce, twice as much as Pepsi had spent on the earlier Jackson commercials.[52]

Two commercials were released late in October of 1987, first airing on MTV, both continuing the "new generation" theme. The first, called "Concert," was a ninety-second spot that showed Jackson live in concert. The other, "Backstage," depicted Jackson in his dressing room meeting a young fan; both commercials use the song "Bad" (example 7.2). *Advertising Age*'s reviewer's report was less than enthusiastic, and made fun of Jackson's album title, *Bad*: "They're bad, they're bad. But it don't make no never mind. Ooh." Describing the long-awaited commercials as "surprisingly ordinary" and highly reminiscent of the previous round of commercials from 1984, the reviewer averred that the long delays in the release of the album were simply an attempt to build up anticipation for it.[53] The second phase of the campaign was first aired during the 1988 Grammy Awards broadcast in March.

Not everyone in the advertising world liked the show business–ization of the advertising industry (one longtime composer I interviewed referred to it derisively as "starfucking"). Some believe that the infatuation with music and musicians threatened to overwhelm the sales pitch. *Advertising Age*'s review of a Diet Coca-Cola commercial featuring George Michael said in early 1989, "You can certainly see how the millions of dollars behind this ad will accrue to the benefit of George Michael. Product as hero? This is product as extra."[54] The reviewer later attacked the commercial-celebrity system, likening it to the old payola system, in which record labels paid radio DJs to play their recordings:

> Used to be, a singer cut a record and some sleazoid promoter paid bribes to get the thing airplay. And if payer and payee got caught—well, Faustian bargains can have infernally unpleasant consequences.

But now the whole system is turned topsy-turvy. These days, boffo recording artists get *paid* lotto-jackpot sums to plug their own songs on TV—with the
sole proviso they be photographed in proximity to a major soft drink. . . .
      Payola is old hat. This is the PayCola age.[55]

But the attachment to the youth market and infatuation with hip and cool
ideology that had begun to be established in the 1960s had become too en-
trenched to jettison; the use of popular music continued, even rose. A late
1980s report in *Advertising Age* noted the increased role played by popular
music in commercials: "The ad industry, as a whole, has fallen in love with
rock 'n' roll, and for good reason. Its fans—primarily 15-to-44-year-olds—are
the country's largest population segment, wielding more purchasing power
than any other age group. Marketers from every product category are eager to
cash in on the avid consumerism of the demographic group."[56]

By the late 1980s, even hip-hop began to be used in commercials as major brands such as McDonald's, Denny's, and Coca-Cola attempted to reach
urban youth. Part of the appeal seems to have been that a good deal of information could be imparted by rapping the lyrics.[57] A survey of teenagers in
this period revealed that nearly 80 percent of them believed hip-hop to be in
vogue, which was a higher score than for any other kind of music. Demon-
strations of the music's appeal to white teenagers were the deciding factor for
many advertisers, though most were reluctant to employ hip-hop musicians
who hadn't "thrown off some of the 'street,'" according to the president of the
African-American Marketing and Media Association in 1993. Russell Simmons, one of the founders of Def Jam record label, said that the use of hip-hop
in advertising wasn't selling out (as it would have been perceived from a white,
middle-class rock viewpoint), because

> black kids want to be sold out, as in "there ain't no more records left, no more
> tickets for your concert." Black people like to see people large. The more cars
> and houses and places rappers go, the badder they are. Being a starving artist is
> not that cool in the ghetto.[58]

Simmons articulated what many African American musicians had long felt:
that permitting their music to be used in commercials was a sign of mainstream acceptance and thus was to be welcomed.

Corporatization

Within the advertising industry itself, the business-friendly environment nur-
tured by Ronald Reagan changed the industry substantially; advertising agencies became, as described by Bill Backer in our interview, "pawns in a Wall
Street game of mergers and acquisitions."[59] A couple of people I interviewed
said that while they liked to work for independent music houses, after the
mergers of the 1980s, many of the creative people that they had worked with
were being let go in favor of younger people who were thought to be more in
touch with youth culture.[60]

The effect of the mergers and acquisitions of this period meant that the
bottom line became increasingly important to the multinational corporations
that owned advertising agencies. Budgets diminished considerably. While it
was common to hire many live musicians in the heyday of the jingle in the
1960s and 1970s—many people I interviewed recalled working with twenty-
to forty-piece orchestras—the rise of digital technologies that emerged in the
1980s and 1990s changed that. Compounding this change was a late 1980s
SAG/AFTRA strike that had the effect of teaching advertising agencies and
advertisers that music could be produced much more cheaply in "right to
work" states and abroad. Once the strike was over, Nick DiMinno told me,
things were never the same.[61]

And music was increasingly tested, increasingly brought into a rationalized
business framework. Anne Phillips, a singer/composer, told me how demoral-
izing all of this testing was, not just testing about the efficacy of jingles but testing of every jingle, every commercial. This was part of the reason she decided
to leave the business.[62] She wrote an unpublished article in 1981 about this
experience, describing how commercials were once beautifully crafted with
skill and care, but

> then something began to happen. More and more campaigns began to mysteri-
> ously die somewhere between creation and broadcast. . . . [The rise of testing
> meant that] soon it seemed that the people who once got excited about new
> campaigns had gotten knocked down so many times by the numbers that they
> just couldn't believe in or fight for an idea anymore. . . . Today if I write 30
> commercials and one finally makes it through the maze of client presentations,
> marketing analysis, legal, testing, etc., I consider it a miracle. . . .

It's as though the rug of basic pride in our work and faith in our experience, talent and professionalism was slowly pulled out from under us. The basis for decision, if you call what is in truth non-decision, "decision," is no longer one's wisdom and ability to make sound judgments. It is numbers.[63]

The advertising and music industries were becoming more like businesses in this era, more exclusively concerned with profits, and advertising agencies realized that they could potentially increase profits by hiring stars or licensing known songs. The kind of money that the increasingly corporatized world of advertising was spending on stars such as Jackson provides examples of just how important marketing through music had become in the 1980s. One of the biggest campaigns of this type occurred in the late 1980s when Burger King mounted a massive radio campaign costing between twenty-two million and thirty million dollars that featured musicians in sixty-second radio commercials, ranging from John Lee Hooker, the Fabulous Thunderbirds, the Neville Brothers, Take Six, Was (Not Was), Mel Tormé, Tone-Lōc, and Paul Shaffer and the World's Most Dangerous Band. According to the senior vice president–creative director at the advertising agency that produced the commercials, who got to play with the musicians, "We got to work with people we liked. We weren't looking for Michael Jackson. We're not looking for the Who; we're not looking for the Rolling Stones. We're looking for bands that have something to say, that have an identifiable musical style who also are known for breaking the rules a little bit." The senior VP–sales and marketing at the Radio Advertising Bureau praised the campaign because "everyone wants to get into specific targeting," at which radio was unparalleled.[64] The campaign, called "Sometimes You've Gotta Break the Rules," began airing on 1 October 1989, three days before the launching of the TV campaign. *Advertising Age* reported that the commercials were "a long way from hard sell, barely mentioning the name Burger King and never mentioning Whoppers, French fries or milk shakes." The ads were intended to "capture an attitude," according to the senior vice president–account director.

Sounding more like a music producer than an advertising music producer, Susan Hamilton, president of the music production company HB&B, said:

One of the reasons we were even able to touch a lot of the artists that we had was that we told them we were not interested in having them sing our jingle

and sound like us. We were interested in having their artistry, their talent, their
words, their music, their sound, their personality be the driving force behind
the performance.

If we had told them to stand up and sing our song, a number of them would
have told us to take a flying leap.[65]

Rather strangely, the television commercials in this campaign did not use this,
or any, music. "We did not want to do a traditional jingle campaign. No matter
how good the music is, and it is, the minute you start putting pictures against
it, it's something you've seen before," said the senior VP–creative director at
the advertising agency.[66]

In 1989, the R. J. Reynolds Tobacco Company began what its marketing
company described as "the largest fully-integrated music-marketing program
in history." This effort included advertising, promotional events in nightclubs,
a direct-mail record and tape club, and a bimonthly music magazine. Reynolds was attempting to recapture some of its younger consumers for its Salem
brand, and it clearly understood the importance of music to younger Americans. "Since we are the leading menthol in the country, there's great potential
with young adult smokers because music is a major element in their lifestyles,"
according to a Reynolds spokesman. This promotional effort was based in
part on the use of what the magazine called a "purchase behavior database"
of menthol cigarette smokers that was built on the responses to offers of free
merchandise.[67]

Clearly, the music and marketing industries were becoming increasingly
interdependent in the 1980s, and both industries became increasingly corporatized. In 1989, *Marketing through Music* included a rare column, by Mitchell Berk, president of Entertainment Marketing Inc., who wrote of the trend
since the beginning of the 1980s of what in his business is called "marketing
through entertainment." At first, he said, companies simply derived goodwill
from this practice. But soon corporate marketers wanted more—they wanted
to be able to make the marketing efforts "help them accomplish specific marketing goals and objectives." His case study was of country music star Kenny
Rogers and Dole Food Company, which had recently signed a deal with the
singer. It paid him a sizable fee ("which still amounts to only a small percentage of the company's yearly marketing budget"), and would sponsor Rogers's
tour for at least three years. Rogers would also appear in television and radio
commercials and "at a select number of Dole VIP functions." Additionally,

every Kenny Rogers concert city becomes a target market for Dole and its field marketing team. For several weeks before a performance, local retail markets are turned into Dole promotional headquarters, with an ongoing appearance by a six foot Kenny Rogers standee, which appears in stores throughout the market.

There were also many different contests and promotions intended to "tactfully, yet permanently associate Dole products with Kenny Rogers"; and one radio station in each market was to air a one-hour music and interview special with Rogers. And still more.[68]

Corporate sponsorship of musicians was one of the signs of the growing convergence of popular music and advertising, and corporate sponsorship of rock music tours reached new heights by the end of the 1980s, when many top musicians were expected to negotiate lucrative deals for sponsorship of their tours. Such deals often included the musician making commercials; Pepsi sponsored Michael Jackson's overseas tours.[69] Paul McCartney received a seven-figure fee to appear in a commercial for Visa, which also sponsored his 1990 tour; McCartney had never appeared in advertising before. The president of Entertainment Marketing and Communications / RockBill said, "In the mid-'70s, when music sponsorships really began, the corporate side was very fearful of the countercultural image of rock 'n' roll, and most of Madison Avenue shared the sentiment. Today, most of the senior and middle-level managers in the agency and client world are products of the baby-boom era. They grew up with rock 'n' roll."[70]

Not surprisingly, marketers were acquiring tour sponsorships with greater alacrity than in the past and thus demanding more from musicians. A vice president at a promotion group said, "In the early 1980s, an advertiser would pay a relatively small amount to have its name printed on tickets and posters. Now advertisers want the umbilical cord to be shortened. They want artists to do things that will have the greatest possible impact on their target demographics, such as TV commercials, special concerts and merchandising programs."[71] At the same time, however, in this era, when many fans worried about whether or not their favorite musicians were sellouts, marketers had to be careful not to be too intrusive. This same vice president said, "If an advertiser over-commercializes the sponsorship, it compromises the value of the star in the eyes of his fans and reduces the value of the sponsorship. People relate to an artist because he's different, he's cool, he's special. [Marketers] have to be careful not to kill the goose that laid the golden egg."[72]

In June 1989, *Marketing through Music* reported on a deal struck between Fuji Photo Film USA and Enigma Entertainment Corporation that the newsletter calls unprecedented. Fuji was to sponsor several Enigma acts on tour, include Enigma cassette samples in Fuji promotions at retail sites, provide the record label with tape for duplication, and sponsor some music specials on cable television. The agreement was based on Fuji's realization of the importance of the youth market.[73]

And musicians increasingly wrote songs for brands. In the summer of 1987, Adidas launched a Run-D.M.C. Sportswear line, after the hip-hop artists wrote a song called "My Adidas" (example 7.3), which reached number 5 on *Billboard*'s black singles chart.

> My Adidas
> walk through concert doors
> and roam all over coliseum floors
> I stepped on stage, at Live Aid
> All the people gave an applause that paid
> And out of speakers I did speak
> I wore my sneakers but I'm not a sneak
> My Adidas cuts the sand of a foreign land
> with mic in hand I cold took command
> my Adidas and me both askin P
> we make a good team my Adidas and me
> we get around together, rhyme forever
> and we won't be mad when worn in bad weather
> My Adidas . . .
> My Adidas . . .
> My Adidas

This was the culmination of a long relationship with Adidas, which had been supplying the musicians with promotional items for three or four years previously. The person responsible for promoting the relationship between the band and Adidas said, "The beauty about the whole thing is that when they began they bought Adidas because they simply loved the shoes. Now, I think Run-D.M.C. is almost synonymous with Adidas."[74]

And in the fall of 1987, Pontiac launched a new campaign aimed at a younger audience. General Motors sponsored a twenty-seven-city tour in

1988 organized by MTV. Seven and a half million fans were expected to see Pontiac's 2.5-minute commercial. The first television commercial in the campaign featured a "feverish new theme song" dubbed "Ride Pontiac," which, in the somewhat overheated prose of *Advertising Age,* "accompanies quick visual intercuts of a band performing the music in concert, hard-charging cars and sultry scenes such as a woman who shrugs off an oversize shirt to reveal her swimsuit as she runs past her LeMans on the beach."[75]

Given the continuing obeisance to the youth market and the ideology of the hip and the cool, finding out what youth were listening to was ever more important. And the new trend toward the use of existing popular music in advertising meant that some companies began to study popular music assiduously. A report in the *Wall Street Journal* in 1985 said that Coca-Cola studied the lyrics of the top 20 songs each week in an attempt to ascertain which music young people like. The senior vice president for marketing said, "Because there are fewer teenagers than in the 1970s, competition for their attention is fiercer, and targeting them demands greater precision than ever before."[76]

A *Marketing through Music* article from April 1989 said that a study in which over two thousand twelve- to nineteen-year-olds were polled showed that teens looked to music and musicians when making their purchasing decisions.[77] Such studies were part of an increasing desire to follow trends in the popular culture of youth. "Commercial music has to follow the trends," according to David Horowitz, president of David Horowitz Music. "They check out the trends and fads before they plug into anything. Millions of dollars are being spent to buy time so they have to be sure that the way the message is cloaked will be acceptable by the pop music culture. After all, we're not selling art, we're selling a product."[78]

Licensing

Big corporate money wasn't being spent just on musicians recording commercials but also to license preexisting music as recordings, not just covers (or parodies as they were known).[79] This practice had existed sporadically before that decade, however, as we have seen, and, in fact, by the late 1970s, articles began to appear on the use of existing songs in commercials.[80] In 1978, an industry insider said that licensing was "at an all-time high. There was a slight surge at the end of the '60s, but it's nothing like what it's been in the last three or four years." One advantage of using known music, according to another

insider, was that "it has a built-in safety factor. The song doesn't need testing; you need only test the campaign and the identification of the song with
the product. There's no guesswork that you would have with a new tune. Will
the public catch on to something it's never heard before? Who knows?"[81] Licensing of original songs was still on the rise in 1980; the agency that issued
licenses and oversaw the collection of fees from record companies on behalf
of music publishers saw licensing income from TV/radio commercials double
from 1978 to 1979.[82]

In May 1984, Sprint aired a TV commercial using Stevie Wonder's "I Just
Called to Say I Love You." Calls to Sprint were up 25 percent in three days,
which had a greater impact than anything the advertising agency had ever
done for Sprint, according to an executive at the advertising agency that produced the commercial. The senior vice president of sales and marketing at
the company said, "Music puts us firmly on the leading edge of contemporary
lifestyles."[83] The success of this commercial was such that in late 1984, CBS,
several music publishers, and United Artists and Unart banded together to
market songs and images to potential licensors in a twenty-two-minute video
presentation entitled "Songs that Make Commercials Sing," which was perhaps the first time that sound and film had been used to seek licensors.[84]

Other advertisers tampered with lyrics of original songs, however, when
they made covers, or remakes, of them. A 1985 article from *Madison Avenue*
described "parody fever"—the use of preexisting popular songs to sell—which
was sweeping the industry; some in the industry referred to the 1980s as the
Re-Decade. Popular songs were tested for their memorability and then employed in commercials; using existing songs makes research and testing easier
since the songs are already known.[85] Examples include the Platters' "Only You,"
which became "Only Wendy's"; the Diamonds' "Little Darlin'" became Ken-
tucky Fried Chicken's "Chicken Little"; Buddy Holly's "Oh Boy" became "Oh
Buick!"; Jerry Lee Lewis's "Whole Lotta Shakin' Goin' On" became Burger
King's "Whole Lotta Breakfast Goin' On"; Danny and the Juniors' "At the
Hop" became "Let's Go Take a [Granola] Dip"; "Mack the Knife" became
"It's Mac Tonight"; and "Look What They've Done to My Song, Ma" became
"Look What They've Done to My Oatmeal."[86]

A 1985 article in *Forbes* noted the new trend of using preexisting music in
commercials, articulating a widespread belief in the industry in this period: "It
is an attempt to sway the viewer toward a product by enlisting the good feelings he or she already has for a popular song."[87] The head of a music produc-

tion company in New York that specialized in turning 1960s hits into jingles noted that, while existing popular music had been used for commercial purposes in the past, it was a much bigger business in the mid-1980s, and that one of the main differences from earlier usages of popular music was the decrease in lag time between the release of a popular song and its appearance in a commercial. When an oldie is used as a jingle, he said:

> You're buying all the associations people have for that song. Those songs define the listeners' life style, so advertisers can really target their audience that way. The risk is if the advertiser misunderstands, misrepresents or doesn't follow through on those associations. They can alienate the very people they want to impress.[88]

Inevitably, new services arose to feed the new demand. *Marketing through Music* wrote in March 1988 that SBK Entertainment (a music publisher and entertainment services company) was to begin offering free catalogs of its extensive library to music professionals.[89] This may be the first time that potential licensors were courted.

The licensing craze did not seem to harm the music production business at first; *Marketing through Music* reported in June 1988 of the licensing boom: "Commercial music has been dramatically affected by the rising popularity of music marketing. The jingle business, once dominated by a handful of New York–based music houses, has become big business with 500 or so commercial music production facilities doing business in major cities across the country." The magazine interviewed several workers at Smythe and Company, a six-month-old jingle house in New York City.[90]

Revolution? Or Devolution?

Perhaps the most celebrated—and condemned—of the early licensing of songs occurred in the spring of 1987, when Nike bought the rights to the Beatles' "Revolution" for a reported $250,000 to EMI and another $250,000 to SBK Entertainment World for the copyrights (example 7.4). This was to be the first time, according to Nike, that the Beatles' recorded music would be used in a commercial.[91] Nike's use of the song was part of a $7- to $10-million campaign (depending on which trade press report one accepts).[92] Nike purchased the rights from SBK, owned by Michael Jackson, to use the original song. The director of public relations and communications for EMI Music, North America (EMI/Capitol owns the recordings) said, "Nike approached Yoko Ono because 'Revolution' is a John Lennon song. It was referred to us through Yoko's office with the understanding that Yoko was in favor of allowing the use of the song in the ad campaign. The deal was structured in such a way that it was used tastefully."[93] *Adweek* said that the commercial was "quietly redefining" TV advertising, in part because of its look, but also because there was no announcer, no real sales pitch, and the logo barely appeared.[94] The video showed clips of athletes young and old, famous and amateur, and Nike products, all in a quick cutting style.

Former music video producers Peter Kagan and Paul Greif, who had been making commercials for only a year, oversaw the production of the ad. They shot it in black and white with a handheld Super 8 camera and employed the music video technique of numerous quick cuts, which made it resemble a home movie. A partner in the advertising agency said, "Clients tend to want very predictable things. To turn everything over to 8mm was very radical. But when the idea of using 'Revolution' came up, we thought it would be terrific to use Kagan & Greif and get that honesty and reality they bring to film." The filmmakers claimed, "This is the right time for progressive advertising."[95] Their response to the prospect of filming a commercial with the iconic 1960s song was, "We were both pleased and nervous dealing with this piece of John Lennon music in advertising. There it is—the anthem—and we all know it had nothing to do with sneakers when it was written." Kagan said, "To voice over John Lennon would not only have been busy, but sacrilegious, impolite and insulting to him. We knew we were trying to do justice to the music."[96]

Nonetheless, there was an outcry over the commercial, which was seen by many as desecrating not just the Beatles and the song but the 1960s revolutionary spirit the song articulated. An *Advertising Age* editorial acknowledged the outrage, but, the author said, the owner of the Beatles songs, Michael Jackson, is not running a charity, and "we lost our innocence about such deals well before 1967 when TWA began using the Fifth Dimension's 'Up, Up and Away,' so we expect many an advertiser to tell Michael Jackson, 'Count me in.'"[97]

A letter to the editor described Jackson's "exploitation" of the Beatles' music as "obnoxious," and suggested that Beatles fans found a charity organization to purchase the music themselves, thus "saving the finest pop songs ever written from becoming fodder for mindless Madison Avenue 'jinglemongers.'"[98] Historian Jon Wiener wrote an article in the *New Republic* in May of 1987[99] that was excerpted in *Advertising Age* on 29 June 1987, which generated a letter to the editor by a staff artist from a corporate advertising department, noting that Wiener and others had neglected to ask the main question: "Do such ads work?"[100]

> By any standard, I would be considered a prime target for such advertising, yet I have been largely unimpressed. The assumption seems to be that my heart will melt when I hear one of those "Good Old Songs" and I will become kindly disposed toward the product. However, when the time comes for me to part with my hard-earned income, I couldn't care less about the background music. I would much rather be intelligently informed about what the seller has to offer.[101]

This position reflects the age-old tension between "reason why" and other forms of advertising.

In July 1987, the Beatles' music company, Apple Records Inc., sued, claiming that Nike "wrongfully traded on the good will and popularity of the Beatles" by using the song. The lawsuit sought up to fifteen million dollars in damages.[102] The lawsuit was based not on copyright infringement, since the Beatles no longer owned the song, but that the Beatles' "persona and goodwill" had been damaged. The attorney for Apple told *Marketing through Music*:

> The Beatles want this lawsuit to be a warning to advertisers that if you think you are going to use Beatles recordings to peddle, promote and endorse your commercial products, we are going to sue you. For 25 years, no Beatles original recording has been used to promote or endorse any product. Nike and EMI are well aware of the fact that this is the first time it has ever been done. Our position is that EMI can sell recordings, but can't license our recordings to push other people's commercial products.

EMI countered that the commercial had been made with Yoko Ono's permission, but Apple's lawyer said that Apple requires all four of its "directors"— that is, Ono and the remaining Beatles—to sign off on such usages.[103] Apple's lawyer also claimed, "The Beatles didn't write and record their music to sell commercial products. Any advertiser that tries to use a Beatles record to sell a product does so at [its] own peril and will be sued." Apple not only wanted money but also demanded that Nike discontinue its advertising campaign,

and that Capitol and EMI return the Beatles' master recordings.[104] Nike, mean-
while, claimed not to have broken any laws. On 6 August 1987, Nike published
a newspaper advertisement in Chicago, Los Angeles, New York, Portland, Or-
egon, and in *USA Today* labeling Apple's lawsuit a publicity stunt.[105] It continued to produce new commercials with the song.[106]

In April 1988, *Marketing through Music* reported that Nike pulled the Beatles' "Revolution"; the fourth and last television usage of the song ceased on
March 22 of that year.[107] Nike didn't exercise its option to renew the song for
a second year, saying that it was simply a business decision.[108] This, however,
did not staunch the animus. Paul McCartney told *Rolling Stone* that he wasn't
pleased with Nike's campaign, "because the Beatles never did any of that. We
were offered Disney, Coca-Cola and the hugest deals in Christendom and beyond. And we never took them, because we thought, 'Nah, kind of cheapens
it.' It cheapens you to go on a commercial, I think,'" even though he did a few
years later.[109] The lawsuit was settled out of court in 1989, terms undisclosed.

A later editorial in *Advertising Age* acknowledged that many fans don't like
the licensing of popular songs to sell goods.

> As these grumblers vow never to buy the products thus advertised, we might
> point out that in most instances the use of the music in commercials puts a
> few more bucks into the pocket of those who wrote the tunes. And since most
> songs that make it to the charts are written to make money, it seems unfair to
> insist the songwriters not benefit from their talent once the record sales fade
> away. They might even be thus inspired to pen more songs that bring pleasure
> to pop music fans.[110]

Despite fans' complaints, the use of familiar songs in commercials continued to rise.[111] Memorability, positive associations with the original song,
and affection for the music were the driving forces behind the licensing trend,
especially in attempts to reach baby boomers. In its July 1988 issue, *Marketing through Music* presented on its first page a graph that showed the success
of commercials with music: Eric Clapton for Michelob, Linda Ronstadt for
Coke, Michael Jackson for Pepsi, Bon Jovi for Coors, and U2 for Kodak. Its
data showed that these commercials with music garnered more positive reactions than negative.[112] Data were presented a few months later in the same
year, and this time, more was made of the data instead of simply displaying a
graph:

In a national survey of more than 1,400 music consumers conducted during January 1988, Soundata asked consumers to name the best commercials they'd seen in the past 3 months. Music-based campaigns—California Raisins, Levi's 501 Blues and Michael Jackson spots—came out on top.[113]

Yet complaints continued. Many, even some in the advertising industry, decried the practice of licensing. A Chicago-based advertising copywriter wrote in a 1986 article in *Advertising Age*, "I'm being manipulated and I don't think I like it." She professed to be a "real" baby boomer, not one of the "new boomers," the twenty-five- to thirty-five-year-olds, and, since she could re-member the original versions of songs that were being covered, wasn't happy about it.[114]

In the spring of 1989, *Advertising Age* interviewed many advertising and commercial music personnel about their favorite, and most disliked, uses of music in television commercials. Predictably, opinions varied on specific songs, as well as on more general questions. One interviewee said, "I don't think there is any music too sacred for appropriate use in a commercial. It depends on the product and the usage. It is very easy to be crass and blasphe-mous." The perennial question about the efficacy of using preexisting music in commercials was also raised. One composer said, "To use existing music in a commercial detracts from that music's original meaning. I understand the value that a well-known piece of music can add to a commercial, but at what price? The music loses value, creativity is stifled and often the consumer is insulted and boycotts the product that ruined his favorite song." Another ob-served, "The use of hit songs in advertising is here to stay. Rather than belittle that fact, we jingle composers should try harder to be the ones who write to-morrow's hit songs."[115]

One advertising agency music director, justifying the use of 1960s music in commercials, said, "You get some kind of immediate awareness when a voice comes on that you or I might know. You turn around and run back to your TV and say, 'Wow! What the hell is that?'"[116] The president of a group that measures psychological response to advertising said of the use of 1960s music:

When you get into the music of the 1960s, it triggers a time in the listener when defenses were much lower than they are now. It was a time of lessened discipline, when people were concerned with protest and getting high. When you use the voices of that time in a commercial, it induces a state of increased receptivity to stimuli.[117]

Baby boomers and others with memories of these songs were thus efficiently targeted with music, as were youths with their music.

In the mid-1990s, Mercedes attempted to reach a clientele younger than its fifty-one-year-old male median by lowering its prices and licensing Janis Joplin's "Oh, Lord, Won't You Buy Me a Mercedes Benz." A thirty-eight-year-old San Francisco banking executive who had bought his first Mercedes in 1994 said of the ad that "it's a riot; my wife sang right along with the ad" the first time they heard it.[118] Licensing continues to the present, with the music industry happily complicit, charging fee after fee; I will discuss this practice in greater detail in the following chapter.[119]

Let's recall, by way of conclusion, how the practice of licensing not only represents the growing closeness of the music and marketing industries, motivated by increased attention to the bottom line in the decade of the 1980s. The revitalized emphasis on consumption in the 1980s also meant a greater attention to profits. Market segmentation, facilitated by the rise of cable television, was a strategy to increase profits. The fascination for the hip and the cool was so powerful that it reshaped not only advertisements and the corporate culture that produced them, but capitalism itself, as discussed in the previous chapter. Today, as one music production company worker told me, most such companies barely break even, and that is the norm. Money is still being made, of course, but only at the very top. Virtually everyone else, including musicians, is struggling.

What's-his-name painted the Sistine Chapel not because he
was a religious nut but because that was his job. I don't understand the concept of selling out.
                    —Lance Jensen, co-owner of Modernista!, 2001

Marketers are increasingly becoming the Medicis of music.
                    —Stuart Elliott, *New York Times*, 2009

8

Conquering (the) Culture

The Changing Shape of the Cultural Industries
in the 1990s and After

Introduction

While popular musicians had been involved with the advertising industry for decades before the 1980s, because of the
effect of MTV and the popularity of portable stereo units
such as the Sony Walkman, released in the United States in
1980, the use of music in advertising was on the rise in the
mid-1980s, including the use of music with known musicians, as the previous chapter examined. One advertising
agency executive said that nearly all of his agency's commercials contained music in the mid-1980s, whereas just
five years previously, only about half of its commercials
had music.[1] So much music was employed for advertising that in the late 1980s, *Advertising Age's* resident critic
Bob Garfield complained about the music having become

ubiquitous in commercials: "It is now one of the five elements: earth, water, wind, fire and jingle." Claiming that 90 percent of commercials featured music, Garfield said that the result was a "terrible cacophony, with a half-dozen competing melodies diluting the impact of any single one." Garfield predicted that some commercials would eschew music altogether only to cut through the clutter, but he advocated a middle road of choosing music that was totally integrated into the commercial.[2]

The rise of the use of music in the 1980s meant that in this period there were increasing signs of the growing closeness of the music and advertising industries. A creative supervisor at the advertising agency Muller Jordan Weiss said, "There's a real meeting of minds between people in the recording industry and the advertising business now. Advertising people and record people talk the same musical language. More and more, I think the two groups are going to become interchangeable."[3] One author noted the number of popular musicians who had been heard in commercials (Sammy Davis Jr., Ray Charles, Frank Sinatra); songwriters such as Richard Adler and Sammy Cahn; and pop/rock stars such as Barry Manilow, Paul Williams, and Melissa Manchester.[4] As composer Billy Davis said in 1984, "Music and advertising are coming closer and closer together. But both sides can do a lot more to help each other communicate a more meaningful message on life."[5]

Some in the industry were beginning to speak increasingly of commercials as recordings in their own right. Gerry Dolezar of Radio Kings, a company that promoted musicians for commercial use, said in 1985:

> I want to get to the point in commercials when bands are listening to my commercials and saying, "Man, did you hear that drum sound? Did you hear how they did this? Did you hear how they did that?" Recording artists are realizing that it's not only doing a bit of music and making a living but trying new things to bring to the record business, or vice versa.[6]

This chapter considers this growing closeness of the advertising and music industries, which was the result of a complex of factors from changes in the law to shifting attitudes toward consumption in American culture, and how the infatuation with the hip and the cool has become not just the conquest of cool, as Thomas Frank has argued, but the conquest of the culture itself: making advertising cool.[7]

Changes in the Cultural Industries

Let me begin with a consideration of the passage of the 1996 Communications Act, which lessened restrictions on radio station ownership. There was inevitably a trend toward monopoly, with the top four radio station owners broadcasting to almost half of all listeners, and the top ten owners broadcasting to almost two-thirds of listeners a decade later.[8]

This consolidation has had a number of other ramifications: local DJs are disappearing as the monopolies attempt to cut costs by prerecording DJ talk and broadcasting it in several cities; playlists have been greatly restricted as a result of increasing market research; few stations venture beyond playing the same handful of hits;[9] Clear Channel coerces musicians into performing at its concert venues by threatening to withhold airplay. Most artists comply.[10] Also in the broadcasting field, MTV is playing fewer videos and airing more programs, further limiting musicians' access to the airwaves.[11]

The consolidation of playlists and decline in videos aired by MTV has meant that the old stigma about allowing one's music to be used in commercials evaporated almost overnight. The executive creative director of Deutch, Los Angeles, observed in 2005, "The biggest change is the willingness. The sell-out stigma is gone."[12] Peter Nicholson at Deutch, New York, added, "The old cliché that the artist 'sold out' doesn't apply in this situation, because it is a harmonious relationship that is built on the truth of popular culture's perception of the music and the brand. The music is cool. The brand is cool. And both can become part of the DNA of how a person defines him- or herself."[13] This has meant that advertising agencies are more in control of musicians' work than in the past. The creative director at Arnold Worldwide said in 2002, "When artists fight with agencies because they think they're compromising their art, that lasts about two seconds. We're paying way too much for that kind of prima donna [behavior]."[14] So pervasive has the use of preexisting popular music—and even new songs—been in the media that the new measure of success for popular musicians today is no longer registered in radio airplay or even sales, charts, or signing a contract with a major record label; one artist's manager told a music producer at an advertising agency in New York in 2008 that his client had had a terrific year—"a 'Grey's Anatomy' [television show] placement, two ad placements and a possible film license."[15]

Finally, another shift was technological. While advertising musicians of a generation ago probably had some classical music training and could read and write music, the rise of digital music technologies in the 1980s meant that those who knew them best could better compete for commercial music jobs, as noted in chapter 5. Most of the people I interviewed for this project who had been in the business for more than a couple of decades mentioned technology as one of the biggest changes they witnessed during their time in the industry, transitioning from frequent live recording dates to many fewer. Early adopters of these new technologies tended to be in the realm of popular music; they viewed writing for commercials as something other than their main work, and would frequently play in bands, produce recordings, and perform other kinds of labor in the commercial music world. This flexibility of labor was another factor that hastened the introduction of contemporary popular musics to advertising.

Taken together, these changes mean that there is less variety of music being broadcast than in the past, making it much harder for musicians to find their way to the airwaves.

The picture is not much better in the music industry, which, like radio, is in a state of near monopoly. Yet this industry is in trouble. For a variety of reasons, there has been a noticeable drop in CD sales. It is not clear how much this is due to the decline in variety of music played on the radio or digital piracy, but the statistics are striking: there has been a steady decrease since 2000 in sales of CDs, down nearly 50 percent in 2008 from 1999, and the decline is continuing.[16]

Other factors were at play in the music industry in this period. The development of high-end digital technology meant that operating a professional recording studio is more expensive than ever, with the result that the cost of producing an album is higher than ever. In the past, labels could offset production costs such as these by using their high-selling acts to subsidize those musicians who sold moderately well, but the music industry has by and large dropped bands it doesn't expect to make much money in order to concentrate instead on blockbusters. And, finally, record labels have tightened promotion budgets, making it harder for bands to find an audience.

Enter Alternative Music

And licensing of preexisting music continues.[17] A new surge in licensing occurred beginning in the 1980s in part because of the entrance of rock and pop musicians into the realm of advertising. Licensing has become an important aspect of the advertising music business, another way of effecting Frank's "conquest of cool," the conversion by the advertising industry of rebellion into hip salesmanship.[18] Licensing to some extent displaced advertising music specialists, who either left the business or learned how to become more flexible workers in the commercial music realm. By 2002, if not earlier, record labels were hiring "strategic marketing" executives whose job is to place recordings in films and television shows.[19] Advertising agencies learned to be on the lookout for new music.

The Warner Special Products A&R (artists and repertoire) film and TV manager said in 2000:

> It's funny, you have creative guys at ad agencies in New York scouring used record bins in record stores and taking albums that just look interesting even though they have no idea what they sound like. They'll take them home, listen to them and, if they like it, call us. That's how you get a Buzzcocks song on a TV commercial. We have gotten some really interesting requests, such as an Aphex Twin track for a Bank of America commercial. It worked really well.[20]

Newer music, rather than music from baby boomers' youth, started to make its way into commercials by the 1990s as a younger generation of workers in advertising began to assume positions of authority. The signal event for putting nonmainstream music on the mental maps of advertisers was Lollapalooza II, a traveling music festival of alternative music groups that toured twenty-seven cities in the summer of 1992. Bob Chippardi, president of Concrete Marketing Inc., in New York City, which promotes alternative bands, said at the time, "I would think there would be some smart marketers and advertising guys on Madison Avenue who saw Lollapalooza and said, 'Hey, why don't we tap into that?'"[21]

And tap into it they did. With the structural, bureaucratic, legal, and technological changes described earlier, all the pieces were in place for alternative musics to enter the mainstream—not via record label marketing, radio, or MTV, but commercials, a development unthinkable only a few years prior. Additionally, new advertising strategies that sold lifestyles rather than products helped television commercials start to become much more interesting beginning in the 1980s, rendering commercials so much more artistic that musicians were less reluctant to permit their music to be used in them.

Mainly, however, it was the lack of a radio outlet that made many musicians feel as though they had no option but to license their music for use in commercials. According to one independent ("indie") rock musician whose decision to license his music saved his band, "Radio is controlled by this huge industry. Ads are controlled by a few creative people. They probably did art in college. Maybe they were college radio programmers."[22]

Jim Powers, cofounder of the Minty Fresh label, admitted the difficulty of making his bands known in 2002.

> Is it a better world? I don't think so, but meanwhile I have bands that need to tour. My bands now are completely open to having their songs as part of television commercials. Seven or eight years ago, it was unseemly to even bring it up. At the time it didn't seem necessary, because there was still a sense that radio was willing to take a chance on adventurous music. That's not true anymore, so you have to look for other ways to get the music out there.[23]

The alternative musics used in television commercials were occasionally composed for a particular ad. But most of the time the music was licensed, and independent record labels (the main purveyors of this music) found that licensing is a growing part of their business. A senior vice president of visual marketing and licensing of Astralwerks, a small record label with some major bands such as the Chemical Brothers, said in 2002:

> In the past two years [advertising] is one of the areas that has been exploding. The money [in the music business] is not what it used to be. And there is more money in advertising than in licensing to film and TV. Subsequently [sic] artists are lending themselves to sponsorship and product endorsement. . . . Record labels have to look into other ways to generate revenue and ad companies spend a lot of money in media. . . . [Also] television commercials have become a lot more worldly and edgy. There are some amazing commercials that people want to see.[24]

Advertising agency creative personnel defend their use of alternative musics, most claiming that it is simply a form of corporate sponsorship. Lance Jensen, who cofounded a hot agency and is a fan of alternative music, said, "What's-his-name painted the Sistine Chapel not because he was a religious nut but because that was his job. I don't understand the concept of selling out. If you've been taking guitar lessons since you were five years old, why shouldn't you make some money?"[25]

It was probably *Play*, the 1999 album by Moby, one of the biggest names in techno music, that alerted musicians to the promise of licensing. V2, Moby's label, signed over a hundred licenses for songs on *Play* in North America alone, garnering nearly one million dollars for Moby; the album went multi-platinum.[26] Elsewhere, early in 2003, an official at the label said, "One year ago, and even with Moby's success, none of my co-workers were focusing on this area. But this has drastically changed internally. Now I'm being asked why Underworld's music or Puretone's 'Addicted to Bass' are not being used in commercials. It's been a complete 180."[27] One British advertising agency, Bartle Bogle Hegarty (BBH), even established an in-house publishing company so it could license its songs to other advertisers and reuse them.[28]

Advertisers also realized that if they made an obscure band into a hit, their taste and perspicacity would enhance their standing in the eyes of potential customers. According to an executive producer / creative director at a music production company in California in 2003, "Breaking bands [i.e., introducing them to the public] in commercials is definitely the new trend. It brought labels and advertising closer together. Advertisers are now, more than ever, interested in finding and breaking bands because it brings more attention to their brand."[29] It also brought more attention to advertisers as arbiters of taste, a position they increasingly seemed to enjoy and acknowledge. Emblematic of this position was the July 2004 cover of *Creativity*, one of the main trade magazines of the advertising industry, which showed the 1980s band Survivor serenading a pajama-clad New York City advertising agency creative director in his kitchen, seeking work.

The advertising industry isn't simply breaking bands, however. In the face of the diminished opportunities provided by radio and MTV, some people in advertising were attempting to reconfigure television commercials as an alternative site for presenting new music. For example, Saatchi & Saatchi licensed a track by the DJ Fatboy Slim designed to appeal to teenagers. A music director at the agency said in 1999, "It was music that our target market would recognize, but it wasn't something you were going to find at the top of the charts. In some ways that makes it more interesting to the teens. It's just the fact that you're buying into the equity of a piece of music that teens are going to think is cool."[30] By this point in the history of marketing, teenagers were being marketed to with great efficiency.

Yet musicians and others in the music industry wondered how much their own creativity was being affected. A president/owner of a music production company asked in 2003, "Are we trying to make commercials, or are we trying to make pop promos? The record business is rubbishy at the moment, so record companies have found the best way of exposure is through commercials. It starts becoming more of a commercial for the band than the product."[31]

Music

Among alternative musics, techno music was hot for a time, and was mainly, though not exclusively, employed in automobile commercials. Examining the use of its music at the peak of its trendiness—the late 1990s and early 2000s—gives evidence of how music frequently associated with the underground was finding its way to television commercials.[32] One advertising creative staffer who had used techno in advertisements said proudly in 2002, "The music you hear in automobile commercials is better than most of the music you can hear on the radio."[33] Techno musics of various kinds became so ubiquitous as the sound of the underground in automobile commercials that in the fall of 2002, the L.A. Office RoadShow, an annual gathering of companies with licensable properties and firms looking for a deal, had to move to a bigger venue; the organizer said that all the record labels asked how many car companies were coming.[34]

Volkswagen

By all accounts, it was Volkswagen that set the trend of using new and interesting music in television advertisements. For years, Volkswagen had been experiencing lagging sales in North America and wanted to attempt a comeback. It hired Arnold Worldwide of Boston in 1995 to bring its sales and brand image out of the doldrums. Arnold assembled the usual market research information on Volkswagen's audience and discovered that Volkswagen drivers tended to be younger than its competitors, earned more money, and possessed more education. Arnold devised a campaign to appeal to these existing buyers, strategically targeting this group rather than attempting to reach a broad market.[35]

It was perhaps the commercials for the New Beetle in 1998 that awakened viewers to Volkswagen's new "Drivers Wanted" campaign. Liz Vanzura, director of marketing for Volkswagen, North America, said in 1998:

We definitely wanted music that was contemporary and that had broad appeal. That's why we did five spots. We wanted to be sure that we covered with certain of our spots our baby-boomer contingency, the folks who had some recall or affiliation with Volkswagen, but we also wanted to have some types of music that had some appeal to the youth market as well. . . . There's really no nostalgic-oriented music in this. . . . We used very contemporary songs, but things that we thought, no matter what age, no matter what demographic you were, you'd think this was cool.[36]

The music of these five ads was eclectic, to say the least, provided by five UK acts: Hurricane #1, Stereolab, the Orb, Spiritualized, and Fluke.

Perhaps the most remarked-upon of the new VW ads featured music by the late English musician Nick Drake, used in an ad that demonstrates Arnold Worldwide's changing attitude toward music.[37] Jonathan Dayton (now famous for codirecting the 2006 hit film *Little Miss Sunshine*), who cofilmed the Volkswagen commercial, envisioned Drake's song "Pink Moon" not as selling a car but as a song that people in the ad might be listening to themselves, a strategy that is employed in all the ads in the "Drivers Wanted" campaign. Dayton said in 2001, "It's acknowledging the place music has in people's lives. It's not meant as an endorsement."[38] The commercial employs Drake's intensely personal and introspective music accompanying nocturnal scenes of young people driving and enjoying the night sky, arriving at a restaurant, then, presumably, departing without entering, back on the road (example 8.1).

By any measure, Volkswagen's commercials in the "Drivers Wanted" campaign were hugely successful. Sales were way up, as was brand loyalty and what is known in the industry as "brand buzz." The buzz generated by the music used in the ads resulted in a 2001 CD entitled *Street Mix: Music from Volkswagen Commercials* (volume 1), which was for a time available from Volkswagen's website for ten dollars. This disc contains ten tracks that are well known from their advertisements, including Nick Drake's, as well as music by the techno band Hooverphonic, Charles Mingus, and others. The liner notes contain little information except some details about the songs (though without saying which albums they're from). There is an introductory note, however, that is suggestive: "We chose these bands because they had something to say, because they felt like kindred spirits. When our creative team set forth to convey the essence of Volkswagen, we needed music that had soul. Well, we got soul and here's 12 tracks of it. Enjoy."[39]

Volkswagen also began an online radio station at its website (which has since been removed). If you visited it, you would have seen the text: "MUSIC'S BEEN GOOD TO US. So we thought we'd return the favor."[40] Volkswagen offered four channels with music from its advertisements, as well as music not on its ads. While the music played, the album cover appeared in the corner of the tuner application, and you could click on it to purchase. You could also click on links that recalled old advertisements, though the website wouldn't play those ads' music.

Mitsubishi

As startling as Volkswagen's successes with music were, it may be that Mitsubishi, whose advertising agency Deutch LA essentially imitated Arnold Worldwide's strategy, had achieved more notice for its advertising music.

In 2002, reflecting on the success of its campaign called "Wake Up and Drive," Pierre Gagnon, president and chief operating officer of Mitsubishi Motor Sales of America, said, "We realized that Generation Y would be reaching driving age soon. We knew if we were going to grow, we needed to reach them."[41] Gagnon said that Mitsubishi had the second-youngest demographic of all foreign automakers in the United States, behind only Volkswagen: the average age of Mitsubishi owners at the time was thirty-eight; 38 percent of its customers were under thirty-five. Gagnon said, "Our cars are for people who think young. People who drive Mitsubishis may look different, but they all have a common youthful spirit. They're part of a club or family of Mitsubishi drivers."[42]

Eclipse: "Fun" (2001)

Eric Hirshberg, executive creative director of the advertising agency Deutch LA, said in 2001, "We had this very simple idea: Let's make the Mitsubishi owners into a cool club. If they were all singing a Britney Spears song, the specialness of driving a Mitsubishi would have gone away."[43] Instead, Deutch used a song called "Start the Commotion" by the British hip-hop/big-beat band the Wiseguys, in an ad for the Mitsubishi Eclipse that debuted in March 2001. (Big beat is a subgenre of techno that emerged in the 1990s and was meant as a return to simple dance music as opposed the more intellectual kind of techno in vogue earlier in the 1990s; the Wiseguys was a "band" consisting of Touche [real name Theo Keating] and Regal [real name Paul Eve], whose music consisted only of samples—that is, exact digital copies of recorded music.)[44]

Deutch's strategy stemmed from the simple desire to attempt to use music in ads that drivers might actually listen to. Its concept was to show what people, especially young people, actually do in their cars, such as singing along with the stereo, as in its ad called "Start the Commotion," which shows actors moving to the music. Deutch LA executives actually drove around in their cars and thought about the music they were listening to. According to Eric Hirshberg, "You can't find great driving songs in a conference room. You have to find them in your car."[45] The "Fun" commercial shows young people grooving to the Wiseguys' music in their Mitsubishis (example 8.2).

Mike Sheldon, the general manager of Deutch LA who was the producer of the commercial, claimed that viewers are invited into the hip Mitsubishi club with ads that say, "'Either you take a youthful look on life. Or you buy a Toyota and give up.'"[46] Significantly, the ads in the "Wake Up and Drive" campaign end with the tagline: "Are You In?" Hirshberg said, "Talk to consumers about cars and they rarely talk about the things car companies talk about— even handling and acceleration. They talk about what image they want to project through their cars: which one is me? We've turned Mitsubishi into the first fashion car brand. It's emotional territory that Mitsubishi can, and does, own."[47] *Affinity marketing* is the term used for this kind of advertising. The strategy is to have customers discover the music and then latch onto the car brand to become part of an in-crowd, a peer group of those in the know.

Gagnon said that Mitsubishi's use of popular music was successful. "The most powerful proof is when a DJ comes onto the radio and says, 'And now, the Mitsubishi song.' It's hard to explain the phenomenon. What we're so pleased with is we know we're breaking through when these songs become more popular."[48] And its use of popular music was successful in terms of sales. In the spring of 2003, Mitsubishi claimed that in the past four years—since the company began using popular music in its commercials, sales grew 81 percent.[49] Hirshberg said that his company's aim was for Mitsubishi to be "woven into the popular culture," and it appeared to work.[50] The Wiseguys' album was released in 1999 but wasn't represented on the *Billboard* charts until heard on the Mitsubishi commercial in March 2001.[51] Then, "Start the Commotion" was on *Billboard* magazine's Hot 100 chart for twelve weeks, peaking at number 31 on 25 August 2001.

Eclipse: "Days Go By" (2002)

Later, Dirty Vegas' (a British house music trio) "Days Go By" was used in a Mitsubishi Eclipse ad; the song became a top 15 hit in the summer of 2002. Vincent Picardi, senior vice president and associate creative director at Deutsch LA, the company that developed Mitsubishi's "Are You In?" campaign, says that the idea was to convey the company's youthful image. "We had to find the music that fit the brand; it's a brand that's more youthful. With the Eclipse, using Dirty Vegas (the commercial), was literally moving. It was about having so much fun tooling around and the music comes on that causes some people to sing, and in her case [a young woman passenger in the commercial], break out dancing and pop locking."[52] All while in a Mitsubishi, of course (example 8.3).

According to Hirshberg, using the Dirty Vegas song "gives street cred to Mitsubishi and shows that they are not just a corporation with a big budget, but a brand cool enough to tell you what's new."[53] Vincent Picardi, senior VP / associate creative director of Deutsch, the advertising agency that produced the Mitsubishi ads, said, "We see it as the perfect marriage of commerce and art. Music spurs sales of Mitsubishi cars and vice versa. Mitsubishi understands the eclectic nature of music and how it works with their brand. Artists and labels see what this exposure does for them."[54] Frances Oda, vice president for marketing at Mitsubishi Motor Sales of America, said, "The music has enabled us to get to our target—affluent buyers looking for a more youthful, styled driving experience. We definitely feel it's been working."[55]

For their part, the musicians were pleased. Paul Harris, a member of Dirty Vegas, said, "The ad [for the Mitsubishi Eclipse] helped push our record into everybody's living room. Only now is radio in America starting to play more dance music. So, people seeing the ad on TV, and hearing our music, contacted their local radio stations wanting to hear the song. The power of the people is what helped propel our song to success."[56]

To reinforce its image as a purveyor of hip music, Mitsubishi, like Volkswagen, also produced a compact disc in 2002, using the campaign tagline as its title.

Advertising and the Cultural Industries

These are all relatively clear-cut examples of licensing: one industry purchasing the temporary use of music from another. But in the new millennium, the production of advertising music in commercials had become increasingly intertwined with the production of popular music more generally. Advertising workers weren't simply remembering music of their youth to employ in commercials but were avidly seeking new and unusual music, essentially playing the role that DJs once performed on the radio. As one composer at a New York City music production company told me in 2006, there is no counterculture anymore; there is only culture, and it is made by commercial interests. That is overstating the case, I think, but it is nevertheless clear that the advertising industry enjoys a greater influence over the making of popular culture, perhaps, especially, music—and American culture more generally—than at any time in its history, to the extent that it increasingly drives popular music production. And its ideology of the cool and trendy is becoming increasingly dominant.

Even though many tens of billions of dollars are spent annually on advertising in the United States, the industry was experiencing difficulties even before the onset of the Great Recession in 2007. Because of TiVo and other time-shifting video-recording devices, by the early twenty-first century, advertisers and the advertising industry began to worry that television commercials were no longer being viewed, paving the way for product placement, or what began to be called "advertainment" or "branded entertainment." "The aim," according to an advertising trade press report in 2002, "is to get viewers to actually choose to view ad content by making it as compelling as the programming."[57] In that year, TiVo began offering "advertainment" to its customers. Spending on branded entertainment was over $4 billion in 2005, up from the $3.45 billion spent in 2004; in 1999, by contrast, spending totaled $1.93 billion.[58] In 1994, American Express spent 80 percent of its marketing budget on television advertising, whereas in 2004 it spent only 35 percent. John Hayes, the chief marketing officer at American Express, said, "We have moved out of the 'buying' world and entered the world of content and channel integration in a significant way."[59] Insiders in every corner of the cultural industries seem to be in agreement that this convergence is occurring. Josh Rabinowitz, a senior vice president=director for music producer at Grey Worldwide, who has produced a few commercial recordings (not just recordings of commercials), believes:

> More artists are going to be broken through corporations, with the agencies as
> talent scouts.... The agencies are kind of like the A&R [artists and repertoire,
> a function once assumed by record companies], and the client's blessing is the

green light. My theory is that sooner or later, the record companies will be cut out of part of the process.[60]

Additionally, while workers in the advertising industry have long employed the trope of creativity to describe their own work, they wield the term today as means of arguing for their natural affinity with the entertainment industry. Not until the twenty-first century did this rhetorical strategy appear to gain traction outside the world of advertising. At a 2002 meeting of advertising and content providers, an advertising agency executive told the assembled crowd, "We're not in the business of content or commerce but in creativity. We are in the business of creating brand experiences. Brands are the central focus of what we do. Our industries are moving independently but in the same direction."[61] In 2007, Peter Nicholson, a partner/chief in the advertising agency Deutch, New York concluded an opinion piece in *Billboard* magazine (the main American music trade press weekly, one of many signs of the convergence of the advertising and music industries) by invoking the creativity trope, writing:

> I will end on my bias as to why an ad agency makes for a great partner if you are
> an independent band: creatives [workers on the creative side of the industry,
> as opposed to the business side]. Most agency creatives are artists at heart. And
> in some agencies, they actually get to be more artist than marketer. Creatives
> spend a lot of time making ideas that take on a bit of their own personality.
> So the work becomes personal and not commercial. Or, as I like to say, a lot
> of care has gone into the work. The creatives share the same understanding
> that any artist has: your work is precious and it is personal and must always be
> respected.[62]

The Conquest of Culture

An early example of this latest phase of the convergence of commerce and content occurred in Arnold Worldwide's Volkswagen commercials, which employed Ben Neill, a "downtown" New York City musician well known in the experimental music scene. Neill says that people at Arnold knew his earlier music and that he was hired to produce his sound for their Volkswagen commercials (example 8.4). In the course of writing music for these ads, Arnold produced an extended version of Neill's songs. Then, says Neill, "I got the idea to turn them all into full-length songs. It's a new model for artists to get their work out, in working with labels, brands, and ad agencies."[63] The result was a CD called *Automotive*, which, according to a cover slipped over the disc, "features expanded arrangements of music Ben Neill composed for a series of groundbreaking VW television ads."[64] On the album, there are live vocals and flute, plus Neill and his electronically manipulated trumpet, accompanying animated black-and-white scenes of father and child in and out of the car. Arnold Worldwide designed the cover art for the album, which is a colorized still picture from one of its ads called "Nite Nite." And it designed the liner notes as well, which include a fictitious encounter between Neill and his employers at Arnold, who are represented as hip and easygoing.[65] "Nite Nite" the commercial was recognized by the International Automotive Advertising Awards in 2000.

Neill seemingly rejected a time-honored "downtown" New York position, claiming, "There is no difference between something that is considered art and something that is a commercial. My album is a statement of that."[66] Neill also said:

> It's a real convergence between a brand, an ad agency and a record company and it has worked out really well for me. . . . It gives my music a lot more exposure. That was one of the things that appealed to me when I was doing it because having my music on television means millions of people are becoming familiar with it.[67]

Since these commercials aired, the relationship between popular music and brands has become ever closer. The first major project that marked this new form of the convergence of content and commerce in the realm of popular music was English rock star Sting's decision to appear in a commercial for Jaguar in 2000. The singer's popularity had waned somewhat since his days with the Police, but, nonetheless, as a rock star, he possessed the qualities that advertisers and their agencies frequently seek to exploit. Sting's then manager, Miles Copeland, said that when he first saw the music video of "Desert Rose" (from the album *Brand New Day*), he realized that it was a car commercial, and sent the video to Jaguar's advertising agency, Ogilvy & Mather. Copeland said he presented the deal this way: "If you will make the commercial look like an ad for my record, I'll give it to you free." It was the first time, Copeland said, that a known artist had promoted an unknown song in this way.[68] Jaguar's worldwide director of sales and marketing said, "Once we saw it, we realized the enormous opportunity to produce a television advertisement using footage from the video. Sting was delighted to become part of Jaguar's mystique."[69] The singer, in a press release, said, "The director proposed a number of cars to be used in the video and I chose the Jaguar S-type. It's a beautiful car and it evokes the feeling of style and success we were trying to achieve."[70] The agreement was that Sting appeared without a fee, in return for excerpts of the video of the song being used in the commercial. The resulting commercial looks much like a music video, with Sting, musicians, and dancers given as much time as the car (with Sting in it, of course; example 8.5). The commercials' titles read: "Everyone dreams of becoming a rock star / What then do rock stars dream of?" In 2003, an *Advertising Age* article entitled "Sting-Jaguar Deal Still Serves as Model for the Music World" wrote of the "reverent references" people in the industry still make to this arrangement.[71]

The marketing expenditures in this case tell an equally interesting story. The label had planned to spend $1.8 million just to market the "Desert Rose" single, which included $800,000 to produce a video of it. Jaguar spent $8 million to broadcast the commercial, much more than is usually spent in music marketing. According to *Advertising Age*, the song received little airplay before the commercial was broadcast, and the sales expectations for the album were about a million copies. But after the commercial was aired, sales soared, and it became Sting's biggest solo album at that time, selling four million copies in the United States alone. Jaguar enjoyed a surge in sales as well, particularly among younger buyers.[72]

Subsequent campaigns have insinuated brands ever more completely into music production and vice versa. For example, on the Coors Light "Love Songs" spot from 2002, which garnered a good deal of attention in the industry, the musicians omitted any reference to the beer. One of the musicians, John Godsey, said that they wanted to make the performance "sound like a real band" so that "people would respond to it as a song, not an ad" (example 8.6).[73] Writing songs instead of jingles isn't that new, going back at least to the early 1970s (the most famous example being "I'd Like to Teach the World to Sing" for Coca-Cola in 1971), but songs that don't mention the product are a twenty-first-century trend.

Major brands have also embarked on promotion and sponsorship deals with musicians on a scale much larger than those discussed earlier. In 2002, Toyota promoted Phil Collins's CD *Testify* and one of its songs, which was used in a commercial for the brand's Avalon model. Toyota employed a caption in the style of MTV to identify the song "Can't Stop Loving You" in the first few seconds of its commercial. The record company affixed Toyota stickers on five hundred thousand copies of the CD, Toyota's logo appeared on posters advertising the CD as well as on related merchandise, and the record company located promotional materials in record stores advertising the Avalon. According to the senior vice president for marketing at the record company, because of the decline in music sales, "We are looking for new and innovative ways to get the music out to the public. We are very proactive in this area. Toyota is the most collaborative partner we ever had. This is real co-marketing."[74] A year later, DaimlerChrysler signed a fourteen-million-dollar multiyear contract with singer Céline Dion, who appeared in its TV commercials (example 8.7); the company also sponsored her long-running show in Las Vegas with its name emblazoned on the marquee.[75]

Following arrangements such as these, musicians' relationships to major brands began to become even more complex and intertwined. In 2003, musicians Common and Mýa recorded "Real Compared to What" for a Coca-Cola commercial, a cover of a 1960s protest song by Eugene McDaniels with new lyrics by Mýa (just one of many commercial adaptations of 1960s political music; example 8.8[76]). She released the full version of the song on her subsequent album, *Moodring*, the same year. Steve Berman, the head of marketing for Interscope/Geffen/A&M, who is a proponent of the convergence of the advertising and music industries, said, "We went to Mýa and Common, not with a product endorsement, but with an idea that would give them exposure while giving Coca-Cola something that would be at the core of their message. From our perspective, it's not a commercial; it's a record and a visual interpretation of that message." Berman acknowledged the decline in CD sales because of illegal downloading and file sharing, but noted, "Music is more popular than ever, but figuring out how to monetize that is difficult. . . . If you tap into a culture, the market is still there." The solution to coping with the decline of sales, he said, was to forge alliances with marketers. "We've decided to work with strong brands where we're targeting a similar audience. We're always challenged by budgets and have to come up with alternative ways to market our artists. A record company can't compete on traditional marketing platforms. For a major release, the entire TV budget might not equal one prime-time spot."[77]

A different approach was employed in an ad for Sprite called "Liquid Freedom," launched in 2005. The commercial shows sweaty basketball players jumping onto the court that morphs into a swimming pool (example 8.9). Human Worldwide was commissioned to write an original song for the commercial, which employed the standard thirty-second version of the song. The song became so popular that Coca-Cola, which owns Sprite, "got excited and wanted to get behind it," according to Marc Altshuler of Human.[78] Human shared the proceeds with Coke. "Instead of paying us the traditional fee for a 30-second spot, which doesn't really apply, they wanted to figure out a way to use their network—POP [point-of-purchase], packaging—to drive people to get this music, and split everything 50–50. It's a pretty unbelievable deal and it was a lot of work," he said.[79] The arrangement Coke struck with Human was to have Sprite's point-of-sale and packaging in over two hundred countries direct people to a website where the song would be available for download. This spot worked well because there was no dialogue, which meant it could play in various countries; Altshuler describes it as a music video. He also attributes the success of the video to web-based searches, which make such videos easy to find; "people discussed 'Pool' in chatrooms, advertising chatrooms, and on blogs," he wrote. And he quoted the director–creative development, Asia, at Coca-Cola, who argued, "Brand content is not pushed at people but requested, downloaded, collected or shared." Altshuler went on to say, "Brands now can drive the culture via the underground and the Internet. Websites such as YouTube, Google and eBay can function as two-way streets for brands: Brands discover who their consumers really are, and consumers let brands know what they want."[80]

Another development is that, while advertisers and marketers have occasionally employed hip-hop music since at least the mid-1980s, the music has become increasingly common. In the spring of 2003, Pepsi sponsored a series of radio programs called *Project X*, a hip-hop show aimed at the elusive Generation Y demographic (elusive in part because observers place people born anywhere between the mid-1970s and the early 2000s in it). Every commercial was for Pepsi, and the musicians sprinkled the brand's name in their broadcast conversations. "DJs are the key influencers in hip-hop—they dictate trends," said the executive in charge.[81] At least eight of the top twenty *Billboard* hip-hop singles that year referred to Pepsi.[82] McDonald's tried something of the same strategy in 2005 when it hired an entertainment-marketing firm to encourage hip-hop musicians to incorporate references to the Big Mac into their songs. Said the director of brand entertainment strategy at McDonald's,

"The stars of hip-hop have become brands. This partnership reflects our appreciation and respect for the most dominant youth culture in the world." This strategy drew criticism from the Campaign for a Commercial-Free Childhood, however, which felt that the resulting commercials would target children, who "won't know the rappers are being paid to push Big Macs—these 'adversongs' are inherently deceptive." McDonald's, of course, disagreed: "We believe that the McDonald's brand is so omnipresent already in America that having it in music, having it in TV, having it in movies, is no more intrusive than anything else children experience nowadays."[83] The deal Maven Strategies (a firm that brings together musicians and marketers) made with McDonald's and the musicians was that the musicians could choose for themselves how to mention the sandwich in their songs, but McDonald's would have final approval.[84] Maven is paid as a consultant in these arrangements; the musicians receive nothing up front, but receive one dollar to five dollars each time the song is played on the radio.[85]

The popular music practice of remixing—taking a preexisting track and modifying it digitally by adding other sounds and altering it in other ways—has also found its way into advertising music. *Advertising Age*, in a story about the ten most successful product launches in 2003, listed the Sprite ReMix as its number 9: "Coca-Cola re-established the hipness of the flagging Sprite brand with a smart PR-drive launch for its tropically-flavored extension. Backed with a Memorial Day launch infused with rule-breaking hip-hop icons and a 50-city sampling tour that included a remix recording studio, the line helped boost trademark Sprite by 7% through November."[86] The premise behind Sprite ReMix is that it is like a musical remix: it is always different. Before Sprite ReMix was launched, Coca-Cola distributed the drink through DJs, giving away three million bottles at various events, and hosted a party with P. Diddy at the MTV Music Video Awards. This strategy of giving the product to people who are called "lifestyle influencers" resulted in a 90 percent awareness with children twelve to eighteen and increased sales by 8.6 percent.[87] Coca-Cola and its advertising agency have even been willing to give up the most valued commodity in the world of marketing—brand stability, which is thought to engender brand loyalty—in order to sell their product. Willingness to jettison this hallowed idea grew out of Sprite's conversations with young people about the drink and popular culture. "With kids today, things change so quickly, it really does tie back to developing a brand that's about change. It almost doesn't matter if it's a berry flavor or a tropical flavor [the first two flavors of the drink]—

it's the whole image of ReMix," said Rob Stone of Cornerstone Promotion, which handled the Sprite campaign (example 8.10).[88] The commercial depicts Latinos, African Americans, Muhammad Ali, a DJ, all quickly intercut, and accompanied by hip-hop music.

In a bid to lure consumers deeper into the web spun by brands, in the summer of 2008, McDonald's resurrected its famous "Two all-beef patties, special sauce . . ." jingle from the mid-1970s, but instead of enticing professional musicians to cover it, remix it, or incorporate it somehow into their music, McDonald's attempted to cash in on viewers' memories of the commercial by inviting consumers to make their own remixes of it, which is becoming an increasingly common strategy.[89] A 2007 survey of one thousand Americans revealed that 80 percent know the ingredients of a Big Mac, which the jingle lists.[90] McDonald's chief marketing officer said that the jingle was "something that many of us grew up with," and that reusing it is "a great way to capture the fun and the personality of Big Mac and the brand, so we're very excited." McDonald's advertising agency produced an updated version of the jingle for a television commercial that advertised the jingle contest, directing viewers to a MySpace website where there were multiple versions of the updated jingle by various artists in different styles.[91] Viewers of the website were encouraged to make their own remix of the jingle, and all visitors to the site could vote on their favorites. A panel of three judges decided on the winner, whose version of the jingle was to be used in a television commercial.[92] The MySpace website sorted the uploaded videos by "genre"—country, Latino, hip-hop, R&B, and rock. Those interested in making their own remix could download an "audio kit" that included the updated version of the jingle, as well as many snippets of beats and other sounds that could be incorporated into one's own remix. Those I listened to (a random sample) tended to eschew these prefabricated sounds and simply devised their own version of the jingle. The winner, out of 12,280 entries, was a hip-hop version, which was aired for a week on MTV in July 2008 (example 8.11).[93]

The erosion of meaningful distinctions between the advertising and music industries has resulted in a convergence not only of content and commerce but also of the marketing of popular musicians. According to Stuart Elliott, it is timing that distinguishes the practices of the present from those of the past, for popular musicians today time the release of recordings with advertising campaigns in which they appear. Elliott cites as an example a commercial for Hewlett-Packard that featured the music of Gwen Stefani and included her and two other members of her band, wearing much the same clothes as in her music video; the same person directed the music video and the commercial (example 8.12).[94]

The 2008 Chris Brown top 10 song "Forever" employed the phrase "Double your pleasure, double your fun," a famous line from a jingle for Wrigley's Doublemint gum. The video was nominated for an MTV Video Music Award's Music Video of the Year. Wrigley in fact commissioned the song; later, a commercial for the gum featuring Brown appeared (example 8.13). According to a trade press article, this was the first time that a song had been "seeded" in a "real" song before being employed in a commercial.[95] According to the marketer who brokered the deal, "Using entertainment assets to introduce products is a platform that needed to get exploited. The lines needed to be blurred. When done correctly, there's consumer acceptance."[96] Elsewhere, he defined selling out as creating an inauthentic relationship between popular culture and a product.[97] The commercial was later pulled after Brown was arrested for assaulting his girlfriend, to which he subsequently pleaded guilty.[98]

Record labels and advertising agencies have moved closer together in yet another way. Sony BMG started an in-house advertising agency called Arcade Creative Group, which opened in April 2008. It can draw on the label's vast catalog of recordings to use in commercials it produces.[99] In July of the same year, the advertising agency Euro RSCG acquired a majority stake in a firm called The:Hours, an independent record label.[100] And new companies are springing up that produce both recordings and advertisements. Decon, one such firm, employs workers who have backgrounds in both the advertising and music industries, and the company produces recordings as well as commercials. Its cofounder described the firm's approach thus: "Our whole model now is to figure out how to incorporate what we've developed with our music and entertainment relationships and apply it to branded content to connect with the youth market. We want to use brands as a launching pad for our talent, and vice versa."[101]

What the foregoing shows is that there are now myriad ways that advertising, through its association with musicians from many different genres, is infiltrating the world of popular music production and dissemination: sponsoring tours, commissioning songs that are not obviously advertising music, inviting consumers to be a part of the music-making process through remixing, promoting musicians' recordings, and still more.[102] Through this penetration of the field of production of popular music, the advertising industry is able to continue to promote its ideology of the importance of trendiness by attaching itself to the hip, the cool, or even, as I will discuss next, creating trends.[103]

Trendspotting → Trendsetting

Until this moment of the convergence of comment and content, advertising agencies saw their job as following and attempting to capitalize on trends; as one executive who worked on the Pepsi account said bluntly in the late 1970s, "Pepsi doesn't create trends, it follows them."[104] Advertising agencies expend a great deal of effort trying to keep up with trends, though the Internet has made researching them easier than in the past. But spending time with real youth still matters. Tom Julian, a trend analyst at Fallon in New York, said in 2004, "We have to go from Tucson to Los Angeles to Vegas to Pittsburgh and live in student unions vicariously, [and] spend time in retail settings."[105]

To help identify existing trends, the advertising and marketing industry has increasingly turned toward social scientists and social science methodologies such as ethnography ("Ethnography is hot," proclaimed a special supplement to *Advertising Age* in the midst of this trend); there is a growing number of publications on this subject aimed at audiences in the advertising and marketing industry, and there are more and more articles devoted to the subject in the trade press.[106] There is also a growing number of scholarly or semischolarly guides that are edited by and/or include articles by trained anthropologists.[107]

A 2007 article noted the increased problem for marketers in focus groups: so many Americans are now so complexly identified, with multiple self-representations (with "different profiles posted on MySpace, Match.com and Wikipedia," wrote an academically trained anthropologist now in the advertising industry), that it is difficult for marketers to know just whom they are dealing with in focus groups. Thus, according to this same writer, "in this environment, ethnography is more vital than ever in helping marketers understand what's really going on in the subcultures where brands live, flourish, fade and regenerate."[108]

The search for trends has produced a new industry that serves the advertising and marketing industry and whose sole function is to spot trends and provide information for marketers. Irma Zandl, one of the founders of this industry, owns a firm that recruits three thousand people between the ages of eight and twenty-four to investigate what is cool and trendy. These workers are sought out mostly in malls, where they fill out questionnaires about their tastes. The staff at the Zandl Group publishes the results in a "Youth Market / Young Adult Trend Tracking Report" or "The Hot Sheet"; subscription costs are eighteen thousand dollars per year.[109] The *Hot Sheet* is a slick publication that features stories on hot musicians, beverages, and so forth, as well as brief profiles of young people, including their taste in music, beverages, and much more.[110] As a the consumer insights director at McCann/Erickson in Thailand said at a symposium on "The Selling Power of Song" in 1999, teenage behavior can be affected in four ways: "belonging, sources of cool, hanging out, and language. You can access all these things through music."[111]

It is clear, however, that the gold standard for an advertising agency is for its client's brand to become part of popular culture, not simply to emulate it; workers in the industry speak of this in matter-of-fact terms. An article in *Adweek* from late 2004 said, "Considering its ephemeral nature, advertising might be the perfect venue for tapping into—even creating—fads and trends."[112] Industry insiders say much the same thing. A cofounder of an advertising agency in Boston asked in 2001, "Did Pepsi sell more the day after Britney Spears's 90-second Super Bowl commercial? I don't know. But Pepsi's job is to be part of the pop culture."[113] In trying to reach a younger crowd by sponsoring various popular culture acts and events, the president and chief executive at a major advertising firm said in 2005, "We want the pop culture dialogue to include Burger King. . . . The mission is not about generating awareness of Burger King . . . because everyone knows Burger King. We want to make a connection. We want to make Burger King the kind of brand people would want to wear on a T-shirt."[114]

And people in advertising agencies increasingly view themselves not just as supporting but as being part of, contributing to, popular culture. Peter Nicholson, Deutch, New York partner/chief, said in 2007:

> The pulse of pop culture isn't dead; it's very much alive and being nurtured in advertising agencies. . . . [Advertising] has always been in touch with popular culture, but now, more than ever, advertising agencies have become more in tune with the beat of pop culture and how that applies to the brands. And, all brands have a role in popular culture. Some have niche roles; others have a broader, more significant reach.

Nicholson decries the old assumption in which music was the "starlet" and "sponsorship was the groupie that got a prime photo op to flaunt around."

> That old model always annoyed me because it discounted the importance of the brand's stature in popular culture. . . . The brand's position in pop culture is more powerful than the music or the artist. So the right brand and music in partnership would provide better and faster exposure for the music and the brand.[115]

Other people in the industry take what one could call a historical-revisionist view, as does Josh Rabinowitz. "Historically, the worlds of branding and advertising have been the underwriters of much of pop culture. In 2008 and beyond, much of pop culture, especially music, may begin to underwrite and rewrite the path of advertising and branding, changing the dynamics of that equation from subsidizer to the subsidized."[116]

It is now the case that musicians can try to attach themselves to brands for qualities that they desire instead of the other way around. In the late 2000s, hip-hop star Common struck a deal with Microsoft, which sponsored his tour and featured him in commercials. When asked why he wanted to work with Microsoft, Common, who seems to regard himself as a brand, said that

> Microsoft is classy, it's a timeless brand, and it means something to the world, internationally, and I felt like that's the direction of what I want Common to be, to be honest. I want to be timeless, I want to be international and those are the things I feel like I'm working toward now. I was able to team up with them for some of those reasons. . . . I liked creatively where they wanted to go.[117]

And Will.I.Am, of the Black Eyed Peas, was named director of creative innovation for Intel in 2011. Said Johan Jervoe, the company's vice president for creative marketing:

> I don't want him to be the promo man. This is not meant for him to say, "Here's the latest and greatest product from Intel and go buy it." There's an overlapping creativity, understanding, desire and expertise that he brings with him. While he may go out and talk about some of the products we'll be coming up with, it was clear to both of us that he needed to be an employee and at the center of these products' creation.[118]

Musicians are thus branding themselves as any other commodity; appearing in commercials, or allowing their music to be used in commercials, is part of the branding process. Selling out is no longer an issue; some in the industry are saying that it's no longer possible.

While advertising agencies do attempt to follow trends so closely that they might be able to set trends, introduce previously unknown or little-known music to a broad public, most of the time, the use of advertising music in commercials is part of a complex series of negotiations between advertiser and audiences. Music is chosen not simply to appeal to a targeted demographic but to signal to that demographic that the advertiser knows it. A marketing executive told Joyce Kurpiers that with the music his company uses in its commercials, "we want them to know we understand who they are and what they need."[119] And, despite the limitations of VALS and other forms of market research, they pretty much do.

Having spent over a decade researching and writing this book, I have slowly come to the conclusion that there is no longer a meaningful distinction to be made between "popular music" and "advertising music"—virtually all musics today that are heard outside the school or church (or Irish bars) are produced in commercial circumstances. My students now tell me that only when the lyrics begin do they realize that a radio commercial is a commercial and not a "real" song. The sounds of capitalism are everywhere.

The point of a proper and effective intersection of the labels, publishers and advertisers is on the not too distant horizon. Hopefully, the actual music, as opposed to the commodity of the music, will be king again.

—Josh Rabinowitz, senior vice president / director for music
at Grey Worldwide (advertising agency), 2007

If you don't have originality, you're not in the advertising business.

—Steve Karmen, interview by author, 2009

9

New Capitalism, Creativity, and the New Petite Bourgeoisie

In this final chapter, I analyze the world of the production of advertising music as a field of cultural production in Pierre Bourdieu's sense, a field populated mainly by what Bourdieu has called the new petite bourgeoisie, whose members adhere to ideologies of creativity and the hip and the cool and who, because of their influence on the culture more generally, are involved in a project of reshaping today's capitalism—which, drawing on Richard Sennett, I will call new capitalism—according to their ideologies, tastes, and practices.[1] A central ideological trope is that of creativity, which serves not art but as a form of symbolic capital, an ideological marker of the privileged members of this group.

The New Petite Bourgeoisie

First, let me address the question of the social group involved in making advertisements and music for them, at least for the period of the last few decades, since people in the industry in this period have been available for interviews. One of the first treatments of this new group appeared in 1979, when Barbara Ehrenreich and John Ehrenreich advanced the notion of the "professional-managerial class," or PMC, which they define as "salaried mental workers who do not own the means of production and whose major function in the social division of labor may be described broadly as the reproduction of capitalist culture and capitalist class relations."[2] Their list of professions includes, interestingly enough for my purposes, workers in advertising. For the Ehrenreichs, the PMC began in the late nineteenth to early twentieth centuries, but articulated strongly with the New Left and the student movement of the 1960s.

Many other writers followed with similar characterizations. Scott Lash and John Urry, for example, considered the American service class, which possesses many of the same characteristics as the PMC.[3] For others, this group was the new middle class.[4] And some have noted that this group has a generational cast: it is baby boomers, who, when they first started to emerge as a distinct class in the 1980s, were referred to as yuppies.[5] Still others have posited a new social group that is similarly involved in cultural production, whether Robert Reich's "symbolic workers" or Richard Florida's "creative class."[6]

There are thus many names and characterizations of this group, which does seem to indicate a consensus that it exists, whatever one labels it. I prefer Bourdieu's conception of the new bourgeoisie and new petite bourgeoisie, which, like many of these other characterizations, includes cultural workers such as advertising agency personnel. Bourdieu described these groups in great detail in *Distinction*, and it is worth reviewing some of his claims. Bourdieu notes that these members of the new petite bourgeoisie possess an ambivalent relationship with the educational system, which includes "a sense of complicity with every form of symbolic defiance," including cultivating a fascination for "the avant-garde underground, which is their monopoly . . . as a challenge to legitimate culture."[7]

The new petite bourgeoisie is also comprised of "rising individuals who have not obtained all the educational capital which, in the absence of social capital, is needed to escape the most limited of middle positions."[8] I have found this to be the case among the people I have interviewed, though there is a split between musicians and producers; producers tend to possess less educational and cultural capital; none of those I interviewed who attended college had studied at institutions as prestigious as those of most of the musicians. Musicians, on the other hand, tend to be the more déclassé group (many of those I interviewed had attended private colleges and universities, some quite prestigious), and were usually the children of professionals. One small firm in New York City is comprised entirely of such people: Two are the children of doctors; the third is the son of an international banker. All three attended private, elite eastern colleges.[9]

Bourdieu's argument that the new petite bourgeoisie operates against high culture helps point out that the baby boomers' introduction of their music for use in advertising in the 1980s wasn't simply a matter of taste, or changes in technology that brought more rock musicians into the realm of advertising. It was also a reaction against what had been dominant in advertising music: music by trained musicians who were adept at scoring music for orchestras, bands, and choruses.

Bourdieu also observes that the new petite bourgeoisie is involved in cultural production, frequently acts as a cultural intermediary, and has devised a series of middlebrow genres halfway between what he calls "legitimate culture" and "mass production."[10] As many have noted, commercials beginning in the 1980s became more artistic, more aesthetic. Advertising agency creative personnel's discourse on their work has changed with this shift. For example, the vice president and associate creative director of Deutch LA, who oversaw the Mitsubishi commercials discussed in the previous chapter, acknowledged in 2002 that "people hate commercials," and that what Deutch wanted to do was "make little pieces of entertainment."[11] It was in part this new attitude that prompted many musicians to make their music available for commercial use.

Bourdieu's analysis of the new petite bourgeoisie as a cultural intermediary is dependent on high culture's claim to prestige, and thus he makes a good deal of the new petite bourgeoisie's middling class position. The new petite bourgeoisie mediates between high and low culture, but its mediating, and the cultural forms that result—such as advertisements—are never seen as being as consequential or prestigious as "legitimate culture." The new petite bourgeoisie is a popularizer of high culture, Bourdieu says, but does not possess the competence of legitimate simplifiers and popularizers such as academics. The new petite bourgeoisie has to invent for itself something resembling the authority of the author apart from the modes of competence that mark the legitimate popularizers, resulting in a role of what Bourdieu calls the "presenter," which he says is "devoid of intrinsic value."[12] Luc Boltanski and Ève Chiapello, in a recent and important book on today's capitalism, similarly write of what they call "managers," people with a talent for "sniffing things out," who must rely on what the management literature (which they surveyed exhaustively) calls "intuition." The success of holders of "intuition" is related not to skill or expertise, but to their affinity with the target group, which is extremely important in the ageist world of advertising.[13] Many advertising agencies today have become presenters of obscure popular musics. Bourdieu is in effect describing the decades-old dilemma of the advertising man (and they are mostly men): they consider themselves to be highly creative, but what they create is rarely valued by the culture.

One last observation of Bourdieu's is worth noting here, and it concerns the new petite bourgeoisie's concern not simply with the production of symbols, as in advertising, or the mediation of cultural forms, but consumption as well. The new petite bourgeoisie, writes Bourdieu, is engaged in struggles "over everything concerned with the art of living, in particular, domestic life and consumption."[14] The new petite bourgeoisie, then, is not necessarily involved with the production of goods, but is intimately concerned with how goods are made to insinuate themselves into people's lives.

Generational Shift

But what are these presenters, these intermediaries, sniffing out and mediating? It is rarely art; the advertising trade press is replete with discussions of the importance of mistaking advertising for art.[15] Rather, it is the hip, the cool, the trendy, as we have seen. Thus, despite its usefulness, it is necessary to update Bourdieu's analysis of the new petite bourgeoisie, because time has passed since *Distinction* was first published in 1979 in French; another generation enjoys a position of authority in the new petite bourgeoisie. What does this group look like now? As a class with certain structural characteristics such as those analyzed by Bourdieu, I think the new petite bourgeoisie is reasonably stable, but with some changes; the update and amplification concerns this issue of mediating cultural forms and, additionally, the attitudes toward consumption held by this younger generation in the new petite bourgeoisie, as Bourdieu saw it was beginning to take shape.

The baby boomers in the advertising industry, who were responsible for bringing about the demise of the jingle and the rise of the practice of licensing music, are being superseded by late or post–baby boomers, who now hold sway in advertising agencies and, thus, the authority to choose the musical selections to license in advertising. These are frequently people who listened to alternative radio in college or may have been involved in college radio themselves; perhaps they played in a band. According to one longtime ad industry member, "These guys are people who grew up with The Cure, with The Police, with The Smiths and they're bringing their taste to Madison Avenue and consequently to the rest of America."[16] Time and again, this latest generation of the new petite bourgeoisie is shown to possess large amounts of knowledge of the hip and the cool—their form of capital—that can be employed in their field of cultural production.

I want to consider briefly who these people are in this new petite bourgeois today and their relationship to techno and alternative music more generally. In the early 1990s, when I taught a class on popular music for the first time, my students were obsessed with arguing about which musicians or bands were sellouts and which weren't. They had a set list of criteria: a sellout was someone who (1) signed a contract with a major label, or (2) appeared on MTV, or (3) allowed his or her music to be used for commercial purposes. This was a period when "alternative"—that is, nonmainstream—music was all the rage, when many young people in college or just out were turning their backs on "corporate music" and seeking something that they felt was less commercially compromised.

Many of these people are in the new petite bourgeoisie, and they retain their attitudes to some extent. They still have no tolerance for what they view as commercial music, and have latched onto alternative music as one of the kinds of noncommercial music that they like, for some of it has a good deal of credibility as underground music. At the same time, however, they have no compunction about using this music for commercial purposes. For them, this does not compromise the music: they believe their motives to be altruistic, in that they are helping obscure musicians survive, and they effectively wield discourses that argue for the artistic worth of commercial production, as we have seen. For example, Apples in Stereo, an indie band with deep anticommercial tendencies, decided to allow its music to be used in a Sony commercial because a friend who worked as a sound designer suggested its music for Sony's

ad. Band member Robert Schneider said in 2001, "You imagine that it's a crass
process. But it's not like Sony used our song in the commercial, which is how
it looks to the indie kid. It's just one guy who liked our music."[17]

Musicians and postboomers in advertising are using the music for their
own ends, not simply accepting what the industry gives them. For this younger
new petite bourgeoisie, controlling how their music is used, controlling how
they consume, is all-important.[18] Controlling consumption is a way of making it manageable, acceptable, which marks another more general difference
between today's new petite bourgeoisie and the one Bourdieu studied nearer
its beginning. Today's has a much less ambivalent attitude toward consumption generally. Even though it was the baby boomer generation that began the
practice of licensing, the practice was quite controversial. The chief strategy
officer for the advertising agency Portland Wieden+Kennedy, a late baby
boomer, said:

> I grew up with the Clash, and the idea of the Clash making a ton of money by
> being commercial was horrifying, OK? [I thought] they should not sell out. We
> used to talk about people selling out. Well, that's not what's going on in youth
> culture today. They fully embrace the entrepreneurial and the business side of
> it. Being entrepreneurial—"It's a business, make it a success"—all of that's got a
> lot of credibility among the young.[19]

Members of today's late and post–baby boomer generations aren't just
shoppers, or even consumers of goods and the sign-values that the culture
attaches to them, but are in effect consumer/participants. Television commercial viewers/listeners are not simply "presented" with factual materials
about automobiles, as in early ads; they are not simply being shown a lifestyle
they can identify with, as in more recent ads. Instead, in many commercials
today, they are being invited to participate, to join the hip club; they are shown
scenes they can imagine themselves in, as in the Mitsubishi commercials discussed in the previous chapter.

This kind of advertising is instrumental in forming a new kind of consumer,
as well as a new kind of relationship to goods. Marketing to yuppies marked
the rise of this mode of advertising. "Before yuppies," observes anthropologist
Grant McCracken, "there was no compelling connection between the Rolex
and the BMW."[20] Today, it is not simply that there is thought to be a connection between a car and a watch—and social class, habitus, lifestyle, and so

forth. Contemporary consumption practices are more integrated into every-day life than before, as many have observed, and today's young consumers consume unabashedly and unapologetically, while they (occasionally) discur-sively protect certain arenas—such as their music—from the taint of com-mercialism, even if that music is commercial through and through.[21]

The members of the new petite bourgeoisie who work in advertising are uniquely situated in that they, like all consumers, possess the identifiable tastes of their social group, but they have the power to share, and promote, their tastes in particularly influential ways. Bourdieu argues that each faction of the bourgeoisie wants to impose its tastes on the other, each wants to be he-gemonic. In addition to their altruistic motivation of helping struggling musi-cians, these members of the new petite bourgeoisie are attempting to educate audiences by promulgating their musical tastes to the masses: they control the use of their music in an attempt to manipulate the tastes of others.

And they are, by and large, successful. Many observers of the music scene have noted the rise of interesting music on television, thanks to workers in the advertising industry. Joan Anderman of the *Boston Globe* wrote in 2001, "The Ad Guys—historically derided as smarmy salesmen—are suddenly the hippest DJs around."[22] Barry Walters included Dirty Vegas' "Days Go By," dis-cussed in the previous chapter, in his list of the top 10 dance music tunes of 2002 in *Rolling Stone*, observing, "Madison Avenue is the new MTV."[23] And fans write in to Internet newsgroups wondering about the music they're hear-ing in commercials; some enterprising fans compile lists of ads and the music used on them, though this activity has largely been superseded by a commer-cial site, adtunes.com. Record labels affix stickers to the cellophane of CDs saying, "As heard on the such-and-such commercial." CD "reviewers" at ama-zon.com write how they discovered a particular band through a commercial.

Last, and most suggestive in my efforts to detail the new generation of the new petite bourgeoisie, for these post–baby boomers, "legitimate culture" is of no import or interest; Lance Jensen didn't know Michelangelo's name (as recounted in the previous chapter), even as he compared advertising work to painting the Sistine Chapel: creative work made to order.[24] The new petite bourgeoisie attempts to confer legitimacy upon itself not by brokering high culture or importing techniques associated with high culture into the produc-tion of advertisements. They remain intermediaries, or presenters in Bour-dieu's sense, but are instead presenters of hip, underground culture, not high culture. Their capital isn't opposed to legitimate cultural capital; it is slowly supplanting it. The structure and practices identified by Bourdieu are intact, since the new petite bourgeoisie still performs a mediating function, but it is mediating not high culture, but hip and the cool. The new petite bourgeoisie in advertising is not educating mainstream viewers about the glories of art, but instead is introducing them to the sounds of the underground. While Bourdieu understood the changing cultural landscape of France when he studied it as increasingly displaying a conflict between "legitimate culture" and more commercial values, this next chapter in the story he began doesn't simply argue that commercial values have become ascendant—even dominant—but that the new petite bourgeoisie has retained its mediating function, its taste-making function, although its taste is organized not around "legitimate culture" but around the hip and the cool.

Now, as musician Ben Neill (born in 1957) said, "There is no difference between something that is considered art and something that is a commercial."[25] Whether or not this statement is "true" is not the point: the point, rather, is that musicians like Neill are increasingly common, and their practices are organized around these kinds of statements and positions.

Advertising employs people of a particular social group in a particular field of cultural production who have the power to extend their tastes beyond this group. In doing so, they help demonstrate that advertising is not simply part of a "top-down" process by which the faceless cultural industries impose their wares on an unsuspecting public. The advertising industry is populated by real people on whom structures act, and they, with their increasingly important role not just in the purveyance but also in the production of popular culture, possess the ability to influence structures themselves, bringing their taste for hip music to the mainstream. Today, unlike what Bourdieu described in *Distinction*, the new petite bourgeoisie in the advertising industry and other parts of the cultural industries has managed to make its own ideology of the relationship to goods—the hip, the cool, the trendy—increasingly dominant, crowding but not yet replacing the bourgeoisie's use of art, by aligning itself with DJs, independent record labels, popular musicians, and so forth. The yardstick by which taste is measured is now more likely to be knowledge of the trendy than knowledge of high art.[26]

I am thus not describing, as Bourdieu was in *Distinction*, a struggle within the dominant group over the definition of legitimate culture (between the old bourgeoisie with links to the past, and the new, which was more technocratic and commercially oriented) but, rather, the ascendance of the values of the new petite bourgeoisie in its struggle to capture legitimacy from the dominant group. The new petite bourgeoisie's quest for legitimacy is increasingly effective as it erodes the value of high culture and as its credibility as mediators, or discoverers—or even creators—of the trendy grows.

The New Petite Bourgeoisie and the New Capitalism

I have tried in the preceding chapters to present a historical narrative of music in advertising, though not a strictly chronological one, since this history is multiple, with many of its parts simultaneously intersecting and diverging. Clearly, however, as is well known, capitalism seems to be endlessly adaptable and flexible. One can make that generalization, and another: that capitalism, at least in the United States, is always encroaching—another well-known point.

What I think this study has shown is that the advertising and marketing industry has proved to be endlessly inventive in devising ways to encourage people to participate willingly in consumer culture and to purchase commodities. The industry hasn't just supported consumer culture, it has played a powerful, and perhaps the principal, role in making consumer culture what it is through the three major phases I have examined here. Through increased market segmentation and niche marketing, today's capitalism—whether one calls it late, postindustrial, neoliberal, global, post-Fordist, disorganized, new, or something else altogether—has insinuated itself ever more effectively into people's everyday lives.[27] If we increasingly inhabit a world of commodities, those very commodities seem to be almost like intimates, as they are marketed to us in terms of our lifestyles and animated, and given meanings by advertising as well as social uses. Consumption has become, therefore, far more than the simple acquisition of goods, but the mean mode of relating to goods, and to one another, a point made some time ago by Jean Baudrillard in his influential attempts to understand the new capitalism in France, positions that are arguably more relevant in the United States today.[28]

It is clear that people in the advertising music industry are not simply making (or choosing) music that they and/or their clients believe to be appropriate for a particular commercial, but that they are attempting to affect listeners—not just trying to get them to make a purchase, but on a deeper level. The term for this is *impact*, defined by Joyce Kurpiers as "an audience member's physical, physiological or emotional response to audiovisual stimuli infused with meanings and values."[29]

Some have argued that this new capitalism relies more heavily than ear-lier ones not just on the production of knowledge but on the production of culture. Scott Lash and John Urry, early articulators of this position, noted in 1994 how "economic and symbolic processes are more than ever interlaced and interarticulated; that is, that the economy is increasingly culturally in-flected and that culture is more and more economically inflected."[30] Subse-quent authors have pursued much the same line. Allen J. Scott, for example, posits what he calls the "cognitive-cultural economy," in which today's econ-omy is driven by certain key sectors such as technology, services, and "cultural products industries."[31] Another author argues for a new "promotional culture" that has increasingly suffused every aspect of contemporary life.[32] The cultural industries are influential not simply for the goods they produce in capitalist cultures but for the ideologies they purvey, ideologies of consumption, and of the importance of youth and the hip and the cool.

Creativity as Calling in the New Capitalism

In addition to intuition, noted above, central to many different considerations of today's capitalism is the question of creativity (or talent, as Richard Sennett writes[33]), and it is indeed a dominant theme in the discourses of advertising workers, and workers in the cultural or "creative industries" more generally.[34] For most in the industry, advertising clearly isn't viewed as art, but it is seen as a product of creativity, an ideology that arose with the advent of our modern conception of art in the late eighteenth and early nineteenth centuries.[35] It was the Creative Revolution of the 1960s that was most important in bequeathing to today's industry the creativity trope as it is now understood. Now-legendary figures such as William Bernbach believed that advertising could be an art—and advertisements should be produced with this in mind.

> What you have to say, however right it is, will not even be noticed unless you say it in a way that hasn't been said before. How do you break through? Only with ideas that reach people, that move them, that they respond to, that they listen to because they want to hear. And the talent to do that is the talent of an artist.[36]

As Stephen Fox writes of this period, "Gray-flannel anonymity gave way to personal expression."[37] The new attitudes of the Creative Revolution influenced the production of music, though first this influence was more discursive than sonic, since it took some time for popular musics to find their way into advertising music, as discussed in chapter 7. Nonetheless, the trade press and how-to guides latched onto the idea of creativity fairly quickly. One musician said in 1962, "Things in the jingle jungle are looking up. . . . People are beginning to realize that jingle writing is a highly creative art and in many instances, the jingle is the springboard for an entire campaign."[38] And the first-published how-to guide is clear: "I simply can't emphasize too strongly that our tool of success is creativeness [sic]."[39]

Today, discourses and ideologies of creativity completely suffuse the world of advertising. There is the creative process, Creative Revolution, the trade magazine *Creativity*; there are creative directors, creative teams, creative fees, creative conferences, and still more; virtually everyone I interviewed used the term. Andy Bloch, for example, told me:

> The creative level . . . you know it's just a dishwashing liquid, but we have to get a great director, and we have to make it look great, and we're going to do something cool and different, and the music . . . we don't want it to sound ad-y at all, it's got to sound cool. As far as I'm concerned, the music that we make, and other people in this industry make on the high end, is probably . . . more cutting-edge, more interesting than pop music. Or it's as good, and sometimes they take more chances.[40]

Anthony Vanger was more blunt: "Advertising is a way to be creative, and you get paid a lot of money for it."[41]

Even producing a cover version of an existing song for a commercial is thought of as creative, as Josh Rabinowitz told me:

> I'm from kind of an objectively creative standpoint. . . . It's kind of cool to come up with a new creative thing. If it's taking an old song and doing a rearrangement of it, a cover version of it, to me that's a pretty cool thing. Sometimes you come up with something . . . you're taking a great song and making it your own. We did that with a Sony spot, a year ago, the song "Carry On" by Crosby, Stills, Nash. . . . That was a great opportunity to do something, and work with a really gifted artist, Alana Davis. To me, that's being really creative, . . . taking a song, making it, contemporizing it a little bit, but certainly making it Sony's own song, Sony Electronics' own song.[42]

Figure 9.1 Andy Bloch. (Courtesy of Andy Bloch.)

Dissenters, I should point out, are rare. David Ogilvy said that *creativity* was too grandiose a word to describe what advertising people do. He acknowledged that he had gotten credit for being "original" and "creative," but he was proudest of an advertisement he wrote to attract industry to Puerto Rico that was very successful. It wasn't "creative," he said; it just did its job. He does not like advertising that tries to be art, tries to take on the aesthetic trappings of art.

I don't like aesthetic advertising and I don't like clever advertising. . . . I'm not out to produce commercials which appeal to your aesthetic or intellectual taste at all. That's not the object of the exercise. I'd go broke if I do that. I just want to sell you / [get you to] try my product tomorrow, you see. And you know that can be done painlessly and pleasantly and not offensively. I want you to say,

"What a very interesting thing. I never knew that about that product. I think I have to try it." That's the reaction I'm looking for all the time.[43]

And Bernie Krause, who was the only one of my interviewees who offered a critique of what advertising musicians do, told me that he got out of the business because,

> after blowing through hundreds of spots, I just got to the point where I didn't want to contribute to any more commercials. I could not find a single compelling reason to spend another creative moment writing music, the purpose of which was to compel folks to buy more things they just don't need, you know—like another pair of 501s or a lipstick or a Big Mac....
>
> If you value your creative work and your level of expertise, soon enough you'll get to a point in your life where you'll begin to take stock of what you've done. The question for me was, "Did I want my legacy to be an archive of sixty, thirty, or twenty seconds worth of jingles?" Just thinking about that option was giving me hemorrhoids. Luckily, I found a much more life-affirming path.[44]

Yet even Krause uses the words *creative* and *creating* to describe this labor.

Figure 9.2 Bernie Krause. (Courtesy of Bernie Krause.)

Both Ogilvy and Krause, however, belong to different generations from workers in today's industry, for whom creativity is the central trope used to describe what those involved with music in advertising (or the "creative" side of things more generally) do. The term is so fetishized, invested with so much potency and meaning, that it needs to be thought through further. Perhaps because asking whether or not advertising is art would too often result in a negative answer, advertising workers focus instead on the concept of creativity. That is, they know they don't make art, but, like artists, they do possess creativity. "Art" is distanced, unobtainable—like God—but can still be paid homage to through worldly activity as labor in advertising, and it is "creativity" that constitutes this labor, standing for duty to God. As Fritz Doddy, creative director at Elias Arts, told me in 2004, "I have to remind these guys that it really is, it's commercial art. It's art. It's commercial art. It doesn't mean that it's any less or any more. You have to aspire toward art, and those are the rewards that you get."[45]

What is interesting in this field of cultural production is the way that musicians and other creatives in advertising are drawn to being creative as though called, in the Weberian sense. But the master they serve is not God or Art but Creativity; the justification for what they do is not spiritual but an almost mystical belief in the significance of their work as creative people as being somehow remote from the world of selling and crass commercial culture. In this context, I have found useful Max Weber's discussion of the calling, which he traces from Martin Luther, establishing that this conception can be found among most Protestants.[46] What was new with this conception, writes Weber, was "the valuation of the fulfillment of duty in worldly affairs as the highest form which the moral activity of the individual could assume."[47] In this sense, "The only way of living acceptably to God was not to surpass worldly morality in monastic asceticism, but solely through the fulfillment of the obligations imposed upon the individual by his position in the world. That was his calling."[48] Weber's position is neatly characterized by Derek Sayer, who writes, "What matters is not *what* one does, but the *spirit* in which one does it."[49] Given the assumptions that what one does in advertising is (according to most) not art, what matters in this context is not what one does—make advertising—but the creative spirit in which one does it. It must be remembered that the origins of the modern understanding of creativity are akin to the divine, as Christine Battersby writes.[50]

While I'm not sure if there are many people called to advertising, there are many people in and out of advertising who feel called to be creative and who use the concept to justify what they do, to valorize it. Further, the ends to which advertising is put in such a (Weberian) system are salutary since, after all, the acquisition of property is the fruits of labor, and the labor of these people is constructed as creative. Advertising agencies make money on their creative labor, and they can justify the sale of the goods that they sell and the consumer culture they fortify. Weber writes that the concept of the calling gave entrepreneurs a clear conscience, for it allowed them to do what they did in the knowledge that they would receive eternal salvation.[51] Today, divorced from religious asceticism, "victorious capitalism" has resulted in a culture in which the idea of duty toward one's calling is deeply sedimented, even for those whose work cannot be seen as being among the most elevated pursuits.[52]

The constant dynamic between the business side and the creative side of the industry, the world of numbers and the world of ideas (another important trope in the industry), gives an almost mystical power and authority to the idea of creativity for those on the creative side of the advertising business, for this is what they believe separates them from the business side. The creative side possesses creativity; it creates and gives sustenance to ideas. William Bernbach said that research, which creatives see as an unacceptable intrusion of the rational into their creative processes, would get in the way of the creative impulse in making an ad; "I consider *research* the major culprit in the advertising picture. It has done more to perpetuate creative mediocrity than any other factor."[53]

In a sense, to continue the Weberian framework, the frequent battles between the business and creative sides of the industry represent a contest between a highly rationalized and bureaucratized wing of the business and its opposite—the creative side—attempting desperately to remain, or at least seem, ineffable, mystical, enchanted. Yet even creativity is subject to the ideological workings of the marketplace, for as many have written, once workers in the industry have aged out of the main target demographic of the product they purvey, their opinions count less, no matter how creatively fecund they might actually be.

The struggle over creativity could seem to make advertising agency creative workers appear to be heroes of a sort, despite their role in selling needless commodities and further inculcating the ideologies of consumption in their listeners and viewers. Theirs is a way of attempting to survive the un-

precedented voracity of capitalism and the iron cage of rationalization that
accompanies it, even as they serve capitalism.

In concluding this book in this way, I am attempting, as I have throughout
these pages, neither to celebrate nor to condemn what musicians and other
creative workers in the advertising industry do: both, and neither. These workers are part of the myriad contradictions of today's capitalism with which we
are all, to varying degrees, complicit. For it has become impossible not to be.

NOTES

Introduction

1. Lizabeth Cohen, *A Consumer's Republic: The Politics of Mass Consumption in Postwar America* (New York: Knopf, 2003); Gary Cross, *An All-Consuming Century: Why Commercialism Won in Modern America* (New York: Columbia University Press, 2000); and Charles F. McGovern, *Sold American: Consumption and Citizenship, 1890–1945* (Chapel Hill: University of North Carolina Press, 2006). For more general and/or theoretical discussions, see, among many others, Colin Campbell, *The Romantic Ethic and the Spirit of Modern Consumerism* (Cambridge, MA: Basil Blackwell, 1989); Martyn J. Lee, *Consumer Culture Reborn: The Cultural Politics of Consumption* (New York: Routledge, 1993); Grant McCracken, *Culture and Consumption: New Approaches to the Symbolic Character of Consumer Goods and Activities* (Bloomington: Indiana University Press, 1988), and *Culture and Consumption II: Markets, Meaning, and Brand Management* (Bloomington: Indiana University Press, 2005); Daniel Miller, *Material Culture and Mass Consumption* (Malden, MA: Blackwell, 1991); and Don Slater, *Consumer Culture and Modernity* (Malden, MA: Polity, 1997).

2. Karl Hagstrom Miller, *Segregating Sound: Inventing Folk and Pop Music in the Age of Jim Crow* (Durham, NC: Duke University Press, 2010); and David Suisman, *Selling Sounds: The Commercial Revolution in American Music* (Cambridge, MA: Harvard University Press, 2009).

3. Stuart Ewen, *Captains of Consciousness: Advertising and the Social Roots of the Consumer Culture* (New York: McGraw Hill, 1976); Jackson Lears, *Fables of Abundance: A Cultural History of Advertising in America* (New York: Basic, 1994); and Roland Marchand, *Advertising the American Dream: Making Way for Modernity, 1920–1940* (Berkeley: University of California Press, 1985). A single exception is Lawrence R. Samuel, *Brought to You By: Postwar Television Advertising and the American Dream* (Austin: University of Texas Press, 2001).

4. See Robert Goldman, *Reading Ads Socially* (New York: Routledge, 1992); Robert Goldman and Stephen Papson, *Sign Wars: The Cluttered Landscape of Advertising* (New York:

Guilford, 1996); Sut Jhally, *The Codes of Advertising: Fetishism and the Political Economy of Meaning in the Consumer Society* (New York: Routledge, 1990); and Judith Williamson, *Decoding Advertisements: Ideology and Meaning in Advertising* (New York: Marion Boyars, 1978).

5. For useful treatments of Sombart, see Arjun Appadurai's introduction to *The Social Life of Things: Commodities in Cultural Perspective* (New York: Cambridge University Press, 1986); and Chandra Mukerji, *From Graven Images: Patterns of Modern Materialism* (New York: Columbia University Press, 1983).

Much has been made of the disagreements between Sombart and Max Weber, but their foci were quite different, Weber's on the religious ideologies of a small but ultimately influential group of religious zealots; and Sombart's on the consumption of luxury goods by the wealthy, a practice that came to shape the development of modern capitalism in Europe in his estimation. Sombart was careful not to claim simply that it was consumption of luxury goods alone that explains the rise of capitalism, but that there were various causes. This argument wasn't necessarily incompatible with Weber's; he notes, for example, "In the management of personal affairs *haute finance* is just as remote from the penny-pinching shopkeeper as is the feudal aristocracy. The notion of thrift is as little known to the one as to the other. The lower-middle-class views, which later spread to all ranks of the middle class, are foreign to the wealthy strata of the capitalist era, that is to say, at least to those strata which accounted for luxury consumption in those days." Werner Sombart, *Luxury and Capitalism*, trans. W. R. Dittmar (Ann Arbor: University of Michigan Press, 1967), 87. More generally, he argues, "Development never takes an absolutely linear course, not even within one and the same cultural circle, for now and then the direction is diverted by countertendencies" (ibid., 43).

6. For a useful treatment of the origins of capitalism, see Ellen Meiksins Wood, *The Origins of Capitalism: A Longer View* (New York: Verso, 2002).

7. Joyce Appleby, *The Relentless Revolution: A History of Capitalism* (New York: Norton, 2010), 222.

8. George Lipsitz, "Consumer Spending as State Project: Yesterday's Solutions and Today's Problems," in *Getting and Spending: European and American Consumer Societies in the Twentieth Century*, ed. Susan Strasser, Charles McGovern, and Matthias Judt (Cambridge: Cambridge University Press, 1998), 142.

9. For a useful and representative collection of Adorno's writings on music, see Theodor W. Adorno, *Essays on Music*, ed. Richard Leppert, trans. Susan H. Gillespie (Berkeley: University of California Press, 2002).

10. Jacques Attali, *Noise: The Political Economy of Music*, trans. Brian Massumi (Minneapolis: University of Minnesota Press, 1985).

11. Pierre Bourdieu, *The Logic of Practice*, trans. Richard Nice (Stanford, CA: Stanford University Press, 1990).

12. Raymond Williams, *Marxism and Literature* (New York: Oxford University Press, 1977).

13. Excluding my own contributions, the published literature consists of David Allan, "An Essay on Popular Music in Advertising: The Bankruptcy of Culture or the Marriage of Art and Commerce?," *Advertising and Society Review* 6 (2005), http://muse.jhu.edu/journals/asr; Nicholas Cook, "Music and Meaning in the Commercials," *Popular Music* 13 (1994): 27–40; David Huron, "Music in Advertising: An Analytic Paradigm" *Musical Quarterly* 73 (1989): 557–74; Bethany Klein, *As Heard on TV: Popular Music in Advertising* (Burlington, VT: Ashgate, 2009); Ronald Rodman, "And Now an Ideology from Our Sponsor: Musical Style and

Semiosis in American Television Commercials," *College Music Symposium* 37 (1997): 21–48; Linda M. Scott, "Understanding Jingles and Needledrop: A Rhetorical Approach to Music in Advertising," *Journal of Consumer Research* 17 (1990): 223–36; and Anna Lisa Tota, "'When Orff Meets Guinness': Music in Advertising as a Form of Cultural Hybrid," *Poetics* 29 (2001): 109–23.

14. Thomas Frank, *The Conquest of Cool: Business Culture, Counterculture, and the Rise of Hip Consumerism* (Chicago: University of Chicago Press, 1997).

15. See Alexander Russo, *Points on the Dial: Golden Age Radio beyond the Networks* (Durham, NC: Duke University Press, 2010). For writings on the South, see Pat Ahrens, "The Role of the Crazy Water Crystals Company in Promoting Hillbilly Music," *JEMF Quarterly* 6 (Autumn 1970): 107–8; Chad Berry, ed., *The Hayloft Gang: The Story of the National Barn Dance* (Urbana: University of Illinois Press, 2008); Pamela Grundy, "From *Il Trovatore* to the Crazy Mountaineers: The Rise and Fall of Elevated Culture on WBT-Charlotte, 1922–1930," *Southern Cultures* 1 (Fall 1994): 51–73, and "'We Always Tried to Be Good People': Respectability, Crazy Water Crystals, and Hillbilly Music on the Air, 1933–1935," *Journal of American History* 81 (March 1995): 1591–1620; Craig Havighurst, *Air Castle of the South: WSM and the Making of Music City* (Urbana: University of Illinois Press, 2007); Tracy E. W. Laird, *Louisiana Hayride: Radio and Roots Music along the Red River* (New York: Oxford University Press, 2004); Bill C. Malone, "Radio and Personal Appearances: Sources and Resources," *Western Folklore* 30 (July 1971): 215–25; Kristine M. McCusker, "'Dear Radio Friend': Listener Mail and the *National Barn Dance*, 1931–1941," *American Studies* 39 (Summer 1998): 173–95; Timothy A. Patterson, "Hillbilly Music among the Flatlanders: Early Midwestern Radio and Barn Dances," *Journal of Country Music* 6 (Spring 1975): 12–18; Richard A. Peterson and Paul DiMaggio, "The Early Opry: Its Hillbilly Image in Fact and Fancy," *Journal of Country Music* 4 (Summer 1973): 39–51; Ivan M. Tribe, "The Economics of Hillbilly Radio: A Preliminary Investigation of the 'P.I.' System in the Depression Decade and Afterward," *JEMF Quarterly* 20 (1984): 76–83; and Daniel W. Wayne, "The National Barn Dance on Network Radio: The 1930s," *Journal of Country Music* 9 (1983): 47–62.

Chapter 1

1. For a treatment of this earlier period, see Timothy D. Taylor, introduction to "Radio," in *Music, Sound, and Technology in America: A Documentary History of Early Phonograph, Cinema, and Radio*, ed. Timothy D. Taylor, Mark Katz, and Tony Grajeda (Durham, NC: Duke University Press, 2012).

2. Joan Shelley Rubin, *The Making of Middlebrow Culture* (Chapel Hill: University of North Carolina Press, 1992), 24.

3. Norman J. Ware, *Labor in Modern Industrial Society* (Boston: D. C. Heath, 1935), 101.

4. See Martha L. Olney, *Buy Now, Pay Later: Advertising, Credit, and Consumer Durables in the 1920s* (Chapel Hill: University of North Carolina Press, 1991). See also Robert S. Lynd and Helen Merrell Lynd, *Middletown: A Study in Modern American Culture* (New York: Harcourt Brace Jovanovich, 1929), for an ethnographic study of the changes in consumption patterns in the 1920s.

5. Gary Cross, *An All-Consuming Century: Why Commercialism Won in Modern America* (New York: Columbia University Press, 2000), 29. See also William Leach, *Land of Desire: Merchants, Power, and the Rise of a New American Culture* (New York: Vintage, 1993).

6. See Stewart Ewen, *All-Consuming Images: The Politics of Style in Contemporary Culture*

(New York: Basic, 1988); and Roland Marchand, *Advertising the American Dream: Making Way for Modernity, 1920–1940* (Berkeley: University of California Press, 1985), ch. 5.

7. See Neil Harris, "The Drama of Consumer Desire," in *Yankee Enterprise*, ed. Otto Mayr and Robert C. Post (Washington, DC: Smithsonian Institution, 1981).

8. Leach, *Land of Desire*, 372.

9. Herbert Hoover, "Advertising Is a Vital Force in Our National Life," *Advertising World*, August 1925, 77.

10. Quoted by Daniel Horowitz, *Morality of Spending: Attitudes toward the Consumer Society in America, 1875–1940* (Chicago: Ivan R. Dee, 1985), 137.

11. Edward A. Filene, *Successful Living in This Machine Age* (New York: Simon and Schuster, 1932), 1; emphases in original.

12. "Messenger to the King," *Collier's*, 3 May 1930, 78, quoted by Jackson Lears, *Fables of Abundance: A Cultural History of Advertising in America* (New York: Basic, 1994), 229. The "king is the people" metaphor seems to have been common; Roland Marchand calls it the "parable of the democracy of goods" (Marchand, *Advertising the American Dream*, 217–22) and elsewhere quotes a document from Barton, Durstine and Osborne in the early 1920s that employs much the same language (ibid., 31).

13. Lears, *Fables of Abundance*, 205.

14. "Senator Borah on Marketing" (editorial), *Printers' Ink*, 2 August 1923, 152.

15. Leverett S. Lyon, "Advertising," *The Encyclopedia of the Social Sciences*, vol. 1 (1922), 475, quoted by Stuart Ewen, *Captains of Consciousness: Advertising and the Social Roots of the Consumer Culture* (New York: McGraw Hill, 1976), 57.

16. George Harrison Phelps, *Tomorrow's Advertisers and Their Advertising Agencies* (New York: Harper and Brothers, 1929), 251, quoting Robert Updegraff in *Advertising and Selling*.

17. Herbert W. Hess, "History and Present Status of the 'Truth-in-Advertising' Movement as Carried on by the Vigilance Committee of the Associated Advertising Clubs of the World," *Annals of the American Academy of Political and Social Science* 101 (May 1922): 211.

18. Lynn Dumenil, *The Modern Temper: American Culture and Society in the 1920s* (New York: Hill and Wang, 1995), 90.

19. A 1931 study for the Columbia Broadcasting System focused on toothpastes, shaving creams, soaps, cigars, and cigarettes; the dominance of personal hygiene goods is telling. Robert F. Elder, *Does Radio Sell Goods?* ([New York]: Columbia Broadcasting System, 1931). The *Variety Radio Directory* compiled figures from 1936 by type of business, revealing that after "Foodstuffs" and "Miscellaneous," the next two categories were "Toilet goods" and "Drugs and pharmaceuticals." "Broadcast Advertising by Type of Sponsoring Business (1936)," *Variety Radio Directory, 1937–1938* [n.p.: Variety, 1937], 689.

20. See Edwin L. Dunham, Lecture 11, Library of American Broadcasting, Hedges Collection 10: Music in Broadcasting (A–F), box 1, file 21; see also Leon Lichtenfeld, interview by Layne R. Beaty, 29 May 1988, Library of American Broadcasting, Transcripts AT 1336, University of Maryland, College Park.

21. Ray Perkins, interview by Ed Dunham, 3 December 1965, Library of American Broadcasting, Transcripts AT 36, University of Maryland, College Park.

22. For a discussion of the efforts to inform the public about radio, see Timothy D. Taylor, "Music and the Rise of Radio in Twenties America: Technological Imperialism, Socialization, and the Transformation of Intimacy," in *Wired for Sound: Engineering and Technology in Sonic Cultures*, ed. Paul Greene and Thomas Porcello (Middletown, CT: Wesleyan University Press, 2004).

23. Raymond Francis Yates, "What Is Wrong with Radio?," *Nation's Business*, quoted in "The Radio Business," *Literary Digest*, 5 May 1923, 28.

24. M. H. Aylesworth, "Radio's Accomplishment," *Century Magazine*, June 1929, 219.

25. National Broadcasting Company, *Broadcast Advertising*, vol. 1, *A Study of the Radio Medium—the Fourth Dimension of Advertising* (New York: National Broadcasting Company, 1929), 25. For more on the rise of psychological techniques used in advertising in this period, see Gillian Dyer, *Advertising as Communication* (New York: Methuen, 1982); and T. J. Jackson Lears, "From Salvation to Self-Realization: Advertising and the Therapeutic Roots of the Consumer Culture, 1880–1930," in *The Culture of Consumption: Critical Essays in American History, 1880–1980*, ed. Richard Wightman Fox and T. J. Jackson Lears (New York: Pantheon, 1982).

26. Edith Lewis, "The Emotional Quality in Advertisements," J. Walter Thompson News Bulletin, April 1923, 11–14, quoted by Lears, *Fables of Abundance*, 227.

27. See, for example, National Broadcasting Company, *Musical Leadership Maintained by NBC* (New York: National Broadcasting Company, 1938).

28. Quoted by Erik Barnouw, *The Sponsor: Notes on a Modern Potentate* (New York: Oxford University Press, 1978), 26; emphasis Barnouw's.

29. Letter to Philip Kobbé Company Inc., 17 February 1925, National Broadcasting Company Archive, box 3, folder 124, Wisconsin Historical Society, Madison.

30. J. Walter Thompson Company Staff Meeting Minutes, box 1, folder 5, 11 July 1928, John W. Hartman Center for Sales, Advertising, and Marketing History, Duke University, Durham, NC.

31. Gerard Chatfield, "Advertising Agency Should Recognize and Use Radio," J. Walter Thompson Company, *News Letter*, vol. 10, no. 8, 15 September 1928, p. 1, Newsletter Collection, Main Newsletter, box A, J. Walter Thompson collection, John W. Hartman Center for Sales, Advertising, and Marketing History, Duke University, Durham, NC.

32. Letter from George W. Hill to Merlin H. Aylesworth, 1928, Library of American Broadcasting, Hedges Collection 315, Client Testimonials (A–M), University of Maryland, College Park. Hill was the model for the authoritarian and intimidating Evan Llewellyn Evans in Frederic E. Wakeman's best-selling novel on the advertising industry, *The Hucksters* (New York: Rinehart, 1946). For more on Hill, see Stephen Fox, *The Mirror Makers: A History of American Advertising and Its Creators*, 2nd ed. (Urbana: University of Illinois Press, 1997).

33. An example is Dr. Strasska's Toothpaste, which sponsored a program in Cleveland featuring a Mr. [Charles W.] Hamp, "who sang, played instruments, cracked jokes and otherwise stirred up the air for twelve weeks during the dinner hour," every day. Joslyn and John Reber, who was soon to replace Joslyn as head of the radio department, both agreed that the show was terrible and that Hamp "has no particular form or class." But then, this ultimately did not matter because "the people who buy toothpaste like it." The radio show, combined with a program in some department stores that gave away free samples of the then-unknown toothpaste, resulted in 8,412 requests for samples; local stores sold 47,500 tubes. J. Walter Thompson Company Staff Meeting Minutes, box 1, folder 7, 3 April 1929, John W. Hartman Center for Sales, Advertising, and Marketing History, Duke University, Durham, NC.

34. *Improving the Smiles of a Nation! How Broadcast Advertising Has Worked for the Makers of Ipana Tooth Paste* (New York: National Broadcasting Company, 1928). Merchandising was an important consideration for sponsors; in 1929, NBC produced a booklet for potential advertisers. The first volume was all about broadcasting and programs. In 1930, a second volume appeared: *Broadcast Advertising*, vol. 2, *Merchandising* (New York: National Broadcasting Company, 1930). This booklet contained many more merchandising ideas than NBC promoted

in its Ipana Troubadours pamphlet, including program theme song sheet music, a personal budget book, pamphlets about programs, and more.

35. "I Believe in Broadcast Merchandising," *Broadcast Merchandising*, August 1933, 13.

36. Francis Chase Jr., *Sound and Fury: An Informal History of Broadcasting* (New York: Harper and Brothers, 1942), 24.

37. Douglas Duff Connah, *How to Build the Radio Audience* (New York: Harper and Brothers, 1938), 192.

38. National Broadcasting Company, *Broadcast Merchandising: Reprints from August 1933 to August 1936* (New York: National Broadcasting Company, n.d.), 3.

39. See Susan Smulyan, *Selling Radio: The Commercialization of American Broadcasting, 1920–1934* (Washington, DC: Smithsonian Institution Press, 1994).

40. Quoted by Carrie McLaren and Rick Prelinger, "Salesnoise: The Convergence of Music and Advertising," *Stay Free!*, Fall 1998, last accessed 11 August 2010, http://www.stayfree magazine.org/archives/15/timeline.html.

41. Alice Goldfarb Marquis, "Written on the Wind: The Impact of Radio during the 1930s," *Journal of Contemporary History* 19 (1984): 387.

42. M. H. Aylesworth, "Forces That Push Radio Forward," *New York Times*, 22 September 1929, § 12, p. 8.

43. Orrin E. Dunlap Jr., *Advertising by Radio* (New York: Ronald Press, 1929), 94.

44. Carl Dreher, "As the Broadcaster Sees It," *Radio Broadcast*, July 1928, 161. The Four Indian Love Lyrics are by Amy Woodforde-Finden (1860–1919), an American known for composing exoticist songs who was married to a British soldier in India.

45. Dunlap, *Advertising by Radio*, 90–91.

46. "Radio's Magic Carpet; Extensive Printed Advertising Reinforces Broadcast Campaign," *Broadcast Advertising*, July 1929, 26. Most of the music played was the familiar panoply of light classics, though the program's theme was entitled "The Call of the Desert" (composed, I believe, by Howard Coates).

47. George C. Biggar, "Broadcasting Barn Warmings Boosts Jamesway Barn Equipment," *Broadcast Advertising*, July 1930, 12.

48. Henry Volkening, "Abuses of Radio Broadcasting," *Current History* 33 (December 1930): 397.

49. V. M. Wallace, "Mexican Orchestra Plays 432 Weeks for Chili Account," *Broadcasting*, 15 April 1934, 16.

50. P. H. Pumphrey, "Writing, Casting and Producing the Radio Program," *Broadcast Advertising*, August 1931, 17, 42. Such a practice denied many musicians the opportunity to perform under their own names, however, and their careers suffered as audiences struggled to keep up with musicians who changed jobs, and thus names. For example, one of the most popular acts in early radio was a singing duo of Billy Jones and Ernest Hare, first known as the Happiness Boys for the Happiness Candy Company, later known as the Interwoven Pair when they sang for the Interwoven Socks Company. See "Branded Men and Women: Pioneers Who Paved the Way and Paid with Personal Oblivion," *Radio Guide*, 3 March 1932, 1, 13; "Problem for the Industry: Swapping of Talent by Sponsors Causes Confusion," *Newsweek*, 19 September 1939, 22; and Susan Smulyan, "Branded Performers: Radio's Early Stars," *Timeline* 3 (1986–87): 32–41. Also, broadcasters had an interest in keeping former names before the public, but this clashed with advertisers' desires; an internal memo at NBC from 18 February 1932 said, "In a telephone conversation today with Miss Birney of Benton and Bowles [a major advertising agency] she expressed a desire, on the part of Mr. Benton, that in all of our releases concern-

ing Billy Jones and Ernie Hare we refrain from any mention of their former titles, such as 'Happiness Boys' and the 'Interwoven Pair.'" National Broadcasting Company Archive, box 11, folder 19, Jones and Hare ("Happiness Boys"), Wisconsin Historical Society, Madison.

51. "An Appraisal of Advertising Today," *Fortune*, September 1932, 37.

52. "Pepper and Salt," *Wall Street Journal*, 9 June 1938, 4.

53. See, for example, Dunlap, *Advertising by Radio*, 73.

54. Frank A. Arnold, *Broadcast Advertising: The Fourth Dimension* (New York: Wiley, 1931), 29.

55. Ibid., 30.

56. P. H. Pumphrey, "Choosing the Program Idea," *Broadcast Advertising*, July 1931, 40. On the importance of music in early radio broadcasting, see also George Burton Hotchkiss, *An Outline of Radio Advertising: Its Philosophy, Science, Art, and Strategy* (New York: Macmillan, 1935).

57. J. Walter Thompson Company Staff Meeting Minutes, box 1, folder 7, 3 April 1929, John W. Hartman Center for Sales, Advertising, and Marketing History, Duke University, Durham, NC.

58. Edgar H. Felix, *Using Radio in Sales Promotion: A Book for Advertisers, Station Managers and Broadcasting Artists* (New York: McGraw-Hill, 1927), 134. There was a public discussion of how radio was changing tastes, with the terms *highbrow, lowbrow,* and even *middlebrow* being bandied about with some frequency. See "Are You a 'Middlebrow'?," *Popular Radio*, June 1923, 619; Mary Jordan, "Radio Has Made 'High-Brow' Music Popular," *Radio News*, February 1928, 884, 932, 934; "Mr. Average Fan Confesses That He Is a 'Low Brow,'" *Radio Revue*, December 1929, 30-32; "Mr. Fussy Fan Admits That He Is a 'High-Brow,'" *Radio Revue*, January 1930, 16-18, 46; and William D. Murphy, "High Hats for Low Brows," *Printers' Ink*, 8 February 1934, 61-62.

59. Jarvis Wren, "The Musical vs. Dramatic Radio Program," *Advertising and Selling*, 6 August 1930, 27, 46.

60. Russell Byron Williams, "This Product Takes That Program," *Broadcast Advertising*, May 1931, 10-11.

61. *Radio Advertising Rates and Data*, Standard Rate and Data Service, December 1936, quoted by Neil H. Borden, *Problems in Advertising* (New York: McGraw-Hill, 1937), 642.

62. For more on the legitimation of advertising, see Marchand, *Advertising the American Dream*. On the question of uplifting the taste of the nation, it is interesting to note that landmark classical broadcasts were repeatedly reported as news and editorialized about in the *New York Times* and other papers. And there were many published arguments about radio uplifting tastes. For just a few, see John C. Freund, "Excerpts from an Address Broadcasted from WJZ," *Wireless Age*, May 1922, 36; Lee de Forest, "Opera Audiences of To-Morrow," *Radio World*, 5 August 1922, 13; "Radio Fan Goes to See Opera after Broadcast," *Radio World*, 14 April 1923, 29; C. M. Tremaine, "Radio, the Musical Educator," *Wireless Age*, September 1923, 39-40; "Radio Cultivates Taste for Better Music," *Radio World*, 19 July 1924, 24; Charles Orchard Jr., "Is Radio Making America Musical?" *Radio Broadcast*, October 1924, 454-55; John Wallace, "The Listeners' Point of View," *Radio Broadcast*, April 1926, 667-68; Jordan, "Radio Has Made 'High-Brow' Music Popular"; Paul Kempf, "What Radio Is Doing to Our Music," *Musician*, June 1929, 17-18; Walter Damrosch, "Music and the Radio," *Annals of the American Academy of Political and Social Science* 177 (January 1935): 91-93; Howard Hanson, "Music Everywhere: What the Radio Is Doing for Musical America," *Etude*, February 1935, 84, 118; and Peter W. Dykema and Karl W. Gehrkens, "Radio as a Potential Force in Music Education," in *The Teach-*

ing and Administration of High School Music (Boston: C. C. Birchard, 1941). For a thoughtful, less boosterish consideration of the subject, see Robert A. Simon, "Giving Music the Air," *Bookman* 64 (1926): 596–99. For interesting discussions of a "lowbrow" product attempting to sponsor "highbrow" music, see Frank Finney, "Grand Opera, Symphonies and Cigarettes," *Printers' Ink*, 25 January 1934, 13–16; Allan P. Ames, "In Defense of Mr. Hill," *Printers' Ink*, 1 February 1934, 53–56; and Murphy, "High Hats for Low Brows." For a scholarly treatment of the larger notion of taste and civilization in the face of mass culture, see Warren I. Susman, "Culture and Civilization: The Nineteen-Twenties," in *Culture as History: The Transformation of American Society in the Twentieth Century* (New York: Pantheon, 1984).

63. P. H. Pumphrey writes, "In the current state of collected data on this subject [of type of music used in programs], the choice of music is really more likely to depend on the musical taste of the advertisers' president, chairman of the board, sales manager, advertising manager, and others who make up the committee on strategy" (Pumphrey, "Choosing the Program Idea," 40). Alice Goldfarb Marquis writes that the music played by Guy Lombardo and His Royal Canadians was selected by the wife of the advertising manager for General Cigar Company. Marquis, "Written on the Wind," 392, citing Carroll Carroll, *None of Your Business: Or My Life with J. Walter Thompson (Confessions of a Radio Writer)* (New York: Cowles Book Company, 1970), ix.

64. Susan J. Douglas, *Listening In: Radio and the American Imagination . . . from Amos 'n' Andy and Edward R. Murrow to Wolfman Jack and Howard Stern* (New York: Times Books, 1999); and Michele Hilmes, *Radio Voices: American Broadcasting, 1922–1952* (Minneapolis: University of Minnesota Press, 1997).

65. See Frederick H. Lumley, *Measurement in Radio* (Columbus: Ohio State University Press, 1934), 27–29, for a discussion of the flaws of many surveys of radio audiences; his hypothetical example is of a musical case.

66. Alfred P. Sloan, letter to M. H. Aylesworth, 2 January 1935, National Broadcasting Company Archives, General Motors–1935, box 37, folder 7, Wisconsin Historical Society, Madison.

67. Alfred P. Sloan, letter to M. H. Aylesworth, 10 January 1935, National Broadcasting Company Archives, General Motors–1935, box 37, folder 7, Wisconsin Historical Society, Madison. Thanks are due to Ronald Radano and Scott Carter for acquiring the two Sloan letters for me.

68. "Radio Listeners Vote for Favorite Composers," *Radio News*, December 1927, 606. The complete list, in order of popularity, is: Richard Wagner: Overture to *Tannhäuser*, Franz von Suppé: *Poet and Peasant* Overture, Franz Schubert: "Marche Militaire," Ludwig van Beethoven: Fifth Symphony, Franz Schubert: Unfinished Symphony, Charles Gounod: Ballet Music from *Faust*, Jules Massenet: Meditation from *Thaïs*, Fritz Kreisler: "Liebesfreud," Sir Arthur Sullivan: *H.M.S. Pinafore*, Peter Tchaikovsky: *Nutcracker* Suite, Rudoph Friml: *The Firefly*, Peter Tchaikovsky: Symphonie Pathetique, Victor Herbert: "Dagger Dance" from *Natoma*, Edvard Grieg: "In the Morning," Carl Maria von Weber: "Invitation to the Dance," Wolfgang Amadeus Mozart: Overture to *The Marriage of Figaro*, Nikolai Rimsky-Korsakov: *Scheherazade*, Edwin Poldini: "Poupée Valsante."

69. Felix, *Using Radio in Sales Promotion*, 123.

70. Ibid., 123.

71. A 1931 article wrote of a questionnaire sent to radio stations asking for lists of requests and the sentiments expressed in fan mail and concluded much the same. "Jazz Music Is Preferred by Listeners, Stations Report," *Broadcast Advertising*, April 1931, 7, 21.

72. M. H. Aylesworth, "Broadcast Advertising," National Broadcasting Company Archive, box 6, folder 38, Wisconsin Historical Society, Madison.

73. Dunlap, *Advertising by Radio*, 86.

74. Ibid., 87.

75. Ibid., 90. It is not entirely clear which Maxwell House program Dunlap was referring to, for there were several in the late 1920s.

76. Eldridge Peterson, "Music on Lucky Strike 'Hit Parade' Is Part of Advertisement," *Printers' Ink Monthly*, May 1941, 30.

77. Ibid., 44.

78. Sherman G. Landers, "Putting a Cigar on the Air," *Broadcast Advertising*, June 1929, 5.

79. Ibid., 6.

80. National Broadcasting Company, *Making Pep and Sparkle Typify a Ginger Ale* (New York: National Broadcasting Company, 1929), 6.

81. James H. Collins, "Giving Folks What They Want by Radio," *Saturday Evening Post*, 17 May 1924, 11.

82. Arnold, *Broadcast Advertising*, 55.

83. Reser (1896–1965) was a spectacular banjo virtuoso. For a compilation album, see *Banjo Crackerjax, 1922–1930*, Yazoo 1048, 1992.

84. Dunlap, *Advertising by Radio*, 88.

85. In the 1950s, the program returned for a time; a recording is available: *Harry Reser and the Clicquot Club Eskimos*, Bauer Studios 981014, n.d.

86. National Broadcasting Company, *Making Pep and Sparkle*, 8.

87. Ibid., ii.

88. The last page of the sheet music of Reser's "Clicquot Fox Trot March" is an advertisement for Paramount banjos and lists the instrumentation of the group: Paramount tenor banjo, two Paramount plectrum banjos, Paramount melody banjo, Paramount B-flat melody banjo, saxophone, piano, tuba, drums, and Paramount tenor harps.

89. National Broadcasting Company, *Making Pep and Sparkle*, 17.

90. Ibid., 5. The sleigh bells and barking dogs are not represented in the published version of the "Clicquot Club March."

91. Gerard Chatfield, "Advertising Agency Should Recognize and Use Radio," J. Walter Thompson Company, *News Letter*, vol. 10, no. 8, 15 September 1928, p. 1, in the J. Walter Thompson collection, Newsletter Collection, Main Newsletter, box A, John W. Hartman Center for Sales, Advertising, and Marketing History, Duke University, Durham, NC.

92. J. Walter Thompson Company Staff Meeting Minutes, box 1, folder 7, 3 April 1929, John W. Hartman Center for Sales, Advertising, and Marketing History, Duke University, Durham, NC. J. Rosamond Johnson (1873–1954) was the brother of James Weldon Johnson, who had a distinguished career as a composer and performer; Taylor Gordon (1893–1971) was a vaudevillian and singer of spirituals.

93. "Aunt Jemima on the Radio," J. Walter Thompson Company, *News Letter*, vol. 10, no. 25, 15 December 1928, John W. Hartman Center for Sales, Advertising, and Marketing History, Duke University, Durham, NC.

94. J. Walter Thompson Company Staff Meeting Minutes, 16 April 1930, box 2, folder 3, John W. Hartman Center for Sales, Advertising, and Marketing History, Duke University, Durham, NC.

95. This impulse has its roots in print advertising earlier in the twentieth century; see Lears, *Fables of Abundance*, 291–94.

256 Notes to Pages 38-44

96. Warren I. Susman, "'Personality' and the Making of Twentieth-Century Culture," in *Culture as History*, 277.

97. See Taylor, "Music and the Rise of Radio in Twenties America," for a discussion of the crowd and radio.

98. Susman, "'Personality,'" 280; the Fitzgerald quotation is from *The Great Gatsby*, p. 2, quoted by Rubin, *Making of Middlebrow Culture*, 24.

99. David Suisman, *Selling Sounds: The Commercial Revolution in American Music* (Cambridge, MA: Harvard University Press, 2009).

100. Dumenil, *Modern Temper*, 78.

101. Waldemar Kaempffert, "The Social Destiny of Radio," *Forum* 71 (June 1924): 769.

102. James C. Young, "Broadcasting Personality," *Radio Broadcast*, July 1924, 246. Rothafel's program was *Roxy and His Gang*, one of the earliest hit radio programs, a musical variety show broadcast from 1927 to 1931. Later he became known as the guiding hand behind the building of Radio City Music Hall. For a report on fans thronging at a Roxy concert, see Taylor, Katz, and Grajeda, *Music, Sound, and Technology in America*. For studies of Rothafel, see Ross Melnick, "Rethinking Rothafel: Roxy's Forgotten Legacy," *Moving Image* 3 (2003): 62–95, and "Station R-O-X-Y: Roxy and the Radio," *Film History: An International Journal* 17 (2006): 217–33, and "Roxy and His Gang: Silent Film Exhibition and the Birth of Media Convergence," PhD diss., University of California, Los Angeles, 2009.

103. Olive Palmer, "Requirements of the Radio Singer," *Etude*, December 1931, 849.

104. Roy Durstine, "We're on the Air," *Scribner's Magazine*, May 1928, 631.

105. William B. Benton, "Building a Program to Get an Audience," address before the annual meeting of the Association of National Advertisers Inc., White Sulphur Springs, WV, 6–8 May 1935; Library of American Broadcasting, Hedges Collection, 22, Advertising Agencies' Part in Broadcasting's Growth (A–Q), box 4, file 6, p. 10, University of Maryland, College Park.

106. "Radio Rays," J. Walter Thompson Company newsletter no. 1 (1 January 1928), 20–21, quoted by Lizabeth Cohen, *Making a New Deal: Industrial Workers in Chicago, 1919–1939* (New York: Cambridge University Press, 1990), 139.

107. Found in the Archive of the National Broadcasting Company, box 2, folder 82, Wisconsin Historical Society, Madison. This form is reprinted in Taylor, Katz, and Grajeda, *Music, Sound, and Technology in America*.

108. National Broadcasting Company, *Broadcast Advertising*, 1:31.

109. National Broadcasting Company, *Making Pep and Sparkle*, 24.

110. Ibid., 5.

111. National Broadcasting Company, *Improving the Smiles of a Nation!*, 24; emphasis in original.

112. For a discussion of music and personality in the television era, see "Successful Commercial Jingles Sell by Expressing a Product's Personality," *Printers' Ink*, 28 March 1958, 36–37.

Chapter 2

1. National Broadcasting Company, *Making Pep and Sparkle Typify a Ginger Ale* (New York: National Broadcasting Company, 1929), 6.

2. Such as Susan J. Douglas, *Listening In: Radio and the American Imagination . . . from Amos 'n' Andy and Edward R. Murrow to Wolfman Jack and Howard Stern* (New York: Times Books, 1999).

3. Quoted by T. J. Jackson Lears, "From Salvation to Self-Realization: Advertising and the

Therapeutic Roots of the Consumer Culture, 1880–1930," in *The Culture of Consumption: Critical Essays in American History, 1880–1980*, ed. Richard Wightman Fox and T. J. Jackson Lears (New York: Pantheon, 1982), 8; emphasis in original.

4. Orange Edward McMeans, "The Great Audience Invisible," *Scribner's Magazine*, April 1923, 416.

5. Ibid., 411.

6. Roy Durstine, "We're on the Air," *Scribner's Magazine*, May 1928, 625.

7. M. H. Aylesworth, "Radio's Accomplishment," *Century Magazine*, June 1929, 216.

8. "The March of Radio: What Radio Broadcast Is Trying to Do," *Radio Broadcast*, May 1923, 12.

9. See also Jackson Lears, *Fables of Abundance: A Cultural History of Advertising in America* (New York: Basic, 1994), 230–31.

10. "American Man-in-the-Street" (editorial), *Fortune*, December 1942, 142.

11. Some companies gave away massive amounts of free products; the George Ziegler Company gave away twenty-seven tons of candy in five weeks in 1930, for example. See "Musical Contest Program Sells 27 Tons of Candy in Five Weeks," *Broadcast Advertising*, October 1930, 12, 300.

12. Chet Crank, "Gilmore Radio Circus Boosts Gasoline Sales 9500% in Three Years," *Broadcast Advertising*, February 1931, 12.

13. Letter from E. P. H. James to Harcourt Parrish, 13 July 1931, National Broadcasting Company Archive, box 4, folder 17, p. 2, Wisconsin Historical Society, Madison.

14. Roy Durstine, "Audible Advertising," in *Radio and Its Future*, ed. Martin Codel (New York: Harper and Brothers, 1930), 54.

15. Frederick H. Lumley, *Measurement in Radio* (Columbus: Ohio State University Press, 1934), 50–51.

16. Letter from James to Parrish, 2.

17. Ibid., 4.

18. Martin L. Davey, "Secrets of a Successful Radio Program," *Broadcasting*, 1 July 1932, 9.

19. Ibid., 9. The broadcast scripts reveal that the music wasn't all that highbrow, though much of it was played by well-known organist Chandler Goldthwaite; other selections were sung by the "Davey Male Quartet" or some other pickup ensemble. Selections from the program broadcast 5 January 1930, for example, include the program's theme song, "Just a Song at Twilight"; "Anitra's Dance," attributed to Edvard Grieg; "Carry Me Back to Old Virginny"; "Jingle Bells"; "Rosary" by Ethelbert Nevin; Fritz Kreisler's "Liebesfreud"; "Annie Laurie" by Lady John Scott; "Soldier's Chorus" from Charles Gounod's *Faust*; "When You and I Were Young, Maggie"; and "When Johnny Comes Marching Home Again"; concluding with "Auld Lang Syne." J. Walter Thompson Company, As Broadcast Scripts, reel 10, John W. Hartman Center for Sales, Advertising, and Marketing History, Duke University, Durham, NC.

20. J. Walter Thompson Company Staff Meeting Minutes, 14 January 1930, box 2, folder 3, p. 7, John W. Hartman Center for Sales, Advertising, and Marketing History, Duke University, Durham, NC.

21. Davey, "Secrets," 9.

22. Whatever the makeup of the audience, however, sales improved with this program. In April 1930, John Reber reported that sales for February 1930 (the month after advertising began) were double the previous February's; March sales were double the previous March's. Reber claimed that Davey had never had an increase of more than 15 percent. J. Walter Thompson Company, Staff Meeting Minutes, 16 April 1930, box 2, folder 3, p. 5, John W. Hartman

Center for Sales, Advertising, and Marketing History, Duke University, Durham, NC. Orrin E. Dunlap Jr. says that sales increased by 20 percent during the first four months of advertising, which, he says, provides evidence that "jazz and ultra-modern melody" are not necessarily "essential elements" of a radio program. Orrin E. Dunlap Jr., *Radio in Advertising* (New York: Harper and Brothers, 1931), 143. For more on this program, see Timothy D. Taylor, Mark Katz, and Anthony Grajeda, eds., *Music, Sound, and Technology in America: A Documentary History of Early Phonograph, Cinema, and Radio* (Durham, NC: Duke University Press, 2012).

    23. Davey, "Secrets," 9.

    24. Merrill Denison, "Why Isn't Radio Better?" *Harper's Magazine*, February 1934, 580.

    25. "Fan Mail: Letters Are More Bread and Butter to Stars of Microphone," *Literary Digest*, 22 May 1937, 21.

    26. See "What the Public Likes in Broadcasting Programs Partly Shown by Letters," *Radio World*, 21 July 1923, 11; James L. Palmer, "Radio Advertising," *Journal of Business of the University of Chicago* 1 (October 1928): 495–96; E. F. McDonald, "What We Think the Public Wants," *Radio Broadcast*, March 1924, 382–84; "Replies to WJZ Questionnaire on Listeners' Tastes Show Classical Music More Popular Than Jazz," *New York Times*, 21 February 1926, § 8, p. 17; Herman S. Hettinger, *A Decade of Radio Advertising* (Chicago: University of Chicago Press, 1933). See also Affie Hammond, "Listeners' Survey of Radio," *Radio News*, December 1932, 331–33; and "Favorite Musical Numbers of the Farm Audience," *Broadcast Advertising*, June 1929, 25–27.

    27. See Douglas's chapter "The Invention of the Audience," in *Listening In*; and Charles Henry Stamps, *The Concept of the Mass Audience in American Broadcasting: An Historical-Descriptive Study* (1957; repr., New York: Arno Press, 1979).

    28. McDonald, "What We Think the Public Wants," 383.

    29. Daniel Starch, "A Study of Radio Broadcasting Based Exclusively on Personal Interviews with Families in the United States East of the Rocky Mountains" (unpublished manuscript commissioned by NBC, 1928), 24. See also "Sizing Up the Radio Audience," *Literary Digest*, 19 January 1928, 55.

    30. Edgar A. Grunwald, "Program-Production History, 1929–1937," in *Variety Radio Directory, 1937–1938* (n.p.: Variety, 1937), 19.

    31. P. H. Pumphrey, "Choosing the Program Idea," *Broadcast Advertising*, July 1931, 40. Pumphrey credits the tables in his article to Herman Hettinger without a citation, but they are clearly from Herman S. Hettinger and Richard R. Mead, *The Summer Radio Audience: A Study of the Habits and Preferences of Summer Radio Audiences in Philadelphia and Vicinity* (Philadelphia: Universal Broadcasting Company, 1931). Inexplicably, however, Pumphrey's figures are, without exception, different from Hettinger's, even though all of the horizontal and vertical labels are the same.

    32. Hettinger and Mead, *Summer Radio Audience*, 32.

    33. Pumphrey, "Choosing the Program Idea," 40.

    34. Ibid.

    35. Ralph M. Hower, *The History of an Advertising Agency: N. W. Ayer & Son at Work, 1869–1949* (Cambridge, MA: Harvard University Press, 1949), 153.

    36. For more on market segmentation in this era, see Jason Chambers, *Madison Avenue and the Color Line: African Americans in the Advertising Industry* (Philadelphia: University of Pennsylvania Press, 2009); Charles F. McGovern, *Sold American: Consumption and Citizenship, 1890–1945* (Chapel Hill: University of North Carolina Press, 2006); Richard Ohmann, *Selling Culture: Magazines, Markets, and Class at the Turn of the Century* (New York: Verso, 1996); and

Joseph Turow, *Breaking Up America: Advertisers and the New Media World* (Chicago: University of Chicago Press, 1997).

37. "Boston Survey Shows It's the Program Not the Station That Gets the Listeners," *Broadcast Advertising*, June 1930, 9.

38. "An Appraisal of Advertising Today," *Fortune*, September 1932, 37.

39. The audience-as-commodity idea is known as the "blind spot" debate in Marxist theories of communication, first forwarded by Dallas W. Smythe in *Dependency Road: Communications, Capitalism, Consciousness, and Canada* (Norwood, NJ: Ablex, 1987), 27; see Dallas W. Smythe, "Communications: Blindspot of Western Marxism," *Canadian Journal of Political and Social Theory* 1 (Fall 1977): 1–27, for his first treatment of this idea. A lively dialogue ensued after the publication of Smythe's article. See Graham Murdock, "Blindspots about Western Marxism: A Reply to Dallas Smythe," *Canadian Journal of Political and Social Theory* 2 (Spring–Summer 1978): 109–19; Bill Livant, "The Audience Commodity: On the 'Blindspot' Debate," *Canadian Journal of Political and Social Theory* 3 (Winter 1979): 91–106; Dallas Smythe, "Rejoinder to Graham Murdock," *Canadian Journal of Political and Social Theory* 2 (Spring–Summer 1978): 120–27; and Sut Jhally, "Probing the Blindspot: The Audience Commodity," *Canadian Journal of Political and Social Theory* 6 (Spring 1982): 204–10.

For a thoroughgoing exploration of the notion of the audience as commodity, see Sut Jhally, *The Codes of Advertising: Fetishism and the Political Economy of Meaning in the Consumer Society* (New York: Routledge, 1990). See also Ien Ang, *Desperately Seeking the Audience* (New York: Routledge, 1991); Kathy M. Newman, *Radio Active: Advertising and Consumer Activism, 1935–1947* (Berkeley: University of California Press, 2004); and James G. Webster and Patricia F. Phalen, "Victim, Consumer, or Commodity? Audience Models in Communication Policy," in *Audiencemaking: How the Media Create the Audience*, ed. James S. Ettema and D. Charles Whitney (Thousand Oaks, CA: Sage, 1994).

40. William S. Paley, *Radio as a Cultural Force* (n.p., 1934), 5.

41. Durstine, "Audible Advertising," 51.

42. William Paley, *As It Happened: A Memoir* (Garden City, NY: Doubleday, 1979), 44.

43. Ibid., 45.

44. "And All Because They're Smart," *Fortune*, June 1935, 82.

45. Ibid., 148.

46. Ibid., 146; emphasis in original.

47. Ibid., 160.

48. Paley, *As It Happened*, 50.

49. J. Walter Thompson Company Staff Meeting Minutes, box 4, folder 4, 15 September 1931, p. 11, John W. Hartman Center for Sales, Advertising, and Marketing History, Duke University, Durham, NC.

50. National Broadcasting Company Archive, box 4, folder 47, *Music That Satisfies*, Wisconsin Historical Society, Madison.

51. Stamps, *Concept of the Mass Audience*, 165.

52. "Outline of Strategic Radio Presentation for Borden—Draft October 14, 1948," National Broadcasting Company Archive, box 188, folder 34, Wisconsin Historical Society, Madison; uppercase word in original.

53. Columbia Broadcasting System, *Vertical Study of Radio Ownership: An Analysis, by Income Levels, of Radio Homes in the United States* (New York: Columbia Broadcasting System, 1933), and *Markets in Radio Homes, by Income Levels and Price Levels* (New York: Columbia Broadcasting System, 1934).

54. Columbia Broadcasting System, *Ears and Incomes* (New York: Columbia Broadcasting System, 1934), 3.

55. Ibid., 6; emphases in original.

56. CBS, *Ears and Incomes*, 24.

57. Princeton Radio Research Project, foreword to H. M. Beville Jr., *Social Stratification of the Radio Audience* (Princeton, NJ: Princeton Office of Radio Research, 1939), v.

58. This figure appears in H. M. Beville Jr., "The ABCD's of Radio Audiences," *Public Opinion Quarterly*, June 1940, 205. Despite research such as this, sophisticated for its time, old assumptions persisted about what particular social groups wanted to hear. One article from 1946 writes matter-of-factly, "Generally, farm people like Western music or some of the older ballads." Victor J. Dallaire, "Music Helps Select Your Audience," *Printers' Ink*, 27 December 1946, 32.

59. "Talent Expenditures," *Variety Radio Directory, 1937–1938* (n.p.: Variety, 1937), 183.

60. Jascha Heifetz, "Radio, American Style," *Harper's Monthly Magazine*, October 1937, 502.

61. Phil Spitalny, "'The Hour of Charm,'" *Etude*, October 1938, 639.

62. Warren B. Dygert, *Radio as an Advertising Medium* (New York: McGraw-Hill, 1939), 89.

63. Ibid., 96.

64. Charles Magee Adams, "A Hand for Radio," *North American Review*, September 1933, 208.

65. Hadley Cantril and Gordon W. Allport, *The Psychology of Radio* (New York: Harper and Brothers, 1935), 42–43.

66. See Roland Marchand, *Advertising the American Dream: Making Way for Modernity, 1920–1940* (Berkeley: University of California Press, 1985), for a discussion of "tempo" in this period.

67. "Reproduce Product's Tempo in Program, Says Woolley," *Broadcast Advertising*, May 1931, 26.

68. Ibid., 26, 28.

69. On crooning as effeminate, see Allison McCracken, "'God's Gift to Us Girls': Crooning, Gender, and the Re-creation of American Popular Song, 1928–1933," *American Music* 17 (Winter 1999): 365–95.

70. Marchand, *Advertising the American Dream*, 336.

71. There is conflicting information about when this first program aired. Vallée's autobiography says that the first airdate was 29 October 1929. Rudy Vallée, *My Time Is Your Time: The Rudy Vallée Story*, with Gil McKean (New York: Ivan Obolensky, 1962), 86. A 1946 J. Walter Thompson Company document says 24 October 1929. W. M. Davidson, memo to Fanny Bell, 9 July 1946, The Colin Dawkins Papers, J. Walter Thompson Company Archive, box 14, TV-Radio Department 1930–1964 and n.d., John W. Hartman Center for Sales, Advertising, and Marketing History, Duke University, Durham, NC. I am using the earlier date based on an internal J. Walter Thompson Company document detailing the history of the program. J. Walter Thompson Company Archive, Accounts–Standard Brands–Fleischmann, box 17, John W. Hartman Center for Sales, Advertising, and Marketing History, Duke University, Durham, NC.

72. Staff Meeting Minutes, 26 August 1929, J. Walter Thompson Company Archive, box 2, folder 1, p. 12, John W. Hartman Center for Sales, Advertising, and Marketing History, Duke University, Durham, NC.

73. "Fleischmann's Yeast—Rudy Vallee," J. Walter Thompson Company Archive, JWT Account Files, box 17, John W. Hartman Center for Sales, Advertising, and Marketing History, Duke University, Durham, NC.

74. Vallée with McKean, *My Time Is Your Time*, 87.

75. Letter from John F. Royal to G. F. McLelland, 31 July 1931, National Broadcasting Company Archive, box 3, folder 31, Wisconsin Historical Society, Madison.

76. Most of the writing about Vallée was the stuff of fanzines, but see Martha Gellhorn, "Rudy Vallée: God's Gift to Us Girls," *New Republic*, 7 August 1929, 310–11. Despite the huge amount of ink used about Vallée at the height of his popularity, there is still little scholarly work on him.

77. In late 1930 and/or early 1931, the J. Walter Thompson Company, evidently concerned about the longevity of Rudy Vallée's popularity, hired an investigator to observe Vallée's live performances on tour in a number of American cities for two and a half months. The unnamed investigator—and, one assumes, his bosses—didn't think to interview audience members, but audiences were observed, and theater personnel interviewed. There were clearly concerns about the gender of Vallée's audience (Vallée's appeal was assumed to be much greater for women than men; his supposed appeal to women listeners was legendary, the subject of many articles in the radio and other popular press). The results were highly scientized. Exact attendance figures were reported, as were the number of tickets sold that were above average; numbers of people standing were also recorded, as was the percentage of performances at which patrons stood. Applause ("character of response") was rated, whether Exceptional, Outstanding, Excellent, Good, or Satisfactory, based on the factors of Volume, Intensity, Frequency, Extent of duration, and Degree maintained at original intensity. And percentage of men and women was tallied, down to the last individual, so that the investigator could report that the combined audiences were 38.8 percent men and 61.2 percent women. J. Walter Thompson Company, Research Department, New York, "A Study of the Public's Reaction to Rudy Vallee during His Ten Weeks Tour of the Paramount Publix Theaters," May 1931, Rudy Vallee Collection, Business-10, Standard Brands: Audience Study 1931, Thousand Oaks Library, Thousand Oaks, CA.

78. William B. Benton, "Building a Program to Get an Audience," address before the annual meeting of the Association of National Advertisers Inc., White Sulphur Springs, WV, 6–8 May 1935, Library of American Broadcasting, Hedges Collection, 22, Advertising Agencies' Part in Broadcasting's Growth (A–Q), box 4, file 6, p. 4, University of Maryland, College Park.

79. Rudy Vallée, *Vagabond Dreams Come True* (New York: Grosset and Dunlap, 1930), 69.

80. J. Walter Thompson Company, Staff Meeting Minutes, 12 August 1930, box 2, folder 5, p. 3, emphasis and ellipses in original, John W. Hartman Center for Sales, Advertising, and Marketing History, Duke University, Durham, NC.

81. Faulkner's boss, Robert T. Colwell, explicated these points about showmanship in "The Program as an Advertisement," in *The Advertising Agency Looks at Radio*, ed. Neville O'Neill (New York: D. Appleton, 1932).

82. William L. Bird Jr., *"Better Living": Advertising, Media, and the New Vocabulary of Business Leadership, 1935–1955* (Evanston, IL: Northwestern University Press), 5–6.

Chapter 3

1. Quoted in Studs Terkel, *Hard Times: An Oral History of the Great Depression* (New York: Pantheon, 1986), 61.

2. Erik Barnouw, *The Golden Web: A History of Broadcasting in the United States*, vol. 2, 1933–53 (New York: Oxford University Press, 1968), 17.

3. Memorandum from Bertha Brainard to William S. Rainey, 2 March 1933, National Broadcasting Company Archive, box 90, folder 13, Wisconsin Historical Society, Madison.

4. See Jackson Lears, *Fables of Abundance: A Cultural History of Advertising in America* (New York: Basic, 1994), 237.

5. Barnouw, *Golden Web*, 36.

6. Douglas B. Craig, *Fireside Politics: Radio and Political Culture in the United States, 1920–1940* (Baltimore: Johns Hopkins University Press, 2000), 12; and Gary Cross, *An All-Consuming Century: Why Commercialism Won in Modern America* (New York: Columbia University Press, 2000), 71.

7. Cross, *All-Consuming Century*, 71.

8. Ibid., 73.

9. Ibid.

10. Lears, *Fables of Abundance*, 237; Cross, *All-Consuming Century*, 77.

11. Roy Dickinson, "Freshen Up Your Product," *Printers' Ink*, 6 February 1930, 163.

12. *A Primer of Capitalism* (New York: J. Walter Thompson Company, 1937), 10; emphases in original.

13. Lears, *Fables of Abundance*, 238.

14. Ibid., 238–39.

15. "An Appraisal of Advertising Today," *Fortune*, September 1932, 37.

16. Earnest Elmo Calkins, "The New Consumption Engineer, and the Artist," in *A Philosophy of Production: A Symposium*, ed. J. George Frederick (New York: Business Bourse, 1930), 125–26.

17. Ibid., 128–29. For more on questions of the visual arts and advertising in this period, see Michele H. Bogart, *Artists, Advertising, and the Borders of Art* (Chicago: University of Chicago Press, 1995).

18. Barry Manilow, telephone interview by author, 24 August 2009. There is a live recording of Manilow singing a medley of jingles, some of which he wrote himself: *Barry Manilow Live*, Arista A2CD 8049, 1986. Thanks go to John T. Carr III for telling me of this medley.

19. *The Oxford English Dictionary*, 2nd ed., 1989, *OED Online* (Oxford University Press, 1989), 12 April 2000, s.v. *jingle*.

20. See at least Brooks McNamara, *Step Right Up* (Garden City, NY: Doubleday, 1976); and "Jingles Have Long History, Stracke Says," *Advertising Age*, 13 February 1967, 20–21.

21. Jean-Rémy Julien, *Musique et publicité: Du Cri de Paris . . . aux messages publicitaires radiophoniques et télévisés* (Paris: Flammarion, 1989), 21–24.

22. See Julien, *Musique et publicité*.

23. Frank Presbrey, *The History and Development of Advertising* (New York: Doubleday, Doran, and Company, 1929), 374. Thanks are due to Linda Scott for informing me of this book.

24. Quoted by Presbrey, *History and Development of Advertising*, 374.

25. *Dry Goods Economist*, 10 February 1894, quoted by Presbrey, *History and Development of Advertising*, 376.

26. Presbrey, *History and Development of Advertising*, 378–79.

27. For more on Phoebe Snow, see Margaret Young, "On the Go with Phoebe Snow: Origins of an Advertising Icon," *Advertising and Society Review* 7 (2006), http://muse.jhu.edu/journals/asr.

28. Frank Rowsome Jr., *The Verse by the Side of the Road: The Story of the Burma-Shave Signs and Jingles* (New York: Penguin, 1965), 72.

29. The Burma Shave verses did have a life on television; see "Burma Shave Adapts Road-side Jingles to TV," *Advertising Age*, 4 September 1967, 4.

30. Charles Austin Bates, *Good Advertising* (New York: Holmes, 1896), 201.

31. Presbrey, *History and Development of Advertising*, 377

32. For a collection of early sheet music advertising, see Bella C. Landauer, *Striking the Right Note in Advertising* (New York: New-York Historical Society, 1951). For a discussion of this practice, see Rick Reublin, "The American Capitalist Initiative, Advertising in Music," *Parlor Songs*, August 2000, last accessed 22 July 2011, http://www.parlorsongs.com/insearch/vanitymusic/vanitymusic.asp.

33. Ed. Rice, interview by Dana Ulloth, 30 July 1979, Library of American Broadcasting, Transcripts AT-540, University of Maryland, College Park.

34. See Maurice Zolotow, "The Troubadour of Trouper Hill," *Saturday Evening Post*, 30 May 1942, 21, 52, 54, 57; and Carol A. McCafferty and Susan E. King, "Harry Frankel: Singin' Sam, More Than the Barbasol Man," *Traces* (Winter 2005), 26–35. One source said the jingle began airing in 1920, but this is highly unlikely since commercial broadcasting began in that year. "Barbasol Jingle Is Back on Radio," *Advertising Age*, 3 April 1961, 2.

35. "Advertising and Marketing," *New York Times*, 7 March 1953, 27.

36. Warren B. Dygert, *Radio as an Advertising Medium* (New York: McGraw-Hill, 1939), 96.

37. Herman S. Hettinger and Walter J. Neff, *Practical Radio Advertising* (New York: Prentice-Hall, 1938), 22.

38. Letter from E. P. H. James to Harcourt Parrish, 13 July 1931, National Broadcasting Company Archive, box 4, folder 17, Wisconsin Historical Society, Madison.

39. Orrin E. Dunlap Jr., *Advertising by Radio* (New York: Ronald Press, 1929), 87.

40. John F. Schneider, "The NBC Pacific Coast Network," last accessed 11 August 2010, http://www.bayarearadio.org/schneider/nbc.shtml.

41. Frank W. Spaeth, *Radio Broadcasting Manual* (New York: Sales Promotion Division of the National Retail Dry Goods Association, 1935), 75.

42. "Fitch Uses the Air to Sell Care of the Hair," *Broadcast Merchandising*, April 1936, 97. For more on Hall, see F. C. Fritz, "Wendell Hall: Early Radio Performer," in *American Broadcasting: A Source Book on the History of Radio and Television*, ed. Lawrence W. Lichty and Malachi C. Topping (New York: Hastings House, 1975).

43. Reginald T. Townsend, "Fun for Millions—and Millions for Pebeco," *Broadcasting*, 15 January 1936, 12.

44. See "$100,000 Re-run for a 1936 Jingle," *Sponsor*, 11 July 1959, 42, for a story of a regional jingle from this year.

45. Ed. Rice, interview by Dana Ulloth. The Novachord was introduced by Hammond Organ Company in 1939 and was an all-tube, early polyphonic synthesizer.

46. "National Archives Sound Recordings Named to National Recording Registry," press release, National Archives, January 30, 2003, last accessed 14 March 2010, http://www.archives.gov/press/press-releases/2003/nr03-22.html.

47. Quoted by James Gray, *Business without Boundary: The Story of General Mills* (Minneapolis: University of Minnesota Press, 1954), 160.

48. Ibid.

49. This jingle was derived from the chorus of a 1919 hit song, "Jazz Baby," made popular by Marion Harris.

50. Quoted by Gray, *Business without Boundary*, 162.

51. Gray *Business without Boundary*, 163. See also *General Mills: 75 Years of Innovation Invention Food & Fun* (Minneapolis: General Mills, 2003).

52. "The Advertising Century: Top 100 Campaigns," *Advertising Age*, last accessed 1 August 2010, http://adage.com/century/campaigns.html; and J. C. Louis and Harvey Z. Yazijian, *The Cola Wars* (New York: Everest House, 1980), 68.

53. "New Pepsi Jingle Has No Rime, Some Reason," *Printers' Ink*, 9 May 1958, 12.

54. Presumably, this was a flyer given away free to customers who asked. Demand must have been high, for a slightly later version of the jingle was circulated that was much less lavishly produced.

55. Walter Mack and Peter Buckley, *No Time Lost* (New York: Atheneum, 1982), 134–35; emphasis in original.

56. Thomas Whiteside, "I Can Be Had—for PELF," *New Republic*, 16 February 1948, 22.

57. Louis and Yazijian write that Mack paid the duo twenty-five hundred dollars, and twenty-five hundred dollars more later (Louis and Yazijian, *Cola Wars*, 68).

58. There is a letter to this effect from the Pepsi-Cola Company to a music publisher dated April 1940, National Broadcasting Company Archive, box 79, folder 51, Wisconsin Historical Society, Madison.

59. Randy Cohen, "Songs in the Key of Hype: Jingles Sweeten Sales Pitch with Pop Tunes, Catchy Cliches," *More*, July–August 1977, 12.

60. "Pepsi-Cola Theme Song Now Heard over 8 Stations," *Bayside Times*, 14 December 1939, 2.

61. "Pepsi-Cola's Walter Mack," *Fortune*, November 1947, 176.

62. Ibid.

63. Harry Lewis Bird, *This Fascinating Advertising Business* (Indianapolis: Bobbs-Merrill, 1947), 231.

64. Liner notes to *A Tribute to the Friends of Radio: Your Program Guide to 65 Years of Great Radio Advertising* (Atlanta: McGavren Guild Radio, 1988).

65. Letter from Niles Trammell to Walter S. Mack Jr., 13 March 1941, National Broadcasting Company Archive, box 85, folder 102, Wisconsin Historical Society, Madison.

66. Mack and Buckley, *No Time Lost*, 136.

67. Walter Mack, interview by Scott Ellsworth, New York City, 16 December 1985, Pepsi Generation Oral History and Documentation Collection, 1938–1986, no. 111, Archives Center, National Museum of American History, Smithsonian Institution, Washington, DC.

68. Louis and Yazijian, *Cola Wars*, 69.

69. Ibid.

70. Al Graham, "Jingle—or Jangle," *New York Times* magazine, 29 October 1944, 26.

71. Liner notes to *Tribute to the Friends of Radio*.

72. Warren E. Kraemer, "Millions in Nickels: Loft's Pepsi-Cola Is a Dynamic Speculation, Coca-Cola a Solid Investment," *Magazine of Wall Street*, 23 March 1940, 737.

73. William L. Bird Jr., *"Better Living": Advertising, Media, and the New Vocabulary of Business Leadership, 1935–1955* (Evanston, IL: Northwestern University Press, 1999), 4.

74. The song appeared on a 1925 recording to induce people to purchase phonographs that could play recordings that had been produced using electrical microphones. "Using a microphone suspended over the Metropolitan Opera House stage, its engineers recorded the British hunting song 'Do You Ken John Peel,' by 850 members of fifteen metropolitan-area clubs, gathered there for a concert by the Associated Glee Clubs of America. 'Adeste Fideles,' sung by the entire group—4,850 singers, according to the company's magazine advertising—was

issued jointly with 'John Peel' on a twelve-inch Columbia record in June. Public response was commensurate with the company's enthusiasm." Russell Sanjek, *American Popular Music and Its Business: The First Four Hundred Years*, vol. 3, *From 1900 to 1984* (New York: Oxford University Press, 1988), 67. Nowadays, the song can still be heard as a children's ditty on some recordings.

75. Alan Bradley Kent and Austen Croom-Johnson, foreword, "How to Create a Hit Radio Jingle—Fourteen Steps," in Charles Hull Wolfe, *Modern Radio Advertising* (New York: Funk and Wagnalls / Printers' Ink, 1949), 563.

76. Philip Hinerfeld, interview by Scott Ellsworth, Boca Raton, FL, 7 November 1984, Pepsi Generation Oral History and Documentation Collection, 1938–1986, no. 111, Archives Center, National Museum of American History, Smithsonian Institution, Washington, DC.

77. Ibid.

78. "Strange People Make Strange Songs to Market Their Wares on the Air," *Life*, 7 October 1940, 78.

Singer, actress, and songwriter Hank Fort says that she wrote a jingle in the mid-1930s, "Royal Crown Cola Hits the Spot," which was used on the *Ripley's Believe It or Not Show* and she played it for Johnson before he cowrote "Pepsi-Cola Hits the Spot." Hank Fort, interview by Edwin Dunham, 12 January 1966, Library of American Broadcasting, Transcripts AT-154, University of Maryland, College Park.

79. Graham, "Jingle—or Jangle," 26; Sylvia Weiss, "It Isn't Shakespeare but It Pays," *New York Times*, 19 December 1943, 7.

80. Whiteside, "I Can Be Had," 20.

81. Ibid., 22. See also "Jingle All the Way," *Time*, 21 August 1944, 75.

82. "WQXR Extends Its Ban," *New York Times*, 31 March 1944, 23.

83. "Specialist," *New Yorker*, 4 October 1947, 27.

84. Tom Morris, "Today's Radio Jingle Makes Listeners Tingle," *Advertising Age*, 8 April 1957, 77.

85. Edgar Kobak, "Singing Commercials," *Music Journal*, September–October 1944, 19. For yet another complaint, see Volney D. Hurd, "Singing Commercials," *Christian Science Monitor Magazine*, 10 March 1945, 5.

WQXR wasn't the only station to ban jingles. A 1955 article from *Time* magazine describes a case in which station WGMS, Washington, DC's "Good Music Station," featured a medley of southern songs performed by the National Gallery Orchestra. Later, Columbia Records brought out a recording of the music, and the radio station broadcast the LP. Mitch Miller, head of A&R (artists and repertoire) at Columbia Records in this era, was approached and thought that one of the songs, "The Yellow Rose of Texas," might have the potential to be a hit, so he made (or had made) a more up-tempo arrangement. Then, people at the J. Walter Thompson Company, for which Miller consulted, decided that this newer version could employ new lyrics to help sell the 1956 Ford. But when this commercial found its way to WGMS, which had a ban against jingles, the station didn't broadcast it, even though the earlier incarnation had been first heard on the station. According to *Time*, "Station executives took another look at the situation—and at the Ford check and capitulated." "The Yellow Rose of Ford," *Time*, 19 September 1955, 87.

86. Bill Backer, *The Care and Feeding of Ideas* (New York: Times Books, 1993), 112.

87. "Outline for Strategic Radio Presentation for Borden—Draft October 14, 1948," National Broadcasting Company Archive, box 118, folder 34, Wisconsin Historical Society, Madison.

88. "Sound Ads Cause Apprehension," *New York Times*, 16 August 1948, 26.

89. "Jingle All the Day," *Newsweek*, 10 June 1940, 65.

90. Several such commercials were produced, with titles such as "Chiquita Banana Goes North," "Chiquita Banana Helps the Pieman," and "Chiquita Banana and the Cannibals." Some of these are viewable at "Chiquita Banana Commercial," last accessed 31 August 2010, http://wn.com/Chiquita_Banana_Commercial.

91. "Bananas, Yes," *Time*, 23 July 1945, 66; the figure of 376 stations is from "That Great Jingle," last accessed 14 October 2006, http://www.chiquita.com (page no longer available); the other figures are from "It Shouldn't Happen to a Banana," *Results from Radio* 3, National Association of Broadcasters, Department of Broadcast Advertising, Library of American Broadcasting, pamphlet 1964 (College Park: University of Maryland, 1945).

92. "Chiquita Banana," *Tide*, 1 February 1946, 23.

93. Carrie McLaren and Rick Prelinger, "Salesnoise: The Convergence of Music and Advertising," *Stay Free!*, Fall 1998, last accessed 11 August 2010, http://www.stayfreemagazine.org/archives/15/salesnoise.html. See also "Tunesmiths, Admen Can Commingle—When There's Green Stuff in a Jingle," *Advertising Age*, 29 May 1961, 6.

94. "Chiquita Banana," *Tide*, 23.

95. "It Shouldn't Happen to a Banana."

96. Charles Hull Wolfe, *Modern Radio Advertising* (New York: Funk and Wagnalls / Printers' Ink, 1949), 563.

97. "BBDO Newsletter," *Printers' Ink*, 12 January 1945, 3.

98. "It Shouldn't Happen to a Banana."

99. Harry Walker Hepner, *Effective Advertising*, 2nd ed. (New York: McGraw-Hill, 1949), 361.

100. "It Shouldn't Happen to a Banana."

101. Ibid.; emphases and ellipsis in original. Although not attributed, I think this quotation is from literature of the United Fruit Company.

102. Ibid.; emphasis in original.

103. "That Great Jingle." For an earlier update, see Patricia Strnad, "Modern Chiquita," *Advertising Age*, 26 February 1990, 4. (Words and music by Garth Montgomery, Leonard Mackenzie, and William Wirges. Copyright © 1945 [renewed] by Music Sales Shawnee, a Division of Tom Cat Music Inc. International copyright secured. All rights reserved. Reprinted by permission.)

104. Kent and Croom-Johnson, foreword, "How to Create a Hit Radio Jingle," 561.

105. Wolfe, *Modern Radio Advertising*, 563.

106. Ibid., 564.

107. Ibid., 565.

108. "Agency Head Irv Olian Jingles While Driving, Doesn't Get Paid for It," *Advertising Age*, 25 January 1954, 40.

109. Joseph J. Seldin, "Selling the Kiddies," *Nation*, 8 October 1955, 305. For a history of advertising to children, see Lisa Jacobson, *Raising Consumers: Children and the American Mass Market in the Early Twentieth Century* (New York: Columbia University Press, 2004).

110. "Specialist," 27.

111. Ibid.

112. Fairfax M. Cone, *With All Its Faults: A Candid Account of Forty Years in Advertising* (New York: Little, Brown, 1969), 209.

113. Thomas Whiteside, "The Relaxed Sell," *New Yorker*, 3 March 1950, 79.

114. Whiteside, "I Can Be Had," 23.

115. Whiteside, "Relaxed Sell," 80.

116. Eugene Feehan, "The Sound of TV Music," *Television Magazine*, February 1967, 48.

117. Whiteside, "Relaxed Sell," 79.

118. Lawrence R. Samuel, *Brought to You By: Postwar Television Advertising and the American Dream* (Austin: University of Texas Press, 2001), 43.

119. Lincoln Diamant, *Television's Classic Commercials: The Golden Years, 1948–1958* (New York: Hastings House, 1971), 181. Short jingles such as this were known as "tag" jingles, complete in six or seven seconds, named because they could serve to end a longer commercial. See Arthur Bellaire, *TV Advertising: A Handbook of Modern Practice* (New York: Harper and Brothers, 1959), 168. Pierre Martineau writes that a study of this jingle revealed, "As soon as women heard the first half of the jingle . . . they had an unconscious compulsion to finish it. . . . The total couplet was fixed in their minds like an unforgettable tune." Pierre Martineau, *Motivation in Advertising: Motives That Make People Buy* (New York: McGraw-Hill, 1957), 111.

This jingle was made into a commercial hit by the Jumpin' Jacks in 1956; the genesis of it, along with sales figures, was reported in Fairfax M. Cone, *The Blue Streak: Some Observations, Mostly about Advertising* (n.p.: Crain Communications, 1973), 81. Other jingles were turned into popular songs in this era; see Feehan, "Sound of TV Music," 44; "New Lyrics Turn Ad Jingles into Pop Records for the Juke Box Trade," *Advertising Age*, 19 April 1954, 72; and "Sell It with Music," *Time*, 14 June 1954, 52.

120. Cone, *With All Its Faults*, 240.

121. Ibid., 241.

122. Ibid., 241–42.

123. Cone, *Blue Streak*, 75.

124. Stephen Fox, *The Mirror Makers: A History of American Advertising and Its Creators*, 2nd ed. (Urbana: University of Illinois Press, 1997), 120.

125. Kent and Croom-Johnson, foreword, "How to Create a Hit Radio Jingle," 557.

Chapter 4

1. See Jackson Lears, *Fables of Abundance: A Cultural History of Advertising in America* (New York: Basic, 1994); Roland Marchand, *Advertising the American Dream: Making Way for Modernity, 1920–1940* (Berkeley: University of California Press, 1985); Charles F. McGovern, *Sold American: Consumption and Citizenship, 1890–1945* (Chapel Hill: University of North Carolina Press, 2006); and Daniel Pope, *The Making of Modern Advertising* (New York: Basic, 1983).

2. Lizabeth Cohen, *A Consumer's Republic: The Politics of Mass Consumption in Postwar America* (New York: Knopf, 2003), 8.

3. See Luc Boltanski and Ève Chiapello, *The New Spirit of Capitalism*, trans. Gregory Elliott (New York: Verso, 2005), 442.

4. The figures were calculated from Stephen Fox, *The Mirror Makers: A History of American Advertising and Its Creators*, 2nd ed. (Urbana: University of Illinois Press, 1997), appendix.

5. Arno H. Johnson, *Huge New Markets: Unprecedented Opportunities Offered by Today's Explosive Economic Pressures*, 1955, J. Walter Thompson Company Archive, JWT: Company Publications, 1955–1958, box 12: *Huge New Markets*, 1955, 1–2, emphases in original, John W. Hartman Center for Sales, Advertising, and Marketing History, Duke University, Durham, NC.

6. Ibid., n.p.; emphasis in original.

7. Sherry B. Ortner, *New Jersey Dreaming: Capital, Culture, and the Class of '58* (Durham, NC: Duke University Press, 2003), 34–35. For more on this subject, see Glen O. Gabbard and

Krin Gabbard, *Psychiatry and the Cinema*, 2nd ed. (Washington, DC: American Psychiatric Press, 1999).

8. See Ernö Rapee, *Motion Picture Moods for Pianists and Organists* (New York: G. Schirmer, 1924), for the first publication of music that addressed specific moods. For studies of music and silent films, see Rick Altman, *Silent Film Sound* (New York: Columbia University Press, 2004); and Gillian B. Anderson, *Music for Silent Films, 1894–1929: A Guide* (Washington, DC: Library of Congress, 1988).

9. See Michele Hilmes, *Hollywood and Broadcasting from Radio to Cable* (Urbana: University of Illinois Press, 1990).

10. Hadley Cantril and Gordon W. Allport, *The Psychology of Radio* (New York: Harper and Brothers, 1935), 217. See also Herman S. Hettinger and Walter J. Neff, *Practical Radio Advertising* (New York: Prentice-Hall, 1938), for a discussion of the question of mood that shows little knowledge of music.

11. David Bennett, "Getting the Id to Go Shopping: Psychoanalysis, Advertising, Barbie Dolls, and the Invention of the Consumer Unconscious," *Public Culture* 17 (2005), 11. This useful article has been important to my understanding of Dichter's work. See also Daniel Horowitz, "The Emigré and American Consumer Culture," in *Getting and Spending: European and American Consumer Society in the Twentieth Century*, ed. Susan Strasser, Charles McGovern, and Matthias Judt (Cambridge: Cambridge University Press, 1998).

12. Ernest Dichter, "A Psychological View of Advertising Effectiveness," *Journal of Marketing* 14 (July 1949): 63.

13. Rena Bartos, "Ernest Dichter: Motive Interpreter," *Journal of Advertising Research* 26 (February–March 1986): 15. For another overview, see Martin Mayer, *Madison Avenue U.S.A.: The Extraordinary Business of Advertising and the People Who Run It* (Lincolnwood, IL: NTC Business Books, 1992).

14. Ernest Dichter, "Psychology in Market Research," *Harvard Business Review* 25 (1947): 441.

15. Ernest Dichter, "Scientifically Predicting and Understanding Human Behavior," in *Consumer Behavior and Motivation*, ed. Robert H. Cole (Urbana: Bureau of Economic and Business Research, College of Commerce and Business Administration of the University of Illinois, 1956), 33; emphasis in original.

16. Dichter, "Psychology in Market Research," 443.

17. Pierre Martineau, *Motivation in Advertising: Motives That Make People Buy* (New York: McGraw Hill, 1957), 6.

18. Ibid., 6–7.

19. Ibid., 112.

20. Vance Packard, *The Hidden Persuaders* (New York: David McKay, 1957), 3.

21. Betty Friedan, *The Feminine Mystique* (New York: Laurel, 1983); see also Bennett, "Getting the Id to Go Shopping."

22. See Clark M. Agnew and Neil O'Brien, *Television Advertising* (New York: McGraw-Hill, 1958); and Arthur Bellaire, *TV Advertising: A Handbook of Modern Practice* (New York: Harper and Brothers, 1959).

23. "P&G Soap Drab in Color . . . Great for Washing Hands," last accessed 30 July 2011, http://www.old-time.com/commercials/1940's/L-A-V-A.htm.

24. "Motivation in TV Spots Hikes Use of Music," *Advertising Age*, 22 June 1959, 18.

25. Sidney Lawrence, memorandum to Helen Fledderus, 31 May 1960, J. Walter Thompson Company Archive, Advertising Vertical File, 1950–1994, box 8: Adv-Commercials-Jingles,

John W. Hartman Center for Sales, Advertising, and Marketing History, Duke University, Durham, NC.

26. George Wyland, "Music Can Have a Special, Selling Language of Its Own," *Broadcasting*, 27 February 1961, 20.

27. "Beneficial Users 'Parade' Psychology," *Sponsor*, 17 September 1962, 35.

28. Ibid.

29. "Tin Pan Alley: Lyres for Hire," *Time*, 21 April 1961, 69.

30. Robert Alden, "Advertising: Commercial Music in Discord," *New York Times*, 3 July 1960, §F, p. 10.

31. Everett G. Martin, "Beware of Background Music on TV Ads: The Tunes May Be 'Fixed,'" *Wall Street Journal*, 13 November 1959, 1.

32. "Should You Pre-score Your TV Commercials?," *Sponsor*, 11 July 1959, 44.

33. Walter Carlson, "Advertising: Composer with a Commercial," *New York Times*, 26 June 1966, 122. See also "Bring Musicians in on Ad Planning, Leigh Urges," *Advertising Age*, 4 May 1959, 14.

34. "Gold Pan Alley," *Newsweek*, 15 August 1966, 64.

35. "Tip Top Jingle Money Makers," *Sponsor*, 30 April 1962, 33.

36. "Music to Sell by Hits $18-Million Note," *Business Week*, 8 September 1962, 70.

37. "What Are the Advantages of Original Scores in TV Commercials?," *Sponsor*, 31 May 1958, 44.

38. Mitch Leigh, telephone interview by author, 16 February 2007.

39. Martin, "Beware of Background Music," 1.

40. "Backstreet Blues" is on a Music Makers demonstration disc, MM-D1158, n.d.

41. Martin, "Beware of Background Music," 1.

42. Carlson, "Advertising: Composer with a Commercial," 122.

43. Mitch Miller, "Jingles in Television and Radio Commercials," American Association of Advertising Agencies, *Papers from the 1956 Regional Conventions*, p. 26, Library of American Broadcasting, Hedges Collection: 22: Advertising Agencies Put in Broadcasting Growth (R=Z), box 4, file 7, University of Maryland, College Park.

44. "Everybody's Singing along with Mitch," *Broadcast Advertising*, 10 April 1961, 40.

45. Ibid.

46. For more on Eaton, see Jason Chambers, *Madison Avenue and the Color Line: African Americans in the Advertising Industry* (Philadelphia: University of Pennsylvania Press, 2009).

47. "Composer Finds Challenge and Success in Agency Music Field," *Sponsor*, 10 June 1963, 46.

48. Roy Eaton, telephone interview by author, 4 August 2009.

49. Albert R. Kroeger, "Music for the Golden Minute," *Television Magazine*, December 1960, 66, 69.

50. Ibid., 40.

51. Ibid., 41; emphasis in original.

52. Ibid., 66.

53. Ibid.

54. Dorothy Ferenbaugh, "Television's Musical Jingles," *New York Times*, 22 December 1963, §X, p. 21.

55. Eugene Feehan, "The Sound of TV Music," *Television Magazine*, February 1967, 47.

56. Martin Rossman, "If Beethoven Were Alive, He Could Score Big at Agencies," *Los Angeles Times*, 15 February 1971, §D, p. 11.

57. "The Making of a Commercial," *Today's Film Maker*, June 1974, 39.

58. William Meyers, *The Image-Makers: Secrets of Successful Advertising* (London: Macmillan, 1984), 119–20.

59. William A. Henry III, "Mirror, Mirror, on the Tube," *Time*, 17 August 1981, 85.

60. Meyers, *Image Makers*, 121.

61. Esther Thorson, "Emotion and Advertising," in *The Advertising Business: Operations, Creativity, Media Planning, Integrated Communications*, ed. John Philip Jones (Thousand Oaks, CA: Sage, 1999), 209.

62. Meyers, *Image Makers*, 121.

63. John McDonough and Allan Ross, "Jingle Jangle: Who Makes Singing Commercials and Why," *High Fidelity*, November 1976, 85.

64. Tamar Crystal, "The Men Who Make the Music That Makes Madison Avenue Move," pt. 1, *Millimeter*, April 1977, 36.

65. Cyndee Miller, "They Write Songs That Jingle, Jangle, Jingle," *Marketing News*, 6 November 1989, 6.

66. Joyce Rutter, "Kuby Conducts," *Advertising Age*, 1 August 1988, 15S.

67. Raymond Serafin, "'Heartbeat': New Ads Pump Life into Chevy's 'American' Image,'" *Advertising Age*, 12 January 1987, 3.

68. Ibid.

69. Bill Meyer, "Is Music Drowning Out the Pitch?," *Adweek*, 14 September 1981, 17.

70. See Eric Pace, "There's a Song in Their Art," *New York Times*, 2 May 1982, §F, p. 4.

71. Sidney Hecker, "Music in Advertising—What the Data Don't Tell Us," *ARF Conference Report*, November 1982, 14; emphases in original.

72. Chuck Reece, "Creatives Grapple with Music and 15s," *Adweek*, 31 March 1986, C.P. 22. For more on Ciani's electronic advertising music, see Timothy D. Taylor, "The Avant-Garde in the Family Room: Advertising and the Domestication of Electronic Music in the 1960s and 1970s," in *The Oxford Sound Studies Handbook*, ed. Karin Bijsterveld and Trevor Pinch (New York: Oxford University Press, 2012).

73. This line appears in David Ogilvy, *Ogilvy on Advertising* (New York: Vintage, 1985), 111.

74. Edmond M. Rosenthal, "Civilization Comes to the Jingle Jungle as Music Houses Pull Together for a Better Deal," *Television/Radio Age*, 23 May 1977, 34.

75. Randy Cohen, "Songs in the Key of Hype: Jingles Sweeten Sales Pitch with Pop Tunes, Catchy Cliches," *More*, July–August 1977, 14.

76. For a description of how clients use library music, see Joyce Kurpiers, "Reality by Design: Advertising Image, Music and Sound Design in the Production of Culture," PhD diss., Duke University, 2009, 139–46.

77. For some examples, see Judy I. Alpert and Mark I. Alpert, "Music Influences on Mood and Purchase Intentions," *Psychology and Marketing* 7 (Summer 1990): 10–35; Gordon C. Bruner II, "Music, Mood, and Marketing," *Journal of Marketing* 54 (1990): 94–104; James J. Kellaris and Anthony D. Cox, "The Effects of Background Music in Advertising: A Reassessment," *Journal of Consumer Research* 16 (1989): 113–18; James J. Kellaris, Anthony D. Cox, and Dena Cox, "The Effect of Background Music on Ad Processing: A Contingency Explanation," *Journal of Marketing* 57 (October 1993): 114–25; Patricia A. Stout and Roland T. Rust, "The Effect of Music on Emotional Reponses to Advertising," in *The Proceedings of the 1986 Conference of the American Academy of Advertising*, ed. Ernest F. Larkin (Norman: School of Journalism, University of Oklahoma, 1986); and Patricia A. Stout, John D. Leckenby, and Sidney Hecker,

"Viewer Reactions to Music in Television Commercials," *Journalism Quarterly* 67 (Winter 1990): 887–91.

78. Gerard J. Tellis, *Effective Advertising: Understanding When, How, and Why Advertising Works* (Thousand Oaks, CA: Sage, 2004), 164.

79. Buddy Scott, "The Magic of Jingles and the Audio Image," *Broadcasting*, 8 August 1983, 24.

80. Meyer, "Is Music Drowning Out the Pitch?," 18.

81. Howard G. Ruben, "They Second That Emotion," *Advertising Age*, 7 September 1987, C15.

82. Fritz Doddy, interview by author, New York City, 14 April 2004.

83. Andrew Knox, interview by author, New York City, 14 May 2004.

84. Phil Dusenberry, *Then We Set His Hair on Fire: Insights and Accidents from a Hall-of-Fame Career in Advertising* (New York: Portfolio, 2005), 171–72.

85. Ron Tindiglia, *Make Money as a Jingle Composer* (Harrison, NY: Tindiglia Enterprises, 1984), 4.

86. Al Stone, *Jingles: How to Write, Produce and Sell Commercial Music* (Cincinnati: Writer's Digest Books, 1990), 3.

87. Norm Richards, "The Myth of Memorability in Commercial Music," *Advertising Age*, 23 July 1979, S-23–S-24; emphases in original. See also "Jingle Men Make Artistic Strides," *Back Stage*, 25 July 1980, 1, 12.

Chapter 5

1. Tom Kemp, *The Climax of Capitalism: The U.S. Economy in the Twentieth Century* (New York: Longman, 1990), 131.

2. Bill Backer, telephone interview by author, 4 May 2004.

3. "Most Agencies Buy Singing Commercials Outside, Study Finds," *Advertising Age*, 30 November 1959, 54.

4. "Things to Know in Buying Jingles," *Sponsor*, 27 February 1960, 37.

5. "Tin Pan Alley: Lyres for Hire," *Time*, 21 April 1961, 69.

6. "Tip Top Jingle Money Makers," *Sponsor*, 30 April 1962, 34, 32.

7. Susan Loesser, *A Most Remarkable Fella: Frank Loesser and the Guys and Dolls in His Life* (New York: Donald I. Fine, 1993), 228.

8. In 1957–58, Loesser signed a one-year agreement with Young and Rubicam to "act as a musical consultant and make arrangements with other composers to furnish original music jingles." The music that resulted was to become the property of the advertising agency (rather than the advertiser, the normal arrangement). Memo from Sigrid H. Pederson to Jack Devine, 15 October 1958, J. Walter Thompson Company Archive, JWT: Radio TV Dept., Devine, box 10: NY Office: Talent, Rights and Contracts: ASCAP, 1958, John W. Hartman Center for Sales, Advertising, and Marketing History, Duke University, Durham, NC.

9. "The Jingle Jangle," *Time*, 6 May 1957, 50.

10. Clark M. Agnew and Neil O'Brien, *Television Advertising* (New York: McGraw-Hill, 1958), 134.

11. "Jingle Jangle," 50.

12. "J. Walter Thompson's Hit Parade," *Television Magazine*, July 1959, 105.

13. Letter from Charles Vanda to Carroll Carroll, 21 August 1958, J. Walter Thompson Company Archive, JWT Radio TV Department Papers of the Administrator, John E. Devine,

box 11: Hollywood Office: Memos, Reports and Correspondence, 1957–1958, John W. Hartman Center for Sales, Advertising, and Marketing History, Duke University, Durham, NC.

14. "Tip Top Jingle Money Makers," 32.

15. Agnew and O'Brien, *Television Advertising*, 135.

16. Arthur Bellaire, *TV Advertising: A Handbook of Modern Practice* (New York: Harper and Brothers, 1959), 103.

17. Memo from Dick Neff to Joe Stone and Dan Seymour, 17 December 1956, J. Walter Thompson Company Archive, Papers of Dan Seymour, box 1, 1956, Oct.=Dec., and 1956, John W. Hartman Center for Sales, Advertising, and Marketing History, Duke University, Durham, NC.

18. "Oratorios for Industry," *Time*, 24 July 1964, 42.

19. Joey Levine, telephone interview by author, 17 October 2009.

20. "Tip Top Jingle Money Makers," 34.

21. The form of the mature jingle encompassed several types in this era: the "donut," a sixty-second commercial with vocals at the beginning and the end, leaving the middle free for a voice-over. The first twenty seconds are called the "front"; the middle section, the "bridge," or "hole"; and the final section, the "tag." A "lift" is any section of the commercial that can be edited out and used as a stand-alone entity; one jingle guidebook author's example is "LAVA" for Lava soap. Antonio Teixeira Jr., *Music to Sell By: The Craft of Jingle Writing* (n.p.: Berklee Press, 1974), 4. There is also a commercial known as a "weave job," in which the musical message weaves around the voice-over. Also, according to composer and guidebook author Al Stone, there are "bumps" or "spikes": "similar to a weave in that a word or a line simply jumps out of context. . . . The bump or spike is used as an interruption of the flow of the jingle without destroying the overall effect of the track. The point is to accent or emphasize a key word or phrase the advertiser feels is critical to its campaign." Last, the "stingers" or "buttons," which are "simply a short jingle usually just singing the advertiser's name or slogan." Al Stone, *Jingles: How to Write, Produce and Sell Commercial Music* (Cincinnati: Writer's Digest Books, 1990), 10.

22. Philip Hinerfeld said all he wanted was "something to move her ass by." Philip Hinerfeld, interview by Scott Ellsworth, Boca Raton, FL, 7 November 1984, Pepsi Generation Oral History and Documentation Collection, 1938–1986, no. 111, Archives Center, National Museum of American History, Smithsonian Institution, Washington, DC.

23. Sid Ramin's music for Pepsi had sixty-five commercial recordings made of it, according to Terry Galanoy, *Down the Tube, or Making Television Commercials Is Such a Dog-Eat-Dog Business It's No Wonder They're Called Spots* (Chicago: Henry Regnery, 1970), 177; see also "Girl Watch Tune from Pepsi Enters Pop Music Arena," *Advertising Age*, 26 December 1966, 23. Burland's Alka-Seltzer jingle is discussed in chapter 6. Ramin recorded a version with Andy Williams with lyrics by Tony Velona. Ramin says that he was directed by BBDO to write something that sounded close to Herb Alpert but not so close that the company would be sued; Alpert ended up recording a version of the tune, which was derived from a television theme song to *The Trials of O'Brien* that Ramin had written. Sid Ramin, interview by Scott Ellsworth, New York City, 18 December 1984, Pepsi Generation Oral History and Documentation Collection, 1938–1986, no. 111, Archives Center, National Museum of American History, Smithsonian Institution, Washington, DC.

24. Teixeira, *Music to Sell By*, 6. More complex taxonomies emerged a little later, such as this one from the late 1970s:

1. Big and showy music. When you are trying to make your idea larger than life, the sound of big music can be of great help. . . .

2. Music to shoot to. A whole category of picture-montage commercials originate, not on a storyboard, but with a music track to which a storyboard is drawn. . . .

3. Music as bookends and a rug. This method takes a music-and-word phrase to open a commercial, continues the theme music under the body of the commercial (like a musical rug) and then closes the commercial with the second bookend, the reprise of the music-and-word phrase.

4. Using somebody else's hit music. . . .

5. Music for mood. If the broadcast idea you are trying to portray is based on emotional response rather than copy points and hard facts, music can guide you into a most separate world of persuasion. (Hooper White, "Striking a High Note: Music in TV Production," *Advertising Age*, 12 November 1979, 67, 70)

25. Brian Albano, interview by author, Lynbrook, NY, 11 March 2004. Albano's band, the Forum Quorum, was the main case study in a book by Leslie Lieber, *How to Form a Rock Group* (New York: Grosset and Dunlap, 1968).

26. Louis Gorfain, "Jingle Giants," *New York*, 23 April 1979, 50–53.

27. See "The Singing Saleswoman," *Ebony*, April 1964, 143; "Oratorios for Industry"; and Sal Nuccio, "Advertising: Treasure in the Jingle Jungle," *New York Times*, 8 November 1964, §F, p. 14, for more on jingle singer salaries.

28. Linda November, telephone interview by author, 28 July 2009.

29. Janie Fricke, telephone interview by author, 4 August 2009.

30. November, telephone interview by author, 28 July 2009. For more on this jingle, see Tom McFaul, "How the Pussy Learned to Sing," 1 April 2002, last accessed 11 August 2010, http://www.classicthemes.com/50sTVThemes/singingPussy.html.

31. Mitch Miller, "Jingles in Television and Radio Commercials," American Association of Advertising Agencies, *Papers from the 1956 Regional Conventions*, p. 25, Library of American Broadcasting, Hedges Collection: 22: Advertising Agencies Put in Broadcasting Growth (R–Z), box 4, file 7, University of Maryland, College Park.

32. Ibid.

33. "Everybody's Singing along with Mitch," *Broadcast Advertising*, 10 April 1961, 40.

34. See "McGuires Join Sales Ranks in Deal with Coke," *Advertising Age*, 12 January 1959, 58, for an article on the growing number of singers recording commercials in this era.

35. These materials no longer appear to be in the archive.

36. Letter from Jack Reeser to Robert V. Ballin, 18 May 1954, quoted by Herman Land, "The Diary of Ford's 'This Ole House' Jingle," *Sponsor*, 10 January 1955, 41.

37. Letter from Joe Stone to Jack Reeser, 22 June 1954, quoted in Land, "Diary," 41, 97.

38. Letter from Robert V. Ballin to Jack Reeser, 7 August 1954, quoted in Land, "Diary," 98.

39. Letter from Jack Reeser to Joe Stone, 4 September 1954, quoted in Land, "Diary," 100.

40. Letter from Joe Stone to Robert V. Ballin, 13 September 1954, quoted in Land, "Diary," 101.

41. Letter from W. Eldon Hazard to Joe Stone and Dwight Davis, 20 October 1954, quoted by Land, "Diary," 103.

42. "J. Walter Thompson's Hit Parade," 105.

43. "A Commercial about Growing up—and How It Grew," *J. Walter Thompson Company*

News, 19 April 1961, J. Walter Thompson Company Archive, Newsletter Collection, Main Series, 1961–1964, box 8, John W. Hartman Center for Sales, Advertising, and Marketing History, Duke University, Durham, NC.

44. "'The Times of Your Life': The Why and How of the Kodak Song," J. Walter Thompson Company Archive, The Granger Tripp Papers, box 1: Eastman Kodak Series, Subject Files, Songs, "The Times of Your Life" 1974–78, John W. Hartman Center for Sales, Advertising, and Marketing History, Duke University, Durham, NC; emphases in original.

45. All letters are contained in the J. Walter Thompson Company Archive, The Papers of Granger Tripp, box 1: Eastman Kodak Series, Subject Files, Songs "Turn Around," 1961–65, John W. Hartman Center for Sales, Advertising, and Marketing History, Duke University, Durham, NC.

46. "Jack O'Brian Says," *New York Journal-American,* 17 April 1961, 22.

47. "Kodak's 'Sellevision' Marathon," *Kodak Dealer News,* September–October 1962, 16.

48. "Jingle Music Freeing Itself from Current Disk Trends: Lucas," *Variety,* 17 November 1976, 57.

49. Steve Karmen, *Who Killed the Jingle? How a Unique American Art Form Disappeared* (Milwaukee: Hal Leonard, 2005), 99.

50. This issue was addressed in some detail in a trade press article: Marion Preston, "Monday Memo," *Broadcasting,* 9 January 1978, 14.

51. Norm Richards, "The Myth of Memorability in Commercial Music," *Advertising Age,* 23 July 1979, S-24.

52. Dan Aron, "The End (?) of the Boring Jingle," *Back Stage,* 20 April 1984, 16B.

53. Judith Topper, "Creatives Try to Change Score," *Back Stage,* 20 April 1984, 58.

54. Randy Cohen, "Songs in the Key of Hype: Jingles Sweeten Sales Pitch with Pop Tunes, Catchy Cliches," *More,* July–August 1977, 17.

55. Steve Karmen told me that in the 1970s, advertisers began to request "a major, original piece of music that fits behind, and supports all the different concepts an advertiser may need in their commercials"—this was an anthem. Steve Karmen, telephone interview by author, 2 September 2009.

56. Even with the successes that jingle proponents could point to, by the end of the 1940s, there were serious questions about jingles' efficacy and their intrusiveness. Veterans like Alan Bradley Kent and Austen Croom-Johnson acknowledged that there were a lot of bad jingles on the air, which would "end up by killing the goose that laid the golden egg," and that radio stations and advertising agencies needed to be much more careful about what they put on the air. Quoted in Charles Hull Wolfe, *Modern Radio Advertising* (New York: Funk and Wagnalls / Printers' Ink, 1949), 557. In 1945, *The Christian Science Monitor* published a rant by Harlow Shapley, a Harvard professor, who wrote vividly of an experience listening to a broadcast of Arturo Toscanini:

> Our attentive listening had, in a sense, made us communicants in a majestic ethereal cathedral. We had collaborated in a timeless divine service. And then suddenly, as our applause registered deep gratitude . . . before we could defend ourselves a squalling, dissonant, hasty singing commercial burst in on the mood. . . . What we got was a hideous jingle about soap, and we could not protect ourselves. The great art had been prostituted in the interest of immediate cash return to the broadcasting industry and its commercial patron. . . . Toscanini and the listeners had more than wasted the afternoon. (Volney D. Hurd, "Singing Commercials," *Christian Science Monitor,* 10 March 1945, 5; ellipses in original)

Six years later, *Science News Letter* described a device that people could attach to their radios to silence singing commercials. "Singing Commercials Cut from Radio by Device," *Science News Letter*, 31 March 1951, 204.

A study conducted by Harry Field and Paul F. Lazarsfeld in the mid-1940s revealed many listeners' distaste for jingles, even though they admitted that such commercials could be attention-getting devices. Lazarsfeld and Field reprinted several responses to jingles from their subjects: "'Them singing ditties. They just kinda make you happy.' (Wife of laborer, Texarkana, Tex.) . . . ; 'Singing commercials are so silly—about the mentality of a six-year-old.' (Wife of engineer, Tacoma, Wash.); 'Ivory Soap. Like to sing the song. Children enjoy it.' (Wife of elevator operator, Bronx, N.Y.); 'The singing, the jingles—the whole thing is ridiculous.' (Wife of welder, Belleville, N.J.)." Paul F. Lazarsfeld and Harry Field, *The People Look at Radio* (Chapel Hill: University of North Carolina Press, 1946), 31. Lazarsfeld and Field's data also showed that 18 percent of listeners believed there were too many jingles on the air, and 15 percent believed that there was too much singing in commercials (ibid., 36).

57. Melvin S. Hattwick, *How to Use Psychology for Better Advertising* (New York: Prentice-Hall, 1950), 254.

58. "Jingle Facts: How Effective Are Television Commercials with Jingles?" J. Walter Thompson Company Archive, JWT: Advertising Vertical File, 1950–1994, box 8, John W. Hartman Center for Sales, Advertising, and Marketing History, Duke University, Durham, NC; emphases in original.

59. Schwerin Research Corporation Bulletin, May 1964, "Music in Commercials," J. Walter Thompson Company Archive, Advertising Vertical File, 1950–1994, box 8: Adv-Commercials-Jingles, John W. Hartman Center for Sales, Advertising, and Marketing History, Duke University, Durham, NC

60. See "Jingles vs. Spoken Commercials: Which?" *Sponsor*, 22 June 1964, 42–45; "Does Music Add to a Commercial's Effectiveness," *McCollum/Spielman Topline*, October 1978; Michael L. Rothschild, *Advertising: From Fundamentals to Strategies* (Lexington, MA: D. C. Heath and Company, 1987), from data in Keith L. Reinhard, "I Believe in Music," Needham, Harper and Steers Inc.; and David W. Stewart and David H. Furse, *Effective Television Advertising: A Study of 1000 Commercials* (Lexington, MA: Lexington Books, 1986).

61. Robert T. Colwell, "America's Attitudes toward Advertising," Atlanta Advertising Institute, 9 April 1965, J. Walter Thompson Company Archive, Writings and Speeches Collection, box 2: Colwell, Robert T., John W. Hartman Center for Sales, Advertising, and Marketing History, Duke University, Durham, NC.

62. Arguments against the jingle could be just as impressionistic. Best known among them was the legendary David Ogilvy, whose famous dictum "If you have nothing to say, sing it" resonated through many publications of the 1950s, 1960s, and 1970s. David Ogilvy, *Ogilvy on Advertising* (New York: Vintage, 1985), 111. *Ogilvy on Advertising* provided a list of what not to do in commercials, including:

> *When you have nothing to say, sing it.* There have been some successful commercials which sang the sales pitch, but jingles are below average in changing brand preference.
>
> Never use a jingle without trying it on people who have not read your script. If they cannot decipher the words, don't put your jingle on the air.
>
> If you went into a store and asked a salesman to show you a refrigerator, how would you react if he started singing at you? Yet some clients feel short-changed if you don't give them a jingle. (Ogilvy, *Ogilvy on Advertising*, 111; emphasis in original).

In *Confessions of an Advertising Man,* Ogilvy wrote, "Don't *sing* your selling message. Selling is a serious business." David Ogilvy, *Confessions of an Advertising Man* (New York: Atheneum, 1963), 133.

In an interview from the 1980s, Ogilvy said, "I hate music. I hate sound commercials. And I have always said, my God, if you have nothing to say, sing it. But there have been a few sound commercials that have sold products. Very, very few. People who use sung commercials are lunatics. If you want to buy a frying pan, you come into my store and come up to my counter and say, 'I want a frying pan,' and I start singing to you in Alexandrian couplets, you'll think I'm a lunatic and you'll run like hell. Why do people ... ? Because they're *entertaining*. They're *not* selling, they're entertaining." Pepsi Collection no. 111, National Museum of American History, series 4, subseries a, box 33, Archives Center, National Museum of American History, Washington, DC. This material was probably misfiled in this location; this seems to have been the audio portion of a documentary on advertising from the 1980s.

63. Rich Meitin, "Creative and Effective Use of Music in Advertising," presentation to J. Walter Thompson, Chicago, October 1990, J. Walter Thompson Company Archive, Information Center, Vertical Files 2000–0283, series B: Advertising and Marketing Subject Files, box 3, Advertising Appeals-Music, Jingles, John W. Hartman Center for Sales, Advertising, and Marketing History, Duke University, Durham, NC.

64. Patricia Winters Lauro, "Forget Jingles. Viewers Prefer Familiar Tunes in Commercials," *New York Times,* 8 November 1999, §C, p. 1.

65. Roy Schecter, personal communication, 21 February 2003.

66. Spencer Michlin, personal communication, 28 July 2009.

67. Karmen, *Who Killed the Jingle?,* 140.

68. Steve Karmen, *Through the Jingle Jungle: The Art and Business of Making Music for Commercials* (New York: Billboard Books, 1989), 120–21.

69. Karmen, *Who Killed the Jingle?,* 177–78.

70. For a treatment of the rise of electronic music in advertising, see Timothy D. Taylor, "The Avant-Garde in the Family Room: Advertising and the Domestication of Electronic Music in the 1960s and 1970s," in *The Oxford Sound Studies Handbook,* ed. Karin Bijsterveld and Trevor Pinch (New York: Oxford University Press, 2012).

71. Karmen, *Who Killed the Jingle?,* 21; emphasis in original.

72. Jean Baudrillard, "Simulacra and Simulation," in *Selected Writings,* ed. Mark Poster (Stanford: Stanford University Press, 1988), 170.

73. Ibid.

Chapter 6

1. James P. Forkan, "Tunes That Sing Songs of Sales," *Advertising Age,* 23 July 1979, S-1.

2. "Kingston Trio Selling 7-Up," *Billboard,* 17 October 1960, 4.

3. "Ford Summer Series Builds TV Show on Advertising Motif," *Advertising Age,* 30 July 1962, 95.

4. Dillon reiterates many of the points of this white paper in Tom Dillon, interview by Scott Ellsworth, New York City, 23 May 1984, Pepsi Generation Oral History and Documentation Collection, 1938–1986, no. 111, Archives Center, National Museum of American History, Smithsonian Institution, Washington, DC.

5. J. C. Louis and Harvey Z. Yazijian, *The Cola Wars* (New York: Everest House, 1980), 138.

6. Phil Dusenberry, *Then We Set His Hair on Fire: Insights and Accidents from a Hall-of-Fame Career in Advertising* (New York: Portfolio, 2005), 125.

7. Louis and Yazijian, *Cola Wars*, 138.

8. James Forkan, "Pepsi Generation Bridges Two Decades," *Advertising Age*, 5 May 1980, 41, 43.

9. "Pepsi-Cola Plans Big Radio-TV Splash," *Broadcasting*, 13 February 1961, 33.

10. Ibid.; see also "Advertising: Epitaph for 'Makin' Whoopee,'" *New York Times*, 8 February 1961, 49.

11. "New Pepsi Jingle Has No Rime, Some Reason," *Printers' Ink*, 9 May 1958, 13.

12. "Pepsi Localizes Its Second Flight of Radio Jingles," *Advertising Age*, 8 May 1961, 38.

13. Dillon, interview by Ellsworth, 23 May 1984.

14. "Pepsi Doubles Already Big Radio Budget," *Broadcasting*, 15 January 1962, 30.

15. Sommers recorded a special birthday song from Pepsi, which, after playing, would be followed by a list of local teenagers' birthdays (ibid., 32).

16. Thomas Frank, *Conquest of Cool: Business Culture, Counterculture, and the Rise of Hip Consumerism* (Chicago: University of Chicago Press, 1997), ch. 8.

17. Mary Jo Kaplan, "Cola Wars and Remembrance: Coca-Cola," *Advertising Age*, 1 August 1988, 31S.

18. Louis and Yazijian, *Cola Wars*, 233–34. "Rum & Coca-Cola" was originally a calypso composed by Lord Invader and Lionel Belasco that was recorded by many musicians and became a hit for the Andrews Sisters in 1945.

19. "Coke Meets Its Goal: 'In' Not 'Way Out,'" *Broadcasting*, 29 June 1964, 46.

20. Kaplan, "Cola Wars and Remembrance," 31S.

21. Louis and Yazijian, *Cola Wars*, 233.

22. Anne Phillips, telephone interview by author, 9 October 2009.

23. Hilary Lipsitz, interview by Scott Ellsworth, New York City, 19 April 1985, Pepsi Generation Oral History and Documentation Collection, 1938–1986, no. 111, Archives Center, National Museum of American History, Smithsonian Institution, Washington, DC.

24. Kaplan, "Cola Wars and Remembrance," 31S. Many of these versions are collected on *Great Cola Commercials*, vol. 1, Vox 1, 1996; and *Great Cola Commercials*, vol. 2, Vox 2, 1996. Musicians include Chicago, Ray Charles, Nancy Sinatra, the Newbeats, Warner Mack, Fontella Bass, the Tremeloes, Brooklyn Bridge, Freddie Cannon, and many more.

According to Hooper White, "music for commercials is of greatest value when it can be 'pooled up,' with many different tempos, arrangements, and versions," though it can be expensive because of all the arranging and musicians needed. Hooper White, *How to Produce Effective TV Commercials* (Lincolnwood, IL: NTC Business Books, 1989), 186. This is a strategy that dates at least until the late 1950s. A jingle for Carolina Rice, introduced in 1948, was recorded by Janette Davis "in a sexy southern drawl," and was intended to appeal to "the housewife," "the Negro population," the "Spanish speaking population," "kids," and the "retailer." After a decade of use, however, the company and its advertising agency decided not to scrap the jingle but to have variations of it written. These were incorporated into a single jingle, which included "scraps of classical (for the housewife), Dixieland (for the Negro), and cha-cha (for Spanish)." "Single Jingle Builds 10-Year Success," *Sponsor*, 8 November 1958, 39. Attempting to market to the Spanish-speaking population was unusual in this era, and would be for at least another decade; see "Howard Clothes' New Drive Puts Stress on Radio," *Advertising Age*, 29 February 1960, 211, for another article on the use of Spanish-language advertising that indicates the still unusual nature of this strategy over a decade later.

25. "Music to Buy Media By," *Sponsor*, November 1967, 14. See also "Coke Adds to Teen-Appeal Jingle Singers," *Advertising Age*, 11 October 1965, 19.

26. Dillon, interview by Ellsworth, 23 May 1984.

27. Philip Hinerfeld, interview by Scott Ellsworth, Boca Raton, FL, 7 November 1984, Pepsi Generation Oral History and Documentation Collection, 1938–1986, no. 111, Archives Center, National Museum of American History, Smithsonian Institution, Washington, DC.

28. John Bergin, interview by Scott Ellsworth, New York City, 6 February 1985, Pepsi Generation Oral History and Documentation Collection, 1938–1986, no. 111, Archives Center, National Museum of American History, Smithsonian Institution, Washington, DC.

29. Allen Rosenshine, interview by Scott Ellsworth, New York City, 10 December 1984, Pepsi Generation Oral History and Documentation Collection, 1938–1986, no. 111, Archives Center, National Museum of American History, Smithsonian Institution, Washington, DC.

30. Dillon, interview by Ellsworth, 23 May 1984.

31. "'Pepsi Generation' Jingle Bows in Radio Spot Drive," *Advertising Age*, 3 August 1964, 2.

32. Frank, *Conquest of Cool*, 175.

33. Louis and Yazijian, *Cola Wars*, 139.

34. Frank, *Conquest of Cool*, 171, citing Forkan, "Pepsi Generation Bridges Two Decades," 41.

35. Sid Ramin, personal communication, 22 October 2009.

36. I have been unable to locate such a recording. Sid Ramin, interview by Scott Ellsworth, New York City, 18 December 1984, Pepsi Generation Oral History and Documentation Collection, 1938–1986, no. 111, Archives Center, National Museum of American History, Smithsonian Institution, Washington, DC.

37. Tom Anderson, interview by Scott Ellsworth, New York City, 14 November 1984, Pepsi Generation Oral History and Documentation Collection, 1938–1986, no. 111, Archives Center, National Museum of American History, Smithsonian Institution, Washington, DC.

38. Bergin, interview by Ellsworth, 6 February 1985.

39. "Pepsi Launches All-Out Campaign Promoting 'Generation' Theme," *Sponsor*, 14 September 1964, 19.

40. Frank, *Conquest of Cool*, 176.

41. Jackson Lears, *Fables of Abundance: A Cultural History of Advertising in America* (New York: Basic, 1994).

42. Phillips, telephone interview by author, 9 October 2009.

43. Hilary Lipsitz, interview by Scott Ellsworth, New York City, 7 February 1985, Pepsi Generation Oral History and Documentation Collection, 1938–1986, no. 111, Archives Center, National Museum of American History, Smithsonian Institution, Washington, DC.

44. Frank writes that during this period, Pepsi produced a commercial that was clearly influenced by psychedelia. I have been unable to see this, so will rely on Frank's description of this commercial, a

> fragmented, impressionistic montage of hip urban nightlife that is as naïve and rosy a rendering of the counterculture as anything written by Roszak or Reich. The commercial is very dark throughout with only city lights and a variety of glowing emblems shining through the gloom. Figures are always dim, lit from one side only, or illuminated by a flashing strobe lamp. No one speaks though the entire commercial; even the Pepsi jingle, which drones throughout in a Byrds-like rendering, has to go without lyrics. The spot is held together by the sporadic appearance of a woman wearing fashionably short hair and a sequined minidress. As it opens she is striking poses for the camera; perhaps she is a

model of some sort. Then she is having her face painted with a fluorescent flower design. After shots of Times Square, marquee lights, and a large Pepsi logo rendered in sequins, she is shown drinking from a cup marked with the glowing word 'Pepsi,' holding an oversized lollipop, and dancing to music being played by a rock band. (Frank, *Conquest of Cool*, 178)

See "Psychedelic Jingles to Turn Listeners On," *Broadcasting*, 31 October 1966, 77, for a slightly earlier usage of psychedelic music, which Detroit-based Theme Productions Inc., the music production company, called "Intensodylic Sound," in part because of its electronic genesis.

45. Louis and Yazijian, *Cola Wars*, 139.

46. Rosenshine, interview by Ellsworth, 10 December 1984.

47. Ibid.

48. Lipsitz, interview by Ellsworth, 7 February 1985.

49. Bergin, interview by Ellsworth, 6 February 1985.

50. Louis and Yazijian, *Cola Wars*, 139.

51. "Pepsi's 'Got a Lot to Give' Drive Wins Viewer Praise; Music Sought," *Advertising Age*, 22 December 1969, 2, 34.

52. Frank, *Conquest of Cool*, 182, quoting PepsiCo, *Media Ordering Catalog* for 1970.

53. *Pepsi 70*, Pepsi-Cola Radio PA 1760, 1970; emphasis in original.

54. *Pepsi 1971*, PA 1818, n.d.

55. Rosenshine, interview by Ellsworth, 10 December 1984.

56. Backer provides a detailed history of this commercial in Bill Backer, *The Care and Feeding of Ideas* (New York: Times Books, 1993).

57. Hilary Lipsitz discussed fees paid to major musicians in the 1960s, which were quite low because musicians in this period were paid out of promotion budgets and not advertising, a practice that later changed. Lipsitz, interview by Ellsworth, 19 April 1985. The abstract of this interview includes an undated estimate for three commercials performed by the Union Gap, a band popular in the late 1960s and early 1970s; the fee for musicians was $2,376; the fee for "Talent" was $4,000. Collection 111, Series 2, box 13, Hilary Lipsitz, Archives Center, National Museum of American History, Smithsonian Institution, Washington, DC.

58. Backer, *Care and Feeding of Ideas*, 48.

59. Bill Backer, telephone interview by author, 4 May 2004.

60. This was reported in a clipping reproduced in Backer, *Care and Feeding of Ideas*, 251.

61. Backer, telephone interview by author, 4 May 2004.

62. This was reported in an uncited clipping in Backer, *Care and Feeding of Ideas*, 214.

63. Uncited clipping reprinted in Backer, *Care and Feeding of Ideas*, 205.

64. Backer's *Care and Feeding of Ideas* reprints several clippings on these cover versions and sales.

65. For a later campaign in which Coke targeted youth reminiscent of the "Hilltop" commercial, see Debbie Seaman, "Coke Gives Refresher Course in Singing," *Adweek*, 16 February 1987.

66. Frank, *Conquest of Cool*.

67. C. H. Sandage, Vernon Fryburger, and Kim Rotzoll, *Advertising Theory and Practice*, 11th ed. (Homewood, IL: Richard D. Irwin, 1983), 103.

68. Dan Seymour, keynote address, Art Directors Club of New York, Annual Visual Communications Conference, 14 April 1965, J. Walter Thompson Company Archive, JWT Writings and Speeches Collection, box 32: Seymour, Dan, 1964–1966, John W. Hartman Center

for Sales, Advertising, and Marketing History, Duke University, Durham, NC; emphasis in original.

69. Dan Seymour, "The New Reality of Radio," 10 November 1967, J. Walter Thompson Company Archive, Duke University, JWT Writings and Speeches Collection, box 32: Seymour, Dan, 1967–1968, April, John W. Hartman Center for Sales, Advertising, and Marketing History, Duke University, Durham, NC.

70. Dan Seymour, speech before Distributor Sales Meeting, Indianapolis, 11 September 1967, J. Walter Thompson Company Archive, JWT Writings and Speeches Collection, box 32: Seymour, Dan, 1967–1968, April, John W. Hartman Center for Sales, Advertising, and Marketing History, Duke University, Durham, NC.

71. Fairfax M. Cone, *The Blue Streak: Some Observations, Mostly about Advertising* (n.p.: Crain Communications, 1973), 187.

72. "Music to Buy Media By," 14.

73. "Six (6) Rock Groups to Give Word on Music to AA Workshop," *Advertising Age,* 13 April 1970, 28.

74. "The Biography of a Commercial," *Sponsor,* 5 April 1965, 41; emphasis in original.

75. Edward Buxton, *Creative People at Work* (New York: Executive Communications, 1975), 156; ellipses in original.

76. "Jingles Production Co. in Nashville Gears to Growth," *Billboard,* 29 August 1970, 4.

77. Eugene Feehan, "The Sound of TV Music," *Television Magazine,* February 1967, 28.

78. Terry Galanoy, *Down the Tube, or Making Television Commercials Is Such a Dog-Eat-Dog Business It's No Wonder They're Called Spots* (Chicago: Henry Regnery, 1970), 78.

79. Feehan, "Sound of TV Music," 28–29.

80. Galanoy, *Down the Tube,* 75. See also "Alka-Seltzer 'Stomach' Tune Becomes Pop-Hit—and Not for Belly Dancers," *Advertising Age,* 10 January 1965, 3.

81. See Chuck Wingis, "Songwriter Nichols Bemoans 'Budget' Jingles," *Advertising Age,* 13 September 1976, 116, for a discussion of "We've Only Just Begun."

82. Steve Karmen, *Through the Jingle Jungle: The Art and Business of Making Music for Commercials* (New York: Billboard Books, 1989), 93.

83. Michael J. Arlen, *Thirty Seconds* (New York: Penguin, 1980), 31–39.

84. Arlen, *Thirty Seconds,* 40–41.

85. Paul Cohen, "Twenty Years After: Woodstock Redux," *Back Stage,* 21 April 1989, 2B.

86. Artie Schroeck, telephone interview by author, 28 July 2009.

87. James P. Forkan, "Rockbill Gives Advertisers, Rock Stars Exposure," *Advertising Age,* 20 November 1978, 12.

88. See Pamela G. Hollie, "A Rush for Singers to Promote Goods," *New York Times,* 14 May 1984, §D, p. 1.

89. Eliot Tiegel, "Warner Puts Top-40 Hits in Ads," *Advertising Age,* 26 August 1985, 49.

90. Stuart Elliott, "Can Mick Jagger Deliver Chap Stick to Masses? 'Rolling Stone' Tells All," *Advertising Age,* 29 September 1986, 43.

91. Leslie Savan, *The Sponsored Life: Ads, TV, and American Culture* (Philadelphia: Temple University Press, 1994), 284.

92. Bob Weinstein, "The Medium Music Is the Message," *Madison Avenue,* July 1985, 46.

93. Bill Meyer, "Is Music Drowning Out the Pitch?," *Adweek,* 14 September 1981, 17.

94. "1950s and '60s Rock Still Alive in Radio-TV Jingles," *Billboard,* 26 July 1980, 70.

95. Ben Allen, "Ad Music: One Long Jingle," *Back Stage,* 20 April 1979, 1.

96. Nancy Millman, "They Make the Music That Makes the Ad Sing," *Advertising Age*, 22 September 1980, S-10.

97. Meyer, "Is Music Drowning Out the Pitch?," 1, 17.

98. Judith Topper, "Agency Reveals the Whys, Wheres and Whens of Getting the Score," *Back Stage*, 20 April 1984, 10B.

99. Anthony Vagnoni, "Music Makers Sing Out," *Back Stage*, 20 April 1984, 1.

100. "Good News! Plus: Because Shaving Can 'Hurt So Bad,'" *Marketing through Music*, April 1987, 5.

101. Michael Gross, "Selling to 'The Big Chill' Beat," *Adweek*, 4 February 1985, C.R. 30.

102. Hunter Murtaugh, telephone interview by author, 16 October 2009.

103. John Wall, "Madison Avenue Learns to Rock," *Insight*, 14 April 1986, 54.

104. "Emotion Sells More Than Perfume; It Sells Cars, Too," *Marketing News*, 22 November 1985, 4.

105. Pamela Sherrid, "Emotional Shorthand," *Forbes*, 4 November 1985, 215.

106. "Emotion Sells More Than Perfume," 4.

107. Sherrid, "Emotional Shorthand," 215.

108. "News from the World of Ford," 11 June 1985, J. Walter Thompson Company Archives, Advertising Vertical File, box 8, pp. 1–2, John W. Hartman Center for Sales, Advertising, and Marketing History, Duke University, Durham, NC.

109. Ibid.

110. "New Lincoln-Mercury Campaign Highlights the Distinctive Sound of Rod Stewart," *Marketing through Music*, October 1986, 1. See also Raymond Serafin, "Ford Division Plows into Radio," *Advertising Age*, 1 September 1986, 3.

111. Wall, "Madison Avenue Learns to Rock," 55.

112. Christine Demkowych, "Music on the Upswing in Advertising," *Advertising Age*, 31 March 1986, S-5.

113. Lawrence Graham and Lawrence Hamdan, *Youthtrends™: Capturing the $200 Billion Youth Market* (New York: St. Martin's Press, 1987). The book contains several discussions of music.

114. "New Book Promotes Music in Youth Advertisements," *Marketing through Music*, October 1987, 1, 6.

115. "Godley and Creme Drive L-M into 'New Age,'" *Marketing through Music*, November 1987, 6.

116. "Hitachi Culture Special Presents Kitaro Debut," *Marketing through Music*, November 1987, 6.

117. "Marketers Invited to Take the 'A' Train," *Marketing through Music*, May 1988, 6.

118. "M.T.M. Datafax," *Marketing through Music*, March 1989, 1. For more on New Age music in advertising in this period, see Laura Loro, "New Age Music Scores in Ads," *Advertising Age*, 22 August 1988, 39.

119. Blayne Cutler, "For What It's Worth," *American Demographics*, August 1989, 42.

120. Joyce Rutter, "Kuby Conducts," *Advertising Age*, 1 August 1988, 15S.

121. "Commercials Swing to Music," *Ad Day/USA*, 6 August 1981.

122. Jon Burlingame, "Tyros, Composer and Classics Vie for Ad Time," *Variety*, 29 July–4 August 2002, A4.

123. Jock Baird, "Chevys, Chunkies, & Cheerios," *Musician*, March 1990, 62; emphasis in original.

124. Susan Hamilton, telephone interview by author, 16 October 2009.

125. James Fadden, "HEA Will Drop a Line to Keep Things Fresh," *Back Stage*, 20 April 1984, 12B. See also Walter Bottger and Henry Martin, "Where Goes the Jingle?," *Back Stage*, 20 April 1984, 42B.

126. Fadden, "HEA Will Drop a Line," 12B.

127. "Track Record Enterprises—The 'Un-jingle' Producers," *Back Stage*, 20 April 1984, 14B.

128. Nancy Millman, "Her Road to Fame Was Paved with Commercials," *Advertising Age*, 19 December 1983, M-4.

129. Hooper White, "Beers Battle to Take over the Night," *Advertising Age*, 22 September 1986, 73.

130. Rutter, "Kuby Conducts," 15S.

131. Luc Boltanski and Ève Chiapello, *The New Spirit of Capitalism*, trans. Gregory Elliott (New York: Verso, 2005), 27.

132. Ibid., 38.

133. Ibid., 425.

134. Ibid., 438.

135. Ibid., 443.

136. Joyce Kurpiers, "Reality by Design: Advertising Image, Music and Sound Design in the Production of Culture," PhD diss., Duke University, 2009, 47.

137. Cone, *Blue Streak*.

138. Frank, *Conquest of Cool*.

139. Stephen Fox, *The Mirror Makers: A History of American Advertising and Its Creators*, 2nd ed. (Urbana: University of Illinois Press, 1997), 270.

140. Boltanski and Chiapello, *New Spirit of Capitalism*, 441.

Chapter 7

1. George Lipsitz, "Consumer Spending as State Project: Yesterday's Solutions and Today's Problems," in *Getting and Spending: European and American Consumer Societies in the Twentieth Century*, ed. Susan Strasser, Charles McGovern, and Matthias Judt (Cambridge: Cambridge University Press, 1998). For more on consumption in the 1980s, see Lizabeth Cohen, *A Consumer's Republic: The Politics of Mass Consumption in Postwar America* (New York: Knopf, 2003); and Martyn J. Lee, *Consumer Culture Reborn: The Cultural Politics of Consumption* (New York: Routledge, 1993).

2. Timothy D. Taylor, *Beyond Exoticism: Western Music and the World* (Durham, NC: Duke University Press, 2007).

3. James B. Twitchell, *Lead Us into Temptation: The Triumph of American Materialism* (New York: Columbia University Press, 1999), 18.

4. See Christopher Shannon, *A World Made Safe for Differences: Cold War Intellectuals and the Politics of Identity* (Lanham, MD: Rowman and Littlefield, 2001); and Taylor, *Beyond Exoticism*.

5. Scott Elias, interview by author, New York City, 19 April 2004.

6. Buddy Scott, "The Magic of Jingles and the Audio Image," *Broadcasting*, 8 August 1983, 24.

7. "Music Houses Achieve New Prominence in Music Marketing Era," *Marketing through Music*, March 1987, 6.

8. On the importance of niche marketing, see Scott Lash and John Urry, *Economies of Signs and Space* (Thousand Oaks, CA: Sage, 1994); and Scott Lash and John Urry, *The End of Organized Capitalism* (Madison: University of Wisconsin Press, 1987).

9. For a discussion of other modes of demographic analysis, see Joseph Turow, *Breaking Up America: Advertisers and the New Media World* (Chicago: University of Chicago Press, 1997).

10. Arnold Mitchell, *The Nine American Lifestyles: Who We Are and Where We're Going* (New York: Macmillan, 1983), 5.

11. Ibid., 8.

12. Ibid., 15.

13. See Mitchell, *Nine American Lifestyles*, 63, 176–79. Subsequent data have become even more detailed and sophisticated. "Innovators" are sophisticated, in charge, curious; "Thinkers" are informed, reflective, and content; "Believers" are literal, loyal, and moralistic; "Achievers" are goal-oriented, brand-conscious, and conventional; "Strivers" are contemporary, imitative, and style-conscious; "Experiencers" are trend seeking, impulsive, and variety seeking; "Makers" are responsible, practical, and self-sufficient; and "Survivors" are nostalgic, constrained, and cautious. All of these groups are categorized by a number of factors such as age, percentage of the population, employment status, marriage status, contributions to public broadcasting, and more. Strategic Business Insights, "Sample Demographics and Behaviors," last accessed 31 July 2011, http://www.strategicbusinessinsights.com/vals/demobehav.shtml.

14. James Vail, "Music as Marketing Tool," *Advertising Age*, 4 November 1985, 24.

15. Ed Fitch, "Ad Music Composer Humming a Happy Tune," *Advertising Age*, 28 February 1985, 38.

16. On the former case, see Gary Levin, "Holiday Inns Book Sinatra," *Advertising Age*, 25 May 1987, 1. Sinatra re-recorded his well-known "Here's to the Winners" for these television commercials.

17. Leslie H. Zeifman, "The Sound of Music," *Advertising Age*, 9 November 1988, 62.

18. Bernie Drayton, telephone interview by author, 14 August 2009. For more on the rise of African American advertising agencies, see Stephen Fox, *The Mirror Makers: A History of American Advertising and Its Creators*, 2nd ed. (Urbana: University of Illinois Press, 1997); and Janice Ward Moss, *The History and Advancement of African Americans in the Advertising Industry, 1895–1999* (Lewiston, NY: Edwin Mellen, 2003).

19. Hilary Lipsitz, interview by Scott Ellsworth, New York City, 19 April 1985, Pepsi Generation Oral History and Documentation Collection, 1938–1986, no. 111, Archives Center, National Museum of American History, Smithsonian Institution, Washington, DC.

20. A. Ross, "Monday Memo," *Broadcasting*, 24 September 1979, 16.

21. Ibid.

22. "Muy Rapido," *Television/Radio Age*, 10 December 1984, 30.

23. See, for example, Harry K. Renfro, "Country and Western Consumer: Forgotten Man in Jingle Market," *Broadcasting*, 7 July 1958, 105; "The C&W Sound Captures U.S. Heart & Purse," *Sponsor*, 20 May 1963, 31; "The New Appeal of Country Music," *Broadcasting*, 1 August 1966, 53–68; and Edward Morris, "Commercials' Newest Star Is Country," *Billboard*, 30 May 1981, 9.

24. Scott Elias, interview by author, New York City, 19 April 2004. See also Pamela Sherrid, "Emotional Shorthand," *Forbes*, 4 November 1985, 214–15, for agency professionals speaking on the new importance of visuals with music after MTV.

25. See, for just one example, E. Ann Kaplan, *Rocking around the Clock: Music Television, Postmodernism, and Consumer Culture* (New York: Routledge, 1987).

26. Susan Spillman, "Commercials Dance to Video Beat," *Advertising Age*, 10 January 1985, 48.

27. Ibid.

28. "How MTV Has Rocked Television Commercials," *New York Times*, 9 October 1989, §D, p. 6.

29. Jennifer Pendleton, "Chalk Up Another Victory for Trend-Setting Rock 'n' Roll," *Advertising Age*, 9 November 1988, 160.

30. David W. Freeman, "Honda Rides Music Videos into Advertising," *Advertising Age*, 19 July 1984, 46.

31. "Jerry Garcia, Others Sing Levi's 501 Blues," *Marketing through Music*, September 1987, 5; emphasis in original.

32. As reported by Robert Goldman, *Reading Ads Socially* (New York: Routledge, 1992), 185. Goldman discusses these commercials at some length.

33. "Jerry Garcia, Others Sing Levi's 501 Blues," 5.

34. "Current Collaborations," *Marketing through Music*, July 1988, 2.

35. James P. Forkan, "Pepsi Generation Bridges Two Decades," *Advertising Age*, 5 May 1980, 41.

36. Allen Rosenshine, *Funny Business: Moguls, Mobsters, Megastars, and the Mad, Mad World of the Ad Game* (New York: Beaufort Books, 2006), 91.

37. This comment resonates with one reported by Thomas Frank from an agency head who said in a presentation that "a brand's myth is everyday experience for consumers . . . and 'if you can understand experience, you can *own* it.'" Thomas Frank, *One Market under God: Extreme Capitalism, Market Populism, and the End of Economic Democracy* (New York: Anchor, 2000), 266; emphasis in original.

38. Allen Rosenshine, interview by Scott Ellsworth, New York City, 10 December 1984, Pepsi Generation Oral History and Documentation Collection, 1938–1986, no. 111, Archives Center, National Museum of American History, Smithsonian Institution, Washington, DC.

39. Ibid.

40. Roger Enrico and Jesse Kornbluth, *The Other Guy Blinked: How Pepsi Won the Cola Wars* (New York: Bantam, 1986), 92.

41. Ibid., 94.

42. Ibid., 99; emphasis in original.

43. Ibid., 11.

44. Phil Dusenberry, *Then We Set His Hair on Fire: Insights and Accidents from a Hall-of-Fame Career in Advertising* (New York: Portfolio, 2005), 232–33.

45. Enrico and Kornbluth, *Other Guy Blinked*, 270.

46. "Pepsi's 'Bad' Breaks: Two New Jackson Spots," *Marketing through Music*, December 1987, 1, 6.

47. Enrico and Kornbluth, *Other Guy Blinked*, 270.

48. Nancy Giges, "Pepsi and Jackson in New Link," *Advertising Age*, 5 May 1986, 1.

49. Ibid.

50. Ibid.

51. "Jackson's Pepsi Spots Showcase New Music," *Marketing through Music*, March 1987, 1–2.

52. Nancy Giges, "Pepsi-Jackson 'Spectacular' Set for Spring," *Advertising Age*, 16 February 1987, 2.

53. Bob Garfield, "Cola War's TV Extravaganzas: Jackson Gives Pepsi Bad Rap," *Advertising Age*, 2 November 1987, 3.

54. Bob Garfield, "George Michael's Spot for Diet Coke Lacks Pop," *Advertising Age*, 13 February 1989, 68.

55. Bob Garfield, "Pepsi Should Offer Prayer to Madonna," *Advertising Age*, 6 March 1989, 76; emphasis in original.

56. Zeifman, "Sound of Music," 162.

57. See Marchelle Renise Barber, "Commercial R-a-p," *Advertising Age*, 25 May 1987, 22.

58. Cyndee Miller, "Marketers Tap into Rap as Hip-Hop Becomes 'Safe,'" *Marketing News*, 18 January 1993, 10.

59. Bill Backer, telephone interview by author, 4 May 2004.

60. Artie Schroeck, telephone interview by author, 28 July 2009; and Linda November, telephone interview by author, 28 July 2009.

61. Nick DiMinno, telephone interview by author, 9 September 2009.

62. Anne Phillips, telephone interview by author, 9 October 2009.

63. Anne Phillips, "Why Isn't My Business Fun Anymore?," photocopy, ca. 1981. Thanks are due to Anne for providing me with this.

64. Jon Lafayette, "Burger King Be Jammin': Agency, Client Work with Top Artists for $20m-Plus Radio Effort," *Advertising Age*, 9 October 1989, 28.

65. Lafayette, "Burger King Be Jammin'," 28.

66. Ibid.

67. Gary Levin, "Salem Turns Up the Sound," *Advertising Age*, 24 April 1989, 1.

68. Mitchell Berk, "Kenny Rogers Tour Sponsorship Proves Fruitful for Dole Food Co.," *Marketing through Music*, August 1989, 5.

69. "Michael 'Pepsi' Jackson: Battling Coke Overseas," *Advertising Age*, 28 September 1987, 80; and Julia Michaels and Patricia Winters, "Music Reintroduces Pepsi to Brazil," *Advertising Age*, 28 September 1987, 80. For more on the intertwined nature of popular culture and advertising, see Jib Fowles, *Advertising and Popular Culture* (Thousand Oaks, CA: Sage, 1996).

70. Judith Graham, "Sponsors Line Up for Rockin' Role: Top Stars to Attract Top Marketers," *Advertising Age*, 11 December 1989, 50.

71. Ibid.

72. Ibid.

73. "Fuji & Enigma Ink Sponsorship/Mktg Pact," *Marketing through Music*, June 1989, 1.

74. "Adidas Launches Run-D.M.C. Sportswear Line," *Marketing through Music*, July 1987, 5.

75. "MTV Inspires Pontiac's Ad Effort in '88," *Advertising Age*, 21 September 1987, 84.

76. Ronald Alsop, "Ad Agencies Jazz up Jingles by Playing on 1960s Nostalgia," *Wall Street Journal*, 18 April 1985, 33.

77. "Music Tops Teen Study," *Marketing through Music*, April 1989, 6.

78. Judith Topper, "Creatives Try to Change Score," *Back Stage*, 20 April 1984, 58.

79. For more on the rise of licensing and advertising agency practices, see Bethany Klein, *As Heard on TV: Popular Music in Advertising* (Burlington, VT: Ashgate, 2009).

80. See Paul Grein, "TV & Radio Ad Usage of Pop Hits Up," *Billboard*, 22 May 1978, 3, 96, 110; Dick Nusser, "Radio-TV Jingles Go for Standards," *Billboard*, 22 April 1978, 102; "Old Songs Brew Jingles Gravy," *Billboard*, 4 December 1978, 77; and Roger Rosenblatt, "The Back of the Book: I Re-write the Songs," *New Republic*, 11 February 1978, 36–37.

81. Grein, "TV & Radio Ad Usage," 96.

82. "Setting Commercials to Music a Growing Part of Pop Culture," *Television/Radio Age, 1980 Production Guide*, 12.

83. Pamela Sherrid, "Emotional Shorthand," *Forbes*, 4 November 1985, 214.

84. "Spotting the Music," *Television/Radio Age*, 10 December 1984, 128.

85. Michele Conklin, "Parody Fever," *Madison Avenue*, December 1985, 36.

86. This list of titles is from Carrie McLaren and Rick Prelinger, "Salesnoise: The Convergence of Music and Advertising," *Stay Free!*, Fall 1998, last accessed 11 August 2010, http://www.ibiblio.org/pub/electronic-publications/stay-free/archives/15/salesnoise.html. See also Kim Kinter, "'Stop in the Name of Rock,' DJs Say," *Adweek*, 18 January 1988, 40; John Motavalli, "Turning Old Hits into New Jingles," *Adweek*, 11 January 1988, B.R. 35–B.R. 36; and "Rock Lovers Decry Use of Classics in Commercials," *Marketing News*, 1 February 1988, 21.

87. Sherrid, "Emotional Shorthand," 214.

88. James P. Forkan, "Turning '60s Music into '80s Ads," *Advertising Age*, 25 April 1985, 40.

89. "SBK Entertainment Offers Free Catalogs," *Marketing through Music*, March 1988, 6.

90. "The Jingle Biz: From Music House to Writer's Co-op," *Marketing through Music*, June 1988, 5.

91. "Newsline," *Advertising Age*, 9 March 1987, 8.

92. "Nike Breaks 'Revolutionary' Spots," *Adweek*, 9 March 1987, reports ten million dollars; "Newsline" reports seven million dollars.

93. "Nike Uses Beatles' Song to Launch 'Revolution,'" *Marketing through Music*, April 1987, 6.

94. Barbara Lippert, "Roll Over, John; the Song Fits, and Nike's Wearing It," *Adweek*, 6 April 1987, 23.

95. Sharon Edelson, "They Say They Want a Revolution: New Progressives Kagan & Greif Style Spots with a Music-Video Sensibility," *Advertising Age*, 1 June 1987, C26.

96. Ibid.

97. "Beatles Still Mean Business" (editorial), *Advertising Age*, 18 May 1987, 16.

98. Timothy G. Manners, letter to the editor, *Advertising Age*, 15 June 1987, 20.

99. Jon Wiener, "Beatles Buy-Out," *New Republic*, 11 May 1987, 13–14.

100. Jon Wiener, "Exploitation and the Revolution," *Advertising Age*, 29 June 1987, 18.

101. Tim Donohoe, letter to the editor, *Advertising Age*, 27 July 1987, 20.

102. "Beatles Company Sues over Use of Song in Ad," *New York Times*, 29 July 1987, §C, p. 22.

103. "Apple Records Sues over Nike's 'Revolution' Ads," *Marketing through Music*, September 1987, 1, 5.

104. Marcy Magiera, "Nike to Keep 'Revolution' despite Suit," *Advertising Age*, 3 August 1987, 3.

105. "For the Record," *Advertising Age*, 10 August 1987, 53.

106. "Other Late News," *Advertising Age*, 31 August 1987, 8.

107. "Nike Pulls Beatles Song; Revolution to Continue," *Marketing through Music*, April 1988, 1, 5.

108. "Nike Says It Hasn't Settled," *Adweek*, 29 February 1988.

109. Paul McCartney, interview by Anthony DeCurtis, *Rolling Stone*, 5 November / 10 December 1987, quoted in Marcy Magiera, "Discord on 'Revolution': McCartney Hits Nike, Jackson for Use of Song," *Advertising Age*, 26 October 1987, 36.

110. "New Role for Classic Rock" (editorial), *Advertising Age*, 14 September 1987, 16.

111. For more on composers' complaints about the licensing practices in this era, see Stephen Meyer, "Everybody Must Get Cloned," *Advertising Age*, 5 October 1987, C28.

112. "MTM Datafax," *Marketing through Music*, July 1988, 1.

113. "MTM Datafax," *Marketing through Music*, October 1988, 1.

114. Fran Fruit, "Look What They've Done to My Song, Ma," *Advertising Age*, 21 April 1986, 18.

115. "Claim That Tune," *Advertising Age*, 6 March 1989, 28S.

116. J. Max Robins and Chuck Reece, "Using Hard Rock for Soft Sell," *Adweek/East*, May 1985, M.M. 20.

117. Ibid.

118. Larry Armstrong, "Janis Joplin, Material Girl," *Business Week*, 20 March 1995, 40.

119. See Irv Lichtman, "Comeback Kids," *Billboard*, 13 June 1998, 45, and "Catalog Evergreens Pop Up as Jingles in Increasing Numbers," *Billboard*, 31 October 1998, 38.

Chapter 8

1. Christine Demkowych, "Music on the Upswing in Advertising," *Advertising Age*, 31 March 1986, S-5.

2. Bob Garfield, "Too Much Ad Music Leaves Little Room for Hitting the Right Note," *Advertising Age*, 4 January 1988, 46.

3. Bill Meyer, "Is Music Drowning Out the Pitch?," *Adweek*, 14 September 1981, 17.

4. Ibid., 18.

5. Judith Topper, "Theories, Thoughts and Reasons on Why Agencies Score Their Own," *Back Stage*, 20 April 1984, 6B.

6. Debbie Seaman, "The Serious Business of Writing Commercial Jingles," *Adweek*, 31 August 1987, 34.

7. Thomas Frank, *The Conquest of Cool: Business Culture, Counterculture, and the Rise of Hip Consumerism* (Chicago: University of Chicago Press, 1997).

8. See Peter DiCola, "False Premises, False Promises: A Quantitative History of Ownership Consolidation in the Radio Industry," 13 December 2006, last accessed 14 March 2010, http://www.futureofmusic.org/article/research/false-premises-false promises.

9. Clear Channel claims that there has been an increase in diversity of radio formats—kinds of programs—but a 2002 study by the Future of Music Coalition revealed that there is as much as a 76 percent overlap in playlists among radio formats. Jenny Eliscu, "Why Radio Sucks," *Rolling Stone*, 3 April 2003, 22. See also Jeff Leeds, "Small Record Labels Say Radio Tunes Them Out," *Los Angeles Times*, 16 September 2001, C1.

10. See Eric Boehlert and John Hogan, interview by Terry Gross, *Fresh Air*, National Public Radio, 23 July 2003.

There is also an existing "legal payola" system. It has long been illegal for radio labels to reward radio stations for playing their songs, so an industry of intermediaries known as "indies" performs this function. Major labels hire indies to represent their interests to radio stations. Money is exchanged for "promotional support"—giveaways, free tickets, etc.—but not directly between radio stations and labels. Eric Boehlert, "Pay for Play," *Salon*, 14 March 2001, http://www.salon.com. See also Boehlert's "One Big Happy Channel?," *Salon*, 28 June 2001, http://www.salon.com, and "Radio's Big Bully," *Salon*, 30 April 2001, http://www.salon.com; Chris Doerksen, "Same Old Song and Dance," 28 February 2003, www.washingtoncitypaper.com; and Greg Kot, "Rocking Radio's World," *Chicago Tribune*, 14 April 2002, 1.

11. David Segal, "Pop Music's New Creed: Buy a TV Commercial," *Washington Post*, 27 February 2002, A1.

12. Greg Lindsay, "Ad as Breakout Song Launchpad," *Advertising Age*, 11 July 2005, 26.

13. Peter Nicholson, "Branded for Success: McDonald's, Others Reveal Agency World Clout When It Comes to Music," *Billboard*, 18 August 2007, 4.

14. Allyce Bess, "That New Hit Single Might Hide a Jingle," *Christian Science Monitor*, 9 December 2002, 11; bracketed term in original.

15. Josh Rabinowitz, "With the Brand: A Public Picking: The Process of Choosing a Song for Ad Placement," *Billboard*, 16 February 2008, 16.

16. Recording Industry Association of America, "2008 Consumer Profile," http://www.riaa.com/keystatistics.php?content_selector=MusicConsumerProfile; "The CD Slide: It's Way Worse Than You Think . . . ," *Digital Music News*, 2 June 2011, http://www.digitalmusicnews.com/stories/06021cds.

17. Licensing has received a good deal of coverage in both the trade and mainstream presses. See Ronald Alsop, "Ad Agencies Jazz Up Jingles by Playing on 1960s Nostalgia," *Wall Street Journal*, 18 April 1985, 33; Eric Boehlert, "Bittersweet Synergy," *Rolling Stone*, 19 March 1998, 25–26, and "Singles Meet Jingles," *Rolling Stone*, 11 November 1999, 27–28; Valerie Block, "Jingle Biz Rocked by Licensed Pop in Ads," *Advertising Age*, 3 February 2003, 6; Ann-Christine Diaz, "Them Changes," *Creativity*, July 2003, 26–28; Paul Farhi, "With a Song in Their Spot," *Washington Post*, 4 January 1998, H1; James P. Forkan, "Turning '60s Music into '80s Ads," *Advertising Age*, 25 April 1985, 40; Debra Goldman, "Two-Part Harmony," *Adweek*, 10 November 1997, 62; Stefano Hatfield, "Music to Watch Sales By," *Creativity*, July 2003, 34–35; Bob Kaplan, "POV," *Creativity*, July 2003, 6; Joey Levine, interview by Beatrice Black, National Public Radio, *Marketplace*, 26 February 2003; Carrie McLaren, "Licensed to Sell," *Village Voice*, 28 April 1998, 36–37; Russ Pate, "Those Oldies but Goodies," *Adweek/Southwest*, 9 April 1984, 12; Tom Vanderbilt, "Taste: That Selling Sound, the Strange Musical Accompaniment to Cruise Lines, Cookies, Cars," *Wall Street Journal*, 12 July 2002, W13; John Wall, "Madison Avenue Learns to Rock," *Insight*, 14 April 1986, 54–55; and Richenda Wilson, "Commercial Sounds," *Marketing Week*, 6 May 1999, 47–52.

18. Frank, *Conquest of Cool*, 11.

19. Wayne Friedman, "Music Labels Court Brands," *Advertising Age*, 16 September 2002, 19.

20. Jeff Silberman, "2000 and Beyond," *Billboard*, 4 November 2000, 10.

21. Cyndee Miller, "Marketers Find Alternative Way to Appeal to Young Music Lovers," *Marketing News*, 12 October 1992, 18.

22. John Leland, "Selling Out Isn't What It Used to Be," *New York Times* magazine, 11 March 2001, 50.

23. Greg Kot, "In the Promotion World, Video Ads Killed the Radio Star," *Chicago Tribune*, 6 October 2002, 7.

24. Sandy Brown, "Licensing Music for the Masses," *Boards*, 2 April 2002, 42.

25. Joan Anderman, "Commercial Instinct: Boston's Modernista! and Other Creators of TV Spots Have Become the Hippest DJs Around," *Boston Globe*, 24 June 2001, L1.

26. Leland, "Selling Out Isn't What It Used to Be," 50. Moby was at the vanguard of licensing; some reports say that the tracks on his 1999 album *Play* have been licensed up to six hundred times. Terry Lawson, "Ad Execs Do Music Acts, Fans a Favor," *Detroit Free Press*, 20 May 2001, http://www.freep.com/entertainment/music/lawcol20_20010520.htm. See also Ethan Smith, "Organization Moby," *Wired*, May 2002, 88–95; and Evan Wiener, "For Sale: Moby

(and Every Other Hip Recording Artist on the Planet)," *Business 2.0*, December 2001, http://www.business2.com/articles/mag/0,1640,35037,00.html.

27. Michael Paoletta, "Dance & Electronic Music: Soundtrack to the World?," *Billboard*, 22 March 2003, 39.

28. "BBH's New Music Model," *Advertising Age*, 28 July 2003, S-7.

29. Joshua Ostroff, "Commercial Music: Where It's At," *Boards*, 1 April 2003, 45.

30. Patricia Winters Lauro, "Forget Jingles. Viewers Prefer Familiar Tunes in Commercials," *New York Times*, 8 November 1999, C1.

31. Ostroff, "Commercial Music," 45.

32. On the proliferation of the underground into mainstream advertising, see Anne Elizabeth Moore, *Unmarketable: Brandalism, Copyfighting, Mocketing, and the Erosion of Integrity* (New York: New Press, 2007).

33. Phil Patton, "Like the Song, Love the Car," *New York Times*, 15 September 2002, §12, p. 1.

34. David Bloom, "Music Biz Takes to the Road," *Variety*, 16–22 September 2002, 6.

35. David Kiley, *Getting the Bugs Out: The Rise, Fall, and Comeback of Volkswagen in America* (New York: Wiley, 2002).

36. Chris Morris, "U.S. TV Ads Tap into New Music, as Stigma Fades," *Billboard*, 25 April 1998, 1.

37. This is the commercial used to advertise the Cabrio in 1999.

38. Leland, "Selling Out Isn't What It Used to Be," 51.

39. Liner notes to *Street Mix*, vol. 1, 2001.

40. Volkswagen, http://www.vw.com/musicpillar/listen.htm; uppercase in original. (This URL, active in the late 1990s and early 2000s, is no longer operational.)

41. Tracy L. Scott, "Music Highlights Mitsubishi TV Ads," *Washington Post*, 9 June 2002, Y6.

42. Ibid.

43. Wiener, "For Sale."

44. The video for this song, available on YouTube, shows Touche shuffling through his vinyl collection, followed immediately by images of real musicians executing what is actually sampled in the Wiseguys' track.

45. Michael McCarthy, "Mitsubishi Campaign Starts Commotion," *USA Today*, 24 December 2001, B6.

46. Ibid.

47. Stefano Hatfield, "The Long & Winding Road: Mitsubishi," *Creativity*, May 2003, 30.

48. Mike Huckman, CNBC, *Business with CNBC*, 21 February 2003.

49. "Mitsubishi Motors and Deutch Launch Advertising Program to Introduce Endeavor SUV," 24 March 2003, http://www.theauthochannel.com/news/2003/03/24/158069.html.

50. Jean Halliday, "British Band Makes U.S. Debut in Car Commercial," *Advertising Age*, 11 March 2002, http://www.adage.com/news.cms?newsId=34194.

51. Donna DeMarco, "Pop Artists Go Commercial," *Insight*, 24 June 2002, 27.

52. Cary Darling, "Car Ads Get an Electronic Tune-up," *Montreal Gazette*, 6 March 2003, §D, p. 1.

53. Patton, "Like the Song," §12, p. 1.

54. Paoletta, "Dance & Electronic Music," 39.

55. Wiener, "For Sale."

56. Paoletta, "Dance & Electronic Music," 39.

57. Tobi Elkin, "TiVo Inks Pacts for Long-Form TV Ads," *Advertising Age*, 17 June 2002, 1.

58. Stuart Elliott, "In Branded Entertainment, 'It's the Wild West' as a Marketing Strategy," *International Herald Tribune*, 30 March 2005, 16.

59. Hank Kim, "Just Risk It," *Advertising Age*, 9 February 2004, 1.

60. Lindsay, "Ad as Breakout Song Launchpad," 26.

61. Marc Graser, "Creativity Bonds Mad Ave., Showbiz," *Daily Variety*, 25 November 2002, 14.

62. Nicholson, "Branded for Success," 4.

63. Jason Koransky, "The Drive behind Neill's *Automotive*," *Down Beat*, February 2003, 20.

64. Ben Neill, *Automotive*, six degrees 657036 1077–2, 2002. For more on Neill and *Automotive*, see his website, http://www.benneill.com.

65. Ben Neill, liner notes to *Automotive*.

66. Bess, "That New Hit Single," 11.

67. Huckman, *Business with CNBC*.

68. Scott Donaton, "Sting-Jaguar Deal Still Serves as Model for the Music World," *Advertising Age*, 22 September 2003, 22.

69. Bradford Wernle, "Jaguar S-Type Evokes Feeling of Style and Success, Says Rock Star Sting," *Automotive News Europe*, 27 March 2000, 18.

70. Ibid.

71. Donaton, "Sting-Jaguar Deal," 22.

72. Ibid.

73. Chris Ballard, "How to Write a Catchy Beer Ad," *New York Times* magazine, 26 January 2003, 14–16.

74. Jean Halliday, "Toyota Links with Phil Collins," *Advertising Age*, 14 October 2002, 14.

75. Jean Halliday, "Carmakers Pick Up the Beat," *Advertising Age*, 14 April 2003, §S, p. 4.

76. See Mark Anthony Neal, "'Real, Compared to What': Anti-war Soul," *PopMatters*, 28 March 2003, last accessed 11 August 2010, http://www.popmatters.com/features/030328-iraq-neal.shtml.

77. Scott Donaton, "Steve Berman Hears Music in Alliances with Advertisers," *Advertising Age*, 7 April 2003, 18.

78. "Human and Sprite: Jingle All the Way," *Creativity*, July 2007, 28.

79. Ibid.

80. Marc Altshuler, "Effective and Sustainable Branding Starts with Music," *Advertising Age*, 5 November 2007, 23.

81. Randi Schmelzer, "RPM's New Urban Marketing Tool: The DJ Made Me Do It," *Adweek*, 13 March 2005, 14; see also Rebecca Flass and Katy Bachman, "Pepsi Experiment Gathers Momentum," *Adweek*, 3 February 2003, 10.

82. Schmelzer, "RPM's New Urban Marketing Tool," 14.

83. Marc Graser, "McDonald's on Lookout to Be Big Mac Daddy," *Advertising Age*, 28 March 2005, 123.

84. See the Maven Strategies website at http://mavenstrategies.com.

85. Graser, "McDonald's on Lookout," 123.

86. Quoted in "10 Most Successful Product Launches," *Advertising Age*, 22 December 2003, 26.

87. Kate MacArthur and Jack Neff, "Sprite Shifts Gears in Quest for Street Cred," *Advertising Age*, 26 January 2004, 1.

88. Rob Walker, "Sprite ReMix," *New York Times*, 28 March 2004, §6, p. 24.

89. See Andrew Hampp, "A Reprise for Jingles on Madison Avenue," *Advertising Age*, 6 September 2010, 1.

90. "If There Were a Jingle, We'd Know the Commandments," *St. Petersburg Times*, 11 October 2007, 6A.

91. "Big Mac® Chant-Off," last accessed 16 July 2011, http://www.myspace.com/bigmac chant. See also Charlie Moran, "McDonald's Asks Aspiring Musicians to Bring Their Own Special Sauce," *Advertising Age*, 25 June 2008, http://adage.com/songsforsoap/post?article_id=128001.

92. Charlie Moran, "Jason Harper: King of Big Mac Chants," *Advertising Age*, 22 July 2008, http://adage.com/songsforsoap/post?article_id=129823.

93. Ibid. See also Stephanie Clifford, "2 All-Beef Patties Are Back," *New York Times*, 17 July 2008, §C, p. 1.

94. Stuart Elliott, "Musicians Market Brands to Sell Their Latest Music," *New York Times*, 24 May 2005, §C, p. 5.

95. Mike Tunnicliffe, "The Brand Band Love-in," *Campaign*, 7 November 2008, 27.

96. Chris Lee, "This Music Is Sponsored By . . . ," *Los Angeles Times*, 7 March 2010, §E, p. 1. Thanks are due to Joanna Love-Tulloch, who told me of this article.

97. Eleftheria Parpis, "Profile: Steve Stoute," *Adweek.com*, 25 August 2008.

98. "Wrigley Suspends Brown from Ads," *Adweek.com*, 10 February 2009.

99. Kamau High, "Arcade Creative Group: Agency of Record," *Billboard*, 4 October 2008, 12.

100. Kamau High, "Listen to the Brand," *Billboard*, 19 July 2008, 24–25.

101. Charlie Moran, "The Record Label That's Also a Creative Agency," *Advertising Age*, 27 October 2008, 16.

102. For a discussion of the rise of corporate sponsorship of tours, see Cotton Seiler, "The Commodification of Rebellion: Rock Culture and Consumer Capitalism," in *New Forms of Consumption: Consumers, Culture, and Commodification*, ed. Mark Gottdiener (Lanham, MD: Rowman and Littlefield).

103. This "convergence of content and commerce" has not affected only popular musicians, as the quotation from a New York City music production company owner above indicates; major film composers such as Danny Elfman, David Newman, and Rachel Portman have signed to a company called Groove Addicts, which seeks to connect such figures with commercial opportunities; famed minimalist composer Philip Glass (described in the advertising trade press as "primarily known for work outside the commercial arena") has signed on as well. Tom Soter, "Clear as Glass," *Shootonline*, 24 September 2004. In 2004, Glass scored the music for a Samsung commercial that was aired during the Summer Olympics that year; previously, Glass had written the music for two Altoids commercials. Glass's prestige transfers not only to the advertising world but also to the other composers who toil in it every day; one such composer told me that now they can aim to compete with the best pop artists, classical composers, and so forth. If a client says it wants a "minimalist" sound and it's also talking to Philip Glass, perhaps this composer's firm can win the contract.

104. Patricia McGinnis, "The Jingle Generation," *Marketing Communications*, January 1979, 71.

105. Mae Anderson, "On the Crest of the Wave," *Adweek.com*, 13 September 2004.

106. A good deal of what counts as "ethnography" among marketers is enough to make academic ethnographers cringe; one author characterizes ethnography as the observation of "consumer behavior in a natural environment"; ethnography is described as a "discipline" that "bor-

rows its techniques from the science of anthropology and allows marketers to study consumers in their everyday habitats." Todd Wasserman, "Watch and Learn," *Adweek*, 3 November 2003, 21.

107. Such as Hy Mariampolski, *Ethnography for Marketers: A Guide to Consumer Immersion* (Thousand Oaks, CA: Sage, 2006); John F. Sherry Jr., ed., *Contemporary Marketing and Consumer Behavior: An Anthropological Sourcebook* (Thousand Oaks, CA: Sage, 1995); and Patricia L. Sunderland and Rita M. Denny, *Doing Anthropology in Consumer Research* (Walnut Creek, CA: Left Coast Press, 2007). For a critique of these uses of anthropology and ethnography, see Patricia L. Sunderland and Rita M. Denny, "Psychology vs Anthropology: Where Is Culture in Marketplace Ethnography?," in *Advertising Cultures*, ed. Timothy deWaal Malefyt and Brian Moeran (New York: Berg, 2003).

108. Alison Dumas, "The Limits of Market-Research Methods," *Advertising Age*, 8 October 2007, 27.

109. ZandlGroup, last accessed 18 July 2011, http://www.zandlgroup.com; and Lev Grossman, "The Quest for Cool," *Time*, 8 September 2003, 44–50.

110. For another report on this industry, see Malcolm Gladwell, "The Coolhunt," *New Yorker*, 17 March 1999, 78–88.

111. Thom Duffy, "Songs' Selling Power Examined," *Billboard*, 3 July 1999, 57.

112. Anderman, "Commercial Instinct."

113. Ibid., 1.

114. Stuart Elliott, "Burger King Moves Quickly to Take a Product from TV to the Table," *New York Times*, 21 January 2005, §C, p. 4.

115. Nicholson, "Branded for Success."

116. Josh Rabinowitz, "With the Brand: Jingle in Your Pocket," *Billboard*, 19 January 2008, 17.

117. Charlie Moran, "Rapper Common Learns to Make Music with Microsoft," *Advertising Age*, 13 October 2008, 22; see also Hilary Crosley, "Common: Creative 'Control,'" *Billboard. com*, 6 December 2008.

118. Andrew Hampp, "Will.I.Am Is with the Brands—and Damn Proud of It," *Advertising Age*, 28 February 2011, 10.

119. Joyce Kurpiers, "Reality by Design: Advertising Image, Music and Sound Design in the Production of Culture," PhD diss., Duke University, 2009, 46.

Chapter 9

1. Richard Sennett, *The Corrosion of Character: The Personal Consequences of Work in the New Capitalism* (New York: Norton, 1998), and *The Culture of the New Capitalism* (New Haven, CT: Yale University Press, 2006).

2. John Ehrenreich and Barbara Ehrenreich, "The Professional-Managerial Class," in *Between Labor and Capital*, ed. Pat Walker (Boston: South End, 1979), 12. See also Gérard Duménil and Dominique Lévy, *Capital Resurgent: Roots of the Neoliberal Revolution*, trans. Derek Jeffers (Cambridge, MA: Harvard University Press, 2004).

3. Scott Lash and John Urry, *Economies of Signs and Space* (Thousand Oaks, CA: Sage, 1994).

4. Alvin Gouldner, *The Future of Intellectuals and the Rise of the New Class* (New York: Seabury, 1979).

5. Herbert J. Gans, "American Popular Culture and High Culture in a Changing Class Structure," in *Prospects: An Annual of American Culture Studies* 10, ed. Jack Salzman (New

York: Cambridge University Press, 1985); Richard A. Peterson and Roger M. Kern, "Changing Highbrow Taste: From Snob to Omnivore," *American Sociological Review* 61 (October 1996): 900–907; and Fred Pfeil, "'Makin' Flippy-Floppy': Postmodernism and the Baby-Boom PMC," in *Another Tale to Tell: Politics and Narrative in Postmodern Culture* (New York: Verso, 1990).

6. Robert Reich, *The Work of Nations* (New York: Vintage, 1992); and Richard Florida, *The Rise of the Creative Class* (New York: Basic Books, 2002).

7. Pierre Bourdieu, *Distinction: A Social Critique of the Judgement of Taste*, trans. Richard Nice (Cambridge, MA: Harvard University Press, 1984), 360.

8. Ibid., 384.

9. Georg Bissen, Victoria Gross, and Shahin Motia, interview by author, New York City, 7 April 2004. I should make clear, however, that there is a distinct difference in the advertising world between the "creative" and "business" sides. The creative side produces ads; the business side manages clients and accounts. Judging from my interviews, the creative side is much more populated by people in this group described by Bourdieu; the business side seems to be populated by people who enter the field with less cultural and educational capital.

10. Bourdieu, *Distinction*, 326. See also Mike Featherstone on "new cultural intermediaries." Mike Featherstone, *Consumer Culture and Postmodernism*, 2nd ed. (Thousand Oaks, CA: Sage, 2007).

11. Tracy L. Scott, "Music Highlights Mitsubishi TV Ads," *Washington Post*, 9 June 2002, Y6.

12. Bourdieu, *Distinction*, 326.

13. Luc Boltanski and Ève Chiapello, *The New Spirit of Capitalism*, trans. Gregory Elliott (New York: Verso, 2005), 444. It's not just that the advertising industry is controlled by young people; it is quite ageist. Richard Sennett writes in his book on work that, in the New York City advertising agency where one of his interlocutors worked, "everything in the office focused on the immediate moment, on what was just about to break, on getting ahead of the curve; eyes glaze over in the image business when someone begins a sentence 'One thing I've learned is that . . .'" (Sennett, *Corrosion of Character*, 79–80). One advertising executive acknowledges this orientation, telling a researcher, "If you're in advertising, you're dead after thirty. Age is a killer." "Flexibility equals youth, rigidity equals age," Sennett concludes (ibid., 93). For more on ageism in the advertising industry, see Joyce Kurpiers, "Reality by Design: Advertising Image, Music and Sound Design in the Production of Culture," PhD diss., Duke University, 2009; and, for the British case, which offers many parallels to the American, see Sean Nixon, *Advertising Cultures: Gender, Commerce, Creativity* (Thousand Oaks, CA: Sage, 2003).

14. Bourdieu, *Distinction*, 366.

15. See Arthur Bellaire, *TV Advertising: A Handbook of Modern Practice* (New York: Harper and Brothers, 1959), 161; Marilyn Harris and Mark Wolfram, *Getting into the Jingle Business (a Source Book)* (New York: Sound Studio Publications, 1983), 7; Al Stone, *Jingles: How to Write, Produce and Sell Commercial Music* (Cincinnati: Writer's Digest Books, 1990), 30; Antonio Teixeira Jr., *Music to Sell By: The Craft of Jingle Writing* (n.p.: Berklee Press, 1974), 7; and "Woloshin Taps Classics to Fashion Jingles," *Back Stage*, 20 April 1984, 42B.

16. Bruno Del Grando, "The Art of Selling Out," interview by Pat Kiernan, CNN, 10 February 2003.

17. John Leland, "Selling Out Isn't What It Used to Be," *New York Times* magazine, 11 March 2001, 50.

18. Nick Gadsby, a British-based market researcher, has discovered that today's consumers want to "control the agenda." Nick Gadsby, "Researching the 4th Dimension," *Brand Strategy*,

4 February 2003, 3. Interestingly, Gadsby singles out contemporary electronica music as a new kind of "brand" (or perhaps "b[r]and") naming the British band Aphex Twin as a group that commands the loyalty of underground fans—famously sensitive to questions of selling out, unlike the mainstream groups I have been describing—even as it permits its music to be used for commercial purposes.

19. Nara Schoenberg, "Ad Chic," *Chicago Tribune*, 4 April 2002, 5. An article in *Adweek* in 1985 noted the "deep-rooted suspicion of the corporate sell" possessed by baby boomers, which the use of music from the 1960s was meant to circumvent. J. Max Robins and Chuck Reece, "Using Hard Rock for Soft Sell," *Adweek/East*, May 1985, M.M. 20. Some baby boomers were appalled by the use of licensed music. A particularly notorious ad was Nike's use in 1987 of the Beatles' "Revolution," largely seen as one of the most influential acts of licensing, discussed in chapter 7. As a response to this and other uses of 1960s music, Neil Young wrote an antiadvertising song called "This Note's for You" in 1988.

20. Grant McCracken, *Culture and Consumption: New Approaches to the Symbolic Character of Consumer Goods and Activities* (Bloomington: Indiana University Press, 1988), 121.

21. See, for just two examples, Martyn J. Lee, *Consumer Culture Reborn: The Cultural Politics of Consumption* (New York: Routledge, 1993); and Douglas B. Holt, "Postmodern Markets," in *Do Americans Shop Too Much?*, ed. Juliet Schor (Boston: Beacon, 2000).

22. Joan Anderman, "Commercial Instinct: Boston's Modernista! and Other Creators of TV Spots Have Become the Hippest DJs Around," *Boston Globe*, 24 June 2001, L1.

23. Barry Walters, "2002: The Year in Recordings: The 10 Best Dance Songs," *Rolling Stone*, 26 December 2002, 112. For more on this Dirty Vegas song, see Jean Halliday, "British Band Makes U.S. Debut in Car Commercial," *Advertising Age*, 11 March 2002, http://www.adage .com/news.cms?newsId=34194; Michael Paoletta, "Capitol's Dirty Vegas Gains Popularity as 'Days Go By,'" *Billboard*, 1 June 2002, 44; Kelefa Sanneh, "Music to Drive By: Their Smash-Hit Single Is a Commercial," *New York Times*, 30 August 2002, E2; and Rob Walker, "Dirty Vegas," *Slate*, 19 September 2002, http://www.slate.com.

24. A number of my interviewees made the same analogy.

25. Allyce Bess, "That New Hit Single Might Hide a Jingle," *Christian Science Monitor*, 9 December 2002, 11.

26. See Timothy D. Taylor, "Advertising and the Conquest of Culture," *Social Semiotics* 4 (December 2009): 405–25.

27. See Manuel Castells, *The Information Age: Economy, Society and Culture*, vols. 1–3 (Cambridge, MA: Basil Blackwell, 1996–98); David Harvey, *The Condition of Postmodernity: An Enquiry into the Origins of Cultural Change* (Cambridge, MA: Basil Blackwell, 1989), and *A Brief History of Neoliberalism* (New York: Oxford University Press, 2005); Scott Lash and John Urry, *The End of Organized Capitalism* (Madison: University of Wisconsin Press, 1987); Ernest Mandel, *Late Capitalism*, trans. Joris de Bres (New York: Verso, 1978); and Sennett, *Corrosion of Character*, and *Culture of the New Capitalism*.

28. Jean Baudrillard, "The System of Objects," in Jean Baudrillard, *Selected Writings*, ed. Mark Poster, 21–22 (Stanford, CA: Stanford University Press, 1988).

29. Kurpiers, "Reality by Design," 207.

30. Lash and Urry, *Economies of Signs and Space*, 64.

31. Allen J. Scott, *Social Economy of the Metropolis: Cognitive-Cultural Capitalism and the Global Resurgence of Cities* (Oxford: Oxford University Press, 2008), 65.

32. Andrew Wernick, *Promotional Culture: Advertising, Ideology and Symbolic Expression* (Thousand Oaks, CA: Sage, 1991).

33. Sennett, *Culture of the New Capitalism.*

34. See Scott, *Social Economy of the Metropolis.* "Creativity" seems to be entering the public lexicon more generally as well, as evidenced by a recent cover story in a national news magazine. Po Bronson and Ashley Merryman, "The Creativity Crisis," *Newsweek,* 19 July 2010, 44–49. For considerations of creativity under the rubric of the literature on creative industries, see John Hartley, ed., *The Creative Industries* (Malden, MA: Blackwell, 2005); and Dave Hesmondhalgh, *The Cultural Industries,* 2nd ed. (London: Sage, 2007).

35. Christine Battersby, *Gender and Genius: Towards a Feminist Aesthetics* (Bloomington: Indiana University Press, 1989).

36. Edward Buxton, *Creative People at Work* (New York: Executive Communications, 1975), 219–20.

37. Stephen Fox, *The Mirror Makers: A History of American Advertising and Its Creators,* 2nd ed. (Urbana: University of Illinois Press, 1997), 218.

38. "Tip Top Jingle Money Makers," *Sponsor,* 30 April 1962, 50.

39. Teixeira, *Music to Sell By,* 49.

40. Andy Bloch, interview by author, New York City, 20 April 2004.

41. Anthony Vanger, interview by author, New York City, 15 April 2004.

42. Josh Rabinowitz, interview by author, New York City, 21 April 2004. Rabinowitz is referring to a 2003 commercial for Sony Electronics aired during the Superbowl; the track could be downloaded for ninety-nine cents. See John Leland, "A Chance to Carry On for 130 Million," *New York Times,* 19 January 2003, §9, p. 2. For a discussion of those who make their living choosing music for television programs and films, see Timothy D. Taylor, "Late Capitalism, Globalisation, and the Commodification of Taste," in *The Cambridge History of World Music,* ed. Philip Bohlman (Cambridge: Cambridge University Press, forthcoming).

43. David Ogilvy, interview by unknown interviewer, undated, Pepsi Collection no. 111, Series 4, Subseries a, box 33, National Museum of American History, Washington, DC.

44. Bernie Krause, telephone interview by author, 4 August 2009.

45. Fritz Doddy, interview by author, New York City, 14 April 2004.

46. Max Weber, *The Protestant Ethic and the Spirit of Capitalism,* trans. Talcott Parsons (New York: Charles Scribner's Sons, 1958), 79.

47. Ibid., 80.

48. Ibid.

49. Derek Sayer, *Capitalism and Modernity: An Excursus on Marx and Weber* (London: Routledge, 1991), 30; emphases in original.

50. Battersby, *Gender and Genius,* 2.

51. Max Weber, *Sociological Writings,* ed. Wolf Heyderbrand (New York: Continuum, 1999), 172.

52. Weber, *Protestant Ethic,* 181–82.

53. William Bernbach, quoted in Fox, *Mirror Makers,* 252; emphasis in Fox.

REFERENCES

Archival Resources

Archives Center. National Museum of American History, Smithsonian Institution, Washington, DC.

J. Walter Thompson Company Archive. John W. Hartman Center for Sales, Advertising, and Marketing History, Duke University, Durham, NC.

Library of American Broadcasting. University of Maryland, College Park.

National Broadcasting Company Archive. Wisconsin Historical Society, Madison.

Rudy Vallée Collection. Thousand Oaks Library, Thousand Oaks, CA.

Advertisements

Look & Company. *Advertising Age*, 2 March 1992, 12C–13C.

Discography

Are You In? The Mitsubishi Mix. Vol. 1. Warner Special Products OPCD 1973, 2002.

Clooney, Rosemary. "This Ole House." Columbia 4–40266, 1954.

Fosdick, Johnny. "Swinging the Jingle." Nocturne 3135A-1, n.d.

Great Cola Commercials. Vol. 1. Vox 1, 1996.

Great Cola Commercials. Vol. 2. Vox 2, 1996.

The Happiness Boys. "How Do You Do?" Edison Diamond Disc 51500-R, 1925.

Harry Reser and the Clicquot Club Eskimos. Bauer Studios 981014, n.d.

The Kingston Trio. *Cool Cargo*. 7UP / Capitol Custom NKB-2670, n.d.

Leigh, Mitch. "Backstreet Blues." Music Makers demonstration disc MM-D1158, n.d.

Manilow, Barry. *Barry Manilow Live*. Arista A2CD 8049, 1986.

Murray, Billy. "In My Merry Oldsmobile." Columbia 33061, 1907.

———. "Under the Anheuser Bush." Columbia 32384, 1904.

Neill, Ben. *Automotive*. six degrees 657036 1077–2, 2002.

Pepsi 70. Pepsi-Cola Radio, PA 1760, 1970.

Pepsi 1971. PA 1818, n.d.

Pepsi-Cola Company. Diet Pepsi. "Girl Watchers." A&R 2929, 1966.

Reser, Harry. *Banjo Crackerjax, 1922–1930*. Yazoo 1048, 1992.

———. "The Clicquot Fox Trot March." Columbia 687-D, 1926.

Street Mix: Music from Volkswagen Commercials. Vol. 1. 2001.

The T-Bones. "No Matter What Shape (Your Stomach's In)." Liberty LRP 3439, 1965.

Interviews

Albano, Brian. Interview by author. Lynbrook, NY, 11 March 2004.

Anderson, Tom. Interview by Scott Ellsworth. New York City, 14 November 1984.
Pepsi Generation Oral History and Documentation Collection, 1938–1986, no. 111.
Archives Center, National Museum of American History, Smithsonian Institution,
Washington, DC.

Backer, Bill. Telephone interview by author. 4 May 2004.

Bergin, John. Interview by Scott Ellsworth. New York City, 6 February 1985. Pepsi Generation Oral History and Documentation Collection, 1938–1986, no. 111. Archives
Center, National Museum of American History, Smithsonian Institution, Washington, DC.

Bissen, Georg, Victoria Gross, and Shahin Motia. Interview by author. New York City, 7
April 2004.

Bloch, Andy. Interview by author. New York City, 20 April 2004.

Dante, Ron. Interview by author. Los Angeles, 17 September 2009.

Dillon, Tom. Interview by Scott Ellsworth. New York City, 23 May 1984. Pepsi Generation Oral History and Documentation Collection, 1938–1986, no. 111. Archives
Center, National Museum of American History, Smithsonian Institution, Washington, DC.

DiMinno, Nick. Telephone interview by author. 9 September 2009.

Doddy, Fritz. Interview by author. New York City, 14 April 2004.

Drayton, Bernie. Telephone interview by author. 14 August 2009.

Eaton, Roy. Telephone interview by author. 4 August 2009.

Elias, Scott. Interview by author. New York City, 19 April 2004.

Fort, Hank. Interview by Edwin Dunham. 12 January 1966. Library of American Broadcasting, Transcripts AT-154, University of Maryland, College Park.

Fricke, Janie. Telephone interview by author. 4 August 2009.

Hamilton, Susan. Telephone interview by author. 16 October 2009.

Hinerfeld, Philip. Interview by Scott Ellsworth. Boca Raton, FL, 7 November 1984. Pepsi Generation Oral History and Documentation Collection, 1938–1986, no. 111. Archives Center, National Museum of American History, Smithsonian Institution, Washington, DC.

Karmen, Steve. Telephone interview by author. 2 September 2009.

Knox, Andrew. Interview by author. New York City, 14 May 2004.

Krause, Bernie. Telephone interview by author. 4 August 2009.

Leigh, Mitch. Telephone interview by author. 16 February 2007.

Levine, Joey. Telephone interview by author. 17 October 2009.

Lichtenfeld, Leon. Interview by Layne R. Beaty. 29 May 1988. Library of American Broadcasting, Transcripts AT 1336, University of Maryland, College Park.

Lipsitz, Hilary. Interview by Scott Ellsworth. New York City, 7 February 1985. Pepsi Generation Oral History and Documentation Collection, 1938–1986, no. 111. Archives Center, National Museum of American History, Smithsonian Institution, Washington, DC.

———. Interview by Scott Ellsworth. New York City, 19 April 1985. Pepsi Generation Oral History and Documentation Collection, 1938–1986, no. 111. Archives Center, National Museum of American History, Smithsonian Institution, Washington, DC.

Mack, Walter. Interview by Scott Ellsworth. New York City, 16 December 1985. Pepsi Generation Oral History and Documentation Collection, 1938–1986, no. 111. Archives Center, National Museum of American History, Smithsonian Institution, Washington, DC.

Manilow, Barry. Telephone interview by author. 24 August 2009.

Murtaugh, Hunter. Telephone interview by author. 16 October 2009.

November, Linda. Telephone interview by author. 28 July 2009.

Perkins, Ray. Interview by Ed Dunham. 3 December 1965. Library of American Broadcasting, Transcripts AT 36, University of Maryland, College Park.

Phillips, Anne. Telephone interview by author. 9 October 2009.

Rabinowitz, Josh. Interview by author. New York City, 21 April 2004.

Ramin, Sid. Interview by Scott Ellsworth. New York City, 18 December 1984. Pepsi Generation Oral History and Documentation Collection, 1938–1986, no. 111. Archives Center, National Museum of American History, Smithsonian Institution, Washington, DC.

Rice, Ed. Interview by Dana Ulloth. 30 July 1979. Library of American Broadcasting, Transcripts AT-540, University of Maryland, College Park.

Rosenshine, Allen. Interview by Scott Ellsworth. New York City, 10 December 1984. Pepsi Generation Oral History and Documentation Collection, 1938–1986, no. 111. Archives Center, National Museum of American History, Smithsonian Institution, Washington, DC.

Schroeck, Artie. Telephone interview by author. 28 July 2009.

Vanger, Anthony. Interview by author. New York City, 15 April 2004.

Musical Scores

"The Cantor Cantata." In *Cantor's Comics*. N.p.: Lehn and Fink, 1936.

Croom-Johnson, Austen, and Alan Kent. "Pepsi-Cola Radio Jingle." N.p.: [Pepsi], 1940.

Edwards, Gus, and Vincent P. Bryan. "In My Merry Oldsmobile." New York: M. Witmark and Sons, 1905.

Mackenzie, Len, Garth Montgomery, and William Wirges. "Chiquita Banana (The Banana Song)." New York: Maxwell-Wirges Publications, 1946.

Moulan, Frank, and Will Donaldson. "Hurrah for the Wonder Bakers!" N.p.: Continental Baking Company, 1929.

Rapee, Ernö. *Motion Picture Moods for Pianists and Organists*. New York: G. Schirmer, 1924.

Reser, Harry. "Clicquot Fox Trot March." New York: Harry Reser, 1926.

"Tastyeast Is Tempting." Arranged by Edward Craig. N.p., n.d.

von Tilzer, Harry, and Andrew B. Sterling. "Under the Anheuser Bush." New York: Harry von Tilzer Music Publishing, 1903.

Unpublished Materials

Boehlert, Eric, and John Hogan. Interview by Terry Gross. *Fresh Air*, National Public Radio, 23 July 2003.

Del Grando, Bruno. "The Art of Selling Out." Interview by Pat Kiernan, CNN, 10 February 2003.

Huckman, Mike. CNBC, *Business with CNBC*, 21 February 2003.

Kurpiers, Joyce. "Reality by Design: Advertising Image, Music and Sound Design in the Production of Culture." PhD diss., Duke University, 2009.

Levine, Joey. Interview by Beatrice Black. National Public Radio, *Marketplace*, 26 February 2003.

Melnick, Ross. "Roxy and His Gang: Silent Film Exhibition and the Birth of Media Convergence." PhD diss., University of California, Los Angeles, 2009.

Michlin, Spencer. Personal communication, 28 July 2009.

Ogilvy, David. Interview by unknown interviewer, undated. Pepsi Collection no. 111, Series 4, Subseries a, box 33, National Museum of American History, Washington, DC.

Phillips, Anne. "Why Isn't My Business Fun Anymore?" Photocopy, ca. 1981.

Ramin, Sid. Personal communication. 22 October 2009.

Schecter, Roy. Personal communication. 21 February 2003.

Webography

Adtunes. Last accessed 21 July 2011. http://adtunes.com/.

"Big Mac® Chant-Off." Last accessed 16 July 2011. http://www.myspace.com/bigmacchant.

"Chiquita Banana Commercial." Last accessed 31 August 2010. http://wn.com/
Chiquita_Banana_Commercial.

Maven Strategies. Last accessed 13 August 2011. http://mavenstrategies.com.

http://www.sonymusicfinder.com. This now-inactive URL was operational in the late
1990s– early 2000s.

"National Archives Sound Recordings Named to National Recording Registry." Press
release, National Archives, January 30, 2003. Last accessed 14 March 2010. http://
www.archives.gov/press/press-releases/2003/nr03-22.html.

Neill, Ben. Last accessed 16 July 2011. http://www.benneill.com.

Volkswagen. http://www.vw.com/musicpillar/listen.htm. This now-inactive URL was
operational in the early 2000s.

ZandlGroup. Last accessed 18 July 2011. http://www.zandlgroup.com.

Books and Articles

Adams, Charles Magee. "A Hand for Radio." North American Review, September 1933,
205–12.

"Adidas Launches Run-D.M.C. Sportswear Line." Marketing through Music, July 1987, 1, 5.

Adorno, Theodor W. Essays on Music. Edited by Richard Leppert. Translated by Susan H.
Gillespie. Berkeley: University of California Press, 2002.

"Advertising and Marketing." New York Times, 7 March 1953, 27.

"The Advertising Century: Top 100 Campaigns." Advertising Age, n.d. http://adage.com/
century/campaigns.html.

"Advertising: Epitaph for 'Makin' Whoopee.'" New York Times, 8 February 1961, 49.

"Agency Head Irv Olian Jingles While Driving, Doesn't Get Paid for It." Advertising Age,
25 January 1954, 40.

Agnew, Clark M., and Neil O'Brien. Television Advertising. New York: McGraw-Hill, 1958.

Ahrens, Pat. "The Role of the Crazy Water Crystals Company in Promoting Hillbilly
Music." JEMF Quarterly 6 (Autumn 1970): 107–8.

Alden, Robert. "Advertising: Commercial Music in Discord." New York Times, 3 July 1960,
§F, p. 10.

"Alka-Seltzer 'Stomach' Tune Becomes Pop-Hit—and Not for Belly Dancers." Advertising
Age, 10 January 1965, 3.

Allan, David. "An Essay on Popular Music in Advertising: The Bankruptcy of Culture or
the Marriage of Art and Commerce?" Advertising and Society Review 6 (2005). http://
muse.jhu.edu/journals/asr/.

Allen, Ben. "Ad Music: One Long Jingle." Back Stage, 20 April 1979, 1, 100.

Alpert, Judy I., and Mark I. Alpert. "Music Influences on Mood and Purchase Intentions."
Psychology and Marketing 7 (Summer 1990): 10–35.

Alsop, Ronald. "Ad Agencies Jazz Up Jingles by Playing on 1960s Nostalgia." Wall Street
Journal, 18 April 1985, 33.

Altman, Rick. *Silent Film Sound*. New York: Columbia University Press, 2004.

Altshuler, Marc. "Effective and Sustainable Branding Starts with Music." *Advertising Age*, 5 November 2007, 23.

"American Man-in-the-Street" (editorial). *Fortune*, December 1942, 142–44.

Ames, Allan P. "In Defense of Mr. Hill." *Printers' Ink*, 1 February 1934, 53–56.

"And All Because They're Smart." *Fortune*, June 1935, 80–83, 146, 148, 151–52, 154, 157–58, 160, 163.

Anderman, Joan. "Commercial Instinct: Boston's Modernista! and Other Creators of TV Spots Have Become the Hippest DJs Around." *Boston Globe*, 24 June 2001, §L, p. 1.

Anderson, Gillian B. *Music for Silent Films, 1894–1929: A Guide*. Washington, DC: Library of Congress, 1988.

Anderson, Mae. "On the Crest of the Wave." *Adweek.com*, 13 September 2004.

Ang, Ien. *Desperately Seeking the Audience*. London: Routledge, 1991.

Appadurai, Arjun, ed. *The Social Life of Things: Commodities in Cultural Perspective*. New York: Cambridge University Press, 1986.

Appleby, Joyce. *The Relentless Revolution: A History of Capitalism*. New York: Norton, 2010.

"Apple Records Sues over Nike's 'Revolution' Ads." *Marketing through Music*, September 1987, 1, 5.

"An Appraisal of Advertising Today." *Fortune*, September 1932, 37–44, 91, 93–94, 96, 98.

"Are You a 'Middlebrow'?" *Popular Radio*, June 1923, 619.

Arlen, Michael J. *Thirty Seconds*. New York: Penguin, 1980.

Armstrong, Larry. "Janis Joplin, Material Girl." *Business Week*, 20 March 1995, 40.

Arnold, Frank A. *Broadcast Advertising: The Fourth Dimension*. New York: Wiley, 1931.

Aron, Dan. "The End (?) of the Boring Jingle." *Back Stage*, 20 April 1984, 16B.

Attali, Jacques. *Noise: The Political Economy of Music*. Translated by Brian Massumi. Minneapolis: University of Minnesota Press, 1985.

Aylesworth, M. H. "Forces That Push Radio Forward." *New York Times*, 22 September 1929, §12, p. 8.

———. "Radio's Accomplishment." *Century Magazine*, June 1929, 214–21.

Backer, Bill. *The Care and Feeding of Ideas*. New York: Times Books, 1993.

Baird, Jock. "Chevys, Chunkies, & Cheerios." *Musician*, March 1990, 62–65, 78, 95–97.

Ballard, Chris. "How to Write a Catchy Beer Ad." *New York Times* magazine, 26 January 2003, 14–16.

"Bananas, Yes." *Time*, 23 July 1945, 66.

"Barbasol Jingle Is Back on Radio." *Advertising Age*, 3 April 1961, 2.

Barber, Marchelle Renise. "Commercial r-a-p." *Advertising Age*, 25 May 1987, 22.

Barnouw, Erik. *The Golden Web: A History of Broadcasting in the United States*. Vol. 2, *1933–53*. New York: Oxford University Press, 1968.

———. *The Sponsor: Notes on a Modern Potentate*. New York: Oxford University Press, 1978.

Bartos, Rena. "Ernest Dichter: Motive Interpreter." *Journal of Advertising Research* 26 (February–March 1986): 15–20.

Bates, Charles Austin. *Good Advertising*. New York: Holmes, 1896.

Battersby, Christine. *Gender and Genius: Towards a Feminist Aesthetics*. Bloomington: Indiana University Press, 1989.

Baudrillard, Jean. *Selected Writings*. Edited by Mark Poster. Stanford, CA: Stanford University Press, 1988.

"BBDO Newsletter." *Printers' Ink*, 12 January 1945, 3.

"BBH's New Music Model." *Advertising Age*, 28 July 2003, S-7.

"Beatles Company Sues over Use of Song in Ad." *New York Times*, 29 July 1987, §C, p. 22.

"Beatles Still Mean Business" (editorial). *Advertising Age*, 18 May 1987, 16.

Bellaire, Arthur. *TV Advertising: A Handbook of Modern Practice*. New York: Harper and Brothers, 1959.

"Beneficial Users 'Parade' Psychology." *Sponsor*, 17 September 1962, 34–36.

Bennett, David. "Getting the Id to Go Shopping: Psychoanalysis, Advertising, Barbie Dolls, and the Invention of the Consumer Unconscious." *Public Culture* 17 (2005): 1–26.

Berk, Mitchell. "Kenny Rogers Tour Sponsorship Proves Fruitful for Dole Food Co." *Marketing through Music*, August 1989, 5.

Berry, Chad, ed. *The Hayloft Gang: The Story of the National Barn Dance*. Urbana: University of Illinois Press, 2008.

Bess, Allyce. "That New Hit Single Might Hide a Jingle." *Christian Science Monitor*, 9 December 2002, 11.

Beville, H. M., Jr. "The ABCD's of Radio Audiences." *Public Opinion Quarterly*, June 1940, 195–206.

———. *Social Stratification of the Radio Audience*. Princeton, NJ: Princeton Office of Radio Research, 1939.

Biggar, George C. "Broadcasting Barn Warmings Boosts Jamesway Barn Equipment." *Broadcast Advertising*, July 1930, 12–13.

"The Biography of a Commercial." *Sponsor*, 5 April 1965, 39–43.

Bird, Harry Lewis. *This Fascinating Advertising Business*. Indianapolis: Bobbs-Merrill, 1947.

Bird, William L., Jr. *"Better Living": Advertising, Media, and the New Vocabulary of Business Leadership, 1935–1955*. Evanston, IL: Northwestern University Press, 1999.

Block, Valerie. "Jingle Biz Rocked by Licensed Pop in Ads." *Advertising Age*, 3 February 2003, 6.

Bloom, David. "Music Biz Takes to the Road." *Variety*, 16–22 September 2002, 6.

Boehlert, Eric. "Bittersweet Synergy." *Rolling Stone*, 19 March 1998, 25–26.

———. "One Big Happy Channel?" *Salon*, 28 June 2001. http://www.salon.com.

———. "Pay for Play." *Salon*, 14 March 2001. http://www.salon.com.

———. "Radio's Big Bully." *Salon*, 30 April 2001. http://www.salon.com.

———. "Singles Meet Jingles." *Rolling Stone*, 11 November 1999, 27–28.

Bogart, Michele H. *Artists, Advertising, and the Borders of Art*. Chicago: University of Chicago Press, 1995.

Boltanski, Luc, and Ève Chiapello. *The New Spirit of Capitalism*. Translated by Gregory Elliott. New York: Verso, 2005.

Borden, Neil H. *Problems in Advertising*. New York: McGraw-Hill, 1937.

"Boston Survey Shows It's the Program Not the Station That Gets the Listeners." *Broadcast Advertising*, June 1930, 9, 26.

Bottger, Walter, and Henry Martin. "Where Goes the Jingle?" *Back Stage*, 20 April 1984, 42B.

Bourdieu, Pierre. *Distinction: A Social Critique of the Judgement of Taste*. Translated by Richard Nice. Cambridge, MA: Harvard University Press, 1984.

———. *The Logic of Practice*. Translated by Richard Nice. Stanford, CA: Stanford University Press, 1990.

"Branded Men and Women: Pioneers Who Paved the Way and Paid with Personal Oblivion." *Radio Guide*, 3 March 1932, 1, 13.

"Bring Musicians in on Ad Planning, Leigh Urges" *Advertising Age*, 4 May 1959, 14.

"Broadcast Advertising by Type of Sponsoring Business (1936)." *Variety Radio Directory, 1937–1938*. [N.p.: Variety, 1937], 689.

Bronson, Po, and Ashley Merryman. "The Creativity Crisis." *Newsweek*, 19 July 2010, 44–49.

Brown, Sandy. "Licensing Music for the Masses." *Boards*, 2 April 2002, 42.

Bruner, Gordon C., II. "Music, Mood, and Marketing." *Journal of Marketing* 54 (1990): 94–104.

Burlingame, Jon. "Tyros, Composer and Classics Vie for Ad Time." *Variety*, 29 July–4 August 2002, A4.

"Burma Shave Adapts Roadside Jingles to TV." *Advertising Age*, 4 September 1967, 4.

Buxton, Edward. *Creative People at Work*. New York: Executive Communications, 1975.

Calkins, Earnest Elmo. "The New Consumption Engineer, and the Artist." In *A Philosophy of Production: A Symposium*. Edited by J. George Frederick. New York: Business Bourse, 1930.

Campbell, Colin. *The Romantic Ethic and the Spirit of Modern Consumerism*. Cambridge, MA: Basil Blackwell, 1989.

"The C&W Sound Captures U.S. Heart & Purse." *Sponsor*, 20 May 1963, 31–33, 66.

Cantril, Hadley, and Gordon W. Allport. *The Psychology of Radio*. New York: Harper and Brothers, 1935.

Carlson, Walter. "Advertising: Composer with a Commercial." *New York Times*, 26 June 1966, 122.

Castells, Manuel. *The Information Age: Economy, Society and Culture*. Vols. 1–3. Cambridge, MA: Basil Blackwell, 1996–98.

"The CD Slide: It's Way Worse Than You Think. . . . " *Digital Music News*, 2 June 2011. http://www.digitalmusicnews.com/stories/06021cds.

Chambers, Jason. *Madison Avenue and the Color Line: African Americans in the Advertising Industry*. Philadelphia: University of Pennsylvania Press, 2009.

Chase, Francis, Jr. *Sound and Fury: An Informal History of Broadcasting*. New York: Harper and Brothers, 1942.

"Chiquita Banana." *Tide*, 1 February 1946, 23.

"Claim That Tune." *Advertising Age*, 6 March 1989, 28S.

Clifford, Stephanie. "2 All-Beef Patties Are Back." *New York Times*, 17 July 2008, §C, p. 1.

Cohen, Lizabeth. *A Consumer's Republic: The Politics of Mass Consumption in Postwar America*. New York: Knopf, 2003.

———. *Making a New Deal: Industrial Workers in Chicago, 1919–1939*. New York: Cambridge University Press, 1990.

Cohen, Paul. "Twenty Years After: Woodstock Redux." *Back Stage*, 21 April 1989, 2B–3B.

Cohen, Randy. "Songs in the Key of Hype: Jingles Sweeten Sales Pitch with Pop Tunes, Catchy Cliches." *More*, July–August 1977, 12–17.

"Coke Adds to Teen-Appeal Jingle Singers." *Advertising Age*, 11 October 1965, 19.

"Coke Meets Its Goal: 'In' Not 'Way Out.'" *Broadcasting*, 29 June 1964, 46.

Collins, James H. "Giving Folks What They Want by Radio." *Saturday Evening Post*, 17 May 1924, 10–11, 102, 107, 109.

Columbia Broadcasting System. *Ears and Incomes*. New York: Columbia Broadcasting System, 1934.

———. *Markets in Radio Homes, by Income Levels and Price Levels*. New York: Columbia Broadcasting System, 1934.

———. *Vertical Study of Radio Ownership: An Analysis, by Income Levels, of Radio Homes in the United States*. New York: Columbia Broadcasting System, 1933.

Colwell, Robert T. "The Program as an Advertisement." In *The Advertising Agency Looks at Radio*. Edited by Neville O'Neill. New York: D. Appleton, 1932.

"Commercials Swing to Music." *Ad Day / USA*, 6 August 1981.

"Composer Finds Challenge and Success in Agency Music Field." *Sponsor*, 10 June 1963, 33, 46.

Cone, Fairfax M. *The Blue Streak: Some Observations, Mostly about Advertising*. N.p.: Crain Communications, 1973.

———. *With All Its Faults: A Candid Account of Forty Years in Advertising*. Boston: Little, Brown, 1969.

Conklin, Michele. "Parody Fever." *Madison Avenue*, December 1985, 35–37.

Connah, Douglas Duff. *How to Build the Radio Audience*. New York: Harper and Brothers, 1938.

Cook, Nicholas. "Music and Meaning in the Commercials." *Popular Music* 13 (1994): 27–40.

Craig, Douglas B. *Fireside Politics: Radio and Political Culture in the United States, 1920–1940*. Baltimore: Johns Hopkins University Press, 2000.

Crank, Chet. "Gilmore Radio Circus Boosts Gasoline Sales 9500% in Three Years." *Broadcast Advertising*, February 1931, 12–13.

Crosley, Hilary. "Common: Creative 'Control.'" *Billboard.com*, 6 December 2008.

Cross, Gary. *An All-Consuming Century: Why Commercialism Won in Modern America.* New York: Columbia University Press, 2000.

Crystal, Tamar. "The Men Who Make the Music That Makes Madison Avenue Move." Pt. 1. *Millimeter*, April 1977, 36–38, 42–43, 62–63, 70.

"Current Collaborations." *Marketing through Music*, July 1988, 2.

Cutler, Blayne. "For What It's Worth." *American Demographics*, August 1989, 42.

Dallaire, Victor J. "Music Helps Select Your Radio Audience." *Printers' Ink*, 27 December 1946, 32–33.

Damrosch, Walter. "Music and the Radio." *Annals of the American Academy of Political and Social Science* 177 (January 1935): 91–93.

Darling, Cary. "Car Ads Get an Electronic Tune-up." *Montreal Gazette*, 6 March 2003, §D, p. 1.

Davey, Martin L. "Secrets of a Successful Radio Program." *Broadcasting*, 1 July 1932, 9.

De Forest, Lee. "Opera Audiences of To-morrow." *Radio World*, 5 August 1922, 13.

Deistler, Carol. "Tops with the Pops." *Audio-Visual Communications*, March 1982, 23–25.

DeMarco, Donna. "Pop Artists Go Commercial." *Insight*, 24 June 2002, 26–27.

Demkowych, Christine. "Music on the Upswing in Advertising." *Advertising Age*, 31 March 1986, S-5.

Denison, Merrill. "Why Isn't Radio Better?" *Harper's Magazine*, February 1934, 576–86.

Diamant, Lincoln. *Television's Classic Commercials: The Golden Years, 1948–1958.* New York: Hastings House, 1971.

Diaz, Ann-Christine. "Them Changes." *Creativity*, July 2003, 26–28.

Dichter, Ernest. "A Psychological View of Advertising Effectiveness." *Journal of Marketing* 14 (July 1949): 61–66.

———. "Psychology in Market Research." *Harvard Business Review* 25 (1947): 432–43.

———. "Scientifically Predicting and Understanding Human Behavior." In *Consumer Behavior and Motivation.* Edited by Robert H. Cole. Urbana: Bureau of Economic and Business Research, College of Commerce and Business Administration of the University of Illinois, 1956.

Dickinson, Roy. "Freshen Up Your Product." *Printers' Ink*, 6 February 1930, 3.

DiCola, Peter. "False Premises, False Promises: A Quantitative History of Ownership Consolidation in the Radio Industry." 13 December 2006. http://www.futureofmusic.org/article/research/false-premises-false promises.

Doerksen, Chris. "Same Old Song and Dance." 28 February 2003. www.washingtoncity-paper.com.

"Does Music Add to a Commercial's Effectiveness." *McCollum/Spielman Topline*, October 1978.

Donaton, Scott. "Steve Berman Hears Music in Alliances with Advertisers." *Advertising Age*, 7 April 2003, 18.

———. "Sting-Jaguar Deal Still Serves as Model for the Music World." *Advertising Age*, 22 September 2003, 22.

Donohoe, Tim. Letter to the editor. *Advertising Age*, 27 July 1987, 20.

Douglas, Susan J. *Listening In: Radio and the American Imagination . . . from Amos 'n' Andy and Edward R. Murrow to Wolfman Jack and Howard Stern*. New York: Times Books, 1999.

Dreher, Carl. "As the Broadcaster Sees It." *Radio Broadcast*, July 1928, 161–62.

Duffy, Thom. "Songs' Selling Power Examined." *Billboard*, 3 July 1999, 57.

Dumas, Alison. "The Limits of Market-Research Methods." *Advertising Age*, 8 October 2007, 27.

Duménil, Gérard, and Dominique Lévy. *Capital Resurgent: Roots of the Neoliberal Revolution*. Translated by Derek Jeffers. Cambridge, MA: Harvard University Press, 2004.

Dumenil, Lynn. *The Modern Temper: American Culture and Society in the 1920s*. New York: Hill and Wang, 1995.

Dunlap, Orrin E., Jr. *Advertising by Radio*. New York: Ronald Press, 1929.

———. *Radio in Advertising*. New York: Harper and Brothers, 1931.

Durstine, Roy. "Audible Advertising." In *Radio and Its Future*. Edited by Martin Codel. New York: Harper and Brothers, 1930.

———. "We're on the Air." *Scribner's Magazine*, May 1928, 623–31.

Dusenberry, Phil. *Then We Set His Hair on Fire: Insights and Accidents from a Hall-of-Fame Career in Advertising*. New York: Portfolio, 2005.

Dyer, Gillian. *Advertising as Communication*. New York: Methuen, 1982.

Dygert, Warren B. *Radio as an Advertising Medium*. New York: McGraw-Hill, 1939.

Dykema, Peter W., and Karl W. Gehrkens. "Radio as a Potential Force in Music Education." In *The Teaching and Administration of High School Music*. Boston: C. C. Birchard, 1941.

Edelson, Sharon. "They Say They Want a Revolution: New Progressives Kagan & Greif Style Spots with a Music-Video Sensibility." *Advertising Age*, 1 June 1987, C26.

Ehrenreich, John, and Barbara Ehrenreich. "The Professional-Managerial Class." In *Between Labor and Capital*. Edited by Pat Walker. Boston: South End, 1979.

Elder, Robert F. *Does Radio Sell Goods?* [New York]: Columbia Broadcasting System, 1931.

Eliscu, Jenny. "Why Radio Sucks." *Rolling Stone*, 3 April 2003, 22.

Elkin, Tobi. "TiVo Inks Pacts for Long-Form TV Ads." *Advertising Age*, 17 June 2002, 1.

Elliott, Stuart. "Burger King Moves Quickly to Take a Product from TV to the Table." *New York Times*, 21 January 2005, §C, p. 4.

———. "Can Mick Jagger Deliver Chap Stick to Masses? 'Rolling Stone' Tells All." *Advertising Age*, 29 September 1986, 43.

———. "In Branded Entertainment, 'It's the Wild West' as a Marketing Strategy." *International Herald Tribune*, 30 March 2005, 16.

———. "Musicians Market Brands to Sell Their Latest Music." *New York Times*, 24 May 2005, §C, p. 5.

"Emotion Sells More Than Perfume; It Sells Cars, Too." *Marketing News*, 22 November 1985, 4.

Enrico, Roger, and Jesse Kornbluth. *The Other Guy Blinked: How Pepsi Won the Cola Wars.* New York: Bantam, 1986.

"Everybody's Singing along with Mitch." *Broadcast Advertising,* 10 April 1961, 40–41.

Ewen, Stuart. *All-Consuming Images: The Politics of Style in Contemporary Culture.* New York: Basic, 1988.

———. *Captains of Consciousness: Advertising and the Social Roots of the Consumer Culture.* New York: McGraw Hill, 1976.

Fadden, James. "HEA Will Drop a Line to Keep Things Fresh." *Back Stage,* 20 April 1984, 12B.

"Fan Mail: Letters Are More Bread and Butter to Stars of Microphone." *Literary Digest,* 22 May 1937, 20–22.

Farhi, Paul. "With a Song in Their Spot." *Washington Post,* 4 January 1998, H1.

"Favorite Musical Numbers of the Farm Audience." *Broadcast Advertising,* June 1929, 25–27.

Featherstone, Mike. *Consumer Culture and Postmodernism.* 2nd ed. Thousand Oaks, CA: Sage, 2007.

Feehan, Eugene. "The Sound of TV Music." *Television Magazine,* February 1967, 28–29, 44–48.

Felix, Edgar H. *Using Radio in Sales Promotion: A Book for Advertisers, Station Managers and Broadcasting Artists.* New York: McGraw-Hill, 1927.

Ferenbaugh, Dorothy. "Television's Musical Jingles." *New York Times,* 22 December 1963, §X, p. 21.

Filene, Edward A. *Successful Living in This Machine Age.* New York: Simon and Schuster, 1932.

Finney, Frank. "Grand Opera, Symphonies and Cigarettes." *Printers' Ink,* 25 January 1934, 13–16.

Fitch, Ed. "Ad Music Composer Humming a Happy Tune." *Advertising Age,* 28 February 1985, 38.

"Fitch Uses the Air to Sell Care of the Hair." *Broadcast Merchandising,* April 1936, 97.

Flass, Rebecca, and Katy Bachman. "Pepsi Experiment Gathers Momentum." *Adweek,* 3 February 2003, 10.

Florida, Richard. *The Rise of the Creative Class.* New York: Basic Books, 2002.

"Ford Summer Series Builds TV Show on Advertising Motif." *Advertising Age,* 30 July 1962, 95.

Forkan, James P. "Pepsi Generation Bridges Two Decades." *Advertising Age,* 5 May 1980, 41, 43.

———. "Rockbill Gives Advertisers, Rock Stars Exposure." *Advertising Age,* 20 November 1978, 12.

———. "Tunes That Sing Songs of Sales." *Advertising Age,* 23 July 1979, S-1.

———. "Turning '60s Music into '80s Ads." *Advertising Age,* 25 April 1985, 40.

"For the Record." *Advertising Age,* 10 August 1987, 53.

Fowles, Jib. *Advertising and Popular Culture.* Thousand Oaks, CA: Sage, 1996.

Fox, Stephen. *The Mirror Makers: A History of American Advertising and Its Creators.* 2nd ed. Urbana: University of Illinois Press, 1997.

Frank, Thomas. *The Conquest of Cool: Business Culture, Counterculture, and the Rise of Hip Consumerism.* Chicago: University of Chicago Press, 1997.

———. *One Market under God: Extreme Capitalism, Market Populism, and the End of Economic Democracy.* New York: Anchor, 2000.

Freeman, David W. "Honda Rides Music Videos into Advertising." *Advertising Age,* 19 July 1984, 46.

Freund, John C. "Excerpts from an Address Broadcasted from WJZ." *Wireless Age,* May 1922, 36.

Friedan, Betty. *The Feminine Mystique.* New York: Laurel, 1983.

Friedman, Wayne. "Music Labels Court Brands." *Advertising Age,* 16 September 2002, 19.

Fritz, F. C. "Wendell Hall: Early Radio Performer." In *American Broadcasting: A Source Book on the History of Radio and Television.* Edited by Lawrence W. Lichty and Malachi C. Topping. New York: Hastings House, 1975.

Fruit, Fran. "Look What They've Done to My Song, Ma." *Advertising Age,* 21 April 1986, 18.

"Fuji & Enigma Ink Sponsorship/Mktg Pact." *Marketing through Music,* June 1989, 1.

Gabbard, Glen O., and Krin Gabbard. *Psychiatry and the Cinema.* 2nd ed. Washington, DC: American Psychiatric Press, 1999.

Gadsby, Nick. "Researching the 4th Dimension." *Brand Strategy,* 4 February 2003, 3.

Galanoy, Terry. *Down the Tube, or Making Television Commercials Is Such a Dog-Eat-Dog Business It's No Wonder They're Called Spots.* Chicago: Henry Regnery, 1970.

Gans, Herbert J. "American Popular Culture and High Culture in a Changing Class Structure." In *Prospects: An Annual of American Culture Studies* 10. Edited by Jack Salzman. New York: Cambridge University Press, 1985.

Garfield, Bob. "Cola War's TV Extravaganzas: Jackson Gives Pepsi Bad Rap." *Advertising Age,* 2 November 1987, 3.

———. "George Michael's Spot for Diet Coke Lacks Pop." *Advertising Age,* 13 February 1989, 68.

———. "Pepsi Should Offer Prayer to Madonna." *Advertising Age,* 6 March 1989, 76.

———. "Too Much Ad Music Leaves Little Room for Hitting the Right Note." *Advertising Age,* 4 January 1988, 46.

Gellhorn, Martha. "Rudy Vallée: God's Gift to Us Girls." *New Republic,* 7 August 1929, 310–11.

General Mills. *General Mills: 75 Years of Innovation Invention Food & Fun.* Minneapolis: General Mills, 2003.

Giges, Nancy. "Pepsi and Jackson in New Link." *Advertising Age,* 5 May 1986, 1.

———. "Pepsi-Jackson 'Spectacular' Set for Spring." *Advertising Age,* 16 February 1987, 2.

"Girl Watch Tune from Pepsi Enters Pop Music Arena." *Advertising Age,* 26 December 1966, 23.

Gladwell, Malcolm. "The Coolhunt." *New Yorker,* 17 March 1999, 78–88.

"Godley and Creme Drive L-M into 'New Age.'" *Marketing through Music*, November 1987, 1, 6.

Goldman, Debra. "Two-Part Harmony." *Adweek*, 10 November 1997, 62.

Goldman, Robert. *Reading Ads Socially*. New York: Routledge, 1992.

Goldman, Robert, and Stephen Papson. *Sign Wars: The Cluttered Landscape of Advertising*. New York: Guilford, 1996.

"Gold Pan Alley." *Newsweek*, 15 August 1966, 64.

"Good News! Plus: Because Shaving Can 'Hurt So Bad.'" *Marketing through Music*, April 1987, 1, 5.

Gorfain, Louis. "Jingle Giants." *New York*, 23 April 1979, 50–53.

Gouldner, Alvin. *The Future of Intellectuals and the Rise of the New Class*. New York: Seabury, 1979.

Graham, Al. "Jingle—or Jangle." *New York Times* magazine, 29 October 1944, 26–27, 44.

Graham, Judith. "Sponsors Line Up for Rockin' Role: Top Stars to Attract Top Marketers." *Advertising Age*, 11 December 1989, 50.

Graham, Lawrence, and Lawrence Hamdan. *Youthtrends™: Capturing the $200 Billion Youth Market*. New York: St. Martin's Press, 1987.

Graser, Marc. "Creativity Bonds Mad Ave., Showbiz." *Daily Variety*, 25 November 2002, 14.

———. "McDonald's on Lookout to Be Big Mac Daddy." *Advertising Age*, 28 March 2005, 123.

Gray, James. *Business without Boundary: The Story of General Mills*. Minneapolis: University of Minnesota Press, 1954.

Grein, Paul. "TV & Radio Ad Usage of Pop Hits Up." *Billboard*, 22 May 1978, 3, 96, 110.

Gross, Michael. "Selling to 'The Big Chill' Beat." *Adweek*, 4 February 1985, C.R. 30–C.R. 31.

Grossman, Lev. "The Quest for Cool." *Time*, 8 September 2003, 44–50.

Grundy, Pamela. "From *Il Trovatore* to the Crazy Mountaineers: The Rise and Fall of Elevated Culture on WBT-Charlotte, 1922–1930." *Southern Cultures* 1 (Fall 1994): 51–73.

———. "'We Always Tried to Be Good People': Respectability, Crazy Water Crystals, and Hillbilly Music on the Air, 1933–1935." *Journal of American History* 81 (March 1995): 1591–1620.

Grunwald, Edgar A. "Program-Production History, 1929–1937." In *Variety Radio Directory, 1937–1938*. N.p.: Variety, 1937.

Halliday, Jean. "British Band Makes U.S. Debut in Car Commercial." *Advertising Age*, 11 March 2002. http://www.adage.com/news.cms?newsId=34194.

———. "Carmakers Pick Up the Beat." *Advertising Age*, 14 April 2003, §S, p. 4.

———. "Toyota Links with Phil Collins." *Advertising Age*, 14 October 2002, 14.

Hammond, Affie. "Listeners' Survey of Radio." *Radio News*, December 1932, 331–33.

Hampp, Andrew. "A Reprise for Jingles on Madison Avenue." *Advertising Age*, 6 September 2010, 1.

———. "Will.I.Am Is with the Brands—and Damn Proud of It." *Advertising Age*, 28 February 2011, 10.

Hanson, Howard. "Music Everywhere: What the Radio Is Doing for Musical America." *Etude*, February 1935, 84, 118.

Harris, Marilyn, and Mark Wolfram. *Getting into the Jingle Business (a Source Book)*. New York: Sound Studio Publications, 1983.

Harris, Neil. "The Drama of Consumer Desire." In *Yankee Enterprise*. Edited by Otto Mayr and Robert C. Post. Washington, DC: Smithsonian Institution, 1981.

Hartley, John, ed. *Creative Industries*. Malden, MA: Blackwell, 2005.

Harvey, David. *A Brief History of Neoliberalism*. New York: Oxford University Press, 2005.

———. *The Condition of Postmodernity: An Enquiry into the Origins of Cultural Change*. Cambridge, MA: Basil Blackwell, 1989.

Hatfield, Stefano. "The Long & Winding Road: Mitsubishi." *Creativity*, May 2003, 30.

———. "Music to Watch Sales By." *Creativity*, July 2003, 34–35.

Hattwick, Melvin S. *How to Use Psychology for Better Advertising*. New York: Prentice-Hall, 1950.

Havighurst, Craig. *Air Castle of the South: WSM and the Making of Music City*. Urbana: University of Illinois Press, 2007.

Hecker, Sidney. "Music in Advertising—What the Data Don't Tell Us." *ARF Conference Report*, November 1982, 14.

Heifetz, Jascha. "Radio, American Style." *Harper's Monthly Magazine*, October 1937, 497–502.

Henry, William A., III. "Mirror, Mirror, on the Tube." *Time*, 17 August 1981, 85.

Hepner, Harry Walker. *Effective Advertising*. 2nd ed. New York: McGraw-Hill, 1949.

Hesmondhalgh, Dave. *The Cultural Industries*. 2nd ed. London: Sage, 2007.

Hess, Herbert W. "History and Present Status of the 'Truth-in-Advertising' Movement as Carried on by the Vigilance Committee of the Associated Advertising Clubs of the World." *Annals of the American Academy of Political and Social Science* 101 (May 1922): 211–20.

Hettinger, Herman S. *A Decade of Radio Advertising*. Chicago: University of Chicago Press, 1933.

Hettinger, Herman S., and Richard R. Mead. *The Summer Radio Audience: A Study of the Habits and Preferences of Summer Radio Audiences in Philadelphia and Vicinity*. Philadelphia: Universal Broadcasting Company, 1931.

Hettinger, Herman S., and Walter J. Neff. *Practical Radio Advertising*. New York: Prentice-Hall, 1938.

High, Kamau. "Arcade Creative Group: Agency of Record." *Billboard*, 4 October 2008, 12.

———. "Listen to the Brand." *Billboard*, 19 July 2008, 24–25.

Hilmes, Michele. *Hollywood and Broadcasting from Radio to Cable*. Urbana: University of Illinois Press, 1990.

———. *Radio Voices: American Broadcasting, 1922–1952*. Minneapolis: University of Minnesota Press, 1997.

"Hitachi Culture Special Presents Kitaro Debut." *Marketing through Music*, November 1987, 6.

Hollie, Pamela G. "A Rush for Singers to Promote Goods." *New York Times*, 14 May 1984, §D, pp. 1, 11.

Holt, Douglas B. "Postmodern Markets." In *Do Americans Shop Too Much?* Edited by Juliet Schor. Boston: Beacon, 2000.

Hoover, Herbert. "Advertising Is a Vital Force in Our National Life." *Advertising World*, August 1925, 77–79.

Horowitz, Daniel. "The Emigré and American Consumer Culture." In *Getting and Spending: European and American Consumer Society in the Twentieth Century*. Edited by Susan Strasser, Charles McGovern, and Matthias Judt. Cambridge: Cambridge University Press, 1998.

———. *The Morality of Spending: Attitudes toward the Consumer Society in America, 1875–1940*. Chicago: Ivan R. Dee, 1985.

Hotchkiss, George Burton. *An Outline of Radio Advertising: Its Philosophy, Science, Art, and Strategy*. New York: Macmillan, 1935.

"Howard Clothes' New Drive Puts Stress on Radio." *Advertising Age*, 29 February 1960, 211.

Hower, Ralph M. *The History of an Advertising Agency: N.W. Ayer & Son at Work, 1869–1949*. Cambridge, MA: Harvard University Press, 1949.

"How MTV Has Rocked Television Commercials." *New York Times*, 9 October 1989, §D, p. 6.

"Human and Sprite: Jingle All the Way." *Creativity*, July 2007, 28.

Hurd, Volney D. "Singing Commercials." *Christian Science Monitor Magazine*, 10 March 1945, 5.

Huron, David. "Music in Advertising: An Analytic Paradigm." *Musical Quarterly* 73 (1989): 557–74.

"I Believe in Broadcast Merchandising." *Broadcast Merchandising*, August 1933, 13.

"If There Were a Jingle, We'd Know the Commandments." *St. Petersburg Times*, 11 October 2007, 6A.

"It Shouldn't Happen to a Banana." *Results from Radio* 3. National Association of Broadcasters, Department of Broadcast Advertising. Library of American Broadcasting, pamphlet 1964. College Park: University of Maryland, 1945.

"Jack O'Brian Says." *New York Journal-American*, 17 April 1961, 22.

"Jackson's Pepsi Spots Showcase New Music." *Marketing through Music*, March 1987, 1–2.

Jacobson, Lisa. *Raising Consumers: Children and the American Mass Market in the Early Twentieth Century*. New York: Columbia University Press, 2004.

"Jazz Music Is Preferred by Listeners, Stations Report." *Broadcast Advertising*, April 1931, 7, 21.

"Jerry Garcia, Others Sing Levi's 501 Blues." *Marketing through Music*, September 1987, 1, 5.

Jhally, Sut. *The Codes of Advertising: Fetishism and the Political Economy of Meaning in the Consumer Society*. New York: Routledge, 1990.

——. "Probing the Blindspot: The Audience Commodity." *Canadian Journal of Political and Social Theory* 6 (Spring 1982): 204–10.

"Jingle All the Day." *Newsweek*, 10 June 1940, 65.

"Jingle All the Way." *Time*, 21 August 1944, 75.

"The Jingle Biz: From Music House to Writer's Co-op." *Marketing through Music*, June 1988, 5.

"The Jingle Jangle." *Time*, 6 May 1957, 50.

"Jingle Men Make Artistic Strides." *Back Stage*, 25 July 1980, 1, 12.

"Jingle Music Freeing Itself from Current Disk Trends: Lucas." *Variety*, 17 November 1976, 57, 60.

"Jingles Have Long History, Stracke Says." *Advertising Age*, 13 February 1967, 20–21.

"Jingles Production Co. in Nashville Gears to Growth." *Billboard*, 29 August 1970, 4.

"Jingles vs. Spoken Commercials: Which?" *Sponsor*, 22 June 1964, 42–45.

Jordan, Mary. "Radio Has Made 'High-Brow' Music Popular." *Radio News*, February 1928, 884, 932, 934.

Julien, Jean-Rémy. *Musique et publicité: Du cri de Paris . . . aux messages publicitaires radio-phoniques et télévisés*. Paris: Flammarion, 1989.

"J. Walter Thompson's Hit Parade." *Television Magazine*, July 1959, 105.

Kaempffert, Waldemar. "The Social Destiny of Radio." *Forum* 71 (June 1924): 764–72.

Kaplan, Bob. "POV." *Creativity*, July 2003, 6.

Kaplan, E. Ann. *Rocking around the Clock: Music Television, Postmodernism, and Consumer Culture*. New York: Routledge, 1987.

Kaplan, Mary Jo. "Cola Wars and Remembrance: Coca-Cola." *Advertising Age*, 1 August 1988, 31S.

Karmen, Steve. *Through the Jingle Jungle: The Art and Business of Making Music for Commercials*. New York: Billboard Books, 1989.

——. *Who Killed the Jingle? How a Unique American Art Form Disappeared*. Milwaukee: Hal Leonard, 2005.

Kellaris, James J., and Anthony D. Cox. "The Effects of Background Music in Advertising: A Reassessment." *Journal of Consumer Research* 16 (1989): 113–18.

Kellaris, James J., Anthony D. Cox, and Dena Cox. "The Effect of Background Music on Ad Processing: A Contingency Explanation." *Journal of Marketing* 57 (October 1993): 114–25.

Kemp, Tom. *The Climax of Capitalism: The U.S. Economy in the Twentieth Century*. New York: Longman, 1990.

Kempf, Paul. "What Radio Is Doing to Our Music." *Musician*, June 1929, 17–18.

Kent, Alan Bradley, and Austen Croom-Johnson. Foreword, "How to Create a Hit Radio Jingle—Fourteen Steps." In Charles Hull Wolfe, *Modern Radio Advertising*. New York: Funk and Wagnalls / Printers' Ink, 1949.

Kiley, David. *Getting the Bugs Out: The Rise, Fall, and Comeback of Volkswagen in America.* New York: Wiley, 2002.

Kim, Hank. "Just Risk It." *Advertising Age,* 9 February 2004, 1.

"Kingston Trio Selling 7-Up." *Billboard,* 17 October 1960, 4.

Kinter, Kim. "'Stop in the Name of Rock,' DJs Say." *Adweek,* 18 January 1988, 40.

Klein, Bethany. *As Heard on TV: Popular Music in Advertising.* Burlington, VT: Ashgate, 2009.

Kobak, Edgar. "Singing Commercials." *Music Journal,* September–October 1944, 19, 29.

"Kodak's 'Sellevision' Marathon." *Kodak Dealer News,* September–October 1962, 16–18.

Koransky, Jason. "The Drive behind Neill's *Automotive.*" *Down Beat,* February 2003, 20.

Kot, Greg. "In the Promotion World, Video Ads Killed the Radio Star." *Chicago Tribune,* 6 October 2002, 7.

———. "Rocking Radio's World." *Chicago Tribune,* 14 April 2002, 1.

Kraemer, Warren E. "Millions in Nickels: Loft's Pepsi-Cola Is a Dynamic Speculation, Coca-Cola a Solid Investment." *Magazine of Wall Street,* 23 March 1940, 737–38, 771.

Kroeger, Albert R. "Music for the Golden Minute." *Television Magazine,* December 1960, 40–41, 66, 69–70.

Lafayette, Jon. "Burger King Be Jammin': Agency, Client Work with Top Artists for $20m-Plus Radio Effort." *Advertising Age,* 9 October 1989, 28.

Laird, Tracy E. W. *Louisiana Hayride: Radio and Roots Music along the Red River.* New York: Oxford University Press, 2004.

Land, Herman. "The Diary of Ford's 'This Ole House' Jingle." *Sponsor,* 10 January 1955, 40–41, 97–98, 100–103.

Landauer, Bella C. *Striking the Right Note in Advertising.* New York: New-York Historical Society, 1951.

Landers, Sherman G. "Putting a Cigar on the Air." *Broadcast Advertising,* June 1929, 5–13, 18.

Lash, Scott, and John Urry. *Economies of Signs and Space.* Thousand Oaks, CA: Sage, 1994.

———. *The End of Organized Capitalism.* Madison: University of Wisconsin Press, 1987.

Lauro, Patricia Winters. "Forget Jingles. Viewers Prefer Familiar Tunes in Commercials." *New York Times,* 8 November 1999, §C, p. 1.

Lawson, Terry. "Ad Execs Do Music Acts, Fans a Favor." *Detroit Free Press,* 20 May 2001. http://www.freep.com/entertainment/music/lawcol20_20010520.htm.

Lazarsfeld, Paul F., and Harry Field. *The People Look at Radio.* Chapel Hill: University of North Carolina Press, 1946.

Leach, William. *Land of Desire: Merchants, Power, and the Rise of a New American Culture.* New York: Vintage, 1993.

Lears, Jackson. *Fables of Abundance: A Cultural History of Advertising in America.* New York: Basic, 1994.

Lears, T. J. Jackson. "From Salvation to Self-Realization: Advertising and the Therapeutic Roots of the Consumer Culture, 1880–1930." In *The Culture of Consumption: Critical*

Essays in American History, 1880–1980. Edited by Richard Wightman Fox and T. J. Jackson Lears. New York: Pantheon, 1982.

Lee, Chris. "This Music Is Sponsored By . . . " *Los Angeles Times*, 7 March 2010, §E, p. 1.

Lee, Martyn J. *Consumer Culture Reborn: The Cultural Politics of Consumption.* New York: Routledge, 1993.

Leeds, Jeff. "Small Record Labels Say Radio Tunes Them Out." *Los Angeles Times*, 16 September 2001, C1.

Leland, John. "A Chance to Carry On for 130 Million." *New York Times*, 19 January 2003, §9, p. 2.

———. "Selling Out Isn't What It Used to Be." *New York Times* magazine, 11 March 2001, 48–51.

Levin, Gary. "Holiday Inns Book Sinatra." *Advertising Age*, 25 May 1987, 1.

———. "Salem Turns Up the Sound." *Advertising Age*, 24 April 1989, 1.

Lichtman, Irv. "Catalog Evergreens Pop Up as Jingles in Increasing Numbers." *Billboard*, 31 October 1998, 38.

———. "Comeback Kids." *Billboard*, 13 June 1998, 45.

Lieber, Leslie. *How to Form a Rock Group.* New York: Grosset and Dunlap, 1968.

Lindsay, Greg. "Ad as Breakout Song Launchpad." *Advertising Age*, 11 July 2005, 26.

Lippert, Barbara. "Roll Over, John; the Song Fits, and Nike's Wearing It." *Adweek*, 6 April 1987, 23.

Lipsitz, George. "Consumer Spending as State Project: Yesterday's Solutions and Today's Problems." In *Getting and Spending: European and American Consumer Societies in the Twentieth Century.* Edited by Susan Strasser, Charles McGovern, and Matthias Judt. Cambridge: Cambridge University Press, 1998.

Livant, Bill. "The Audience Commodity: On the 'Blindspot' Debate." *Canadian Journal of Political and Social Theory* 3 (Winter 1979): 91–106.

Loesser, Susan. *A Most Remarkable Fella: Frank Loesser and the Guys and Dolls in His Life.* New York: Donald I. Fine, 1993.

Loro, Laura. "New Age Music Scores in Ads." *Advertising Age*, 22 August 1988, 39.

Louis, J. C., and Harvey Z. Yazijian. *The Cola Wars.* New York: Everest House, 1980.

Lumley, Frederick H. *Measurement in Radio.* Columbus: Ohio State University Press, 1934.

Lynd, Robert S., and Helen Merrell Lynd. *Middletown: A Study in Modern American Culture.* New York: Harcourt Brace Jovanovich, 1929.

MacArthur, Kate, and Jack Neff. "Sprite Shifts Gears in Quest for Street Cred." *Advertising Age*, 26 January 2004, 1.

Mack, Walter, and Peter Buckley. *No Time Lost.* New York: Atheneum, 1982.

Magiera, Marcy. "Discord on 'Revolution': McCartney Hits Nike, Jackson for Use of Song." *Advertising Age*, 26 October 1987, 36.

———. "Nike to Keep 'Revolution' despite Suit." *Advertising Age*, 3 August 1987, 3.

"The Making of a Commercial." *Today's Film Maker*, June 1974, 23–25, 38–39.

Malone, Bill C. "Radio and Personal Appearances: Sources and Resources." *Western Folklore* 30 (July 1971): 215–25.

Mandel, Ernest. *Late Capitalism*. Translated by Joris de Bres. New York: Verso, 1978.

Manners, Timothy G. Letter to the editor. *Advertising Age*, 15 June 1987, 20.

Marchand, Roland. *Advertising the American Dream: Making Way for Modernity, 1920–1940*. Berkeley: University of California Press, 1985.

"The March of Radio: What Radio Broadcast Is Trying to Do." *Radio Broadcast*, May 1923, 3–16.

Mariampolski, Hy. *Ethnography for Marketers: A Guide to Consumer Immersion*. Thousand Oaks, CA: Sage, 2006.

"Marketers Invited to Take the 'A' Train." *Marketing through Music*, May 1988, 6.

Marquis, Alice Goldfarb. "Written on the Wind: The Impact of Radio during the 1930s." *Journal of Contemporary History* 19 (1984): 385–415.

Martin, Everett G. "Beware of Background Music in TV Ads: The Tunes May Be 'Fixed.'" *Wall Street Journal*, 13 November 1959, 1.

Martineau, Pierre. *Motivation in Advertising: Motives That Make People Buy*. New York: McGraw-Hill, 1957.

Mayer, Martin. *Madison Avenue U.S.A.: The Extraordinary Business of Advertising and the People Who Run It*. Lincolnwood, IL: NTC Business Books, 1992.

McCafferty, Carol A., and Susan E. King. "Harry Frankel: Singin' Sam, More Than the Barbasol Man." *Traces* (Winter 2005), 26–35.

McCarthy, Michael. "Mitsubishi Campaign Starts Commotion." *USA Today*, 24 December 2001, B6.

McCracken, Allison. "'God's Gift to Us Girls': Crooning, Gender, and the Re-creation of American Popular Song, 1928–1933." *American Music* 17 (Winter 1999): 365–95.

McCracken, Grant. *Culture and Consumption: New Approaches to the Symbolic Character of Consumer Goods and Activities*. Bloomington: Indiana University Press, 1988.

———. *Culture and Consumption II: Markets, Meaning, and Brand Management*. Bloomington: Indiana University Press, 2005.

McCusker, Kristine M. "'Dear Radio Friend': Listener Mail and the *National Barn Dance*, 1931–1941." *American Studies* 39 (Summer 1998): 173–95.

McDonald, E. F. "What We Think the Public Wants." *Radio Broadcast*, March 1924, 382–84.

McDonough, John, and Allan Ross. "Jingle Jangle: Who Makes Singing Commercials and Why." *High Fidelity*, November 1976, 82–87.

McFaul, Tom. "How the Pussy Learned to Sing," 1 April 2002. http://www.classicthemes.com/50sTVThemes/singingPussy.html.

McGinnis, Patricia. "The Jingle Generation." *Marketing Communications*, January 1979, 69=72.

McGovern, Charles F. *Sold American: Consumption and Citizenship, 1890–1945*. Chapel Hill: University of North Carolina Press, 2006.

"McGuires Join Sales Ranks in Deal with Coke." *Advertising Age*, 12 January 1959, 58.

McLaren, Carrie. "Licensed to Sell." *Village Voice*, 28 April 1998, 36–37.

McLaren, Carrie, and Rick Prelinger. "Salesnoise: The Convergence of Music and Advertising." *Stay Free!* Fall 1998. http://www.stayfreemagazine.org/archives/15/timeline.html.

McMeans, Orange Edward. "The Great Audience Invisible." *Scribner's Magazine*, April 1923, 410–16.

McNamara, Brooks. *Step Right Up.* Garden City, NY: Doubleday, 1976.

Melnick, Ross. "Rethinking Rothafel: Roxy's Forgotten Legacy." *Moving Image* 3 (2003): 62–95.

———. "Station R-O-X-Y: Roxy and the Radio." *Film History: An International Journal* 17 (2006): 217–33.

Meyer, Bill. "Is Music Drowning Out the Pitch?" *Adweek*, 14 September 1981, 1, 17–18.

Meyer, Stephen. "Everybody Must Get Cloned." *Advertising Age*, 5 October 1987, C28.

Meyers, William. *The Image-Makers: Secrets of Successful Advertising.* London: Macmillan, 1984.

"Michael 'Pepsi' Jackson: Battling Coke Overseas." *Advertising Age*, 28 September 1987, 80.

Michaels, Julia, and Patricia Winters. "Music Reintroduces Pepsi to Brazil." *Advertising Age*, 28 September 1987, 80.

Michaelson, Sam. "Matching the Musical Message." *Marketing and Media Decisions*, August 1986, 133–34.

Miller, Cyndee. "Marketers Find Alternative Way to Appeal to Young Music Lovers." *Marketing News*, 12 October 1992, 18.

———. "Marketers Tap into Rap as Hip-Hop Becomes 'Safe.'" *Marketing News*, 18 January 1993, 10.

———. "They Write Songs That Jingle, Jangle, Jingle." *Marketing News*, 6 November 1989, 6.

Miller, Daniel. *Material Culture and Mass Consumption.* Malden, MA: Blackwell, 1991.

Miller, Karl Hagstrom. *Segregating Sound: Inventing Folk and Pop Music in the Age of Jim Crow.* Durham, NC: Duke University Press, 2010.

Millman, Nancy. "Her Road to Fame Was Paved with Commercials." *Advertising Age*, 19 December 1983, M-4, M-28.

———. "They Make the Music That Makes the Ad Sing." *Advertising Age*, 22 September 1980, S-10, S-12.

Mitchell, Arnold. *The Nine American Lifestyles: Who We Are and Where We're Going.* New York: Macmillan, 1983.

"Mitsubishi Motors and Deutch Launch Advertising Program to Introduce Endeavor SUV." 24 March 2003. http://www.theauthochannel.com/news/2003/03/24/158069.html.

Moore, Anne Elizabeth. *Unmarketable: Brandalism, Copyfighting, Mocketing, and the Erosion of Integrity.* New York: New Press, 2007.

Moran, Charlie. "Jason Harper: King of Big Mac Chants." *Advertising Age*, 22 July 2008. http://adage.com/songsforsoap/post?article_id=129823.

———. "McDonald's Asks Aspiring Musicians to Bring Their Own Special Sauce." *Advertising Age*, 25 June 2008. http://adage.com/songsforsoap/post?article_id=128001.

———. "Rapper Common Learns to Make Music with Microsoft." *Advertising Age*, 13 October 2008, 22.

———. "The Record Label That's Also a Creative Agency." *Advertising Age*, 27 October 2008, 16.

Morris, Chris. "U.S. TV Ads Tap into New Music, as Stigma Fades." *Billboard*, 25 April 1998, 1.

Morris, Edward. "Commercials' Newest Star Is Country." *Billboard*, 30 May 1981, 9, 32.

Morris, Tom. "Today's Radio Jingle Makes Listeners Tingle." *Advertising Age*, 8 April 1957, 3, 77.

Moss, Janice Ward. *The History and Advancement of African Americans in the Advertising Industry, 1895–1999*. Lewiston, NY: Edwin Mellen, 2003.

"Most Agencies Buy Singing Commercials Outside, Study Finds." *Advertising Age*, 30 November 1959, 54.

Motavalli, John. "Turning Old Hits into New Jingles." *Adweek*, 11 January 1988, B.R. 35–B.R. 36.

"Motivation in TV Spots Hikes Use of Music." *Advertising Age*, 22 June 1959, 18.

"Mr. Average Fan Confesses That He Is a 'Low Brow.'" *Radio Revue*, December 1929, 30–32.

"Mr. Fussy Fan Admits That He Is a 'High-Brow.'" *Radio Revue*, January 1930, 16–18, 46.

"MTM Datafax." *Marketing through Music*, July 1988, 1.

"MTM Datafax." *Marketing through Music*, October 1988, 1.

"M.T.M. Datafax." *Marketing through Music*, March 1989, 1.

"MTV Inspires Pontiac's Ad Effort in '88." *Advertising Age*, 21 September 1987, 84.

Mukerji, Chandra. *From Graven Images: Patterns of Modern Materialism*. New York: Columbia University Press, 1983.

Murdock, Graham. "Blindspots about Western Marxism: A Reply to Dallas Smythe." *Canadian Journal of Political and Social Theory* 2 (Spring–Summer 1978): 109–19.

Murphy, William D. "High Hats for Low Brows." *Printers' Ink*, 8 February 1934, 61–62.

"Musical Contest Program Sells 27 Tons of Candy in Five Weeks." *Broadcast Advertising*, October 1930, 12, 30.

"Music Houses Achieve New Prominence in Music Marketing Era." *Marketing through Music*, March 1987, 6.

"Music to Buy Media By." *Sponsor*, November 1967, 14.

"Music Tops Teen Study." *Marketing through Music*, April 1989, 6.

"Music to Sell by Hits $18-Million Note." *Business Week*, 8 September 1962, 68–70.

"Muy Rapido." *Television/Radio Age*, 10 December 1984, 30, 34.

National Broadcasting Company. *Broadcast Advertising*. Vol. 1, *A Study of the Radio*

Medium—the Fourth Dimension of Advertising. New York: National Broadcasting Company, 1929.

———. *Broadcast Advertising.* Vol. 2, *Merchandising.* New York: National Broadcasting Company, 1930.

———. *Broadcast Merchandising: Reprints from August 1933 to August 1936.* New York: National Broadcasting Company, n.d.

———. *Improving the Smiles of a Nation! How Broadcast Advertising Has Worked for the Makers of Ipana Tooth Paste.* New York: National Broadcasting Company, 1928.

———. *Making Pep and Sparkle Typify a Ginger Ale.* New York: National Broadcasting Company, 1929.

———. *Musical Leadership Maintained by NBC.* New York: National Broadcasting Company, 1938.

Neal, Mark Anthony. "'Real, Compared to What': Anti-war Soul." *PopMatters,* 28 March 2003. http://www.popmatters.com/features/030328-iraq-neal.shtml.

Neill, Ben. Liner notes to *Automotive.* six degrees 657036 1077–2, 2002.

"The New Appeal of Country Music." *Broadcasting,* 1 August 1966, 53–68.

"New Book Promotes Music in Youth Advertisements." *Marketing through Music,* October 1987, 1, 6.

"New Lincoln-Mercury Campaign Highlights the Distinctive Sound of Rod Stewart." *Marketing through Music,* October 1986, 1–2.

"New Lyrics Turn Ad Jingles into Pop Records for the Juke Box Trade." *Advertising Age,* 19 April 1954, 72.

Newman, Kathy M. *Radio Active: Advertising and Consumer Activism, 1935–1947.* Berkeley: University of California Press, 2004.

"New Pepsi Jingle Has No Rime, Some Reason." *Printers' Ink,* 9 May 1958, 12–13.

"New Role for Classic Rock" (editorial). *Advertising Age,* 14 September 1987, 16.

"Newsline." *Advertising Age,* 9 March 1987, 8.

Nicholson, Peter. "Branded for Success: McDonald's, Others Reveal Agency World Clout When It Comes to Music." *Billboard,* 18 August 2007, 4.

"Nike Breaks 'Revolutionary' Spots." *Adweek,* 9 March 1987.

"Nike Pulls Beatles Song; Revolution to Continue." *Marketing through Music,* April 1988, 1, 5.

"Nike Says It Hasn't Settled." *Adweek,* 29 February 1988.

"Nike Uses Beatles' Song to Launch 'Revolution.'" *Marketing through Music,* April 1987, 1, 6.

"1950s and '60s Rock Still Alive in Radio-TV Jingles." *Billboard,* 26 July 1980, 70.

Nixon, Sean. *Advertising Cultures: Gender, Commerce, Creativity.* Thousand Oaks, CA: Sage, 2003.

Nuccio, Sal. "Advertising: Treasure in the Jingle Jungle." *New York Times,* 8 November 1964, §F, p. 14.

Nusser, Dick. "Radio-TV Jingles Go for Standards." *Billboard,* 22 April 1978, 102.

Ogilvy, David. *Confessions of an Advertising Man*. New York: Atheneum, 1963.

―――. *Ogilvy on Advertising*. New York: Vintage, 1985.

Ohmann, Richard. *Selling Culture: Magazines, Markets, and Class at the Turn of the Century*. New York: Verso, 1996.

"Old Songs Brew Jingles Gravy." *Billboard*, 4 December 1978, 77.

Olney, Martha L. *Buy Now, Pay Later: Advertising, Credit, and Consumer Durables in the 1920s*. Chapel Hill: University of North Carolina Press, 1991.

"$100,000 Re-run for a 1936 Jingle." *Sponsor*, 11 July 1959, 42.

"Oratorios for Industry." *Time*, 24 July 1964, 42.

Orchard, Charles, Jr. "Is Radio Making America Musical?" *Radio Broadcast*, October 1924, 454–55.

Ortner, Sherry B. *New Jersey Dreaming: Capital, Culture, and the Class of '58*. Durham, NC: Duke University Press, 2003.

Ostroff, Joshua. "Commercial Music: Where It's At." *Boards*, 1 April 2003, 45.

"Other Late News." *Advertising Age*, 31 August 1987, 8.

The Oxford English Dictionary. 2nd ed., 1989; *OED Online*. Oxford University Press, 1989, 12 April 2000, s.v. *jingle*.

Pace, Eric. "There's a Song in Their Art." *New York Times*, 2 May 1982, §F, p. 4.

Packard, Vance. *The Hidden Persuaders*. New York: David McKay, 1957.

Paley, William S. *As It Happened: A Memoir*. Garden City, NY: Doubleday, 1979.

―――. *Radio as a Cultural Force*. N.p., 1934.

Palmer, James L. "Radio Advertising." *Journal of Business of the University of Chicago* 1 (October 1928): 495–96.

Palmer, Olive. "Requirements of the Radio Singer." *Etude*, December 1931, 849–50.

"P&G Soap Drab in Color . . . Great for Washing Hands." Last accessed 13 August 2011. http://www.old-time.com/commercials/1940's/L-A-V-A.htm.

Paoletta, Michael. "Capitol's Dirty Vegas Gains Popularity as 'Days Go By.'" *Billboard*, 1 June 2002, 44.

―――. "Dance & Electronic Music: Soundtrack to the World?" *Billboard*, 22 March 2003, 39.

Parpis, Eleftheria. "Profile: Steve Stoute." *Adweek.com*, 25 August 2008.

Pate, Russ. "Those Oldies but Goodies." *Adweek*/Southwest, 9 April 1984, 12.

Patterson, Timothy A. "Hillbilly Music among the Flatlanders: Early Midwestern Radio and Barn Dances." *Journal of Country Music* 6 (Spring 1975): 12–18.

Patton, Phil. "Like the Song, Love the Car." *New York Times*, 15 September 2002, §12, p. 1.

Pendleton, Jennifer. "Chalk Up Another Victory for Trend-Setting Rock 'n' Roll." *Advertising Age*, 9 November 1988, 160.

"Pepper and Salt." *Wall Street Journal*, 9 June 1938, 4.

"Pepsi-Cola Plans Big Radio-TV Splash." *Broadcasting*, 13 February 1961, 32–33.

"Pepsi-Cola's Walter Mack." *Fortune*, November 1947, 126–31, 176, 178, 181–82, 184, 187–88, 190.

"Pepsi-Cola Theme Song Now Heard over 8 Stations." *Bayside Times*, 14 December 1939, 2.

"Pepsi Doubles Already Big Radio Budget." *Broadcasting*, 15 January 1962, 30, 32.

"'Pepsi Generation' Jingle Bows in Radio Spot Drive." *Advertising Age*, 3 August 1964, 2.

"Pepsi Launches All-Out Campaign Promoting 'Generation' Theme." *Sponsor*, 14 September 1964, 19.

"Pepsi Localizes Its Second Flight of Radio Jingles." *Advertising Age*, 8 May 1961, 38–39.

"Pepsi's 'Bad' Breaks: Two New Jackson Spots." *Marketing through Music*, December 1987, 1, 6.

"Pepsi's 'Got a Lot to Give' Drive Wins Viewer Praise; Music Sought." *Advertising Age*, 22 December 1969, 2, 34.

Peterson, Eldridge. "Music on Lucky Strike 'Hit Parade' Is Part of Advertisement." *Printers' Ink Monthly*, May 1941, 30.

Peterson, Richard A., and Paul DiMaggio. "The Early Opry: Its Hillbilly Image in Fact and Fancy." *Journal of Country Music* 4 (Summer 1973): 39–51.

Peterson, Richard A., and Roger M. Kern. "Changing Highbrow Taste: From Snob to Omnivore." *American Sociological Review* 61 (October 1996): 900–907.

Pfeil, Fred. "'Makin' Flippy-Floppy': Postmodernism and the Baby-Boom PMC." In *Another Tale to Tell: Politics and Narrative in Postmodern Culture*. New York: Verso, 1990.

Phelps, George Harrison. *Tomorrow's Advertisers and Their Advertising Agencies*. New York: Harper and Brothers, 1929.

Pope, Daniel. *The Making of Modern Advertising*. New York: Basic, 1983.

Presbrey, Frank. *The History and Development of Advertising*. New York: Doubleday, Doran, and Company, 1929.

Preston, Marion. "Monday Memo." *Broadcasting*, 9 January 1978, 14.

A Primer of Capitalism. New York: J. Walter Thompson Company, 1937.

"Problem for the Industry: Swapping of Talent by Sponsors Causes Confusion." *Newsweek*, 19 September 1939, 22.

"Psychedelic Jingles to Turn Listeners On." *Broadcasting*, 31 October 1966, 77.

Pumphrey, P. H. "Choosing the Program Idea." *Broadcast Advertising*, July 1931, 15, 40, 42–43.

———. "Writing, Casting and Producing the Radio Program." *Broadcast Advertising*, August 1931, 17, 42–44.

Rabinowitz, Josh. "With the Brand: Jingle in Your Pocket." *Billboard*, 19 January 2008, 17.

———. "With the Brand: A Public Picking: The Process of Choosing a Song for Ad Placement." *Billboard*, 16 February 2008, 16.

"Radio Audience Decides Programs." *Wireless Age*, August 1923, 28–31.

"The Radio Business." *Literary Digest*, 5 May 1923, 28.

"Radio Cultivates Taste for Better Music." *Radio World*, 19 July 1924, 24.

"Radio Fan Goes to See Opera after Broadcast." *Radio World*, 14 April 1923, 29.

"Radio Listeners Vote for Favorite Composers." *Radio News*, December 1927, 606.

"Radio's Magic Carpet; Extensive Printed Advertising Reinforces Broadcast Campaign."
    Broadcast Advertising, July 1929, 5–10, 23–26.

Recording Industry Association of America. "2008 Consumer Profile." http://www.riaa
    .com/keystatistics.php?content_selector=MusicConsumerProfile.

Reece, Chuck. "Creatives Grapple with Music and 15s." *Adweek*, 31 March 1986, C.P. 22.

Reich, Robert. *The Work of Nations*. New York: Vintage, 1992.

Renfro, Harry K. "Country and Western Consumer: Forgotten Man in Jingle Market."
    Broadcasting, 7 July 1958, 105.

"Replies to WJZ Questionnaire on Listeners' Tastes Show Classical Music More Popular
    Than Jazz." *New York Times*, 21 February 1926, §8, p. 17.

"Reproduce Product's Tempo in Program, Says Woolley." *Broadcast Advertising*, May 1931,
    26, 28.

Reublin, Rick. "The American Capitalist Initiative, Advertising in Music." *Parlor Songs*,
    August 2000. http://www.parlorsongs.com/insearch/vanitymusic/vanitymusic.asp.

Richards, Norm. "Hints to Make Commercial Music Sing." *Advertising Age*, 23 January
    1978, 50, 54.

———. "The Myth of Memorability in Commercial Music." *Advertising Age*, 23 July 1979,
    S-23–S-24.

Robins, J. Max, and Chuck Reece. "Using Hard Rock for Soft Sell." *Adweek*/East, May
    1985, M.M. 20–M.M. 21.

"Rock Lovers Decry Use of Classics in Commercials." *Marketing News*, 1 February
    1988, 21.

Rodman, Ronald. "And Now an Ideology from Our Sponsor: Musical Style and Semio-
    sis in American Television Commercials." *College Music Symposium* 37 (1997):
    21–48.

Rosenblatt, Roger. "The Back of the Book: I Re-write the Songs." *New Republic*, 11 Febru-
    ary 1978, 36–37.

Rosenshine, Allen. *Funny Business: Moguls, Mobsters, Megastars, and the Mad, Mad World
    of the Ad Game*. New York: Beaufort Books, 2006.

Rosenthal, Edmond M. "Civilization Comes to the Jingle Jungle as Music Houses Pull
    Together for a Better Deal." *Television/Radio Age*, 23 May 1977, 32–34, 66–68.

Ross, A. "Monday Memo." *Broadcasting*, 24 September 1979, 16.

Rossman, Martin. "If Beethoven Were Alive, He Could Score Big at Agencies." *Los Angeles
    Times*, 15 February 1971, §D, pp. 11–12.

Rothschild, Michael L. *Advertising: From Fundamentals to Strategies*. Lexington, MA:
    D. C. Heath and Company, 1987.

Rowsome, Frank, Jr. *The Verse by the Side of the Road: The Story of the Burma-Shave Signs
    and Jingles*. New York: Penguin, 1965.

Ruben, Howard G. "They Second That Emotion." *Advertising Age*, 7 September 1987,
    C15–C16.

Rubin, Joan Shelley. *The Making of Middlebrow Culture*. Chapel Hill: University of North
    Carolina Press, 1992.

Russo, Alexander. *Points on the Dial: Golden Age Radio beyond the Networks*. Durham, NC: Duke University Press, 2010.

Rutter, Joyce. "Kuby Conducts." *Advertising Age*, 1 August 1988, 15S.

Samuel, Lawrence. R. *Brought to You By: Postwar Television Advertising and the American Dream*. Austin: University of Texas Press, 2001.

Sandage, C. H., Vernon Fryburger, and Kim Rotzoll. *Advertising Theory and Practice*. 11th ed. Homewood, IL: Richard D. Irwin, 1983.

Sanjek, Russell. *American Popular Music and Its Business: The First Four Hundred Years*. Vol. 3, *From 1900 to 1984*. New York: Oxford University Press, 1988.

Sanneh, Kelefa. "Music to Drive By: Their Smash-Hit Single Is a Commercial." *New York Times*, 30 August 2002, E2.

Savan, Leslie. *The Sponsored Life: Ads, TV, and American Culture*. Philadelphia: Temple University Press, 1994.

Sayer, Derek. *Capitalism and Modernity: An Excursus on Marx and Weber*. London: Routledge, 1991.

"SBK Entertainment Offers Free Catalogs." *Marketing through Music*, March 1988, 6.

Schmelzer, Randi. "RPM's New Urban Marketing Tool: The DJ Made Me Do It." *Adweek*, 13 March 2005, 14.

Schneider, John F. "The NBC Pacific Coast Network." Last accessed 13 August 2011. http://www.bayarearadio.org/schneider/nbc.shtml.

Schoenberg, Nara. "Ad Chic." *Chicago Tribune*, 4 April 2002, 1, 5.

Scott, Allen J. *Social Economy of the Metropolis: Cognitive-Cultural Capitalism and the Global Resurgence of Cities*. Oxford: Oxford University Press, 2008.

Scott, Buddy. "The Magic of Jingles and the Audio Image." *Broadcasting*, 8 August 1983, 24.

Scott, Linda M. "Understanding Jingles and Needledrop: a Rhetorical Approach to Music in Advertising." *Journal of Consumer Research* 17 (1990): 223–36.

Scott, Tracy L. "Music Highlights Mitsubishi TV Ads." *Washington Post*, 9 June 2002, Y6.

Seaman, Debbie. "Coke Gives Refresher Course in Singing." *Adweek*, 16 February 1987.

———. "The Serious Business of Writing Commercial Jingles." *Adweek*, 31 August 1987, 34.

Segal, David. "Pop Music's New Creed: Buy a TV Commercial." *Washington Post*, 27 February 2002, A1.

Seiler, Cotton. "The Commodification of Rebellion: Rock Culture and Consumer Capitalism." In *New Forms of Consumption: Consumers, Culture, and Commodification*. Edited by Mark Gottdiener. Lanham, MD: Rowman and Littlefield, 2000.

Seldin, Joseph J. "Selling the Kiddies." *Nation*, 8 October 1955, 305.

"Sell It with Music." *Time*, 14 June 1954, 52.

"Senator Borah on Marketing" (editorial). *Printers' Ink*, 2 August 1923, 152.

Sennett, Richard. *The Corrosion of Character: The Personal Consequences of Work in the New Capitalism*. New York: Norton, 1998.

———. *The Culture of the New Capitalism*. New Haven, CT: Yale University Press, 2006.

Serafin, Raymond. "Ford Division Plows into Radio." *Advertising Age*, 1 September 1986, 3.

———. "'Heartbeat': New Ads Pump Life into Chevy's 'American' Image.'" *Advertising Age*, 12 January 1987, 3.

"Setting Commercials to Music a Growing Part of Pop Culture." *Television/Radio Age, 1980 Production Guide*, 10–12.

Shannon, Christopher. *A World Made Safe for Differences: Cold War Intellectuals and the Politics of Identity*. Lanham, MD: Rowman and Littlefield, 2001.

Sherrid, Pamela. "Emotional Shorthand." *Forbes*, 4 November 1985, 214–15.

Sherry, John F., Jr., ed. *Contemporary Marketing and Consumer Behavior: An Anthropological Sourcebook*. Thousand Oaks, CA: Sage, 1995.

"Should You Pre-score Your TV Commercials?" *Sponsor*, 11 July 1959, 40–41, 44.

Silberman, Jeff. "2000 and Beyond." *Billboard*, 4 November 2000, 3, 10.

Simon, Robert A. "Giving Music the Air." *Bookman* 64 (1926): 596–99.

"Singing Commercials Cut from Radio by Device." *Science News Letter*, 31 March 1951, 204.

"The Singing Saleswoman." *Ebony*, April 1964, 143.

"Single Jingle Builds 10-Year Success." *Sponsor*, 8 November 1958, 39.

"Six (6) Rock Groups to Give Word on Music to AA Workshop." *Advertising Age*, 13 April 1970, 28.

"Sizing Up the Radio Audience." *Literary Digest*, 19 January 1928, 54–55.

Slater, Don. *Consumer Culture and Modernity*. Malden, MA: Polity, 1997.

Smith, Ethan. "Organization Moby." *Wired*, May 2002, 88–95.

Smulyan, Susan. "Branded Performers: Radio's Early Stars." *Timeline* 3 (1986–87): 32–41.

———. *Selling Radio: The Commercialization of American Broadcasting, 1920–1934*. Washington, DC: Smithsonian Institution Press, 1994.

Smythe, Dallas W. "Communications: Blindspot of Western Marxism." *Canadian Journal of Political and Social Theory* 1 (Fall 1977): 1–27.

———. *Dependency Road: Communications, Capitalism, Consciousness, and Canada*. Norwood, NJ: Ablex, 1987.

———. "Rejoinder to Graham Murdock." *Canadian Journal of Political and Social Theory* 2 (Spring–Summer 1978): 120–27.

Sombart, Werner. *Luxury and Capitalism*. Translated by W. R. Dittmar. Ann Arbor: University of Michigan Press, 1967.

Soter, Tom. "Clear as Glass." *Shootonline*, 24 September 2004.

"Sound Ads Cause Apprehension." *New York Times*, 16 August 1948, 26.

Spaeth, Frank W. *Radio Broadcasting Manual*. New York: Sales Promotion Division of the National Retail Dry Goods Association, 1935.

"Specialist." *New Yorker*, 4 October 1947, 26–27.

Spillman, Susan. "Commercials Dance to Video Beat." *Advertising Age*, 10 January 1985, 48.

Spitalny, Phil. "'The Hour of Charm.'" *Etude*, October 1938, 639–40.

"Spotting the Music." *Television/Radio Age*, 10 December 1984, 128.

Stamps, Charles Henry. *The Concept of the Mass Audience in American Broadcasting: An Historical-Descriptive Study*. 1957. Reprint, New York: Arno Press, 1979.

Starch, Daniel. "A Study of Radio Broadcasting Based Exclusively on Personal Interviews with Families in the United States East of the Rocky Mountains." Unpublished manuscript commissioned by NBC, 1928.

Stevens, Paul. *I Can Sell You Anything: How I Made Your Favorite TV Commercials with Minimum Truth and Maximum Consequences*. New York: P. H. Wyden, 1972.

Stewart, David W., and David H. Furse. *Effective Television Advertising: A Study of 1000 Commercials*. Lexington, MA: Lexington Books, 1986.

Stone, Al. *Jingles: How to Write, Produce and Sell Commercial Music*. Cincinnati: Writer's Digest Books, 1990.

Stout, Patricia A., John D. Leckenby, and Sidney Hecker. "Viewer Reactions to Music in Television Commercials." *Journalism Quarterly* 67 (Winter 1990): 887–91.

Stout, Patricia A., and Roland T. Rust. "The Effect of Music on Emotional Reponses to Advertising." In *The Proceedings of the 1986 Conference of the American Academy of Advertising*. Edited by Ernest F. Larkin. Norman: School of Journalism, University of Oklahoma, 1986.

"Strange People Make Strange Songs to Market Their Wares on the Air." *Life*, 7 October 1940, 78–80.

Strategic Business Insights. "Sample Demographics and Behaviors." Last accessed 13 August 2011. http://www.strategicbusinessinsights.com/vals/demobehav.shtml.

Street Mix: Music from Volkswagen Commercials. Vol. 1. Liner notes. 2001.

Strnad, Patricia. "Modern Chiquita." *Advertising Age*, 26 February 1990, 4.

"Successful Commercial Jingles Sell by Expressing a Product's Personality." *Printers' Ink*, 28 March 1958, 36–37.

Suisman, David. *Selling Sounds: The Commercial Revolution in American Music*. Cambridge, MA: Harvard University Press, 2009.

Sunderland, Patricia L., and Rita M. Denny. *Doing Anthropology in Consumer Research*. Walnut Creek, CA: Left Coast Press, 2007.

———. "Psychology vs Anthropology: Where Is Culture in Marketplace Ethnography?" In *Advertising Cultures*. Edited by Timothy deWaal Malefyt and Brian Moeran. New York: Berg, 2003.

Susman, Warren I. *Culture as History: The Transformation of American Society in the Twentieth Century*. New York: Pantheon, 1984.

"Talent Expenditures." *Variety Radio Directory, 1937–1938*. N.p.: Variety, 1937.

Taylor, Timothy D. "Advertising and the Conquest of Culture." *Social Semiotics* 4 (December 2009): 405–25.

———. "The Avant-Garde in the Family Room: Advertising and the Domestication of Electronic Music in the 1960s and 1970s." In *The Oxford Sound Studies Handbook*, edited by Karin Bijsterveld and Trevor Pinch. New York: Oxford University Press, 2012.

————. *Beyond Exoticism: Western Music and the World*. Durham, NC: Duke University Press, 2007.

————. "The Changing Shape of the Culture Industry; Or, How Did Electronica Music Get into Television Commercials?" *Television and New Media* 8 (August 2007): 235–58.

————. "Late Capitalism, Globalisation, and the Commodification of Taste." In *The Cambridge History of World Music*, edited by Philip Bohlman. Cambridge: Cambridge University Press, forthcoming.

————. "Music and the Rise of Radio in Twenties America: Technological Imperialism, Socialization, and the Transformation of Intimacy." In *Wired for Sound: Engineering and Technology in Sonic Cultures*. Edited by Paul Greene and Thomas Porcello. Middletown, CT: Wesleyan University Press, 2004.

Taylor, Timothy D., Mark Katz, and Tony Grajeda, eds. *Music, Sound, and Technology in America: A Documentary History of Early Phonograph, Cinema, and Radio*. Durham, NC: Duke University Press, 2012.

Teixeira, Antonio, Jr. *Music to Sell By: The Craft of Jingle Writing*. N.p.: Berklee Press, 1974.

Tellis, Gerard J. *Effective Advertising: Understanding When, How, and Why Advertising Works*. Thousand Oaks, CA: Sage, 2004.

"10 Most Successful Product Launches." *Advertising Age*, 22 December 2003, 26.

Terkel, Studs. *Hard Times: An Oral History of the Great Depression*. New York: Pantheon, 1986.

"That Great Jingle." http://www.chiquita.com/Discover/osjingle.asp (URL no longer active).

"Things to Know in Buying Jingles." *Sponsor*, 27 February 1960, 36–38, 67.

Thorson, Esther. "Emotion and Advertising." In *The Advertising Business: Operations, Creativity, Media Planning, Integrated Communications*. Edited by John Philip Jones. Thousand Oaks, CA: Sage, 1999.

Tiegel, Eliot. "Warner Puts Top-40 Hits in Ads." *Advertising Age*, 26 August 1985, 49.

Tindiglia, Ron. *Make Money as a Jingle Composer*. Harrison, NY: Tindiglia Enterprises, 1984.

"Tin Pan Alley: Lyres for Hire." *Time*, 21 April 1961, 69.

"Tip Top Jingle Money Makers." *Sponsor*, 30 April 1962, 32–33, 50–51.

Topper, Judith. "Creatives Try to Change Score." *Back Stage*, 20 April 1984, 1.

————. "Theories, Thoughts and Reasons on Why Agencies Score Their Own." *Back Stage*, 20 April 1984, 6B.

————. "Agencies Reveal the Whys, Wheres and Whens of Getting the Score." *Back Stage*, 20 April 1984, 10B, 43B.

Tota, Anna Lisa. "'When Orff Meets Guinness': Music in Advertising as a Form of Cultural Hybrid." *Poetics* 29 (2001): 109–23.

Townsend, Reginald T. "Fun for Millions—and Millions for Pebeco." *Broadcasting*, 15 January 1936, 12, 45.

"Track Record Enterprises—The 'Un-jingle' Producers." *Back Stage*, 20 April 1984, 14B.

Tremaine, C. M. "Radio, the Musical Educator." *Wireless Age*, September 1923, 39–40.

Tribe, Ivan M. "The Economics of Hillbilly Radio: A Preliminary Investigation of the 'P.I.' System in the Depression Decade and Afterward." *JEMF Quarterly* 20 (1984): 76–83.

A Tribute to the Friends of Radio: Your Program Guide to 65 Years of Great Radio Advertising. Liner notes. Atlanta: McGavren Guild Radio, 1988.

"Tunesmiths, Admen Can Commingle—When There's Green Stuff in a Jingle." *Advertising Age*, 29 May 1961, 6.

Tunnicliffe, Mike. "The Brand Band Love-in." *Campaign*, 7 November 2008, 27–28.

Turow, Joseph. *Breaking Up America: Advertisers and the New Media World*. Chicago: University of Chicago Press, 1997.

Twitchell, James B. *Lead Us into Temptation: The Triumph of American Materialism*. New York: Columbia University Press, 1999.

Vagnoni, Anthony. "Music Makers Sing Out." *Back Stage*, 20 April 1984, 1, 55.

Vail, James. "Music as Marketing Tool." *Advertising Age*, 4 November 1985, 24.

Vallée, Rudy. *My Time Is Your Time: The Rudy Vallée Story*. With Gil McKean. New York: Ivan Obolensky, 1962.

———. *Vagabond Dreams Come True*. New York: Grosset and Dunlap, 1930.

Vanderbilt, Tom. "Taste: That Selling Sound, the Strange Musical Accompaniment to Cruise Lines, Cookies, Cars." *Wall Street Journal*, 12 July 2002, W13.

Vick, Edward, and Hal Grant. "How to Sell with Music." *Art Direction*, May 1980, 67–68.

Volkening, Henry. "Abuses of Radio Broadcasting." *Current History* 33 (December 1930): 396–400.

Wakeman, Frederic E. *The Hucksters*. New York: Rinehart, 1946.

Walker, Rob. "Dirty Vegas." *Slate*, 19 September 2002. http://www.slate.com.

———. "Sprite ReMix." *New York Times*, 28 March 2004, §6, p. 24.

Wall, John. "Madison Avenue Learns to Rock." *Insight*, 14 April 1986, 54–55.

Wallace, John. "The Listeners' Point of View." *Radio Broadcast*, April 1926, 667–68.

Wallace, V. M. "Mexican Orchestra Plays 432 Weeks for Chili Account." *Broadcasting*, 15 April 1934, 16.

Walters, Barry. "2002: The Year in Recordings: The 10 Best Dance Songs." *Rolling Stone*, 26 December 2002, 112.

Ware, Norman J. *Labor in Modern Industrial Society*. Boston: D. C. Heath, 1935.

Wasserman, Todd. "Watch and Learn," *Adweek*, 3 November 2003, 21–22.

Wayne, Daniel W. "The National Barn Dance on Network Radio: The 1930s." *Journal of Country Music* 9 (1983): 47–62.

Weber, Max. *The Protestant Ethic and the Spirit of Capitalism*. Translated by Talcott Parsons. New York: Charles Scribner's Sons, 1958.

———. *Sociological Writings*. Edited by Wolf Heyderbrand. New York: Continuum, 1999.

Webster, James G., and Patricia F. Phalen. "Victim, Consumer, or Commodity? Audience Models in Communication Policy." In *Audiencemaking: How the Media Create the Audience*. Edited by James S. Ettema and D. Charles Whitney. Thousand Oaks, CA: Sage, 1994.

Weinstein, Bob. "The Medium Music Is the Message." *Madison Avenue*, July 1985, 45–49.

Weiss, Sylvia. "It Isn't Shakespeare but It Pays." *New York Times*, 19 December 1943, 7.

Wernick, Andrew. *Promotional Culture: Advertising, Ideology and Symbolic Expression.* Thousand Oaks, CA: Sage, 1991.

Wernle, Bradford. "Jaguar S-Type Evokes Feeling of Style and Success, Says Rock Star Sting." *Automotive News Europe*, 27 March 2000, 18.

"What Are the Advantages of Original Scores in TV Commercials?" *Sponsor*, 31 May 1958, 44–45.

"What the Public Likes in Broadcasting Programs Partly Shown by Letters." *Radio World*, 21 July 1923, 11.

White, Hooper. "Beers Battle to Take over the Night." *Advertising Age*, 22 September 1986, 73.

———. *How to Produce Effective TV Commercials*. Lincolnwood, IL: NTC Business Books, 1989.

———. "Striking a High Note: Music in TV Production." *Advertising Age*, 12 November 1979, 67, 70.

Whiteside, Thomas. "I Can Be Had—for PELF." *New Republic*, 16 February 1948, 20–23.

———. "The Relaxed Sell." *New Yorker*, 3 March 1950, 70–86.

Wiener, Evan. "For Sale: Moby (and Every Other Hip Recording Artist on the Planet)." *Business 2.0*, December 2001. http://www.business2.com/articles/mag/0,1640, 35037,00.html.

Wiener, Jon. "Beatles Buy-Out." *New Republic*, 11 May 1987, 13–14.

———. "Exploitation and the Revolution." *Advertising Age*, 29 June 1987, 18.

Williams, Raymond. *Marxism and Literature*. New York: Oxford University Press, 1977.

Williams, Russell Byron. "This Product Takes That Program." *Broadcast Advertising*, May 1931, 10–11.

Williamson, Judith. *Decoding Advertisements: Ideology and Meaning in Advertising*. New York: Marion Boyars, 1978.

Wilson, Richenda. "Commercial Sounds." *Marketing Week*, 6 May 1999, 47–52.

Wingis, Chuck. "Songwriter Nichols Bemoans 'Budget' Jingles." *Advertising Age*, 13 September 1976, 116.

Wolfe, Charles Hull. *Modern Radio Advertising*. New York: Funk and Wagnalls / Printers' Ink, 1949.

"Woloshin Taps Classics to Fashion Jingles." *Back Stage*, 20 April 1984, 42B.

Wood, Ellen Meiksins. *The Origins of Capitalism: A Longer View*. New York: Verso, 2002.

"WQXR Extends Its Ban." *New York Times*, 31 March 1944, 23.

Wren, Jarvis. "The Musical vs. Dramatic Radio Program." *Advertising and Selling*, 6 August 1930, 27, 46.

"Wrigley Suspends Brown from Ads." *Adweek.com*, 10 February 2009.

Wyland, George. "Music Can Have a Special, Selling Language of Its Own." *Broadcasting*, 27 February 1961, 20.

"The Yellow Rose of Ford." *Time*, 19 September 1955, 87.

Young, James C. "Broadcasting Personality." *Radio Broadcast,* July 1924, 246–50.

Young, Margaret. "On the Go with Phoebe Snow: Origins of an Advertising Icon." *Advertising and Society Review* 7 (2006). http://muse.jhu.edu/journals/asr/.

Zeifman, Leslie H. "The Sound of Music." *Advertising Age,* 9 November 1988, 162.

Zolotow, Maurice. "The Troubadour of Trouper Hill." *Saturday Evening Post,* 30 May 1942, 21, 52, 54, 57.

INDEX

Bergen, Polly, 89
Bergin, John, 152–54
Berk, Mitchell, 194
Berle, Milton, 152
Berman, Steve, 221
Bernbach, William, 240, 245
"Be Sociable" (Pepsi commercial), 150
Beville, H. M. Jr., 57
Big Chill, The (film), 167–68, 171
Biggar, George C., 24
Billboard charts, 196, 215–16, 218, 222
"Billie Jean" (Michael Jackson song), 189
Bird, William L. Jr., 64, 88
Black Eyed Peas (band), 228–29
Bloch, Andy, 179, 241–42
Blue Velvet (radio program), 30
Blu-Green Gas, 46
Boltanski, Luc, 175–77, 234
Bon Jour Jeans, musical commercials for, 121
Bon Jovi, 202
Boone, Pat and Shirley, 182
Bourdieu, Pierre, 5, 9, 231–34
Brainard, Bertha, 66
branding: advertainment and, 217–18; brand
    loyalty and stability through, 223–24;
    popular culture and, 227–28
Brand New Day (Sting album), 219
"Bring Your Ford Back Home" jingle, 96
Bristol-Myers Corporation, 20
broadcast advertising: advertising agencies and,
    16–20; audience research and growth of,
    57–59; business model adopted for, 50–51;
    classical vs. jazz radio programming and,
    28–30; commodification of mass audience
    and, 51–55; goodwill model and, 22–25;
    merchandising strategies and, 251n34; mu-
    sic and, 11–41; personality-driven strategies
    in, 38–41, 252n50; promotion of radio for,
    14–16; sponsored musical programs, 26–28.
    See also radio; television
Broadcast Advertising magazine, 51
Broadway composers, recycling of music for
    commercials by, 130–31
Brooks, Joe, 154–55
Brown, Chris, 225
Brubeck, Dave, 149
Bryan, Vincent P., 72–73
"Brylcreem" jingle, 98
Burger King: musical commercials for, 119–20,
    140; radio campaign in 1980s for, 193

Burland, Granville (Sascha), 114–15, 162–63
Burma-Shave roadside advertisements, 71–72
Bush, George W., 4
business: as advertising model, 50–51; creativity
    and, 68, 244–46, 293n9

cable television, market segmentation and,
    185–87
Cahn, Sammy, 206
Calkins, Earnest Elmo, 1, 67, 70–71
Campaign for a Commercial-Free Childhood,
    223
Cantor, Eddie, 81–82
"Cantor Cantata, The" (radio song), 81–82
"Can't Stop Loving You" (song), 221
capitalism: advertising as protection for, 67;
    artistic critique of, 175–77; production of
    consumption and, 3–5; youth market and,
    147–48. *See also* new capitalism
Carmichael, Hoagy, 129
Carolina Rice, commercial jingle for, 277n24
Carpenters (music group), 163
Caruso, Enrico, 38
Cash, Johnny, 155
Caswell's National Crest Coffee, 80
"chain break" jingles, 95
Chain Store Management magazine, 16
Charles, Ray, 116, 151, 163, 206
Chatfield, Gerard, 18, 36
C/Hear Services Inc., 114
Chemical Brothers (band), 210
Chesterfield Program, The (radio program), 56
Chevrolet, "Heartbeat of America" commercial
    for, 117
Chiapello, Ève, 175–77, 234
Chicago Tribune, 106
Chippardi, Bob, 209
Chiquita Banana jingle, 7, 91–95
Ciani, Suzanne, 119
citizenship, consumption linked to, 67, 102–3
Clapton, Eric, 202
Clark, Petula, 151
classical music: radio programming us-
    ing, 28–30, 253n62, 257n19; surveys of
    favorite compositions, 28–30, 264n68,
    264n71
class stratification: market segmentation and,
    183–85; new petite bourgeoisie and,
    232–34
Clear Channel company, 207, 287n9